The Character
of Swift's Satire

The Character
of Swift's Satire

A REVISED FOCUS

Edited by Claude Rawson

NEWARK: UNIVERSITY OF DELAWARE PRESS
LONDON AND TORONTO: ASSOCIATED UNIVERSITY
PRESSES

Associated University Presses, Inc.
440 Forsgate Drive
Cranbury, NJ 08512

Associated University Presses Ltd
25 Sicilian Avenue
London WC1A 2QH, England

Associated University Presses
2133 Royal Windsor Drive
Unit 1
Mississauga, Ontario
Canada L5J 1K5

Library of Congress Cataloging in Publication Data
Main entry under title:

The Character of Swift's satire.

  Bibliography: p.
  1. Swift, Jonathan, 1667–1745—Criticism and
interpretation—Addresses, essays, lectures. I. Rawson,
Claude Julien.
PR3727.C47 1983   828'.509   81-72062
ISBN 0-87413-209-6

Printed in the United States of America

Contents

Prefatory Note

Several of the essays in this book are reprinted with revisions from *Focus: Swift* (London: Sphere Books, 1971), which has long been out of print. The present volume differs substantially from its predecessor, though it preserves its main conception. Several of the earlier essays have been omitted and several new ones added. The Bibliography has been brought up to date. All references to *Works* are from *The Prose Works of Jonathan Swift*, ed. Herbert Davis et al., 16 vols. (Oxford: Blackwell, 1939–74).

The essays in this volume, while conforming to a broad editorial plan, represent the views of the contributors rather than a consensus. Thus, Professor Quintana's view of the controversial Fourth Book of *Gulliver's Travels*, in his excellent new essay, differs substantially from the "hard" positions expressed by some other contributors, including the editor, in publications outside the present volume. Similar things might be said about some other opinions expressed in the book, which does not seek to achieve a Procrustean conformity on a difficult and elusive subject, or to blunt the edge of controversy, though the essays as a group proceed from a generally similar outlook and from sympathies broadly shared.

Contributors

J. C. Beckett is professor emeritus of Irish history, Queen's University, Belfast. He is the author of various works on Irish history, including *A Short History of Ireland* (1952; 6th ed. 1979), *The Making of Modern Ireland* (1966; revised ed. 1981), *The Anglo-Irish Tradition* (1976), and of an article on "Swift as an Ecclesiastical Statesman" (1949).

Irvin Ehrenpreis is professor of English at the University of Virginia. His most recent book is *Acts of Implication* (1980). The third and final volume of his life of Swift is in press.

Richard Feingold, University of California, Berkeley, is the author of *Nature and Society: the Later Eighteenth-Century Uses of the Pastoral and Georgic* (1978).

F. P. Lock is senior lecturer in English, University of Queensland, Australia. His publications include *The Politics of "Gulliver's Travels"* (1980), "The Text of *Gulliver's Travels*" (*Modern Language Review*, 1981), and other studies of eighteenth-century authors.

Jenny Mezciems, lecturer in English, University of Warwick, is currently writing a book about *Gulliver's Travels* and has published several essays on utopian fiction and *Gulliver's Travels*. She is assistant editor of the *Modern Language Review* and the *Yearbook of English Studies*.

Ricardo Quintana is professor emeritus of English, University of Wisconsin, Madison. He is the author of several standard works on Swift, of which the best known are *The Mind and Art of Jonathan Swift* (1936, reprinted 1965), *Swift: An Introduction* (1955), and *Two Augustans: John Locke, Jonathan Swift* (1978). He has also written on other eighteenth-century authors.

CLAUDE RAWSON is professor of English at the University of Warwick. His books include *Henry Fielding and the Augustan Ideal Under Stress* (1972) and *Gulliver and the Gentle Reader* (1973). He is an editor of the *Modern Language Review* and the *Yearbook of English Studies* and general editor of the Unwin Critical Library. He is a past president of the British Society for Eighteenth-Century Studies.

PAT ROGERS is professor of English, University of Bristol, England. His works include *Grub Street: Studies in a Subculture* (1972) and books on Pope, Defoe, and Fielding. His edition of Swift's *Poems* in the Penguin English Poets has recently appeared. He is president of the British Society for Eighteenth-Century Studies (1982–83) and the Johnson Society (1982).

JOHN TRAUGOTT is professor of English at the University of California, Berkeley. He is the author of *Tristram Shandy's World* (1954) and has written on Swift, Restoration comedy, Richardson, and Shakespearean comedy.

IAN WATT, the Jackson Eli Reynolds Professor of English at Stanford University, is currently director of the Stanford Humanities Centre. He is the author of *The Rise of the Novel* (1957), and of *Conrad in the Nineteenth Century* (1979), the first of a two-volume study of Joseph Conrad.

The Character
of Swift's Satire

1
Biographical Introduction

Claude Rawson

Jonathan Swift was born on 30 November 1667 in Dublin. His parents were English, and his father's family had settled in Ireland fairly recently. His father, also named Jonathan, died in 1667, a few months before the younger Jonathan was born. His mother was left in straitened circumstances. The Swifts had relations in Dublin, however, and Jonathan was supported by them. After early childhood (during which he may have been, and believed that he had been, abducted to England for three years by his nurse), he was sent, about 1674, to Kilkenny School, the best school in Ireland. He stayed at Kilkenny until 1682. Meanwhile, his mother went to live in Leicester, and, though greatly attached to her, he seldom saw very much of her. A tendency to draw back from full commitment in his later relations with women to whom he felt attached may be traceable to this.

In 1682, he went to Trinity College, Dublin. His academic record was not outstanding, and in 1686 he obtained his B.A., *speciali gratia* (a special dispensation apparently implying poor performance). Before he could take his M.A., the violence that came to Ireland in the wake of the English Revolution of 1688, and that threatened English settlers, caused him (and many others) to leave for England.

By the end of 1689, Swift was installed at Moor Park, in Surrey, in the household of Sir William Temple, the retired politician, diplomat, and man of letters. He served as Temple's secretary, with two long interruptions, until Temple's death in 1699. He termporarily returned to Ireland in 1690, having contracted an illness which was to dog him all his life with fits of giddiness, nausea, and deafness. This trouble has been identified by later medical authorities as Ménière's disease, an illness of the inner ear. There is no connection between this illness and "madness", nor between it and the senility of Swift's very last years (he remained, in any case, mentally alive and vigorous well into his later sixties). On the other hand, some recent descriptions of Swift as an un-neurotic, well-adjusted man of liberal and moderate views, some-thing like a cheerfully tolerant and hygienic campus-parson of our own time, may also be discounted: at times, one almost prefers the demonic misanthrope of the older romancing falsifications.

He returned to Temple's house in 1691, and stayed, this time, until 1694. About then he wrote his early odes, some of them "pindarics" in Cowley's manner. Their elaborate, celebratory style was not really suited (despite a few small triumphs in individual passages) to his genius, and he soon abandoned it. He also did editorial work on Temple's memoirs, essays, and correspondence (later seeing several volumes through the press). The M.A. that he had not taken at Trinity, he now obtained, in 1692, at Hart Hall, Oxford.

Swift's friendship with Esther Johnson (Stella), daughter of Temple's housekeeper, began at Moor Park when she was still a young girl (she was born in 1681). Swift directed her reading and gave her moral instruction, and there developed between them the most important and longest-lived of a series of friendships (in which Swift combined roles of guardian, teacher, and, somewhat prob-lematically, lover) with younger women.

In 1694, having failed to secure a suitable permanent occupation while at Moor Park, Swift again returned to Ireland, where he took Anglican deacon's orders in October and was ordained priest in January 1695. His first parish was Kilroot, near Belfast. He was unhappy there. The district consisted largely of Presbyterians, and his congregation was small. He was geographically isolated, and somewhat demoralized by the fact that his living had recently got rid of a disreputable incumbent, Swift's immediate predecessor. He had an inconclusive attachment with a Belfast girl, Jane War-ing, to whom he made, on 29 April 1696, a proposal of marriage. (Four years later, he effectively refused to marry her, although she then would have liked to marry him.)

He returned to Moor Park in 1696. In the next three years, he wrote the greater part of *A Tale of a Tub*, *The Battle of the Books*, and *The Mechanical Operation of the Spirit* (possibly with more or less extensive collaboration by a cousin, Thomas Swift); but these works were not published until 1704, when they appeared grouped together in one (anonymous) volume. The religious satire in these works was directed principally against the nonconformist sects, but also to a substantial degree against Popery; the satire on learning attacked pedants and hacks in general, but was more specifically conceived as a defense of the "ancient" position in a late phase of an old controversy over the respective merits of ancient and modern civilizations. Swift's patron, Sir William Temple, involved himself in this controversy during the 1690s, and in some ways provided an immediate "occasion" for these Swiftian satires written in the same cause.

Temple died in January 1699. During 1699–1710, Swift held various appointments and livings in the Church of Ireland. He returned to Dublin as domestic chaplain to the Earl of Berkeley, a Lord Justice of Ireland, and was able from then on to maintain contact with the circle at Dublin Castle. His main living was the fairly lucrative vicarage of Laracor. In these years, he visited England several times and acted on behalf of the Church of Ireland in efforts to secure certain financial benefits from the Crown. He also expressed in various writings his opposition to Whig proposals to repeal the Sacramental Test, which restricted members of nonconformist sects from holding public office. In political as distinct from religious affairs, Swift was throughout this period a strong supporter of the Whigs. His first important publication, the *Contests and Dissensions in Athens and Rome* (1701), was in defense of Somers's group of Whig Lords against a House of Commons attack led by the moderate Tory Harley (later Swift's political patron and personal friend). *A Tale of a Tub* was dedicated to the same Lord Somers in 1704 (Somers was, some years later, to be attacked in Swift's posthumously published *History of the Four Last Years of the Queen*). His adherence to the Whigs may have partly been a matter of political expediency, but he did feel at this time that the principles of the Revolution of 1688 were more securely enshrined in the outlook of that party. At the same time, he constantly opposed what he felt to be an over-tolerance by the Whigs of religious nonconformism, regarding dissenting sects as a danger both to the established church, and to the peace of the state. The classic statement of his views on Dissent, and on the limits of toleration, is to be found in the *The Sentiments of a Church-of-England Man, With Respect to Religion and Government*, probably written in 1704. Swift wrote several other works concerned with the place of dissenting sects in the state, and with occasional conformity and the sacramental test, and these topics are part of the immediate background to the brilliant ironic fantasy, *An Argument Against Abolishing Christianity* (written in 1708, but, like the *Sentiments*, not published until 1711), and to the important nonironic pamphlet, *A Project for the Advancement of Religion, and the Reformation of Manners* (1709). When Swift went over to Harley's Tory group, newly in power, in 1710, he was doubtless serving his interest, but he was doing so in a context of growing and amply documented discontent on his part with Whig policy in church affairs. Harley was more accommodating on the question of First Fruits and Twentieth Parts, on which Swift had for years been negotiating with Whig leaders on behalf of the Irish Church. Moreover, Harley's government seemed a moderate and broadly based one, rather than a narrowly partisan group. Swift's support of it was not only compatible with his High Church, anti-Whiggish attitude in church matters, but also with his devotion to the principles of 1688. Thus, the severing of his (never altogether easy) connection with the Whigs in 1710, though not without an element of self-interest, was motivated also by real, consistent, and intellectually respectable principles.

During this period between the death of Temple in 1699 and the acceptance of service under Harley in 1710, Swift was consolidating his position as a literary man. His greatest early work, the *Tale of a Tub*, was published in 1704, though written earlier, and not openly acknowledged. The *Tale* was to be a stumbling block in his career as a churchman. But lesser works of real distinction were also produced in this period, notably several poems in Swift's famous light colloquial manner, and the very amusing series of *Bickerstaff Papers* (1708–09), a mock-astrological hoax at the expense of the quack-astrologer Partridge. Swift was by now moving in literary circles, and became friendly with Addison and Steele. In the next few years, his relations with Steele were to become embittered by political opposition and a fierce pamphlet-war. But at this earlier time, Swift helped Steele to start the *Tatler* (whose ostensible author, Isaac Bickerstaff, was borrowed by Steele from Swift's anti-Partridge hoaxes). Swift's poem, "A Description of the Morning," appeared in *Tatler*, No. 9, 28–30 April 1709, and its companion-piece, "A Description of a City-Shower," followed in No. 238, 14–17 October 1710. Swift also wrote an essay on style, for No. 230, 26–28 September 1710.

In 1701, Swift persuaded Esther Johnson, together with Rebecca Dingley, an older woman also from Temple's household, to settle in Ireland, so as to be near him. The close friendship between Swift and Stella has produced much speculation, and knowledge about it is very incomplete. What is certain is that the friendship was very central in both their lives. In later years, it was to elicit some moving and important poems. Earlier than this, in 1710–13, it produced the series of letters that came to be known as the *Journal to Stella*, which are a vivid record of the new phase of Swift's career, as a political journalist under Harley in London.

This period, continuing strictly until the death of Queen Anne in 1714, is one of the most important in his career as a public and political figure (it is rivaled only by the 1720s, when he wrote most of his major tracts on Irish affairs, this time as an opponent rather than as a spokesman of the government of the day). It begins in 1710, when Harley appointed Swift as editor of the Tory *Examiner*, in which Swift wrote many essays in defense of Harley's Ministry, and against the Duke of Marlborough. His other political writings at this time include the brilliant, vitriolic *Short Character of Thomas Earl of Wharton* (1710), *The Conduct of the Allies* (1711), *Some Advice to the October Club* (1712), *The History of the Four Last Years of the Queen* (largely written in these years but published after Swift's death). An important part of his political campaigning was a justification of the Peace of Utrecht (1713), which the Tories concluded with France, against Whig objections that the Peace threw away important advantages gained by Marlborough's military victories, and that it sacrificed the interests of England's allies in the war against France.

Swift hoped that his political activities would help him to secure a good preferment (a deanery or bishopric) in England. In 1713, he received instead, not to his unmixed satisfaction, the Deanery of St. Patrick's Cathedral in Dublin. He attributed his disappointment to the Queen's hostility, and to the influence of highly placed persons who felt that his (unacknowledged) *Tale of a Tub* was an irreligious work, rather than, as the *Tale's* "Apology" claimed, a defense of true religion against Puritan and Papist "abuses." After his installation as Dean in Dublin, he returned to London, in September 1713. He continued his political activities in the Tory cause, by now much weakened by strong disagreements between Harley (now Earl of Oxford) and his Secretary of State, St. John (now Viscount Bolingbroke). Swift remained faithful to both, and tried hard but unsuccessfully to restore harmony between them. More publicly, he maintained his pamphlet-war against the Whigs. Two powerful and witty tracts, *The Importance of the Guardian Considered* (October 1713), and *The Publick Spirit of the Whigs* (February 1714), attacked Swift's former friend Steele. Swift's political realignment, away from his former literary friends, was accompanied by new and parallel literary friendships. The Scriblerus Club, consisting principally of Swift, Pope, Gay, Arbuthnot, Thomas Parnell and the Earl of Oxford, combined convivial and witty gatherings with the planning of concerted literary activities. Out of this grew not only the collective *Memoirs of Martinus Scriblerus*, which Pope published in 1741, but also *Gulliver's Travels* (1726), Pope's *Peri-Bathous, or of the Art of Sinking in Poetry* and the *Dunciad* (both published in 1728).

The actual meetings of the Scriblerus Club (as distinct from its ultimate influence on the published works of its members) virtually ended, except for a faint revival in 1718, with the Tory collapse and the Queen's death on 1 August 1714. Bolingbroke fled to the Continent, Oxford was imprisoned in the Tower (Swift did not know of a correspondence both men had secretly conducted with the Pretender). Swift retired to his Deanery in Dublin in the second half of 1714, and for several years kept away from public affairs, devoting himself to the administration of his cathedral.

Swift's personal life was complicated in these years by the later and embarrassing stages of his friendship with Esther Vanhomrigh (Vanessa). Swift probably first met this young girl (born in Ireland, of Dutch descent) with her widowed mother during 1707–8 in England. There developed between them a characteristic Swiftian relationship, in which teacher-pupil and father-daughter elements combined with some form of erotic affection. She at least fell deeply in love with him, and she followed him to Ireland after the Queen's death. They probably broke in 1722 and she died in 1723. Swift's famous account of their friendship, in the wry, tender, but somewhat patronizing and self-exculpating poem, *Cadenus and Vanessa* (Cadenus is an anagram of *decanus*, or dean), was written as early as 1713. It was published after Vanessa's death, in 1726. It is not known for certain what attitude Stella took towards this relationship and whether she took a strong part in its unhappy end. Stella's friendship with Swift was certainly the more strongly based, and the longest-lived, whether (as some think) they married or not.

Five or six years after his return to Dublin in 1714, Swift was again active both as a creative writer and as a political pamphleteer. In 1719 he wrote several poems, including "The Progress of Beauty." In 1720 he produced the interesting *Letter to a Young Gentleman, Lately Entered Into Holy Orders*, which yields fascinating insights into Swift's temperament and into his attitudes on much more than mere sermon styles. In 1723 came the brief "Letter to a Young Lady, on her Marriage." Both letters of advice are in a sense antiromantic, expressing plain, unhighfalutin conceptions of morality, religion, literature, and life.

But the great creative period of the 1720s is notable chiefly for a massive burst of pamphleteering on Irish affairs, and for *Gulliver's Travels*. Swift's feelings about Ireland were ambiguous. Though born there, he felt himself an Englishman, and thought of his life there as exile. On the other hand, he felt offended at the underprivileged position that England imposed on Ireland, and at Ireland's internal failure to act in her own interest. Although the Irish political writings may be said to begin with *The Story of the Injured Lady*, written in 1707, the major series began in 1720 with the *Proposal for the Universal Use of Irish Manufacture*, which urged, as Swift repeatedly urged, that the Irish should help their own economy by using Irish goods rather than imported ones from England. In 1724–25, in the assumed character of a Dublin draper, he published the series of *Drapier's Letters*, opposing—successfully—an English plan to let loose on the Irish economy a brass coinage manufactured by an English ironmonger, William Wood. Swift risked his personal safety in this cause, and its success turned him into a popular hero.

In the early and middle 1720s, Swift wrote *Gulliver's Travels*. In 1726, he came to England, for the first time since 1714, in order to arrange for the publication of *Gulliver*. He saw again his old Scriblerian friends, Pope, Arbuthnot and Gay (Parnell and Oxford had died in the meantime), and also Bolingbroke, now returned from Continental exile. He also had an inconclusive meeting with Walpole, the prime minister. He was back in Dublin by the time *Gulliver* appeared in England in October 1726. It was an instant, and enormous, success.

The following year, 1727, Swift came again to London—on his last visit. He discussed with Pope the composition of their joint volumes of *Miscellanies* (four were published between 1727 and 1732). It was an exciting time. Pope's *Dunciad* and Gay's *Beggar's Opera* were both to appear the next year, and Swift knew about, and involved himself in, these projects, in which some of the collaborative atmosphere of the early days of the Scriblerus Club was revived.

Shortly after his final return to Ireland from this visit, Stella died (28 January 1728). Swift wrote an eloquent prayer for Stella and an account of her death. His grief was great. He did, however, continue active in his decanal duties, and in 1728–29 produced a brilliant burst of Irish pamphleteering, of which the two best examples are the biting *Short View of the State of Ireland* (1728) and *A Modest Proposal* (1729), the last of his major prose satires. He continued writing on Irish affairs in the 1730s. In that decade he also produced the satiric compilations *Directions to Servants* (not published until 1745) and *A Complete Collection of Genteel and Ingenious Conversation* (1738), for which he had been gathering materials over many years. In the 1730s he wrote also some of his most impressive and vigorous verse, the notorious *Lady's Dressing Room* (written in 1730 and published in 1732), the *Verses on the Death of Dr. Swift* (written 1731, published 1739), the *Epistle to a Lady* (written 1733, published 1734), *On Poetry: A Rapsody* (1733), and the angry *Legion Club* (1736), attacking the Irish House of Commons.

In 1742, in his mid-seventies, he was senile, and in August of that year was declared of unsound mind. He died on 19 October 1745. He was buried near Stella in St. Patrick's Cathedral. His epitaph, composed by himself, is inscribed over his tomb:

> *Hic* depositum est Corpus
> JONATHAN SWIFT S.T.D.
> Hujus Ecclesiæ Cathedralis
> Decani,
> *Ubi* sæva Indignatio
> Ulterius
> Cor lacerare nequit.
> Abi Viator
> Et imitare, si poteris,
> Strenuum pro virili
> Libertatis Vindicatorem.

Yeats (or rather a character in one of his plays) called it "the greatest epitaph in history." Yeats himself translated it into a fine English poem.

2

The Character of Swift's Satire: Reflections on Swift, Johnson, and Human Restlessness

CLAUDE RAWSON

Restlessness and Doubt

Swift's satire rests on a traditional assumption (especially common perhaps among conservative and authoritarian thinkers) about the human condition: that it is a prey to subversion and unhappiness from within, that men are by mental constitution restless, irrational, and unsatisfied, congenitally prone to false needs and driven to supererogatory and destructive satisfactions. Samuel Johnson was later, and more compassionately than Swift, to speak of this universal mental predicament as "that hunger of imagination which preys incessantly upon life," relentlessly craving new satisfactions:

> Those who have already all that they can enjoy, must enlarge their desires. He that has built for use, till use is supplied, must begin to build for vanity, and extend his plan to the utmost power of human

This essay is a revised and expanded version of the essay that appeared in the original edition under the title of "The Character of Swift's Satire." A few paragraphs concerning Swift and Johnson have been woven into scattered parts of the revised version from my review-article "Jobswell: A Short View of the Johnson-Boswell Industry," *Sewanee Review* 88(1980):106–20. Grateful acknowledgement is due to the editor, George Core, and the publishers, the University of the South, for these few extracts.

The original version of this essay benefited from the learned and generous comments of George P. Mayhew. A few passages that go back to this original version overlap slightly with parts of the subsequently published book, *Gulliver and the Gentle Reader* (London: Routledge & Kegan Paul, 1973).

performance, that he may not be soon reduced to form another wish. (*Rasselas*, 1759, ch. 31 [32])

"Vanity" means both pride and emptiness, and man aptly emerges as both guilty and trapped in a kind of suffering emptiness or unreality, self-inflicted, and incurable:

> There is no man whose imagination does not sometimes predominate over his reason, who can regulate his attention wholly by his will, and whose ideas will come and go at his command. No man will be found in whose mind airy notions do not sometimes tyrannise, and force him to hope or fear beyond the limits of sober probability. All power of fancy over reason is a degree of insanity. (*Rasselas*, ch. 43 [44])

The last few words bring to mind Swift's description of madness, in the famous "digression" in *A Tale of a Tub*, as the state that occurs "when a Man's Fancy gets *astride* on his Reason, when Imagination is at Cuffs with the Senses, and common Understanding, as well as common Sense, is Kickt out of Doors" (*Tale*, sec. 9). The differences may seem more apparent than the similarities, since all that ostensibly links the two passages is a commonplace notion of madness as a state where reason is subdued by fantasy. Swift's words have a zany violence absent in Johnson's definition. Swift's emphasis is satirical, rather than soberly and compassionately descriptive. And Swift is castigating certain groups of men, rather than generalizing about all mankind.

These differences are real, but not as great as they seem, especially the last. The digression on madness has a strange universalizing tendency that somehow (by an irrational feat of irony, rather than by open argument) turns the specific types Swift is castigating, the tyrants, system-builders, occultists, nonconformist sectarians, free-thinkers, and the rest, into examples of a radical human perversity, common to all. The sense of the culpable and compulsive unreality of men's pursuits, the insatiable, self-complicating play of ever-renewed need, is, in the *Tale* as in other works of Swift, not unlike Johnson's. The notion of a radical restlessness is itself common enough: Swift could find it in Hobbes, whom he disliked but with whom he shared many ideas, or in his own patron, Temple, whose essay "Of Popular Discontents," which Swift saw through the press, defined "restlessness of mind" as distinguishing men from beasts.

The latter distinction was not in fact always felt to be very strong. Both Swift and Johnson were deeply impregnated with the old homiletic notion that men very readily lapsed into living "like beasts." Swift's most extreme version of this are the Yahoos. Johnson once, in a more casual context, varied the formula when replying to a lady's complaint about excessive drinkers who made "beasts of themselves": "I wonder, Madam, . . . that you have not penetration enough to see the strong inducement to the excess; for he who makes a *beast* of himself gets rid of the pain of being a man" (*Johnsonian Miscellanies*, ed. G. B. Hill [Oxford, 1897], 2:333). In a way, Johnson is even saying that "being a man" is worse than being a beast. Swift might have said the same, comparing real mankind with the Yahoos to its disadvantage. Johnson's "worse" in this case partly means more unhappy and Swift's mainly means more evil. Both would regard bestial reversion not only as squalid in itself, but (whether "better" or "worse" than the human state) as entailing a radically damaging reflection on that human state. Johnson's compassion does not deny the hard fact, but Swift tends to cut off any possibility of compassion.

For Johnson is under no sentimental illusion about the bestiality of man, and critics have pointed out that his view of man's nature is in some ways that of Hobbes, Swift, or Mandeville. Bate and others have cited from Boswell's Hebridean *Tour* the episode in which "Lady MacLeod asked if no man was naturally good." When Johnson (varying the old adage, also found, incidentally, in Hobbes and Mandeville, about man being a wolf to man) replied "no more than a wolf," the lady commented "This is worse than Swift" (Boswell, *Journal of a Tour to the Hebrides with Samuel Johnson*, Yale Edition [New York: McGraw-Hill Book Company, 1963], p. 170; W. Jackson Bate, *Samuel Johnson* [Harcourt Brace Jovanovich, 1977], pp. 196, 493). It is Swift who is normally "worse" in the sense intended by Lady MacLeod, however, although the difference in their respective treatments of men who make beasts of themselves is superimposed on a common perception in both that the process is lamentably natural.

But the main traditional emphasis that Swift shares with Johnson has to do with man's unregenerate restlessness of spirit, rather than with primitive savagery of the Hobbesian or the Yahoo kind, though these were not, in Swift's imagination, unconnected. For both Swift and Johnson the restlessness was a radical perversity of the human mind. Because the condition was mental rather than circumstantial, they felt it to be incurable, and because it was universal they understood that its reach extended to themselves. Both men had the same self-implicating fear of the human mind left to its own spontaneous motions, with its natural tendency to "free-thinking," which meant not only political and religious subversiveness, and immorality, but intellectual disorder and clinical insanity. Both men dreaded madness in themselves and tended to equate the mad with the bad.

Both also felt compassion for the clinically mad. Swift's was a gruff and dismissive compassion, solidly demonstrated in the financial legacy that he insultingly left for the Irish "To build a House for Fools and Mad" (*Poems*, 2;572). In the imaginative as distinct from the practical dimension, madness in Swift's satire is the viciousness and squalor of the Academy of Modern Bedlam or the Legion Club. Johnson, on the other hand, is notable for a continuously sustained tenderness towards the mentally afflicted in his writings as well as in his personal life. The common factor in the writings of both men on folly and on vice is a feeling, never far from the surface, of "there but for the grace of God go I." Johnson's satirical impulse tends to be contained by this reflection and quickly turns benign, whereas Swift's is exacerbated into added urgencies of rejection. Thus mad scientists serve in both authors as examples of the dangers of free-wheeling unregulated intellect, but the treatment of the Academicians of Lagado, as we shall see, is very different from that of the mad astronomer in *Rasselas*.

Swift shared with Johnson an unusually active and personalized conception of mankind's restlessness. Both were not only quick to feel that their view of a universal "madness" implicated themselves also, but that the dividing-line between the universal malady in which they shared by definition and an individual pathological insanity was very narrow. It is not just that both men happened at times to feel menaced by insanity in themselves, and that Johnson's Imlac could say, poignantly, that "Of the uncertainties of our present state, the most dreadful and alarming is the uncertain continuance of reason" (*Rasselas*, ch. 42 [43]). Less dramatically, and perhaps more importantly, both men felt that even states of ordinary sanity are in a sense precarious and momentary victories of "reason" over "fancy," victories of a vigilance needing constant renewal, perhaps at times a matter not even of "control" or "repression" (the latter word is used idiomatically, of course, and without the technical coloring of Freudian terminology), but of show:

All power of fancy over reason is a degree of insanity; but while this power is such as we can controul and repress, it is not visible to others, nor considered as any depravation of the mental faculties: it is not pronounced madness but when it comes ungovernable, and apparently influences speech or action. (*Rasselas*, ch. 43 [44])

Similarly Swift, in a short undated piece, *Some Thoughts on Free-Thinking*, describes "free-thinking" as an undirected flow of consciousness, of a kind to which all men are subject but which only madmen fail to regulate. He quotes with approval an Irish prelate who

> said, that the difference betwixt a mad-man and one in his wits, in what related to speech, consisted in this: That the former spoke out whatever came into his mind, and just in the confused manner as his imagination presented the ideas. The latter only expressed such thoughts, as his judgment directed him to chuse, leaving the rest to die away in his memory. And that if the wisest man would at any time utter his thoughts, in the crude indigested manner, as they come into his head, he would be looked upon as raving mad. (*Works*, 4:49)

In Swift's approval of the prelate's analysis (Johnson would have endorsed it too) one senses the conscious reasoning behind Swift's exposure of the "author" of *A Tale of a Tub*, that compound of intellectual and religious deviation, and of disordered thought, compulsively confessional and wildly digressive. That "author," and the parodied energies of his stream-of-consciousness, anticipates a powerful mode of the "modern" imagination, those heroes of the wandering mind in Sterne or Beckett whose "repertory of permitted attitudes has never ceased to grow," who have "to overflowing, the exasperated good-will of the over-anxious" (*Molloy, Malone Dies, The Unnamable* [London, 1959], p. 25), and whose mentalities are restlessly indecorous, digressive, disordered. Swift's official attitude is one of uncompromising censure. He would have abhorred Tristram Shandy and seen Molloy, who is for Beckett a pained and witty embodiment of the human condition, as merely another mad modern to be savaged. But if Swift parodied both Sterne and Beckett in advance, they, in turn, were able to assimilate the parody and then to transcend it into primary creations, and Swift may be said to have prepared the way for these creations by a prophetic and imaginative feat of repudiation. The fact suggests an intuitive understanding of the fragmentation of "modern" sensibility and of the literary modes this was to call forth. And Swift's diagnosis seems to have proceeded not merely from the protesting reasonings of a satirist, but also from a kind of sympathetic involvement. At all events, Swift enlarges the bishop's notions in *Some*

Thoughts on Free-Thinking by a self-implicating generalization that is almost Johnsonian in its literalness, its moral determination, and its reductive practicality:

> And indeed, when we consider our thoughts, as they are the seeds of words and actions, we cannot but agree, that they ought to be kept under the strictest regulation. And that in the great multiplicity of ideas, which ones mind is apt to form, there is nothing more difficult than to select those, which are most proper for the conduct of life:

This cool glimpse of the psychological constitution of humankind leads straight to the risks of sectarianism and freethinking:

> So that I cannot imagine what is meant by the mighty zeal in some people, for asserting the freedom of thinking: Because, if such thinkers keep their thoughts within their own breasts, they can be of no consequence, further than to themselves. If they publish them to the world, they ought to be answerable for the effects their thoughts produce upon others.

The pun on "free-thinking," sliding tacitly between a general meaning of "unrestricted flow of thought" and the more usual technical sense of "free exercise of reason in matters of religious belief" (the latter definition is the Oxford English Dictionary's) is not merely disingenuous: sectarian folly, like other kinds (described most exhaustively in *A Tale of a Tub*), is not only "disease" as well as vice, but the product of elementary mental instincts common to us all. Hence the "realistic" acceptance that these instincts cannot be eradicated, but can and must be regulated: by concealment, discretion, discipline, practical sanctions concerned with "the conduct of life." Men's "answerability," not for their thoughts but "for the effect their thoughts produce upon others," entails, says Swift, a need for political restrictions on religious freethinkers (and sectarians) similar to the restrictions that governments employ against those who openly propose "innovations in government." The King of Brobdingnag, after noting "the several Sects among us in Religion and Politicks . . . said, he knew no Reason, why those who entertain Opinions prejudicial to the Publick, should be obliged to change, or should not be obliged to conceal them" (*Gulliver's Travels*, 2:6). The political treatment of the sectarian is exactly parallel to the personal discipline a man must impose on his subversive inner thoughts:

> The want of belief is a defect that ought to be concealed when it cannot be overcome. . . .
>
> I am not answerable to God for the doubts that arise in my own breast, since they are the consequence of that reason which he hath planted in me, if I take care to conceal those doubts from others, if I use my best endeavours to subdue them, and if they have no influence on the conduct of my life. (*Thoughts on Religion*, *Works*, 9:261–62)

The practical stress on the conduct of life, the conception of the limits of "answerability," are the same, down to the use of the same phrases, as in *Some Thoughts on Free-Thinking*. The same language and the same patterns of thought apply to political government and to mental self-government, and the King of Brobdingnag's views (often repeated in Swift's own name) on how to treat religious and political sectarians, echo exactly Swift's views on how to treat his own doubts and subversive thoughts.

One notices in both spheres a recognition of the fact of unceasing tension, of radical "incurability." Because the subversions are *psychologically* determined (as distinct from being seen as bad *behavior* or unhappy *circumstance*, both of which would have seemed easier to put right than a congenital cast of mind), there can be no question of any solution. Swift, in such places as the loaded pun on freethinking, characteristically carries a greater attribution of guilt, not just to freethinkers, but to mankind, than Johnson would normally be inclined to emphasize. But Swift's two "thoughts on religion" may be compared with Johnson's prayer of 12 August 1784:

> teach me by thy Holy Spirit to withdraw my mind from unprofitable and dangerous enquiries, from difficulties vainly curious, and doubts impossible to be solved. (*Diaries, Prayers, and Annals*, Yale Edition, pp. 383–84)

Because neither Swift nor Johnson entertains the possibility that the doubts can be resolved or the "dangerous enquiries" answered, they speak of concealing or trying to subdue them, of preventing their influence upon action or of withdrawing the mind from them, of disciplines rather than solutions. This does not mean that Swift lacked faith or positive values, any more than Johnson did (though Swift, as we shall see, often shied from proclaiming his positives directly). The moral vision of both men rests, with an authoritarian solidity, on some great commonplaces of Christian and humanist thought. Nor does their great complexity of character allow these

positives to be refined away in casuistical subtlety ("refinement" is
one of Swift's favorite terms of abuse), or to evaporate in a luxuri-
ous indulgence of Victorian "honest doubt." "The Grand points of
Christianity ought to be taken as infallible Revelations," Swift said
(*Correspondence*, 4:7). The attitude reaches out to that area of
simplification where controversy is silenced, and the great truths
stand in unassailable and uncomplicated authority. If neither Swift
nor Johnson envisages the inner peace of a full reconciliation between man and the beliefs by which he lives, they do assert the
practical possibility (however strenuous), and the moral necessity,
of living under the rule of these beliefs. Just as in the private mind,
doubts and difficulties must be neutralized, not solved, so also in
the public teaching of religion. In his *Letter to a Young Gentleman,
Lately Entered into Holy Orders* (1720), Swift advocates the disarming
of the controversial and arcane, either by an uppish refusal to busy
oneself "with philosophical Terms, and Notions of the metaphysical or abstracted Kind," or by unquestioning assent:

> I do not find that you are any where directed in the Canons, or
> Articles, to attempt explaining the Mysteries of the Christian Religion.
> And, indeed, since Providence intended there should be Mysteries; I do
> not see how it can be agreeable to *Piety*, *Orthodoxy*, or good *Sense*, to go
> about such a Work. For, to me there seems to be a manifest Dilemma in
> the Case: If you explain them, they are Mysteries no longer; if you fail,
> you have laboured to no Purpose. (*Works*, 9:77)

The *reductio ad absurdum* comes with a characteristic bossiness.
Freethinkers who clamor against the mysteries are like the pedants
who "explain" them: arrogant, obfuscating, divisive—and low, a
kind of mob. The proper alternative for a clergyman "is upon
solemn Days to deliver the Doctrine as the Church holds it."
Swift's *hauteur* is schoolmasterly, but there is moral (and political)
urgency in its simplifying force. It is perhaps unfair to say that the
tenets of "the Christian Religion" seemed to Swift less interesting
for their ideological content or especially for any theological nicety
than for their power to provide imperatives by which behavior can
be regulated and the restless mind sustained. But there is a little of
this tendency at a certain level of thought. A few pages earlier
(p. 73), Swift warns the young gentleman against "the common
unsufferable Cant" by which some clergymen disparage the ancient
"Heathen *Philosophers* " for not knowing certain matters of faith
concerning the Christian God, which had not yet been revealed.
No person with ordinary human faculties can in any case be ex-

pected to grasp inaccessible concepts like "the Nature of God." The ancient philosophers preached a very good morality, and their real lack, "the true Misery of the Heathen World," was "the Want of a Divine *Sanction;* without which, the Dictates of the Philosophers failed in the Point of *Authority*" (my italics).

The instruction to deliver doctrine "as the Church holds it" readily connects with phrases like "received Doctrine" and "what is generally believed," and ultimately with the authority of the Religion of the State. Emphasis on this authority goes back, as Swift knew, to some of the ancient philosophers themselves, notably Plato, though it also had many (and varied) modern exponents. Swift was arguing in some detail in favor of this authority at least as early as 1704, when the *Sentiments of a Church-of-England Man* were probably written. It is clear there that the Religion of the State had for Swift this primary feature, that it offered a pragmatic principle of cohesion, a simplifying and official restraint on the anarchic proclivities of the human mind:

> When a *Schism* is spread in a Nation, there grows, at length, a Dispute which are the Schismaticks. Without entering on the Arguments, used by both Sides among us, to fix the Guilt on each other; it is certain, that in the Sense of the Law, the *Schism* lies on that Side which opposeth it self to the Religion of the State. I leave it among *Divines* to dilate upon the Danger of *Schism*, as a Spiritual Evil; but I would consider it only as a Temporal one. And I think it clear, that any great Separation from the established Worship, although to a new one that is more pure and perfect, may be an Occasion of endangering the publick Peace; because, it will compose a Body always in Reserve, prepared to follow any discontented Heads. (*Works,* 2:11)

One need not question Swift's devotion to the Church of England, or the sincerity of his belief that it is, of all churches, "most agreeable to primitive Institution." But he immediately adds that it is "fittest, of all others for preserving Order and Purity, and under its present Regulations, best calculated for our Civil State" (*Works,* 2:5). And it is clear that Anglicanism would be schismatic, and therefore of subversive tendency, in, say, France. On schism, Swift's speaker confessedly limits his discussion to the *temporal* aspect, but Swift, though seldom patient with the speculations of divines, would endorse the notion that schism, as such, was a "Spiritual Evil" too. The whole issue, in Swift, is not only readily secularized, but psychologized. The "discontented Heads" who lead schismatic movements or who turn to sectarianism and free

thinking, are, to a large extent, social nuisances with secular motives, venal and ambitious self-seekers (*Works*, 2:12) or miscellaneous riff-raff on the fringes of society (one notices again Swift's
dismissive *hauteur*):

> Where then are these Kind of People to be found? Amongst the worst
> Part of the Soldiery, made up of Pages, younger Brothers of obscure
> Families, and others of desperate Fortunes; or else among idle Town-
> Fops; and now and then a drunken "Squire of the Country." (*Letter to a
> Young Gentleman*, *Works*, 9:78)

But such people cannot be completely accounted for by such
merely external explanations, or any similar simplified categorizing
of moral or sociological types. Sectarianism and free thinking
would be disruptive enough even if seen merely thus, but in fact
Swift frequently presents them as a strange amalgam not only of
profit-motive, ambition, mechanical operation, and the like, but of
a more fundamental mental disruptiveness, an innate mental perversity that might be, or might become, very sincere in its schismatic attitudes. The problem, in other words, is not merely a moral
one, implicating only bad men, but a psychological feature of the
human condition, implicating all men, including ultimately Swift.

Madness, Badness, and Politics

Free thinkers, Dissenters, and Schismatics are an example of the
anarchic folly of man in its corporate, institutional, or political
form. In this, they resemble other group-manifestations of man's
wilful disputatiousness, notaby those of secular politics and those
of learned debate. That there is analogy and interpenetration between the private and the public aspects of the universal psychological condition (that *donnée* of Swift's outlook), we have already
seen. A special danger of the public aspect is that it tends to be
worse than the mere sum of its private elements, for a reason upon
which Swift is often insistent, namely that public groupings,

> besides that they are composed of Men with all their Infirmities about
> them . . . have also the ill Fortune to be generally led and influenced by
> the very worst among themselves; I mean, *Popular Orators*, *Tribunes*, or,
> as they are now stiled, *Great Speakers*, *Leading Men*, and the like. (*Works*,
> 1:227)

This statement, from Swift's first political publication, *A Discourse of the Contests and Dissensions in Athens and Rome* (1701; ch. 4), refers to popular political assemblies (parliaments or bodies "of Commons either collective or represented"), but it extends in Swift's mind to many of the other situations in which men attempt to subdue multitudes to their power, their reasons, or their visions (*Tale of a Tub*, sec. 9), especially perhaps to sectarian proselytizing in religion. Many of Swift's arguments for limiting the toleration of Dissenters, in sober discourses like the *Sentiments of a Church-of-England Man* as well as in ironic fantastications like the Digression on Madness and the *Mechanical Operation of the Spirit*, emphasize the snowballing threat posed by sectarian leaders. Swift parodied a Free-Thinker's thoughts in 1713: "It is the indispensable Duty of a *Free Thinker*, to endeavour *forcing* all the World to think as he does, and by that means make them *Free Thinkers* too" (*Works*, 4:36). In secular politics, this process translates itself into a rule that Swift often enunciated, that popular or anarchic governments lead straight to tyranny by "a single Person": the example of Cromwell, in the *Contests and Dissensions*, emphasizes not only the analogy but the interaction between political subversiveness and religious nonconformism (ch. 5; *Works*, 1:230, 231).

The notion that the "rude, passionate, and mistaken Results" emanating from even the best political assemblies arise "from the Influence of private Persons upon great Numbers," provides Swift with the basis for a queer, backhanded compliment to the anarchic and contentious nature of man:

> when we sometimes meet a *few Words* put together, which is called the *Vote*, or *Resolution* of an Assembly, and which we cannot possibly reconcile to *Prudence*, or *publick Good;* it is most charitable to conjecture, that such a Vote hath been conceived, and born, and bred in a private Brain; afterwards raised and supported by an obsequious Party; and then, with usual Methods confirmed by an *artificial* Majority. For, let us suppose five Hundred Men, mixed, in Point of Sense and Honesty, as usually Assemblies are; and let us suppose these Men proposing, debating, resolving, voting, according to the meer natural Motions of their own little, or much Reason and Understanding; I do allow, that Abundance of indigested and abortive, many pernicious and foolish Overtures would arise, and float a few Minutes; but then they would die, and disappear. Because, this must be said in Behalf of human Kind; that common Sense, and plain Reason, while Men are disengaged from acquired Opinions, will ever have some general Influence upon their

Minds; Whereas, the Species of Folly and Vice are infinite, and so different in every Individual, that they could never procure a Majority, if other Corruptions did not enter to pervert Mens Understandings, and misguide their Wills. (*Works*, 1:231–32)

In these effects of political leaders or influential "private Brains" we sense the same strange psychological laws that govern the dissemination of folly in the Digression on Madness, supported no doubt by "mechanical operation" and the forces of material self-interest (the "Corruptions," one supposes, of jobbing, bribery, and the like). If Swift does not here concede anything so positive as the Digression's statement that

the Brain, in its natural Position and State of Serenity, disposeth its Owner to pass his Life in the common Forms, without any Thought of subduing Multitudes to his own *Power*, his *Reasons* or his *Visions* (*Tale*, sec. 9)

neither does he dramatize as vividly and painfully as in the Digression those destructive energies that are let loose "when a Man's Fancy gets *astride* on his Reason . . . and common Understanding, as well as common Sense, is Kickt out of Doors" (*Tale*, sec. 9). And if the individual "brain" of the private man is not seen in the *Contests* as naturally inclined to conformity (see also two pages further, *Works* 1:234), nevertheless the pamphlet tells of a self-regulating quality in man's anarchy that Swift does not always concede elsewhere. For, Swift argues here, the individual variations of folly and vice are so "infinite" that unless men are artificially unified by a perverse leadership, they will find their only principle of cohesion in "common Sense, and plain Reason." If any "publick Conventions" are exempt from the effect of "all the Infirmities, Follies, and Vices of private Men" (compounded by bad leadership), it can only be those which

act by *universal Concert, upon publick Principles, and for publick Ends;* such as proceed upon Debates without *unbecoming Warmths,* or *Influence from particular Leaders and Inflamers;* such whose Members, instead of *canvassing to procure Majorities for their private Opinions, are ready to comply with general sober Results, although contrary to their own Sentiments.* Whatever Assemblies act by these, and other Methods of the like Nature, must be allowed to be exempt from several Imperfections, to which particular Men are subjected. (*Works*, 1:231–32)

The appeal to public principles and public ends is firm and simplifying. It is not that their content will necessarily be able to *persuade*, for Swift expects them to be contrary to the sentiments of some of their supporters, but that they are somehow identified with *"general sober Results."* Swift is, of course, attacking party-factionalism in general theoretical terms, so that specific and detailed examples of the public principles and ends are not at this moment called for, but there is no doubt that the largeness of the conception as such, and especially its power to override (rather than settle) disagreement, are what really excite Swift's imagination.

Behind this conception, however remotely, stands a vision of an ideal society that Swift, many years later, was to fashion into the Houyhnhnmland of *Gulliver's Travels*. Or rather, Swift's notions in the earlier work of what can take place in political assemblies at their best are recognizably embodied in the later Utopian vision of creatures whose political (and other) behavior is *always* at its best. It is not just that a phrase like "without *unbecoming Warmths*" evokes the same aspirations as the picture of the Houyhnhnms conversing without "Interruption, Tediousness, Heat, or Difference of Sentiments" (*Gulliver*, 4.10), or that the Houyhnhnms are notable for what the earlier passage calls *"universal Concert, upon publick Principles, and for publick Ends"* (see *Gulliver*, 4.8, for their public-spirited benevolence towards their "whole Species," and 4.10 for their political asssembly). It is much more that the Houyhnhnms are permanently actuated by criteria that are absolute and simple enough to neutralize the possibility of serious individual disagreement. Swift was always somewhat inclined to see individual disagreement from a general consensus as psychologically rather than rationally motivated, and as tending therefore to the perverse. The Houyhnhnms are not immune from disagreement, as their uncertainty over the proper way to treat Gulliver at the end indicates; and if such disagreements are rare, their theoretical possibility is assumed in the fact, for example,

> that a Decree of the general Assembly in this Country, is expressed by the word *Hnhloayn*, which signifies an *Exhortation;* as near as I can render it: For they have no Conception how a rational Creature can be *compelled*, but only advised, or *exhorted;* because no Person can disobey Reason, without giving up his Claim to be a rational creature. (*Gulliver*, 4.10)

At the same time, the last clause makes clear that no disagreement

can be sustained for very long, and Swift had earlier emphasized that "opinions" and "controversies" are impossible among the Houyhnhnms, because it stands to "reason" that there is only one truth:

> Neither is *Reason* among them a Point problematical as with us, where Men can argue with Plausibility on both Sides of a Question; but strikes you with immediate Conviction; as it must needs do where it is not mingled, obscured, or discoloured by Passion and Interest. I remember it was with extreme Difficulty that I could bring my Master to understand the Meaning of the word *Opinion*, or how a Point could be disputable; because *Reason* taught us to affirm or deny only where we are certain; and beyond our Knowledge we cannot do either. So that Controversies, Wranglings, Disputes, and Positiveness in false or dubious Propositions, are Evils unknown among the *Houyhnhnms*. In the like Manner when I used to explain to him our several Systems of *Natural Philosophy*, he would laugh that a Creature pretending to *Reason*, should value itself upon the Knowledge of other Peoples Conjectures, and in Things, where that Knowledge, if it were certain, could be of no Use. Wherein he agreed entirely with the Sentiments of *Socrates*, as *Plato* delivers them. (*Gulliver*, 4.8)

Obviously there are not, among them, any of those *"unbecoming Warmths"* mentioned in the *Contests*. The Houyhnhnms embody an ideal of social and political health that goes far beyond the modest and pragmatic hope of the *Contests*, that men, in a real world, might be *"ready to comply with general sober Results, although contrary to their own Sentiments."* Despite the possibility of disagreements among the Houyhnhnms, they somehow seem to have no individual sentiments contrary to general sober results, their unifying "reason" being a spontaneous thing operating unerringly through "immediate Conviction." If there is an inconsistency in this, between an absolute reason without disagreements and the theoretical possibility of at least provisional disagreement on some points, it is at most a minor and technical one, and the whole emphasis of the book is on the Houyhnhnms' cool and righteous cohesion. This cohesion is unthinkable in the real world, where other and more terrible spontaneities, those of "Passion and Interest," inevitably hold sway. But Swift's invention of Houyhnhnm society, where a secure and absolute reason exercises so much control over disruptive impulses that these impulses hardly appear at all and the control itself becomes effortless and spontaneous, represents a powerful yearning for a state protected from the tyrant-passions. Orwell saw a "totalitarian tendency" in the Houyhnhnm myth, adding: "In a Society in

which there is no law, and in theory no compulsion, the only arbiter of behaviour is public opinion," and that, Orwell adds, "is less tolerant than any system of law" (*Selected Essays* [Harmondsworth: Penguin Books, 1957], p. 132). Martin Price is right to point out that Houyhnhm conformity is spontaneous rather than enforced, so that, in the fiction, "what, for us, would be defects of liberty" do not arise (*To the Palace of Wisdom* [Garden City, N.Y.: Doubleday, 1965] p. 200). But the fact remains that Swift created the fiction, and it might be argued that such a fiction embodies authoritarian leanings even more radically than a Utopia of socially enforced conformity would have done, as though Swift were saying that the ideal conformism is total and unproblematic.

Not that Swift was opposed to a degree of enforced conformity, especially in religion and politics, as we have seen. The absence of enforcement among the Houyhnhnms depends precisely on the fact that they do not exist in the real world, and that their systematic conformity is only possible in a world whose creatures are reasonable enough to need no sanctions. One of the bleakest implications of the Fourth Book (bleaker perhaps than the Yahoos, or than Gulliver's onslaught upon man, or than our tendency to dislike the Houyhnhnms for their supposed coldness or their "defects of liberty") is that the most thorough-going positive in the entire fiction is tartly established as outside human possibility. If Houyhnhnm cohesion is more complete and better than the limited harmony envisaged in the passage from the *Contests*, it is by the same token much less hopeful. But even in the passage from the *Contests*, in the very place where Swift asserts "that common Sense, and plain Reason, while Men are disengaged from acquired Opinions, will ever have some general Influence upon their Minds," we feel that the infinite "Species of Folly and Vice," like Leavis's Yahoos, "have all the life."

This teeming perversity was for Swift, as we have seen, a psychological condition of the human race. He shared the notion of a radical restlessness with earlier thinkers like Hobbes or Temple, and more profoundly (because in a more poignantly personalized way) with a later individualistic conservative, Samuel Johnson. Swift differs from Johnson, and perhaps comes closer to the earlier writers, however, in the emphasis he placed on the political and social implications of restlessness. Not only did Swift feel more acutely than Johnson the analogy between mental and political states, and therefore between psychological and political government. He was also more frequently given to portraying the universal madness in its collective rather than its private manifestations, and, partly as a result of this, likelier to equate mad with bad.

A relatively lighthearted passage from *Gulliver*, 3.2, illustrates the point. The Laputians have a collective insane anxiety about the supposed threat of great astronomical disasters: they fear, for example, the swallowing up of the earth into the sun, the sun's gradual loss of all its heat, the eventual annihilation of both sun and earth. This echoes some fairly widespread speculations among scientists and divines in the seventeenth and eighteenth centuries. Swift makes exquisite comedy of this Laputian folly: "When they meet an Acquaintance in the Morning, the first Question is about the Sun's Health; how he looked at his Setting and Rising." Laputian folly readily turns very grim, as parts of the Academy of Lagado (*Gulliver*, 3.5–6) show, and I shall return to some of the grimmer side. What I wish to note now is that even when the fun is real and disarming, the absurdity is presented as collective to a whole society, and at the same time emphasized as a deviation from the common forms, a fussy and self-disturbing nonconformism:

> These People are under continual Disquietudes, never enjoying a Minute's Peace of Mind; and their Disturbances proceed from Causes which very little affect the rest of Mortals. . . .
>
> They are so perpetually alarmed with the Apprehensions of these and the like impending Dangers, that they can neither sleep quietly in their Beds, nor have any Relish for the common Pleasures or Amusements of Life. (*Gulliver*, 3.2)

A passage in Johnson's *Idler*, No. 3, 29 April 1758, mocks a similar intellectual folly:

> Many philosophers imagine that the elements themselves may be in time exhausted. That the sun, by shining long, will effuse all its light; and that, by the continual waste of aqueous particles, the whole earth will at last become a sandy desert.

Johnson mentions this absurdity in passing, in an essay not primarily concerned with philosophical vagaries, and it is doubtless largely fortuitous that where Swift converted a particular learned folly into a mad society, Johnson more literal-mindedly confined himself to mentioning "many philosophers." Nor should too much be made of the fact that where Swift signposted a deviation from common ways, Johnson contented himself with noting an irrational absurdity without emphasizing a willful self-isolation from normal-

ity. But even if fortuitous, these slight distinctions do sketch out a
larger difference that is very real.

Johnson is much readier to sympathize and to withhold blame.
As he proceeds, amusingly, to reassure his readers that anxieties
about the end of the world are premature, his irony acquires an
unSwiftian avuncularity, a note of compassion or sympathy for
states of mind afflicted by such worries:

> I would not advise my readers to disturb themselves by contriving
> how they shall live without light and water. For the days of universal
> thirst and perpetual darkness are at a great distance. The ocean and the
> sun will last our time.

He talks as one would comfort a child about some improbable or
remote calamity, a show of confident derision mingling with sympathetic reassurance. When Swift (elsewhere: for example, above,
p. 28) treats his reader as a child, his tone suggests not a comforting
avuncularity but a pedagogue's bossiness. Here, however, Swift
mocks with sharply playful exposure what Johnson treats (almost)
tenderly.

For, although the notions of the "philosophers" seemed as absurd
to Johnson as to Swift, and although both might see them as symptoms of an illness from which no man is strictly free, Swift's focus
on the social dangers of folly yields no possibility of the kind of
compassion that Johnson's passage holds in reserve for individual
sufferers. Behind Johnson's astronomer cranks-is to be discerned
the pathos of such a figure as the mad astronomer in *Rasselas* (written less than a year after the *Idler* paper), a learned man "who has
spent forty years in unwearied attention to the motions and appearances of the celestial bodies, and has drawn out his soul in endless
calculations" (ch. 39 [40]), and whose real skill as a scientist has
curdled into the delusion that he possesses "the regulation of the
weather" (ch. 40[41]). Ironically, and sadly, he is denied the pleasures of this delusion:

> If the task of a king be considered as difficult, who has the care only of a
> few millions, to whom he cannot do much good or harm, what must be
> the anxiety of him, on whom depend the action of the elements, and the
> great gifts of light and heat! . . . I have sometimes turned aside the axis
> of the earth, and sometimes varied the ecliptick of the sun: but I have
> found it impossible to make a disposition by which the world may be
> advantaged; what one region gains, another loses by any imaginable
> alteration, even without considering the distant parts of the solar sys-

tem with which we are unacquainted. . . . The memory of mischief is no desirable fame. (*Rasselas*, ch. 42 [43])

Swift would have placed this astronomer in his rogues' gallery of crazed projectors. Johnson presents him as a morally and intellectually admirable man, whose derangement proceeds from the nature and the solitude of his professional calling, and who exemplifies that "most dreadful and alarming" uncertainty of life, "the uncertain continuance of reason" (ch 42 [43]). He is the subject of a tenderly self-involving tragi-comedy on Johnson's part. His delusion of omnipotence is quite free from the self-congratulation of Swift's hack, as the latter announces that his "Imaginations are hard-mouth'd, and exceedingly disposed to run away with his *Reason*," and *a fortiori* free also from the power-mania that in Swift's same Digression on Madness makes conquerors and other madmen dream of "subduing Multitudes" (*Tale*, 9). In Swift's vision, moreover, fantasy has a dangerous way of spilling into reality. Ambitions of universal conquest, though they start as mental vapors and anal fistulas, turn into a Louis XIV raising "mighty Armies" (*Tale*, sec. 9). Swift's most exact parallel to Johnson's astronomer, who imagines that he can control the weather, is the King of Laputa, who *really can* (with his flying island) do just this:

> as it is in the Power of the Monarch to raise the Island above the Region of Clouds and Vapours, he can prevent the falling of Dews and Rains whenever he pleases. (*Gulliver*, 3.3)

This is no mere science-fiction extravagance, for it turns out that this maneuverability of the flying island is the direct instrument of political tyranny (in particular England's, over the Irish):

> If any Town should engage in Rebellion or Mutiny, fall into violent Factions, or refuse to pay the usual Tribute; the King hath two Methods of reducing them to Obedience. The first and the mildest Course is by keeping the Island hovering over such a Town, and the Lands about it; whereby he can deprive them of the Benefit of the Sun and the Rain, and consequently afflict the Inhabitants with Dearth and Diseases. And if the Crime deserve it, they are at the same time pelted from above with great Stones, against which they have no Defence, but by creeping into Cellars of Caves, while the Roofs of their Houses are beaten to Pieces. But if they still continue obstinate, or offer to raise Insurrections; he proceeds to the last Remedy, by letting the Island drop directly upon their Heads, which makes a universal Destruction

both of Houses and Men. However, this is an Extremity to which the Prince is seldom driven.

The last phrase, of course, softens nothing. Nor is it meant to: for as we read on, we discover that the reasons for holding back, normally, from "a universal Destruction," are cynical reasons of expediency. Johnson's moral writing normally rejects examples of great national catastrophes because he feels that they are easily exaggerated and remote from the experience of most readers. "I cannot bear that querelous eloquence which threatens every city with a siege like that of Jerusalem," says Rasselas to his sister, for such things are usually "found in books rather than in the world" (ch. 28); and in his own voice Johnson said that "histories of the downfall of kingdoms, and revolutions of empires, are read with great tranquillity," since the happiness of private men is seldom affected by great events (*Rambler*, No. 60,13 October 1750; see also Nos. 17 and 68, and *Idler*, No. 84). Even when he is himself writing specifically about the cruelties of war, as in *Thoughts on . . . Falkland's Islands* (1771), he will remind us that "war is not the whole business of life; it happens but seldom. . . ." He once or twice describes carnage with something like a Swiftian generality, but without the more spectacular details and with a stress on the drabness of its miseries, as a realistic reminder to readers deluded by "heroick fiction." The "generality" itself escapes Rasselas's objections, for it has a precise factual validation: Johnson is referring to specific events of the recent past.

The literal-minded insistence that personal distresses are more common than large-scale disasters, or that, among acts of personal wrong-doing, violence and bloodshed occur more seldom than acts of "concupiscible" sin, runs through all his thought. It is a theme of sermon 18 in the Yale Edition of Johnson's *Sermons*. The belief that the more spectacular evils are more uncommon goes hand in hand with a view that they are more remote and therefore less effective as moral examples. The fact that they usually occur "in books rather than in the world" is a warning to the writer to keep them out of *his* books; it confirms Johnson in his preference for factual over fictional genres, his special predilection for biography, and his stress on minute personal detail in biography as more instructively revealing and more moving than public deeds or occurrences.

Related to this is an important difference in satiric style, which is more than merely a difference between Swiftian repudiation and Johnsonian tolerance. That temperamental defensiveness which

built a restless indirection into Swift's most casual utterances and
made his writing bristle with aggressive mystifications and the con-
cealments of ironic obliquity is far removed from the almost compulsively vulnerable, open, literal-minded truthfulness of Johnson.
Irony not only tends towards disguise and indirection. Since it says
something different from what it really means, it is also by
definition *literally untrue*; and Johnson often shows an instinctive
impulse to confute or resist its implied fictions and its distortions of
sheer fact. Some of his talking for victory consists of literalizing
into nonsense the more figured, oblique or "witty" observations of
his friends. Johnson shrank from irony as Swift shrank from plain
statement.

Bate notes that *Marmor Norfolciense* failed because "indirect and
drawn-out irony was never . . . Johnson's forte," and that much
Johnsonian irony resembles that of Hardy rather than that of the
Augustan ironists. He says this is because Johnson's "vision [is]
more essentially tragic than comic" (Bate, *Samuel Johnson*, pp. 201,
279–80), but Swift's irony or that of Pope's *Dunciad* could plausibly
be described as "tragic" too. The crucial difference is surely between an irony that is situational and one that is mainly verbal, and
it is this that gives the analogy with Hardy its pregnant rightness.
Johnson is full of pained instances of the cruel turns of life, life's
little (and not-so-little) ironies, but the relative absence of Bate's
"Augustan" irony comes not mainly from "tragic" vision, but from
the peculiar literal-mindedness of Johnson's nature. It is the product of a rectitude so open and so doggedly committed to plain
palpable fact that it cannot lightly allow itself the distorting obli-
quities of verbal wit and satiric fantasy.

It is partly for this reason that Johnsonian satire "misses" (not of
course misfires), turning into something else. Johnson will, for example, refuse a satiric exaggeration or distortion simply because it
is not factually true, or not so commonly or widely true as the plain
occurrences of private domestic existence. His peculiarly literal-
minded style, by contrast with the ironic negations and fantastications of Swift, is almost in itself a medium of accommodation and
acceptance.

Bate's well-known, acute, and ungrammatical conception of
Johnson's "satire *manqué*" rightly sees it as "a form in which protest
and satire, ridicule and even anger, are essential ingredients at the
start but then, caught up in a larger context of charity, begin to
turn into something else" (*Samuel Johnson*, p. 295). It explains a great
deal. The merely formal aspect of the difference from Swift that I

have been sketching should not, however, be exaggerated. For just as Swift, in some of his lesser works, and less often than has been claimed, sometimes wrote in a plain style devoid of ironic indirection, so Johnson occasionally did the opposite. Two of his early works were conscious exercises in "Swiftian" irony: *Marmor Norfolciense*, and the *Complete Vindication of the Licensers of the Stage*. This early fixation on Swift was also playfully sustained by the parliamentary reports that he concocted for the *Gentleman's Magazine* under the title "Debates in the Senate of Magna Lilliputia," and there were examples of "sarcasm and 'sophistry' " among the political writings of his later years. But these works are exceptional, and the few overt Swiftian imitations may be taken as among the more superficial instances of that deep similarity with Swift that Johnson seems uneasily to have sensed in himself. His dislike of Swift, as Bate observed in an earlier book, may have been partly due to the fact that "he was in some ways temperamentally akin" (*The Achievement of Samuel Johnson* [New York: Oxford University Press, 1961] p. 126). The scarcity of sustained irony and of severe satiric exposure in his mature work may also have been due to a desire to minimize this resemblance to Swift, who certainly became (even if Bate overstates in saying that he "always" was) "a frightening example for Johnson of what not to be" (*Samuel Johnson*, p. 498).

Misfortune, then, seems real for Johnson the less public, the more domestic, it is, and the more literal-mindedly it is described. Swift, on the other hand, makes one feel that huge misfortunes and turpitudes, however extensively spread and however fantasticated in his description, are immediate and indeed almost domestically relevant: think of Ireland beneath the Laputian island, or in the *Modest Proposal*, or the brilliant universalized portrayals in *Gulliver's Travels* of the depravities and devastations of war. What Johnson will describe as a pitiful fantasy of the mind, Swift actualizes as totalitarian terror. If the Laputians are at times charmingly mad, with their abstracted air, their flappers, their substitution of things for words, they are no mere unreal society of harmless academics: their school of political projectors is at times mad with the terrible reality of modern research establishments, of obscenely prying secret services, and of other horrors (*Gulliver*, 3. 6). These tyrannical consequences of the universal madness are a grotesquely concrete counterpart of those political results of "freethinking" that Swift imaged in the parody, already cited, of a freethinker's mind: "*forcing* all the World to think as he does, and by that means make them *Free Thinkers* too" (above, p. 31).

It is not surprising, in view of this, to find that in Swift's satire the notion of madness as something to be punished is expressed with particular vividness. Talking of some of the world's "Grand Innovators," subduers of multitudes, the Digression on Madness remarks

> that several of the chief among them, both *Antient* and *Modern*, were usually mistaken by their Adversaries, and indeed, by all, except their own Followers, to have been Persons Crazed, or out of their Wits, having generally proceeded in the common Course of their Words and Actions, by a Method very different from the vulgar Dictates of *unrefined* Reason: agreeing for the most Part in their several Models, with their Present undoubted Successors in the *Academy* of *Modern Bedlam.* (*Tale*, 9)

Swift then makes his "author" add, in a way that emphasizes both the fitness of severe punishment for madness and the tyrannical bent of the mad "Innovators":

> Of this Kind were *Epicurus, Diogenes, Apollonius, Lucretius, Paracelsus, Des Cartes*, and others; who, if they were now in the World, tied fast, and separate from their Followers, would in this our undistinguishing Age, incur manifest Danger of *Phlebotomy*, and *Whips*, and *Chains*, and *dark Chambers*, and *Straw*. For, what Man in the natural State, or Course of Thinking, did ever conceive it in his Power, to reduce the Notions of all Mankind, exactly to the same Length, and Breadth, and Heighth of his own?

Mad is bad, and a modern reader is struck by the undifferentiated mingling of medical (phlebotomy, or blood-letting) and punitive (whips, etc.) treatments. When, especially in *Gulliver's Travels*, Reason is spoken of as a *moral* faculty, sins and vices come to be seen as deviations from Reason, and therefore, by a familiar buried pun, as forms of *un*reason. The "natural State . . . of Thinking" to which the Digression on Madness refers, means "normal state" in at least three leading (and interpenetrating) senses: 1, fitting, proper, healthy, the state in which all minds ought to be; and therefore, 2, the state in which the mind naturally or spontaneously exists when not interfered with; and 3, the common, usual, ordinary state of men's minds. A large part of the satiric enterprise of *Gulliver's Travels* consists of exposing radical incongruities in the human character, in which these various senses of "nature" and "natural" fail to dovetail: vice is unnatural in sense 1, but man is perversely given to vice, which comes naturally to him in senses 2 and 3. This paradox is elaborated in coils upon coils of painful ironic refinement in *Gulliver*, reinforcing in endless unpredictable ways the grotesque connection between folly and vice, universalizing its reach to the whole of mankind. The passage from the Digression is ostensibly less universalizing, since its point is to distinguish sane minds in their "natural State" from those that are mad-and-bad. The Digression also, however, has some irrational tendencies, in its style rather than its statements, towards a universal applicability to all men, one minor example of which being that *"Academy* of *Modern Bedlam"* whose inmates are turned into types of the various classes and professions of men.[1]

This literal Madhouse reinforces, by an extra ironic twist, the equation of mad-and-bad: for it says not only the conventional thing, that badness is unnatural, perverse, or mad in a *moral* sense, but also that this equation is so deeply true that typical badnesses may be inferred from the literally mad (in a *medical* sense). This added twist is a rhetorical flourish, not a sober truth, and the equation of mad-and-bad, not rare in satire, is part of a satiric fiction or joke. But the readiness (not facility) with which Swift oscillates between mad and bad, the depth of his imaginative commitment to aspects of the equation in the *Tale* and in *Gulliver*, and his insistent politicization of the notion of "universal madness" (in "straight" political arguments as well as in ironic fantasies), show that more is at work than a formulaic exercise.

The tendency to see madness as culpable is perhaps one to which highly tradition-conscious and cohesive societies (in which outsiders are neither pitied very much, nor glorified in a Romantic way) are prone, even if, or especially if, the society's values and cohesiveness are felt to be threatened by the pressures of social change. Swift's was a highly conservative temperament, in an age when conservative temperaments (Pope's was another example) felt particularly acutely that their traditions and culture were in grave jeopardy from "modern" upstart encroachments, notably of arrogant individualists, "innovators," sectarians. They might have felt that their fears had been fulfilled in the sense that, in the eighty or so years after the death of Pope and Swift, the figure of the outsider, the rebel, and man of feeling, the high soul charged with noble frenzy, acquired an increasing and unprecedented respectability and indeed glamour in European society. It is also in roughly the same period that more compassionate and philanthropic attitudes to social outcasts (the insane, fallen women, and others)

established themselves with a new, widespread, and in-
stitutionalized effectiveness. Swift was, in a sense, part of both
movements himself. It is a curious irony, and perhaps not an entirely inappropriate one, that a powerful later tradition should
think of him as a heroic outsider (demonic misanthrope, or Byronic
rebel, or Promethean protester): on this paradoxical feature of
Swift's self-implication in the objects of his own attack I shall have
more to say. Here I wish to note the part he played in the second
and less dramatic of the two movements, the growth of philanthropic sentiments and institutions.

For if Swift equated mad with bad in certain ways, and if his
satiric fictions (as well as contemporary social fact, in some instances) interchangeably inflict upon their victims phlebotomy and
whips, there is another side to the matter. Swift left money to
found a mental hospital in Ireland (showing "by one satyric
Touch,/No Nation wanted it so much," as he wryly commented at
the end of the *Verses* on his own death), and had liberal and farsighted views about the treatment of mental illness.[2] The ambiguity that this implies existed also in Johnson, though in a less starkly
polarized form. If Johnson's notion of the "universal madness" was
by no means free of attribution of sin, he was (though never smug)
more compassionate and more self-tolerant about it. He differed
from Swift not only in feeling less intensely the analogy between
private and political madness, but in being much less concerned
(not unconcerned) to make satiric judgments on men's failures to
submit energy to rule.

Bate reminds us that Johnson had many of the primary characteristics of a satirist: a quickness to sense incongruity and pretense,
a well-developed aggressiveness, a temperamental irritability and
dissatisfaction aggravated by personal suffering, an instinctive re-
ductionist talent not unlike Swift's, and one might add, a certain
violence or immoderation of character combined with a desperate
attachment to the disciplines of moderation and good sense(*Samuel
Johnson*, pp. 489–90, 495). Unlike Swift's however, Johnson's re-
ductions do not *leave* their victim humiliated and crushed: instead
they readily open into afterthoughts that tend to explain and even
defend. The differences are mainly personal, but they have a
chronological aptness. For if both men saw "restlessness" as universal and incurable, and as implicating themselves, it was the earlier
of the two who punished himself and others most uncompromisingly for it, and who most explicitly and systematically proposed

measures to deal with it on the social and political, as well as the private and introspective, planes.

Law, Morals and Hypocrisy

Swift opposed tyranny, whether of the One, the Few, or the Many. We have seen that some of his leanings were authoritarian and that he has sometimes been accused of tyrannical or totalitarian implications. Perhaps this suggests yet another instance of Swift's paradoxical assimilation to the things he attacks. But part of the reason why some modern readers emphasize the totalitarian implications may be that we are more suspicious today of applying a psychological analysis of the human condition too directly in the service of political or social action. Fears of such a direct application would seem less pressingly urgent then than they do to us, with our technologized media of mass-persuasion and our highly developed techniques of individual brainwashing. Psychological accounts of man's nature and condition that have an actual or potential bearing on political programs or ideals are not lacking in our time. But those (like Norman Brown's or Herbert Marcuse's) that command respect are unable to rely on any widespread consensus of moral standards in their own society, and unable therefore to make simple direct connections between the morally good and the politically enforceable. They cannot say as literally as Swift sometimes says that because personal and public "restlessness" are parallel and interpenetrating, therefore the sanctions dressed against both are, at a certain level, the same. Swift's equation sometimes implies greater and more direct legal control over private morals and personal feelings than we are prepared to accept in principle, perhaps because we are less able today to count on rough agreement about the moral standards themselves. In *The Publick Spirit of the Whigs* (1714), Swift jeered at Steele's assertion that *"Men's Beings are degraded when their Passions are no longer governed by the Dictates of their own Mind,"* as

> directly contrary to the Lessons of all Moralists and Legislators; who agree unanimously, that the Passions of Men must be under the Government of Reason and Law; neither are Laws of any other Use than to correct the Irregularity of our Affections. (*Works*, 8:46–47)

The statement is, in itself, a commonplace. But it shows the readiness with which Swift sees Reason and the Law, the inner and the outer sanctions, as parallel and mutually reinforcing regulators of that culpable madness to which all men are prone, and which sects and freethinkers threaten to institutionalize.

Hence Swift's feeling that laws ought not only to be keepers of public order, but guardians of private morals. The authority of princes, Swift says in *A Project for the Advancement of Religion, and the Reformation of Manners* (1709), must be vigorously exercised towards "making it every Man's Interest and Honour to cultivate Religion and Virtue," by insisting on moral virtue as a precondition of professional preferment, and by appointing censors to watch over the moral behavior of public officials, the morality of plays, and the religious orthodoxy of published writings (*Works*, 2:47 ff., 49, 56, 60). In this *Project* (quite wrongly but understandably considered by some critics to be ironical), Swift is almost more concerned with psychological effects, with the control of mental predispositions, than with legal enforcement as such. This concern does not make his insistence on authority or on legal sanctions any less, but the assurance of enforcement is partly seen as a form of mind-bending, or character-molding. Most legal or institutional arrangements have partly a psychological function, as deterrents to bad actions or incentives to good ones, but Swift insists on this function with particular force, and focuses part of his discussion, with an unusually literal-minded practicality, on the mental operations involved.

A notorious example of this is to be found in Swift's handling of the objection that his project is likely to encourage hypocrisy rather than virtue. He does not deny the charge, but claims pragmatically not only that hypocrisy is better than open vice, but that it can be put to psychological use in support of virtue:

> Neither am I aware of any Objections to be raised against what I have advanced; unless it should be thought, that the making Religion a necessary Step to Interest and Favour, might encrease Hypocrisy among us: And I readily believe it would. But if One in Twenty should be brought over to true Piety by this, or the like Methods, and the other Nineteen be only Hypocrites, the Advantage would still be great. Besides, Hypocrisy is much more eligible than open Infidelity and Vice: It wears the Livery of Religion, it acknowledgeth her Authority, and is cautious of giving Scandal. Nay, a long continued Disguise is too great a Constraint upon human Nature, especially an *English* Disposition. Men would leave off their Vices out of meer Weariness, rather than undergo the Toil and Hazard, and perhaps Expence of practising them perpetually in private. And, I believe, it is often with Religion as it is

with Love; which, by much Dissembling, at last grows real. (*Works*, 2:56–57)

It is possible to be shocked at this apparently cynical pragmatism. Irvin Ehrenpreis says of it: "As threadbare cynicism or as muddled psychology, it is equally deplorable and naïve" (*Swift: The Man, His Works, and the Age*, vol. 2: *Dr. Swift* [London: Methuen, 1967], pp. 293–94). The reaction is understandable, especially if one emphasizes, as Ehrenpreis (at a certain level quite correctly) does, the element of practical political exhortation in the *Project*, its place in a tradition of political thought, and its immediate historical context, when Queen Anne actually issued "a royal proclamation 'for the encouragement of piety and virtue, and for the preventing and punishing vice'" (Ehrenpreis, 2:289 ff., 293). But the passage can also properly be viewed in the context of Swift's pessimistic sense of the relentless pressure of vicious impulses, where any stratagem that saved a bit of ground for virtue might seem justified. Perhaps the sentiments seem less shocking when expressed by Johnson, no friend to hypocrites (any more, for that matter, than Swift was):

> With the hypocrite it is not at present my intention to expostulate, though even he might be taught the excellency of virtue, by the necessity of seeming to be virtuous; but the man of affectation may, perhaps, be reclaimed, by finding how little he is likely to gain by perpetual constraint, and incessant vigilance, and how much more securely he might make his way to esteem, by cultivating real, than displaying counterfeit qualities. (*Rambler*, No. 20, 26 May 1750)

Johnson is not advocating a political program, but his "psychology" is similar (his distinction between hypocrisy and affectation is marginal to the present discussion), and it does not seem muddled, deplorable or naïve. It belongs with that same literal-minded acknowledgment of human frailty, and the same practical acceptance of less than absolute remedies, which lead Johnson to say elsewhere, for example, that one should not too readily condemn the hypocrisy of authors who fail, in life, to live up to the principles that they honestly advocate in their writings (e.g., *Rambler*, No. 14, 5 May 1750).

When Johnson makes Imlac tell Rasselas not to be too hasty to admire "the teachers of morality: they discourse like angels, but they live like men" (*Rasselas*, ch. 18), he is engaging in no *mere* stripping of pretenses. Living "like men" is in the end not more than men can do, and Johnson frequently stresses that moralists and men of letters have a duty to "discourse like angels" and to advocate virtue, even if as men they cannot live up to their precepts, a position ultimately close to that from which Swift, in the *Project*, asserted the social value of some such kinds of "hypocrisy," though Swift did so with more dry distaste than charitable understanding. In his satire, the yawning failure of men to live like angels or even Houyhnhnms is hardly palliated by the beastly and uncompromising reality known as living "like men." Johnson said in a sermon that repentant sinners "are not to be excluded from commemorating the sufferings of our Saviour, in a Christian congregation, who would not be shut from heaven . . . and the choirs of angels." The Yale editors (who believe this sermon to be by Johnson despite an element of doubt) cite Johnson's defense to Boswell of the right of a repentant fornicator to be ordained: "A man who is good enough to go to heaven, is good enough to be a clergyman" (*Sermons*, Yale Edition, pp. 97–98 nn.) This may seem to contrast with Swift's emphasis in the *Project* on banning profligates even from *secular* preferments. But both men *begin* with the same literal-minded acknowledgement of a radically peccant world: there is no benign underplaying or softening of that harsh initial fact, as there might be in Chaucer or Dickens, only a partially different response to the fact once noted.

Though no unqualified admirer of Swift, Johnson significantly praised the *Project*, objecting only

> that, like many projects, it is, if not generally impracticable, yet evidently hopeless, as it supposes more zeal, concord, and perseverance than a view of mankind gives reason for expecting. (*Lives of the Poets*, ed. G. B. Hill [Oxford, 1905] 3:13)

Swift would, in fact, certainly accept most of this "objection." He was at bottom no more optimistic than Johnson, and no more given to viewing mankind in any sort of moral "concord," actual or potential. It is precisely because of this that he will settle, like Johnson, for *ad hoc* and pragmatic checks on human unruliness, rather than envisaging total or wholly satisfying solutions: "he that would keep his House in Repair, must attend every little Breach or Flaw, and supply it immediately, else Time alone will bring all to Ruin; how much more the common Accidents of Storms and Rain?" (*Project, Works*, 2:63). The tone is hardly buoyant. If the *Project* is not as "hopeless" as Johnson feels the facts warrant, this is only because its formal business is to *propose* a few of the needed repairs. Swift sardonically confines his proposals within the reach of existing administrative and legal powers: "All other Projects . . . have proved hitherto ineffectual. Laws against Immorality have not been executed," and as to any notions of "introducing new Laws for the Amendment of Mankind," they are just "airy Imaginations" (*Works*, 2:57, 61). In this most literal Swiftian ruefulness, we recognize a sober echo of the crazed accents of those later, *fictional* reformers of mankind, Gulliver and the modest proposer; just as the *Project*'s confidence in its genuinely limited and "modest" program,

> Neither am I aware of any Objections to be raised against what I have advanced (*Works*, 2:56)

anticipates not only the modest proposer's calm assurance, but Gulliver's testy certainty of being

> an Author perfectly blameless; against whom the Tribes of Answerers, Considerers, Observers, Reflecters, Detecters, Remarkers, will never be able to find Matter for exercising their Talents. (*Gulliver's Travels*, 4. 12)

These resemblances do not "prove" that the *Project* is radically ironical, like the *Modest Proposal*. If anything they rather emphasize the closeness of Swift's relation to the rhetorical postures he assumed through his fictional *personae*, a relation that oscillates between direct congruence and the kind of intimate mirror-opposition where self and anti-self complete one another. Irvin Ehrenpreis compares the ironic advocacy of nominal rather than real Christianity in the *Argument Against Abolishing Christianity* ("Written in the year 1708," about the same time as the *Project*, though not actually published until 1711), with the *Project*'s literal tolerance of a degree of "hypocrisy".

> It is one thing for Swift in the *Argument* barely to admit Tartufe as a despicable *pis aller*; it is another thing for him in the *Project* to hold up false godliness as second only to true. (Ehrenpreis, *Swift*, 2:294)

Ehrenpreis's judgment of the *Project* may, as I suggested, seem unduly unsympathetic; but the parallel, as such, is important.

Properly speaking, the *Argument Against Abolishing Christianity* has two principal ironies at the expense of a hypocritical "nominal christianity," both of which enter into a teasing relationship with the literal acceptance of "hypocrisy" in the *Project*. The first is more absolute, and more immediately obvious to the uninstructed modern reader. It says that things have become so bad that the speaker can blandly take for granted that nobody wants real christianity, insisting modestly on the nominal kind as the only one likely to be accepted, and for the crudest reasons of expediency at that: that stocks and shares might otherwise drop, for example (*Works*, 2:38–39). The suggestion at this level is that irreligion—the notion, for Swift, unites atheists and nonconformists indiscriminately—is bad, but a society where irreligion assumes a hypocritical appearance of religion to further its irreligious purposes is worse.

The second and more specific irony is that described by Ehrenpreis. It runs somewhat across the other (no unfamiliar thing in Swiftian satire, which always tends to attack on more than one front, with the victim losing either way), admitting "hypocrisy" as an unworthy second best, or *pis aller*. Swift dislikes "nominal christianity" while writing in defense of the Test Act, which imposed a nominal communion on sectarians and freethinkers in public office. Ehrenpreis (2:284) puts it very well: "occasional conformists are hypocrites; but . . . the true church will be stronger if men are forced into hypocrisy than if they are released into unlimited freedom of worship." Where Dissenters are concerned, some forms of restraint or disguise of "natural" impulses seemed to Swift called for. Moreover, the unillusioned (or "muddled" and "naïve") psychology which claims that sincerity can supervene on a prolonged or determined or externally induced hypocrisy, does not entail an automatic approval of sincerity as such. Puritans may be scorned as mechanical operators of the spirit, but Swift's point, said to be an original contribution to anti-Puritan satire (see Ehrenpreis, *Swift: The Man, His Works, and The Age* [London: Methuen, 1962] 1:246) that some of their "enthusiasm" is "an Effect grown from *Art* into *Nature*," hardly creates respect for their sincerity (*Mechanical Operation of the Spirit*, 1704, *Works*, 1:176). Swift's graphic vision of their grotesque passionate spontaneities adds a further dimension to the *Project*'s tolerance of hypocrisy.

It is clear that the antithesis between the *Project*'s advocacy of "hypocrisy" and that side of the *Argument* which ironically praises but actually deplores it, holds together what in fact are closely connected attitudes—as indeed the *other* implication of the *Argument*, that "occasional conformity" must be enforced, demonstrates. The coexistence in the *Argument* of an attack that both intensifies the distaste for "hypocrisy" and at the same time asserts a practical if contemptuous preference for it, should not surprise us unduly. For it is precisely because Swift felt that an absolute principle or ideal standard was being violated that he was pained into sarcastic (but not unmeaning) praises of an otherwise unacceptable compromise. No man is more tartly and doggedly "realistic" than a certain type of disillusioned idealist, and none more likely to insist that unacceptable compromises are what, in the practical politics of life, one must, finally, settle for. Not only is the "realism" a protest against the betrayal of more absolute expectations, a haughty rubbing-in of the meanness of things: it is also a limiting of moral demands to a scale small enough to satisfy an absolutist temperament instead of oppressing him with dispiriting loose ends. The ideal of perfection embodied in the Houyhnhnms is presented on the assumption that no one can achieve it, and at the same time as a matter of plain utilitarian common sense. It is clear that, in Swift's case at least, the relation between pragmatism and absolutism, between the man who advocates balances of power *(Contests and Dissensions)*, middle ways *(Sentiments of a Church-of-England Man)*, and specific economic expedients (Irish tracts), and the man who invents Houyhnhnmland, is very close.

The *Project* provides a vivid glimpse not only of the pragmatist who will be content with half-measures that support virtue by saving appearances, but also of the absolute moralist who recoils from compromise. There is, for example, a strong passage denouncing polite society's tolerance of "Women of tainted Reputations," as a sign that "Regard for Reputation" is at a low ebb:

> If this be not so; how comes it to pass, that women of tainted Reputations find the same Countenance and Reception in all publick Places, with those of the nicest Virtue, who pay, and receive Visits from them, without any Manner of Scruple? Which Proceeding, as it is not very old among us, so I take it to be of most pernicious Consequence. It looks like a Sort of compounding between Virtue and Vice; as if a Woman were allowed to be vicious, provided she be not profligate: As if there were a certain Point where Gallantry ends, and Infamy begins; or that an Hundred criminal Amours were not as pardonable as Half a Score. (*Works*, 2:46)

There is nothing surprising in the fact that Swift deplored female immorality and the polite world's tolerance of it. The gap between good manners and good morals that the situation exposes exercised many courtesy-writers who, like Swift, wished to insist, more or less emphatically, on the moral basis and the moral function of manners. That it was possible to do this and to value chastity without applying a totally dismissive rigor to "criminal Amours" is variously shown by, for example, Fielding and Chesterfield. Fielding felt that there were many vices worse than lewdness, and that the *Beau Monde* might profitably be humanized by a certain amount of love, even though "criminal" (*Tom Jones*, 14.1), at least where a generosity and mutuality of feeling, and a benevolent expansiveness were involved. Chesterfield spoke, in a more "libertine" and less morally concerned way than Fielding, of the civilizing properties of fashionable women, the importance to best companies of "Women of fashion and character (I do not mean absolutely unblemished)" (letter to his godson, 4 December 1765, *Letters*, ed. Bonamy Dobrée [London, 1932], 6:2688); and one might feel that Chesterfield is perhaps close to being an exponent of the kind of attitude Swift had castigated. Even so, Swift's complaint of a gap between morals and the code of manners would not seem surprising or unacceptable to either Fielding or Chesterfield. But what is notable in Swift's passage is the vividness with which he is shocked at the notion of a social compromise with morality ("a Sort of compounding between Virtue and Vice"), and the way the writing kindles at this into exposing vistas of vacuous absurdity: "as if there were a certain Point where Gallantry ends, and infamy begins." Where Fielding and Chesterfield both seek to narrow the gap between morals and manners, Swift makes use of a logic that inexorably widens this gap until the whole social basis of the compromise is reduced to nullity. In an absolute morality, there can be no chartable point where gallantry ends and infamy begins. One may be sure that for Fielding "an Hundred criminal Amours" were indeed "not as pardonable as Half a Score." Yet it is Swift, the more absolute moralist of the two, who proposes *ad hoc* and practical remedies to patch up the situation, and who, refusing to envisage total changes of heart, recommends the enlisting of hypocrisy and the use of job incentives as viable and not unacceptable aids to morality.

Sound and Moderate Men

From the notion of job incentives for the virtuous to the notion that it is better to employ virtuous than able men is a fairly short step. If state employees were appointed with a regard to their piety and virtue and remained exemplary in the Conduct of their Lives, Things would soon take a new Face, and Religion receive a mighty Encouragement: Nor would the publick Weal be less advanced; since of nine Offices in ten that are ill executed, the Defect is not in Capacity or Understanding, but in common Honesty. (*Project, Works,* 2:48–49)

The matter is taken up in *Gulliver's Travels.* In describing the state of Lilliput in its original Utopian purity (as against the "scandalous Corruptions" it has since fallen into) Gulliver says:

> In chusing Persons for all Employments, they have more Regard to good Morals than to great Abilities: For, since Government is necessary to Mankind, they believe that the common Size of human Understandings, is fitted to some Station or other; and that Providence never intended to make the Management of publick Affairs a Mystery, to be comprehended only by a few Persons of sublime Genius, of which there seldom are three born in an Age: But, they suppose Truth, Justice, Temperance, and the like, to be in every Man's Power; the Practice of which Virtues, assisted by Experience and a good Intention, would qualify any Man for the Service of his Country, except where a Course of Study is required. But they thought the Want of Moral Virtues was so far from being supplied by superior Endowments of the Mind, that Employments could never be put into such dangerous Hands as those of Persons so qualified; and at least, that the Mistakes committed by Ignorance in a virtuous Disposition, would never be of such fatal Consequence to the Publick Weal, as the Practices of a Man, whose Inclinations led him to be corrupt, and had great Abilities to manage, to multiply, and defend his Corruptions. (*Gulliver,* 1.6)

The King of Brobdingnag took a plain moral view of government, in which a similar preference for sound moral principles over the refinements of expertise is rooted simultaneously in an uncomplicated rectitude and a simplifying utilitarianism:

> He confined the Knowledge of governing within very *narrow Bounds;* to common Sense and Reason, to Justice and Lenity, to the Speedy Determination of Civil and criminal Causes; with some other obvious Topicks which are not worth considering. And, he gave it for his Opinion; that whoever could make two Ears of Corn, or two Blades of Grass to grow upon a Spot of Ground where only one grew before; would deserve better of Mankind, and do more essential Service to his Country, than the whole Race of Politicians put together. (*Gulliver,* 2.7)

One recognizes here the familiar lineaments of an aristocratic contempt for the professional, and also of that distantly related and

rather British cult of the sound mediocre all-round man in preference to the highly trained specialist (Even the "Course of Study"
required for certain jobs in Lilliput sounds more like a requirement
of basic competence in those fields where such competence involves
study than any emphasis on a highly developed specialist skill).
Swift's fear is clearly not only of the superior danger of an able
rogue "to manage, to multiply, and defend his Corruptions." There
is too the conception of the expert as a pedant, a fussy distorter of
plain central truths and traditional ways, a multiplier of false needs
and false complications. Mystery, refinement, and similar restless
invitations to intellectual and moral perversion are not the exclusive
preserve of sects, nor of learned moderns, but extend to those who
think of politics as a science or art (*Gulliver*, 2.7). The expert advis-
ers of monarchs are frequently mocked (*Gulliver*, 1.2 and 2.3). By
contrast, free-minded men like Swift may quite properly advise the
great, who, however, will not take advice, for an amusing reason
that Swift explained in *A Letter from Dr. Swift to Mr. Pope*, dated 10
January 1721:

> this pedantry ariseth from a maxim themselves do not believe at the
> same time they practice by it, that there is something profound in
> politicks, which men of plain honest sense cannot arrive to. (*Works*,
> 9:28)

Even good politicians and courtiers, like the Earl of Oxford, are
caught up in a pretense that is not only false, but in which they
disbelieve. Swift's role in offering advice is that of the man "of plain
honest sense," not that of the professional adviser: "I have formerly
delivered my thoughts very freely, whether I were asked or no, but
never affected to be a Councellor, to which I had no manner of call"
(loc. cit.). Swift adds in explanation:

> I was humbled enough to see my self so far out-done by the Earl of
> Oxford in my own trade as a Scholar, and too good a Courtier not to
> discover his contempt of those who would be men of importance out of
> their sphere. (loc. cit.)

These lines must not be taken as a celebration of specialist expertise. Their main force is to say, negatively, that men should not
meddle in what they know nothing about. "My own trade as a
Scholar" is a mock-modest reference to his liberal education, and to
what is expected of a civilized clergyman and man of letters: no
pedantry, nothing which a gentlemen should lack, as witness the

Earl's outdoing Swift in this sphere (part of the phrasing, of course, is accounted for the the wish to speak handsomely of the former chief minister).

Outside specialist departments of government, where mastery of a "Course of Studies" is required, Swift's inclination is then to insist on a general soundness of character rather than specialist skill or even brillant ability in general (although he does praise that in Lord Oxford and others). His ideal is perhaps one in which ability and expertise merge with a larger wisdom and with virtue. This passage about the political projectors in Lagado suggests a reluctance to distinguish too closely between moral and intellectual qualifications, seeming instead to take for granted an ideal in which the two are interfused:

> These unhappy People were proposing Schemes for persuading Monarchs to chuse Favourites upon the Score of their Wisdom, Capacity and Virtue; of teaching Ministers to consult the publick Good; of rewarding Merit, Great Abilities, and eminent Services; of instructing Princes to know their true Interest, by placing it on the same Foundation with that of their People: Of chusing for Employments Persons qualified to exercise them, with many other wild impossible Chimaeras, that never entered before into the Heart of Man to conceive. (*Gulliver*, 3.6)

The list is deliberately headlong, its brisk summarizing irony playing down any separation of morality from talent in good politics. But a passage like this easily shades into a protest against the way talented men remain unrewarded while cautious mediocrities prosper:

> There is no *Talent* so useful towards rising in the World, or which puts Men more out of the Reach of Fortune, than that Quality generally possessed by the the dullest Sort of People, in common Speech called *Discretion;* a Species of lower Prudence, by the Assistance of which, People of the meanest Intellectuals, without any other Qualification, pass through the World in great Tranquility, and with universal good Treatment, neither giving nor taking Offence. . . . And, indeed, as Regularity and Forms are of great Use in carrying on the Business of the World, so it is very convenient, that Persons endued with this Kind of Discretion, should have the Share which is proper to their Talents, in the Conduct of Affairs; but, by no Means, meddle in Matters which require *Genius, Learning, strong Comprehension, Quickness of Conception, Magnanimity, Generosity, Sagacity,* or any other superior Gift of human minds. (*Intelligencer*, No. 5, 1728, *Works,* 12:38)

The discussion slightly later notes that many "Men of eminent Parts and Abilities, as well as Virtues" in many countries have been

> *disgraced*, or *banished*, or *suffered Death*, merely in Envy to their Virtues and superior *Genius*, which emboldened them in great Exigencies and Distresses of State (wanting a reasonable Infusion of this Aldermanly Discretion) to attempt the Service of their Prince and Country, out of the common Forms. (*Works*, 12:39)

One recognizes here the contempt of the man of great talent towards the mediocre, and the "common Forms." But it is precisely because Swift recognized in himself a subversiveness that would throw out the "common Forms" along with their bathwater of mediocrity, and because he saw in a certain kind of rule-bound mediocrity a protection against this subversiveness, that he insisted so often elsewhere on the common forms as a civilized bastion against individualist misrule. Thus Lord Munodi stands out from the mad originals of Gulliver's third voyage in that

> being not of an enterprizing Spirit, he was content to go on in the old Forms; to live in the Houses his Ancestors had built, and act as they did in every Part of Life without Innovation; (*Gulliver*, 3.4)

and the sane, traditionalist man of sense in the Digression on Madness is defined as passing

> his Life in the common Forms, without any Thought of subduing Multitudes to his own *Power*, his *Reasons* or his *Visions*; and the more he shapes his Understanding by the Pattern of Human Learning, the less he is inclined to form Parties after his particular Notions. (*Tale*, sec. 9)

The paradox behind this has been well described by Robert M. Adams, in an important essay on Swift and Kafka:

> One could look for no better example of the placid, adjusted man than Swift's great enemy William Wotton, whose reaction to the *Tale of a Tub* was one of unqualified horror. Although Swift's theological blasphemies may have been exaggerated, his raging contempt for the whole race of moderns can scarcely be overstated; and surely this implies, on the face of it, a considerable contempt for the "common forms." Indeed, a treatise so fantastic, sardonic, and derisive as *A Tale of a Tub* could scarcely culminate in a calm conformity; the expenditure of so much nervous ingenuity merely to endorse the "common forms" would be at the least a paradox, akin to that by which the fourth book of

> *Gulliver* may be read as the most passionate denunciation of passion
> ever penned. (*Strains of Discord: Studies in Literary Openness*, [Ithaca,
> N.Y.: Cornell University Press, 1958], p. 154)

The point is fairly taken, even though Swift might claim that it was
the essence of modernism to subvert the common forms: doubtless
Wotton would lose either way, since whatever adherence to the
common forms one would attribute to him would be described by
Swift as "Aldermanly Discretion." In a sense, the distinction could
resolve itself into "common forms" explicitly identified with old
and solid tradition, as against the cheap simulacrum of convention-
ality with which modern mediocrities disguise their viciousness.
But we return to a familiar circularity. All established states are
good, and what subverts them are not constitutional defects but
"the Corruption of Manners." Thus the Church-of-England Man
does not "think any one regular Species of Government, more
acceptable to God than another . . . few States are ruined by any
Defect in their Institution, but generally by the Corruption of
Manners" (*Sentiments, Works*, 2:14; see also *Project, Works*, 2:44, 57,
63). If the Church-of-England Man is a little gloomy over the fact
that even "the best Institution is no long Security" (2:14) against
corruptions of manners, his point is not that established institutions
need to be changed, but that they must constantly guard against the
relentless subversions of human viciousness. The old and established is *as such*, pragmatically, the best available if imperfect protection, needing constant *ad hoc* repairs, but not revolution or
reconstitution, which merely (the principle is dear to British conservatism, and has links with the preference for the sound over the
brilliant public servant) replaces the old with something "which
may neither be so safe nor so convenient." Thus the final, somewhat Burkeian, words of the *Project for the Advancement of Religion*
demand (in the name of a "Reformation of Manners" rather than of
institutions), great vigilance,

> because the Nature of Things is such, that if Abuses be not remedied,
> they will certainly encrease, nor ever stop till they end in the Subver-
> sion of a Common-Wealth. As there must always of Necessity be some
> Corruptions; so in a well-instituted State, the executive Power will be
> always contending against them, by *reducing Things* (as *Machiavel* speaks)
> *to their first Principles;* never letting Abuses grow inveterate, or multiply
> so far that it will be hard to find Remedies, and perhaps impossible to
> apply them. As he that would keep his House in Repair, must attend
> every little Breach or Flaw, and supply it immediately, else Time alone

will bring it all to Ruin; how much more the common Accidents of
Storms and Rain? He must live in perpetual Danger of his House
falling about his Ears; and will find it cheaper to throw it quite down,
and build it again from the Ground, perhaps upon a new Foundation,
or at least in a new Form, which may neither be so safe nor so convenient as the old. (*Works*, 2:63)

We may note the fatalistic concept of human subversiveness, that is
identified in the metaphor of the endangered house not only with
"the common Accidents of Storms and Rain," but with something
so ineluctable as Time itself.

Abuses in Religion

The threats posed by "modernism" (sects, factious pedants and
their "speculations," politicians, lechers, etc.) are the threats posed
by human nature itself. They reside in that relentless pressure of
misdirected intensities that the *Tale of a Tub* dramatizes: the frenzies
of religious sado-masochism in Peter and Jack, the hack's obses-
sional feats of pseudo-logic and the dazzlingly imaged perversity of
his system-making. The outrageous coruscations of the *Tale* have a
vitality well beyond the scope of mere parody; it is almost fair to
think of it as the greatest of all the bad books it mocks, in the real,
not just the mock-sense. Swift's repudiating mimicry of the subversive intensities of the human mind clearly proceeded from a certain
inwardness of understanding. The moderation and the traditional
centrality of the standards he sets up against these intensities have
an avowedly precarious, or a resolutely self-protective quality, or
both. Hence a tendency to subvert his own positives by irony, and
(as we saw with the common forms) both to praise and to attack the
same things, or things for which he uses uncannily similar language. Many readers of *A Tale of a Tub* have found it difficult to
choose between their instinct to read the work as an attack on
religion and Swift's official claim that it attacked only "Abuses in
Religion"—namely, Popery and Nonconformism, or, more
broadly, "*Abuses . . . such as all Church of England Men agree in*" (*Tale*,
Apology). Martin's Anglican middle way between the excesses of
Peter (the Roman Church) and Jack (Puritanism), and his ecumen-
ical moderation are, however, put forward somewhat ambiguously.
Here it is at its best (a clause is for the moment omitted near the
beginning), in the famous passage where Martin tries to restrain
Jack's frenzy, as he tears his coat to make it seem least like Peter's:

> But *Martin . . . begged his Brother of all Love, not to damage his Coat by any Means; for he never would get such another:* Desired him *to consider, that it was not their Business to form their Actions by any Reflection upon* Peter's, *but by observing the Rules prescribed in their Father's* Will. That *he should remember,* Peter *was still their Brother, whatever Faults or Injuries he had committed; and therefore they should by all means avoid such a Thought, as that of taking Measures for Good and Evil, from no other Rule, than of Opposition to him.* That *it was true, the Testament of their good Father was very exact in what related to the wearing of their* Coats; *yet was it no less penal and strict in prescribing Agreement, and Friendship, and Affection between them. And therefore, if straining a Point were at all dispensable, it would certainly be so, rather to the Advance of Unity, than Increase of Contradiction.* (*Tale,* sec. 6)

This is probably the most straightforwardly sensible thing that anyone says in the entire *Tale,* and comes close to the Church-of-England Man's sentiment about Christian unity:

> As to Rites and Ceremonies, and Forms of Prayer, he allows there might be some useful Alterations; and more, which in the Prospect of uniting Christians might be very supportable, as Things declared in their own Nature indifferent; (*Sentiments, Works,* 2:5)

Even in the *Sentiments,* however, Swift hedges the allowability of "Alterations" with heavy reservations; and the proposal easily turns into its repudiated Whiggish counterpart, which urges Protestant unity (against Papists) in language very close to Martin's or the Church-of-England Man's. Here is the position ironically summarized in the *Argument Against Abolishing Christianity:*

> . . . It is proposed as a singular Advantage, that the Abolishing of Christianity, will very much contribute to the uniting of *Protestants,* by enlarging the Terms of Communion, so as to take in all Sorts of *Dissenters;* who are now shut out of the Pale upon Account of a few Ceremonies, which all Sides confess to be Things indifferent. (*Works,* 2:34)

or again, years later, in the *Intelligencer's* attack on the Whiggish, time-serving clergyman of "Aldermanly Discretion" and

> his dreadful Apprehensions of *Popery;* his great Moderation towards Dissenters of all Denominations; with hearty Wishes, that by yielding somewhat on both Sides, there might be a general Union among Protestants (*Works,* 12:44)

The contradictions would not, on a plane of ideological discourse, be difficult to reconcile. The interesting thing is the similarity in the language, and in the configuration of attitudes, between Martin's correct position, and its Whiggish "Abuse." It is not altogether surprising that Martin's speech comes to us slightly subverted in advance, as may be seen by supplying the clause I omitted in the first sentence of the quotation, which actually begins thus:

> But *Martin*, who at this Time happened to be extremely flegmatick and sedate, *begged*

Martin is still further subverted by the words that follow his speech:

> *Martin* had still proceeded as gravely as he began; and doubtless, would have delivered an admirable Lecture of Morality, which might have exceedingly contributed to my Reader's *Repose, both of Body and Mind:* (the true ultimate end of *Ethicks;*) But *Jack* was already gone a Flight-shot beyond his Patience.

The "admirable Lecture of Morality" and its predicted soporific effect on the reader tend to deflate Martin. The damage should not be exaggerated. Mild ironic underminings of serious statements are common in Augustan writers, as not very damaging (indeed sometimes affectionate) jokes at the speaker's expense, which at the same time release the (real) *author* from too solemn a posture of endorsement. Parson Adams falls asleep during a speech by Joseph Andrews on charity (*Joseph Andrews*, 3.6); Adams himself launches on "a long discourse" in contempt of gold, which the author omits "as most which he said occurs among many authors who have treated this subject" (ibid., 3.8); serious words by Allworthy are followed by "Here Allworthy concluded his sermon" (*Tom Jones*, 1.12 *ad fin.*); Johnson caps Imlac's famous speech on poetry with "Imlac now felt the enthusiastic fit, and was proceeding to aggrandize his own profession, when the prince cried out, 'Enough . . .'" (*Rasselas*, ch. 11).

Such irony came easily to eighteenth-century writers, and its mere presence need not be made much of. In the passages from Fielding and Johnson, however, it is genial and avuncular. Swift's passage, on the other hand, strikes a tart, flattening note: a real sarcasm takes shape at the expense of "modern" laziness of mind and morals, not just because moral discourse puts moderns to sleep, but because they require their "*Ethicks*" to be, above all, *restful*. The apparent escape, that the comment is made not, as in Fielding or

Johnson, by an authorial figure, but by one who is himself under constant parody by Swift, does not really exist as we read. For if part of the ostensible or official sting is directed at the silly speaker (or "author") and at bad modern readers, Swift's interinvolvement with the speakers he derides is always close and intimate, and the intensities and acerbities that proceed from them have a way of being closer to Swift than the comments of the more directly authorial narrators of *Joseph Andrews*, *Tom Jones*, and *Rasselas* are to Fielding and Johnson. There is in the *Tale* no vivid alternative presence that we can hang on to, that will assure us that things are really more sane than the speaker makes out, and the presupposition (so prominent in the satire of Pope or of Fielding) that writer and reader are in healthy and honest complicity against vice and folly is here totally blocked. If the mad speaker assumes that the reader will be lax, complacent, and lazy, we are somehow forced, in part, to take that insult to ourselves.

In a similar way, it is hard in the reading to feel that Swift is not somehow participating in the deflation of Martin: if the reader is made to feel too shallow to attend to Martin's sensible words, it is Swift who not only put the suggestion in his speaker's mouth, but who also generated the ironic slur of "an admirable Lecture of Morality" in the first place. That slur, incidentally, is no sudden shock, no simple and clear-cut betrayal of the reader such as critics are fond of attributing to Swift. Martin's speech, as we saw, is also undermined in advance, and what we feel is no merely momentary cancelation or revision of his creditability after the event, but a more continuous and indefinite uneasiness over how to take all his good sense throughout.

This subversive indefiniteness does not merely depend on hints of moral reservation or on simple stylistic deflations. It is compounded by a tendency to dissolve in an exuberance of zany comedy, occasionally quickened by brief eruptions of violence:

> But *Jack* was already gone a Flight-shot beyond his Patience. And as in Scholastick Disputes, nothing serves to rouze the Spleen of him that *Opposes*, so much as a kind of Pedantick affected Calmness in the *Respondent;* Disputants being for the most part like unequal Scales, where the *Gravity* of one Side advances the *Lightness* of the Other, and causes it to fly up and kick the Beam; So it happened here, that the *Weight* of *Martin's* Arguments exalted *Jack's Levity*, and made him fly out and spurn against his Brother's Moderation. In short, *Martin's Patience* put *Jack* in a *Rage*.

It is not so much that the "weight" of Martin's sensible arguments is morally subverted by the familiar satiric play on "gravity" and "lightness" as that it is comically dissipated in a pseudo-scientific description of weird mechanical interchange. The descriptive device of rendering action in such abstracting terms is old in comic narrative and looks forward to Beckett and the French new novelists. The image of a pair of scales in a mental conflict is also commonplace (see, for example, *Joseph Andrews*, 1. 9). But although what Swift creates (not merely mental processes allegorized in physical terms, but a ragged mental disagreement elaborately enacting the geometrical predictability of a precision-instrument) is commonplace in a way, his passage has a ghoulish vitality special to itself. And just as the reader's sleepiness is forgotten in the sudden eruption of Jack "gone a Flight-shot beyond his Patience" and the decorous movement of the scales quickens at the unseemly violence of Jack's rage, so the disembodied ballet of inner feelings goes richly physical as the narrative returns to Jack's ravaged coat, and the populous world of images which it reminds the "author" of:

> but that which most afflicted [Jack] was, to observe his Brother's Coat so well reduced into the State of Innocence; while his own was either wholly rent to his Shirt; or those Places which had scaped his cruel Clutches, were still in *Peter*'s Livery. So that he looked like a drunken *Beau*, half rifled by *Bullies*; Or like a fresh Tenant of *Newgate*, when he has refused the Payment of *Garnish*; Or like a discovered *Shoplifter*, left to the Mercy of *Exchange-Women*; Or like a *Bawd* in her old Velvet Petticoat, resign'd into the secular Hands of the *Mobile*. Like any, or like all of these, a Meddley of *Rags*, and *Lace*, and *Rents*, and *Fringes*, unfortunate Jack did now appear.

Allegory and satire (of the self-indulgent austerities and destructiveness of Puritan "enthusiasm," of Puritanism's paradoxical kinship with Popery, of the individual social types in the similes, of pompously elaborate or learnedly garrulous similes as such) are maintained throughout, but they operate well below the vitality of the passage at its varied and animated *face-value*. After this, further narrative of Jack's feelings and behavior, and with it a comparatively unruffled thread of allegorical implication, proceed relatively soberly to the end of a longish paragraph. Even there, however, narrative and allegory are from time to time sparked with momentary finalities of wildness, glimpses of crazed intensity on Jack's part that certainly make narrative and allegorical sense, but that arrest us by an energy which spills over the overt and official functions:

> He would have been extremely glad to see his Coat in the Condition of *Martin*'s, but infinitely gladder to find that of *Martin*'s in the same Predicament with his. However, since neither of these was likely to come to pass, he thought fit to lend the whole Business another Turn, and to dress up Necessity into a Virtue. Therefore, after as many of the *Fox*'s Arguments, as he could muster up, for bringing *Martin* to *Reason*, as he called it; or, as he meant it, into his own ragged, bobtail'd Condition; and observing he said all to little purpose; what, alas, was left for the forlorn *Jack* to do, but after a Million of Scurrilities against his Brother, to run mad with Spleen, and Spight, and Contradiction.

This emotional rhythm, of narrative sobriety concluding in a momentary explosive wildness, is repeated in the rephrasing ("To be short") that immediately follows:

> To be short, here began a mortal Breach between these two. *Jack* went immediately to the *New Lodgings*, and in a few Days it was for certain reported, that he had run out of his Wits. In a short time after, he appeared abroad, and confirmed the Report, by falling into the oddest Whimsies that ever a sick Brain conceived.

By now, Martin has regained most of the strictly *moral* status that he had lost in the earlier deflation. He is more straightforwardly the sensible and virtuous foil to Jack's mad antics. But he recovers this dignity only by withdrawing from the center of the stage. If his words are not undercut again by phrases like "an admirable Lecture of Morality," it is because he is given no more words to speak.

But the problem of Martin's presentation in the *Tale* is not, as we have seen, mainly one of moral deflation of an open and straightforward kind. He is much more radically subverted not by direct slurs but by the tear-away energies of the fictional world he is made to inhabit (or, if one prefers, by the strange unpredictable autonomy of Swift's irony, which sometimes simply forgets its positive standards and even momentarily ignores its official enemies). The *Tale* is of a kind that does not easily accommodate positives. Even when Martin is no longer directly implicated in the bad doings of his two brothers (as he had been in the early part of their story, in Section 2), their folly illogically rubs off on him. As Wotton said in his *Observations* (1705) on the *Tale:* "let *Peter* be mad one way, and *Jack* another, and let *Martin* be sober. . . . Yet still this is all Part of a

Tale of a Tub" (*Tale*, ed. A. C. Guthkelch and D. Nichol Smith, 2d
ed. [Oxford: Clarendon Press, 1958], p. 322). Wotton, and many
others, felt that religion itself, not just opponents of the Church of
England, was affected by the satire:

> that he might shelter himself the better from any Censure here in
> *England*, he falls most unmercifully upon *Peter* and *Jack*, i.e. upon *Pop-
> ery* and *Fanaticism*, and gives *Martin*, who represents the *Church of En-
> gland*, extream good Quarter. I confess, Sir, I abhor making Sport with
> any way of worshipping God, and he that diverts himself too much at
> the Expense of the *Roman Catholics* and the *Protestant Dissenters*, may lose
> his own Religion e're he is aware of it, at least the Power of it in his
> Heart. (Ibid., p. 318)

There was little danger of Swift losing "his own Religion," though
one knows what Wotton means. Wotton was understandably
pained (ibid., pp. 321, 323) by the description of the Cross as "an
old *Sign-Post* that belonged to his *Father*, with Nails and Timber
enough on it, to build sixteen large Men of War" (*Tale*, 4, *Works*,
1:74 and n.) and by the assertion that "the Fumes issuing from a
Jakes, will furnish as comely and useful a Vapor, as Incense from
an Altar" (*Tale*, 9). Wotton would not be disarmed by Swift's modern defenders, who might point out quite correctly (as Swift himself might have pointed out) that the first passage refers to the
Papist claim to possess relics of the true cross,[3] and is spoken by
Peter in a fit of megalomaniac exaggeration; and that the second
passage is part of a Digression on Madness. But in refusing to be
disarmed, Wotton would, I feel, be right, though for slightly different reasons. If Swift cannot be accused of losing his religion or
endorsing the language of his speakers, that language does have
energies which resist being neutralized by Swift's mockery of these
speakers. Whether or not Swift was always clearly conscious that
the firm authoritarianism of his religious admonitions was partly
self-protective, he seems as an artist to have sensed that his style, at
its highest pitch of creative expression, not only tended to subversiveness but was not easily given to positive affirmations. Martin's
speech is such an affirmation, but it is almost unique in the book. It
placed Swift in an impasse that he may or may not have acknowledged, but that was nonetheless real. He had either to omit the
direct moral deflation and neutralize the centrifugal vitalities of the
immediate context, so as to let the speech stand on the dignity of its
naked assertion, thus becoming untrue to the book's real manner; or
to sustain that manner, thus subverting Martin and, with him, the

Church of England and, to some extent, religion and God themselves. Swift took, on this occasion, the artist's choice, not the divine's. But he normally evaded the dilemma. Martin appears less circumstantially, for the most part, than his two brothers, and, unlike them, has no separate section devoted to his particular "history" (a spurious abstract of this unwritten history was printed in the edition of 1720, by what Guthkelch and Nichol Smith, ed. cit., p. lxii, call "an imitator of Swift who was hostile to the Church of England"). The reasons for this seem both religious and artistic, the book being one where positive norms, of any sort, are out of place.

Authority and Truth

The ironic subversions of the *Tale* are so universal that they become self-subversions; and the implied appeal to a simplifying authority is itself subverted by that fact. In other writings also, close relationships exist between attitudes that Swift repudiated through ironic mimicry and attitudes that he held literally, and these relationships extend, for example, to the question of "authority" itself. The cynical proponent of the *Argument Against Abolishing Christianity* grants that

> it may perhaps admit a Controversy, whether the Banishing all Notions of Religion whatsoever, would be convenient for the Vulgar. Not that I am in the least of Opinion with those, who hold Religion to have been the Invention of Politicians, to keep the lower Part of the world in Awe, by the Fear of invisible Powers; unless Mankind were then very different from what it is now: For I look upon the Mass, or Body of our People here in *England,* to be Free-Thinkers, that is to say, as stanch Unbelievers, as any of the highest Rank. But I conceive some scattered Notions about a superior Power to be of singular Use for the common People, as furnishing excellent Materials to keep Children quiet, when they grow peevish. (*Works,* 2:34)

The irony of this has many coils, and the speaker puts himself variously in the wrong. But his pondered refusal to accept that Religion is a political instrument "to keep the lower Part of the World in Awe" and his cautious assertion that there is nevertheless something in such a view do not mirror any Swiftian rejection of a political and disciplinarian conception of the role of religion. If anything can be described as the principal target of Swift's attack in this paragraph, it is the fact that the English are nowadays too free

thinking for religion to fulfill this role satisfactorily. It is free
thinkers themselves who oppose such a disciplinarian conception,
and in *Mr. Collins's Discourse of Free-Thinking, Put into plain English,
by Way of Abstract, for the Use of the Poor*, 1713, Swift mimics them
pointedly:

> It is objected (by Priests no doubt, but I have forgot their Names)
> that false Speculations are necessary to be imposed upon Men, in order
> to assist the Magistrate in keeping the Peace, and that Men ought
> therefore to be deceived like Children, for their own Good. I answer,
> that Zeal for imposing Speculations, whether true or false (under which
> Name of Speculations I include all Opinions of Religion, as the Belief
> of a God, Providence, Immortality of the Soul, future Rewards and
> Punishments, &c.) has done more hurt than it is possible for Religion to
> do good. (*Works*, 4:40)[4]

Mr. Collins's mimicked absurdities do not, nowadays, always seem
as absurd as Swift meant, and some passages may, as J. M. Bullitt
says, "fail to evoke contempt" (*Jonathan Swift and the Anatomy of
Satire* [Cambridge, Mass.: Harvard University Press, 1961],
p. 102). But the passage is as ironical as the *Project for the Advancement of Religion* was literal. Swift's position on the peace-keeping
functions of religion might well seem to us a more outrageous
invitation to parody than Mr. Collins's, for he would have agreed
with Bolingbroke's view of free thinkers as

> Men whom I look upon to be the Pests of Society, because their en-
> deavours are directed to losen the bands of it, & to take att least one
> curb out of the mouth of that wild Beast Man when it would be well if
> he was check'd by half a score others. (To Swift, 12 September 1724,
> *Correspondence*, 3:27; Bolingbroke was protesting against Swift's imputa-
> tion of free thinking to him.)

If the scintillating indirections of the *Argument Against Abolishing
Christianity* tempt us to feel superior to the speaker's boneheaded
statesmanliness as he concedes the uses of religion "for the common
People," we cannot dissociate Swift himself from some non-
ridiculed version of the same view. The proponent of the *Argument*
clearly perceives that the proposed abolishing of Christianity rests
not on any doctrinal objections to particular religious beliefs, but to
the status, as a controlling force, of any religion as such:

> And therefore, if, notwithstanding all I have said, it shall still be
> thought necessary to have a Bill brought in for repealing Christianity; I

would humbly offer an Amendment, that instead of the word *Christian-ity*, may be put *Religion* in general; which I conceive, will much better answer all the good Ends proposed by the Projectors of it. For, as long as we leave in Being a God, and his Providence, with all the necessary Consequences, which curious and inquisitive Men will be apt to draw from such Premises; we do not strike at the Root of the Evil, although we should ever so effectually annihilate the present Scheme of the Gospel. For, of what Use is Freedom of Thought, if it will not produce Freedom of Action; which is the sole End, how remote soever, in Appearance, of all Objections against Christianity? And therefore, the Free-Thinkers consider it as a Sort of Edifice, wherein all the Parts have such a mutual Dependance on each other, that if you happen to pull out one single Nail, the whole Fabrick must fall to the Ground. This was happily expressed by him, who had heard of a Text brought for Proof of the Trinity, which in an antient Manuscript was differently read; he thereupon immediately took the Hint, and by a sudden Deduction of a long *Sorites*, most logically concluded; Why, if it be as you say, I may safely whore and drink on, and defy the Parson. From which, and many the like Instances easy to be produced, I think nothing can be more manifest, than that the Quarrel is not against any particular Points of hard Digestion in the Christian System; but against Religion in general; which, by laying Restraints on human Nature, is supposed the great Enemy to the Freedom of Thought and Action. (*Works*, 2:37–38)

If the politic speaker, in the complacency of his moderation, plays fast and loose with all distinction between one creed and the next, so to some extent does Swift himself literally, insofar as he supports religion more as a "curb" (political and psychological) to human subversiveness than as a specific body of doctrine, and insofar as he insists on the overriding authority of established national religions in their respective countries. The anarchic "Freedom of Thought and Action" that (by a familiar paradox) leads straight to tyranny is clearly perceived by Mr. Collins to be most threatened by the state religions. In a passage already quoted in part, he is made to say:

It is the indispensable Duty of a *Free Thinker*, to endeavour *forcing* all the World to think as he does, and by that means make them *Free Thinkers* too. You are also to understand, that I allow no Man to be a *Free Thinker*, any further than as he differs from the received Doctrines of Religion. Where a Man falls in, though by perfect Chance, with what is generally believed, he is in that Point a confined and limited Thinker; and you shall see by and by, that I celebrate those for the noblest *Free Thinkers* in every Age, who differed from the Religion of their Countries in the most fundamental Points, and especially in those which bear any Analogy to the chief Fundamentals of Religion among us. (*Mr. Collins's Discourse, Works,* 4:36–37)

The wild arbitrariness of Mr. Collins's logic, the glimpse it provides of a mental bottomlessness turning into bossy despotism, are a perfect and inventive emblem of the favorite Swiftian paradox, that anarchy leads to tyranny. The particular intellectual nightmare created by Mr. Collins's words proceeds partly from the free thinking claim that, because there are in the world many religions and many scriptures, every man is free to range among them, and "a great deal of *Free-thinking* will at last set us all right, and every one will adhere to the *Scripture* he likes best" (*Works,* 4:32–33). It will not surprise us to see Swift repudiating a religious relativism that proceeds from the singularity of individuals, while, as champion of state religions, defending one that tends to the cohesiveness of separate national communities. But Swift's own position as a Church-of-England Man, not only upholding state religions as such but personally believing in the superiority of what Mr. Collins calls "the chief Fundamentals of Religion among us" (for the "straight" version see *Works,* 2:5), seems in some ways an example of the very situation from which Mr. Collins's derided reasoning flows:

> Here are perhaps twenty Sorts of *Scriptures* in the several Parts of the World, and every Sett of Priests contends that their *Scripture* is the true One.

The reasoning becomes actively disreputable, presumably, at the point where Mr. Collins argues that, since only one of the scriptures can be right and no one can know which that is without "*thinking freely,* every one of us for ourselves,"

> The Parliament ought to be at the Charge of finding a sufficient number of these *Scriptures* for every one of Her Majesty's Subjects, for there are Twenty to One against us, that we may be in the wrong: But a great deal of *Free-thinking* will at last set us all right, etc. (*Works,* 4:32)

My object is not to expose any "contradictions" in Swift's implied position. There is probably no contradiction that cannot be resolved by logical or theological means, and none of which Swift himself was not, in a high-handed way, aware. If, for example, free thinking leads ultimately to tyranny, the free thinker may justly argue that an organized religious conformity does so too. Swift mockingly puts the argument into Mr. Collins's mouth, and evades answering it, in a style reminiscent of *A Tale of a Tub:*

> Besides, if all People were of the same Opinion, the Remedy would be worse than the Disease; I will tell you the Reason, some other time. (*Works*, 4:39)[5]

If Swift is mocking muddled and evasive authors, as often in the *Tale* (e.g., Section 9, *Works*, 1:107 and 113, where the manuscript fails just when a "knotty Point" is to be unraveled, or the "author" simply announces that he will "not farther enlarge" on this or that), the evasion lets Swift out too.

It will not do to conclude too readily that Swift is unconsciously silencing a doubt of his own, since the practice occurs frequently and Swift is not ashamed to signpost it. But in those schoolmasterly bossinesses and arbitrarinesses of his foolish speakers, Mr. Collins haughtily dismissing a knotty problem or Gulliver asserting that no critic can impugn what he has disclosed (4.12), Swift not infrequently indulges an hauteur of his own, transferred to fools but not exorcised by the parody. Behind Mr. Collins's shoddy laxity stands Swift's uppish refusal to get tangled up in an ungentlemanly and subversive complexity of argument, on a matter best solved by a brisk reduction to practicalities: not only are "doubts" best concealed and subdued (*Works*, 9:261, 262) and metaphysical fussiness likely to do more harm than good, but "Violent zeal for truth hath an hundred to one odds to be petulancy, ambition, or pride" (ibid., p. 261). This is doubtless aimed at Dissenters, but Swift's own "zeal for truth" and (for that matter) no lack of "petulancy, ambition, or pride" turns the sarcasm into one of those self-implicating paradoxes that exemplify the moral impasse underlying Swift's cravings for, and his sense of the urgent importance of, "authority" (even in preference to "truth").

In this light, bossy uppishness (whether it silences an argument or diminishes an enemy) ceases to seem merely funny, and becomes, beyond the joke, a primary display of rule. The wittiest, most buoyantly managed hauteurs transcend their element as semi-playful debating points. Consider the celebrated epigram against Steele in *The Importance of the Guardian Considered* (1713):

> What Bailiff would venture to Arrest Mr. *Steele*, now he has the Honour to be your Representative? and what Bailiff ever scrupled it before? (*Works*, 8:14)

This indeed shows Swift at a very high level of inventive play (Leavis quotes it, a shade solemnly, as an example of the way "surprise is a perpetually varied accompaniment of the grave, dispassionate, matter-of-fact tone in which Swift delivers his intensities" [*The Common Pursuit* (Harmondsworth: Penguin Books, 1962), p. 76]). The dazzling epigrammatic turn escapes no one, nor the imputation that Steele had sought election to Parliament as a means of "escaping arrest for debt" (Ehrenpreis, *Swift*, 2:690, and *Works*, 8:21). But what is sometimes overlooked is that the epigram is also a brilliant deflection *ad hominem* of an argument more than half-seriously maintained, that the bailiff might be right in both cases, for official status really deserves special respect: "that supposing the Persons on both Sides to be of equal Intrinsick Worth, it is more Impudent, Immoral, and Criminal to reflect on a *Majority* in Power, than a *Minority* out of Power" (*Works*, 8:14); and that whatever doctrines of his own Swift was contradicting here for polemical purposes (Ehrenpreis, *Swift*, 2:691–92) and whatever qualifications, in political theory, surround the "Maxim . . . that the Prince can do no wrong" (*Works*, 8:23), there is more than a satiric commitment in Swift's rebuke to Steele for attacking

> those Persons, whom Her Majesty has thought fit to place in the highest Stations of the Kingdom, and to trust them with the Management of Her most weighty Affairs: And this is the Gentleman who cries out, *Where is Honour? Where is Government? Where is Prerogative?* Because the *Examiner* has sometimes dealt freely with those, whom the Queen has thought fit to *Discard*, and the Parliament to *Censure*. (*Works*, 8:15)

Swift, an anti-Hobbesian with a Hobbesian view of human nature and a Hobbesian conception of some of the functions of government (on this, see for example Martin Price, *To the Palace of Wisdom* [Garden City, N.J.: Doubleday, 1965], p. 186), opposes Hobbesian and other tyranny, famously and unquestionably. But his irony, even when he is at his most explicit on this point, leaves us unsure that an authoritarian undertone is not present in some form:

> It is a remark of *Hobbes*, that the Youth of *England* are corrupted in their Principles of Government, by reading the Authors of *Greece* and *Rome*, who writ under Commonwealths. But it might have been more fairly offered for the Honour of Liberty, that while the rest of the known World was over-run with the Arbitrary Government of single persons; *Arts* and *Sciences* took their Rise, and flourished only in those few small Territories where the People were *free*. And although *Learning* may

continue after *Liberty* is lost, as it did in *Rome*, . . . yet it hardly ever began under a *Tyranny* in any Nation: Because *Slavery* is of all Things the greatest Clog and Obstacle to *Speculation*. (*Sentiments of a Church-of-England Man, Works*, 2:17–18)

Although in context these words lead to an eloquent plea for "limited Monarchy," arguing that as "Arbitrary Power is but the first natural Step from *Anarchy* or the *Savage Life*," so a maturer process leads to a proper "adjusting *Power* and *Freedom*," they do not leave us unambiguously convinced that the matter ends here. Can the word "Speculation" ever escape altogether the tentacles of Swift's irony? What reader of *A Tale of a Tub*, whose "author" vents his "Speculations . . . for the universal Benefit of Human kind" (*Tale*, 9) in every possible mad and bad way, will be confident that clogs and obstacles to speculation are altogether wrong? and what reader who then comes upon the dead kings in Glubbdubdrib showing

with great Strength of Reason, that the Royal Throne could not be supported without Corruption; because, that positive, confident, restive Temper, which Virtue infused into Man, was a perpetual Clog to publick Business, (*Gulliver*, 3:8)

can be absolutely certain that the sentiments are as utterly discredited as Swift's irony is meant to suggest; or that Virtue's "positive, confident, restive Temper" does not tend to the same condition as the "violent zeal for truth" of the aphorism?

It may be that what Irvin Ehrenpreis said of Swift's conversation applies well to many of his writings:

Commonplace though his views tended to be, he had to display them as his very own . . . he liked to sound publicly witty, daringly unconventional, even if his moral principles were the most hidebound. Actually, it is just because his substance was orthodox that his style grew iconoclastic. (Swift, 2:211)

This hints fruitfully at a possible relation of Swift to the moderation and orthodoxy of, for example, Martin in the *Tale:* a refusal to settle unguardedly for the ordinary, while asserting it with genuine commitment. If the style grew subversive because the ideological substance was orthodox, there may yet be a further loop to the spiral: perhaps the ideological substance was orthodox because beneath it lay a temperament (reflected in the style!) that knew itself to be subversive. The sense of his own recalcitrance from the or-

thodox may have driven Swift to assert it with a passion both
overemphatic and undermining in its sheer unruliness. Or rather,
not so much *assert* it as castigate its opposite. The positive norms,
those standards of central and self-evident human value,

> Anglicanism, humane letters, reason . . . limited monarchy, classical
> literary standards, and rational judgment . . . the virtue and cultivation
> of Graeco-Roman antiquity, improved by Christian ethics and a cheer-
> ing hope of salvation . . . the doctrines of the Church of England and
> the political constitution of 1688 (Ehrenpreis, *Swift*, 1:202–3)

insofar as they purport to be central and self-evident, are difficult to
present except in terms of the deviations that the *Tale* superbly
dramatizes. This is only partly because of the hoary principle according to which vice is easier to make interesting than virtue,
especially *ordinary* virtue: this principle has not deterred such authors as Spenser or Bunyan, for example, from undertaking a direct
presentation of virtue in their most ambitious imaginative works
(nor has it led them necessarily to undercut that presentation with
irony). There are, on Swift's part, reasons also that may be called
"rhetorical": since his claim is that his positive standards are obvious and in the widest sense normal, restating them in detail merely
concedes that they are not, whereas exposing deviations from what
is assumed to be taken for granted by everyone strengthens the
emphasis on the sheer unreason and perversity of vice. Moreover,
Swift's positive standards hold together a great number of things,
"Anglicanism, humane letters, reason . . . limited monarchy . . .
Graeco-Roman antiquity . . . the political constitution of 1688,"
whose coherence (short of elaborate feats of ideological synthesis
that would have been not only rebarbative to Swift's temperament
but unsuited to the satire and fiction he was writing) can only be
asserted through generalized concepts of centrality, moderation,
authority, freedom, reason, common sense, and by confident appeals "to the Lessons of all Moralists and Legislators" (*Works*,
8:47)—that last phrase, from *The Publick Spirit of the Whigs*, 1714, so
typically joining together the notions of tradition and of rule. In the
same work (p. 44), Swift mocks Steele for using the phrase "*reasonable to common Sense;* that is . . . *reasonable* to *Reason.*" The passage
is, really, a piece of trivial polemical word-splitting. But the kind of
inclusive term that united virtue and sense with the plainly obvious
and the agreed opinion of good men in all ages had a particular
appeal for Swift. He was not, of course, the only man of his age to
be fond of such terms, and it is doubtless true that, in an age when

values could be assumed or not too hopelessly desired to be widely shared, generalized ethical terminology might be specially favored. But it is also true that terms like *reason* had a multitude of meanings, that Swift knew this, and that he nevertheless, while fully exploiting the variety in such crucial places as the fourth book of *Gulliver*, liked at the same time bossily to insist that only one real meaning existed, inclusive of all virtue and sense, yet obvious and unhighfalutin. This Reason, as we have seen, is not

> a Point problematical as with us, where Men can argue with Plausibility upon both Sides of a Question; but strikes you with immediate Conviction; as it must needs do where it is not mingled, obscured, or discolored by Passion and Interest. (*Gulliver*, 4:8)

There may be a jokey quixotism, as of the satirist satirized, in the visionary absurdity of proposing to a fallen humanity the notion that argument is improper because there is never more than one truth, or that lying is a mad perversion of speech, since the only function of speech is to communicate the truth. And there is no suggestion that because Reason's imperatives are few, luminously plain, and absolute, its paths will therefore be easy to follow, since, in a non-Houyhnhnm world, vice and folly are always tending to subvert its rule. But the insistence nevertheless is that the concept is simple and easy to grasp, and thus, though in one sense impossible to abide by, nevertheless not too farfetched or ambitious for the moralist to proclaim. It permits Swift, in other words, to demand the absolute while sounding moderate, realistic, and low-pitched. It permits a large abstraction to remain earthbound and pragmatic, unimplicated in "mysteries" of religion or politics, clearly separate from the obscurantism of theology and metaphysics, from "Ideas, Entities, Abstractions and Transcendentals" of which, to Gulliver's chagrin, the sensible and practical Brobdingnagians could not grasp "the least Conception" (*Gulliver*, 2.7). And it is consonant with the fact that in rejecting abstractions and "mysterious" terms, Swift is also rejecting the grandiose.

Lofty Style and Ridiculous Tragedy

For, when Swift told the young gentleman lately entered into holy orders:

> I defy the greatest Divine, to produce any Law either of God or Man,

which obliges me to comprehend the Meaning of *Omniscience, Omnipresence, Ubiquity, Attribute, Beatifick Vision,* with a Thousand others so frequent in Pulpits; any more than that of *Excentrick, Idiosyncracy, Entity,* and the like (*Works,* 9:66)

he was ostensibly only recoiling from "obscure Terms" and "mysterious" concepts, but the terms he rejects in the first list are also, with only one exception, terms of sublime, transcendent or ecstatic import. This "distrust of the celebrative and the sublime," as Martin Price calls it (*To the Palace of Wisdom,* p. 196) goes also with a dislike of grandiose overstatement and of a highly emotional rhetoric. Swift told the young clergyman, approvingly, the comment of a certain "great Person" upon a sermon he had heard by a preacher of his acquaintance:

A Lady asked him, coming out of Church, whether it was not a very moving Discourse? *Yes,* said he, *I was extremely sorry, for the Man is my Friend.* (*Works,* 9:70)

Swift is talking specifically about sermons, and the ideal of a plain sermon style was common among Anglican clergymen from the middle of seventeenth century, parly in reaction to a highly ornamented "metaphysical" style, and partly in avoidance of the nonconformists' "*Fanatick* or *Enthusiastic* Strain" (*Works,* 9:68). Both in the *Letter to the Young Gentleman,* and in the sermon "Upon sleeping in Church," he stresses that "plain convincing Reason" is more lastingly effective and generally more satisfactory than "the Art of wetting the Handkerchiefs of a whole Congregation" (*Works,* 9:70, 217), part of the reason being, as we might expect, the sheer day-to-day practicality of a sermon's function: "to tell the People what is their Duty; and then to convince them that it is so" (*Works,* 9:70). If the reference is specifically to sermons, however, the preference for practicality over high talk is central and characteristic. It extends beyond sermons, as when he refers to the eloquence of Demosthenes and Cicero, concedes that their case is different because their task was to speak in the immediacy of a political or legal situation, yet prefers Demosthenes as the less "rhetorical" of the two, finally returning to a preference for English sermons not only because steady reminders of duty do not need rhetoric, but because phlegmatic Englishmen are unlikely to be stirred by it anyway: "I do not see how this Talent of moving the Passions, can be of any great Use towards directing Christian Men in the Conduct of their Lives, at least in these *Northern* Climates" (*Works*, 9:69). There is something in this affectionate sarcasm not restricted to sermons as a genre, a preference for the placid English above the emotional foreigners of southern Europe (see also the backhanded compliment to the phlegmatic English, above p. 46), an uppishness far removed in its low intensity from Swift's distaste for "enthusiastic" dissenters, yet not, one feels, entirely unrelated. There is, too, about all this, a familiar note of hauteur, again not restricted to sermon styles: "I know a Gentleman, who made it a Rule in Reading, to skip over all Sentences where he spied a Note of Admiration at the End" (*Works*, 9:69).

Nil admirari, then, joins well not only with recent sermon-tradition, but with Swift's temperamental predilection for the practical and low-pitched. As further illustration of the latter, consider Gulliver's praise of the poetry of the Houyhnhnms, where the criteria are justness, exactitude, and moral usefulness, rather than poetic fire:

> In *Poetry* they must be allowed to excel all other Mortals; wherein the Justness of their Similes, and the Minuteness, as well as Exactness of their Descriptions, are indeed inimitable. Their Verses abound very much in both of these; and usually contain either some exalted Notions of Friendship and Benevolence, or the Praises of those who were Victors in Races, and other bodily Exercises. (*Gulliver*, 4.9)

("exalted Notions of Friendship and Benevolence" may seem to sort ill with an avoidance of emotional grandeur; the words, however, imply not grandiose utterance but high moral tone).

Swift is often described, in praise and blame, as speaking in accents of angry majesty. Yeats, in "Blood and the Moon," celebrates him as "beating on his breast in Sibylline frenzy blind" (*Collected Poems* [London: Macmillan, 1952], p. 268), while F. R. Leavis scornfully reminds us that

> *saeva indignatio* is an indulgence that solicits us all, and the use of literature by readers and critics for the projection of nobly suffering selves is familiar. (*The Common Pursuit*, p. 86)

Both seem wrong, not because Swift was not, in his way, both passionate and self-dramatizing, but because the comments are so ill-applied to Swift's persistent refusal of the "lofty Stile" and "Heroick Strain" as being "against my nat'ral Vein" (*Epistle to a*

Lady, 1733, ll. 140, 218, 135–36; *Poems* 2:634, 637). It seems almost permissible to say (the exaggeration would be slight) that *saeva indignatio* was only openly claimed by Swift in his epitaph.

When Swift claimed that the misanthropy of *Gulliver* was not in Timon's manner, he may have been refusing a *manner* only, and not Timonlike feelings (letter to Pope, 29 September 1725, *Correspondence*, 3:103). More widely, Swift's avoidance of other grand manners hardly precluded intense or passionate feelings. The refusal of the manner is, however, very important. Swift offers some explanations, notably the commonplace that in satire raillery is more effective than railing ("Switches better guide than Cudgels"), but also the more intimate fact that in a "lofty Stile . . . I Shou'd make a Figure scurvy" (*Epistle to a Lady*, ll. 202, 218–19). The tone is bantering, but Swift's feelings of vulnerability are seriously involved: to imputations of solemnity, of self-importance, of emotional indiscipline, and, above all, of conceding by a lofty manner that high demands have any viability in a bad world. The "high stilts" that Yeats stood on, Swift from the start rejected in all modern mechanic inventions to rise above the crowd: Dissenters' pulpit, gallows, stage-itinerant (*Tale* 1). Yeats's stilts may be a come-down from the heroic days of his great-granddad: only "fifteen foot, no modern stalks upon higher." But this self-undercutting gives nothing away. If Yeats seems prepared, as the price for "High Talk," to court a certain ridicule, that is because he makes sure of the clown's closeness to sublimity:

> Malachi Stilt-Jack am I, whatever I learned has run wild . . .
> I, through the terrible novelty of light, stalk on, stalk on.
>   (*Collected Poems*, pp. 385–86)

Swift shied from such claims. Stilt-Jack was sinking too low, and the rest talking too high: claim and counter-claim merge at that familiar point where the deepest drop and the highest flight come together, in heroic epiphany for Yeats, climax of folly for Swift.

Swift's refusal of grand manner and high talk cuts, we might say, very deep: deep enough, for example, to extend to serious mock-heroic, that province of the grandiose where other Augustan writers felt sufficiently protected by the built-in irony of the form. There is nothing, in Swift, like *The Dunciad*, nor even like *Le Lutrin*, *The Dispensary*, or *The Rape of the Lock*, but only some octosyllabic burlesques, and that prose foolery, *The Battle of the Books*, where mock-epic is desolemnified not only by the prose medium, but by an admixture of mock-journalese. It is as though Swift shrank from whatever high talk survived in the parody to proclaim positives of lost or betrayed grandeur.

Swift's undercutting of grand satiric rages, postures of Juvenalian majesty, noble self-projections, is thus more radical than that of Pope, whose mock-heroic by its very nature strove, as Pound might say, "to maintain 'the sublime'/In the old sense," and that of Yeats, who, out of clown and beggar, made the sublime new. High self-praise comes much seldomer in Swift than in the other two and takes itself less seriously. It has recently been suggested (by Barry Slepian, *Review of English Studies*, N. S. 14 (1963):esp. 254–56) that even the self-celebration towards the end of the *Verses on the Death of Dr. Swift*, in lines like

> Fair LIBERTY was all his Cry;
> For her he stood prepared to die,
>
> (Ll. 347–48)

or

> Yet, Malice never was his Aim;
> He lash'd the Vice but spar'd the Name,
>
> (Ll. 459–60)

is radically self-mocking and ironical. The suggestion, as Mr. Slepian makes it, seems improbable, even though he is able to point out that some of the things Swift says about himself were (like the last two lines quoted) perhaps untrue. But even if we do not accept that such strong self-discounting takes place in the poem, the self-celebration is qualified both by the lightly chatty Hudibrastic meter, and by the pleasant joke of the author inventing an "impartial" (l. 306) obituarist to say these things for himself. There is, at the very least, the friendly undercutting of a coy leg-pull, and certainly none of the glow of Pope's claim to be actuated by "The strong Antipathy of Good to Bad," or his pride "to see/Men not afraid of God, afraid of me" (*Epilogue to the Satires*, Dial. 2, ll. 198, 208–9)

If such grandeurs of self-praise in Swift are less than *radically* modified by irony, however, the great denunciations are almost totally removed from their own potential sublimity. When this happens, the strength of feeling is, I believe, greater, not less. The disturbing intensities increase in proportion with Swift's success in devising formulas that release him from direct commitment to a majestic role. In the *Modest Proposal*, for example, the emotional

pressure is enormous, and it is reflected in the monstrousness of the
fable: but its intensity proceeds largely from a cunning divorce
between the monstrous fable and its formal semblance as an economic tract (flat statistical style, calm display of concern for the
public good). The mad proposer of cannibal horrors had in the
past, he tells us, proposed "other Expedients," sound measures for
Ireland's benefit that we recognize as those Swift himself had
fought for in the 1720s, in vain. The proposer's present blandness
and assurance of success derive from the fact that his new scheme is
so evil that a morally mad world must accept it as good. His crazed
lucidity is a Swiftian intensity posing as weary sarcasm. Swift is
autobiographically implicated, and the cannibal fiction registers the
violence of his protest: but the proposer's newfound worldliness
frees Swift from the sentimental risks of posing as a lonely defiant
protester, and rant is eschewed without loss of intensity because
the violence of Swift's feelings can be melted into the proposer's
calm.

Gulliver too had hoped to mend the world, and got nowhere.
He, however, is allowed to rant, and Swift's commitment to Gulliver's strident denunciation of man in 4.12 is more teasingly
oblique than his relationship of total ironic opposition to the
speaker in the *Proposal*. Gulliver's outburst is too petulant, too
fraught with a kind of wilful hysteria, for us to be able simply to
identify his voice as Swift's; nor are we accustomed to accord Gulliver our whole-hearted respect. But the volume as a whole has
been establishing, bleakly and massively, the grounds for an attack
on man; and we as readers are left alone with Gulliver's voice at the
end, for Swift has taken care to provide no competing point of view
to help us towards a more comforting perspective. Swift is readily
dissociated from Gulliver's rant, but hardly from the indictment it
embodies. Again, there seems no loss, but rather increase of intensity, for the satirist allows us to discount nothing while remaining
protected against our dismissal of the rant. Or rather, we are left
uncertain how much to discount. Similar uncertainties occur even
when Swift himself is talking: "I hate and detest that animal called
man," "I would hang them if I cou'd" (to Pope, 29 September 1725,
Correspondence, 3:103; *Epistle to a Lady*, l. 170). Flattened and made
elusive by sarcastic overstatement, the denunciation becomes unanswerable by literal denial, because we do not know how to take
it: instead of the clearcut remoteness of the satirist on high stilts,
the uncertainty creates an uneasy intimacy, a sniping aggression on
the reader at close quarters.

Swift's relations with his reader depend, then, not on lofty denunciations from above, but on the strange haughtinesses of a low-pitched intimacy. Gulliver tells the reader, "my principal Design was to inform, and not to amuse thee" (4:12), echoing Swift's own declared aim "to vex the world rather then divert it" (to Pope, 29 September 1725, *Correspondence*, 3:102), but using a personal and familiar *thee*, aimed directly at the reader in familiarity and contempt. Compare Pope's use of the contemptuous thee,

> Has God, thou fool! work'd solely for thy good. . . .
> Is it for thee the lark ascends and sings
>
> (*Essay on Man*, 3:27ff.),

which is aimed not at the reader, but at Man. Nothing illustrates more clearly the difference between the two men's satire, Pope's grandly decorous, public, and resting on a decent relationship with the reader in which intimacy is held in check by a sense of public agreement, a feeling that both are gentlemen and men of the world; Swift's satire operating at close quarters, creating a relationship with the reader that is intimate but (paradoxically) hardly friendly. A good example both of the low-pitched school-masterly haughtiness, and of the intimacy of comic and unpleasant involvement with his satiric victims (and, by an extension that is always felt in Swift, with his readers), are these lines from the *Epistle to a Lady:*

> Let me, tho' the Smell be Noisom,
> Strip their Bums: let CALEB hoyse 'em;
> Then, apply ALECTO's Whip,
> Till they wriggle, howl, and skip,
>
> (Ll. 177–80)

Pope spoke of Swift as "an Avenging Angel of wrath" (letter to Swift, 15 October 1725), and the words are tempting to critics too literally stirred by notions of *saeva indignatio* and Sibylline frenzy blind. But Pope's reference was playful also, and included an image of farce:

> . . . I find you would rather be employ'd as an Avenging Angel of wrath, to break your Vial of Indignation over the heads of the wretched pityful creatures of the World; nay would make them *Eat your Book*, which you have made as bitter a pill for them as possible.
>
> (*Correspondence*, 3:108)

The spirit of this remark, in which noble angers are made to turn

into a farcical spectacle of vials broken on heads, captures well
Swift's refusal of a thoroughgoing tragic role. It is true that Swift
once wrote in a letter that "Life is a Tragedy, wherein we sit as
Spectators awhile, and then act our own Part in it" (to Mrs. Moore,
7 December 1727, *Correspondence*, 3:254). He was consoling a
mother on the death of her child, and the occasion dictated a special
solemnity. His more characteristic and more famous remark to
Pope, that

> The common saying of life being a Farce is true in every sense but the
> most important one, for it is a ridiculous tragedy, which is the worst
> kind of composition (20 April 1731, *Correspondence*, 3:456)

suggests all the tart pessimism, but plays down the majesty. It is an
important remark, synthesizing that desperate gaiety *(vive la
bagatelle)* so vivid in Swift's feats of anarchic mimicry (in the *Tale*
and in some horrible exuberances in *Gulliver's Travels*), with a tight-
lipped severity over the offended decorum. If the remark looks back
to an old tradition of Democritean laughter,

> Like the ever-laughing Sage,
> In a Jest I spend my Rage,
> *(Epistle to a Lady*, ll. 167–68)

it also looks forward to an absurdism which says, with Ionesco, that
"the comic . . . is another aspect of the tragic" (*Notes and Counter-
Notes* [London: 1964, p. 123]). To Ionesco, this complete interpenetration is a fact of the human condition, its old faiths lost, and
with them the viability of fixed categories, of decorums of feeling or
style. Ionesco describes his experience of certain moments of alienation:

> Then the universe seems to me infinitely strange and foreign. At such a
> moment I gaze upon it with a mixture of anguish and euphoria; separate
> from the universe, as though placed at a certain distance outside it; I
> look and I see pictures, creatures that move in a kind of timeless time
> and spaceless space, emitting sounds that are a kind of language I no
> longer understand or ever register. "What is all this?" I wonder, "what
> does it all mean?," and out of this state of mind, which seems to spring
> from the most fundamental part of my nature, is strangely born at times
> a feeling that everything is comic and derisory, at others a feeling of
> despair that the world should be so utterly ephemeral and precarious,
> as if it all existed and did not exist at one and the same time, as if it lay

somewhere between being and not being: and that is the origin of my tragic farces, *Les Chaises*, for example. (*Notes and Counter-Notes*, p. 141)

Swift recognized the condition, and refused it. Life is a "ridiculous tragedy," but that "worst kind of composition" is forbidden by the dramatic canons of his day. Swift's response to the absurd is to hang on to the rules. And although he would have understood modern conceptions of the absurd as a gap between aspiration and bodily fact, between what is and what ought to be, between man's desires and a world that disappoints, he would have concealed, suppressed, disciplined, but not accepted or yielded to, the "doubts" of God and order that these disconnections aroused. For a philosopher of the absurd, like the Camus of the *Myth of Sisyphus*, the absurd is sin without God. For Swift, it resides in man's nature, fallen through disobedience to God. The myths of Sisyphus and of Tantalus, condemned to eternally-repeated torments of effort and desire, are for Camus emblems of an inexplicable universe. For Swift, the restlessness of ever-renewed needs is the price for original sin. Freethinking, in this light, is punningly but aptly seen as part universal madness, part wilful vice. And this attribution of sin, while in one sense it settles nothing and can seldom calm the restless struggle, yet remains fixed in an overriding faith and an uncompromising morality, asserting obligations not of the individual conscience, but of tradition and rule.

Notes

1. For amplification of these comments on *Gulliver* and on the *Tale's* Digression, see *Gulliver and the Gentle Reader*, especially pp. 18ff., 33ff.

2. See the account of "Swift's Philanthropy" by J. N. P. Moore, the director of the hospital Swift founded, in *Jonathan Swift 1667–1967. A Dublin Tercentenary Tribute*, ed. Roger McHugh and Philip Edwards (Dublin, 1967), esp. pp. 140 ff.

3. Calvin remarked that if all the claimed fragments of the true cross were put together, they would fill a large ship. This seems to be a specific part of the background to Swift's joke.

4. The real Anthony Collins, in the *Discourse of Free-Thinking* (1713), which is the object of Swift's parody, had strongly resisted the notion *"That certain Speculations (tho false) are necessary to be impos'd on Men, in order to assist the Magistrate in preserving the Peace of Society: And that it is therefore as reasonable to deceive Men into Opinions for their own Good, as it is in certain cases to deceive Children"* (pp. 111ff.).

5. The real Collins had said:

"It is objected, *That to allow and encourage Men to think freely, will produce endless Divisions in Opinion, and by consequence Disorder in Society.* To which I answer,

1. Let any Man lay down a Rule to prevent Diversity of Opinions, which will not be as fertile of Diversity of Opinions as *Free-Thinking;* or if it prevents Diversity of Opinions, will not be a Remedy worse than the Disease; and I will yield up the Question.

2. Mere Diversity of Opinions has no tendency in nature to Confusion in Society" (p. 101).

He also said: ". . . it is evident Matter of Fact, that a *Restraint upon Thinking* is the cause of all the Confusion which is pretended to rise from Diversity of Opinions, and that *Liberty of Thinking* is the Remedy for all the Disorders which are pretended to arise from Diversity of Opinions" (p. 103).

On pp. 123ff. Collins had spoken of the folly of a slavish adherence to state religions.

3

A Tale of a Tub

JOHN TRAUGOTT

Motley in the Brain?

So giddy are the quick changes of Swift's foolery in *A Tale of a Tub* that few readers from his day to ours have been convinced they know the "enemy." The parodies are brilliant and raucous but they have a habit at odd moments of sounding like Swift himself, and when most thoroughly vulgar and utterly reprehensible they make the keenest comments on the life we must live. Worse by far, as responses to those comments, the serene Augustan assumptions about reason and a gentleman's education, elsewhere encouraged in the reader by the irony towards those lower orders, can come to seem pointless and fatuous. Irony is, after all, a conspiracy of the elite; the reader would seem to have a right to expect from the ironist some regard for class solidarity. Swift seems to delight, however, in leaving the reader, whom he has encouraged to assume his own top-loftiness above the crowd, stranded with what turn out to be merely pompous airs. It is not easy to learn the lesson from a reading of the *Tale* of how not to be a fool among knaves. Officious reason ruins life but Epicurean dilly-dallying is an idiot illusion; meanwhile madmen and fanatics tell us what the world is really like. Whatever advice we have is a madman's or a fool's but we ignore it at our peril. The easiest response—which ought to be rejected almost as soon as it is imagined—is that the giddy speaker, being a "persona" parodying literary hirelings or scholarly worms or metaphysical cabbalists or mad world-makers, is the real target of the satire. That tiresome persona of the critics, complained Professor Herbert Davis in a delightfully petulant essay,[1] is always getting between us and Swift. We *know* perfectly well that we are in the presence of Swift, not of some novelistic fiction. When we hear, "Last week I saw a Woman *flay'd*, and you will hardly believe, how much it altered her Person for the worse," we shiver with the superb ironist who so easily finds out behind the excellent foppery of the world the bloodiness of us all. He has an ear, this ironist, for picking up in the accents of a vagrant voice in the street an epitome of our existence, mimicking here a smart-talking man-about-town's satisfaction in reporting the latest news that beauty may be a whore and the law a brute. Not very pleasant news. A whore does look better with her paint than without her skin. Better to let such things pass with a knowing giggle and not go about asking discommoding questions. Irony leaves the man who is inclined to look into such things to shift for himself, with the pain of finding out what to do with his knowledge. He is one of the unhappy few cursed with eyes to see, ears to hear, and a tongue to speak. But there are rewards as well as pains in joining the ironist. One takes to oneself the wonderful art of Swift in parodying so perfectly the bloody idiocy of the many and thus one escapes the crowd. Listening carefully to the ring of this irony we hear also an echo of Lear's rage at the beadle of the law who whips the whore he hotly lusts after. It is rage stylized by Jonathan Swift for an age of reason. The art of it all bestows upon the reader a pleasurable elevation and there is an instant transfer of allegiance to the author. Few readers have believed themselves superior to this speaker, though in fact he is ostensibly the madman and the object of satire. So distinctions between Swift and his speaker collapse, as they do in all his satires; but here in the *Tale* the problem is especially bedevilling and bemusing as the speaker sets up to wear motley. Presumably Swift does not wear motley in his brain, but even this proposition is not easily demonstrable. The demonic joy with which Swift conjures up his repertoire of voices in the *Tale* and speaks his deepest thoughts in their tongues, the sheer invention and flamboyant virtuosity, seem at times to define a game, civilized though pyrrhonnist and cynical, for would-be ironists, and we could accept it as such were it not for the deadly hatred and rage that show everywhere in odd, sudden bursts that it is not finally a game at all. Even the subject matter, the corruptions in learning and religion, is troubling by its very inconsistency. Corruptions in learning can be taken care of by parody, delivered from a posture of Augustan common sense. We scarcely need be more than snobbish for this sort of thing—or perhaps snobbish with serious artistic purpose, like Pope in the *Dunciad*. But is religion, which assumes the com-

mon body and communion, clarified by irony? Satire of the corruptions in religion could hardly be expected to chime with a
gentleman's reserve towards the new learning. Though that satire
in the *Tale* seems at times to resemble the scurrilous ridicule of a
host of seventeenth-century Church polemicists who had less
Christianity than Thersites,[2] it goes much deeper, into the inevitable psychology of the religious personality, and raises ultimate
questions. Obviously, in reading the *Tale* we need a special attitude
of willingness to follow a diabolist personality and to entertain
sudden glimpses of realities not comprehended in orthodoxies or
class postures. The last thing we need look for is "Sweetness and
Light," that shibboleth of Augustan decorum.

Who was Swift, after all, to talk about "Sweetness and Light"?
When Matthew Arnold appropriated the phrase in his battle for
Culture against Anarchy, he took care to remark, primly but precisely, that the satirist had himself all too little of the first, at least,
of these admirable qualities. Although Arnold was willing to incor-
porate in this way a good deal of the intellectual content of Swift's
Spider and Bee allegory of *The Battle of the Books* (and, indeed, like
Swift to spice it with snobbish disdain of the protestantism of the
protestant, the dissonance of dissent, and the general hurly-burly
of mechanicians, liberals, and people with vulgar names), he did
not want to confuse Swift's motives with his own. In effect he did
not accept Swift's pretension to the Bee's motives. It is hard to
gainsay Arnold.

"Culture hates hatred," says Arnold. "Sweetness and Light" suggests "a finely tempered nature" that "gives exactly the notion of
perfection as culture brings us to conceive it: a harmonious perfection in which the characters of beauty and intelligence are both
present." With such sweetness what has the violent-tempered satirist to do—he who peeps at the soul of man by way of his breech (to
turn, justly, Swift's own figure upon himself)? What has the priest
who hates inspiration, the episcopalian who hates bishops, the patriot who hates his countrymen to do? Only too often Swift's idea
of religion appears to be a judicious conjunction of punctiliousness
with repression. An easy way out from these embarrassing questions for the scholar who thinks to purify Swift of all mixed motives
and thus raise his market in academia is to deny, quite baldly, the
violence—put it down to satiric technique, while rehabilitating the
priest in the most orthodox canonicals by placing him against an
historical "background" of Christian ideas, long forgotten but now
happily recovered by scholarship.[3] The sociology of this phenome-

non of modern academia by which a demonic writer like Swift is "elevated" by being reduced to a proper cleric is beyond the scope of this essay. Suffice it to say that it is a form of the pseudoscientific determinism in scholarship that explains (away) a refractory writer by a system of ideas that were, we are told, his heritage and environment. This Swift comes to seem much like a university lecturer.[4] Nowadays university lecturers, though perhaps atheists, know a good deal more about original sin and other theological puzzles than Swift and his contemporaries cared to contemplate.[5] Such rare knowledge does not lie idle; it is put into the mouth of Swift's ghost, which then responds as obediently as a zombie, easily clarifying the unholy mysteries of the human condition that the living man risked his very sanity to think on. Thus Swift's seeming madness in *A Tale of a Tub*— not only in the bedevilling "Digression concerning Madness" but as well throughout the allegory of the history of the Christian Church—is explained as "Anglican rationalism"; his horror at the Yahoo image of Gulliver in the mirror pool, as "original sin"; his notorious predilection for images of excrement, as traditional Christian denigration of the flesh. Most ingenious of all, the vast abrupt of being that divides the religious personality as manifested in history—Jack and Peter—from reasonable men, or that divides Yahoo from Houyhnhnm, is rationalized as a lesson in the need for "compromise."[6] Little matter that the only wooden figure of the *Tale* is Martin, who represents the compromise, and that the madman of the "Digression concerning Madness" is vital and compelling, the object of every reader's wonder. Little matter that Gulliver faced with a choice between Yahoo and Houyhnhnm seems to go as mad as any Platonic dreamer delivered from the Cave to the Light and is the object of every reader's wonder.[7] Little matter—we are delivered to the insipid moral of "compromise" according to a formula called "classical humanism."[8] One cannot resist attempting to apply this moral. When Jack pisses in the eyes of passersby, when Peter pretends to change stale bread into mutton, should Jack piss more moderately, Peter work a more modest magic? When the Yahoos defecate on their own kind, are we to know that "compromise" suggests defecating on only some of our friends, and only moderately?

But a reading of Swift will always constitute an appeal from the scholars to common sense. Thackeray is the *bête noire* of modern scholars of Swift because the sentimental novelist, apologist for female purity and the sanctity of the family, accused Swift of "lifelong hypocrisy" for taking a priest's vows when his works show so evidently a "consciousness of his own scepticism." Thackeray is sentimental; he hates Swift for being so thoroughly un-English as to be capable of thinking of ladies at stool; he makes of Swift's life a sentimental drama—two pitiful virgins, Stella and Vanessa, betrayed by an imperious cad who is underneath it all a tragically alienated wretch. Yet for all his genuflecting to the household gods, Thackeray perceives with great clarity Swift's paradoxical qualities—the strange mixture of institutional piety with a subversive and fundamentally pyrrhonistic imagination. Swift, he says, did not "hiccop" Church and State in the simple way of "poor Dick Steele and poor Henry Fielding." "A vast genius . . . to seize, to know, to see, to flash upon falsehood and scorch it to perdition, to penetrate into hidden motives, and expose the black thoughts of men—an awful, an evil spirit" *(English Humorists)*. Without succumbing to Thackeray's nervousness, the common reader will understand his point.

Far from resolving the mysteries of the human condition in a table of doctrines and commandments, the *Tale* is a playhouse of illusions. A harlequin author tells a funny story of three brothers, younkers who come to town to be fops. To get on they do what is required—whore, swagger, tattle, get claps, and join a sect that worships the tailor. Here the harlequin digresses for a speculative game in which he invents a fantastic theology depending on the word *clothes* as Christian theology depends on *cross* (one crazy system among several he spins out before he is done); and then in turns he acts out the postures and struttings of each brother going his way to madness, only pausing occasionally to tell his own sad story as a battered but still pert hireling writer under three reigns, for six and thirty factions, now trying the experiment of writing upon nothing. Being such a shifty fellow, naturally he changes voices and motley from time to time; if he begins as a silly hireling, he soon develops a serious allegory, and seems to conclude as a nihilistic madman. The whole performance of parody, allegory, foolery, sententia, paradoxes, and fantastic imaginings hopelessly confuses profane and sacred subjects. It is a *tour de force* of black humor, an opportunity for Swift to mimic grubs who worm their way and philosophers who hoist themselves into the rare air over the crowd, an opportunity as well to ridicule Roman Catholics and Dissenters. Yet the *Tale's* parody of grubs and sectarians is hardly the continuing interest of this harlequinade. Now as then, it is the mind of Swift dreaming terrible truths, radical and destructive, about our culture, our reason, and the will of God, that captures the reader's imagination. Though speaking in tongues, playing the fool, the author of the *Tale* is always Swift, but Swift relieved of responsibility and its decorums and hence liberated and energized. "Good God, what a genius I had when I wrote that book," said Swift, musing over an entire career of tricks on the world. That genius was a natural gift for parody, and once having hit upon the posture and cant of the parodic figure, a further gift for looking at the world through his eyes, thinking his thoughts, calling into question the fondest orthodoxies. It can only be an inward sympathy with the enemy, for its truest, most incisive, and most radical discoveries of the realities of human life come not as satiric parodies of perverse figures but when the author is speaking in the idiom and guise of those figures. The discoveries are theirs.

At this point one example, only typical, will suffice. Because he has spent his life pursuing the main chance, the hireling author knows, he says, that the trick is not to elbow your way in the crowd but to get above it where there is room. To do that all men are compelled by their nature to invent some machine or other—the pulpit is one, the mountebank's stage another, and even the criminal's ladder to the gallows is a way of asserting the ego. Preachers and criminals fall into one category, the category of humankind, and the allegory of Peter and Jack makes clear the radical realities of religious egotism. These radical realities are elaborately worked out, and worked out to the edge of despair, by the allegory's metaphors. They are Swift's convictions, not the cracked notions of a Grub Street hireling, and the satire falls upon the human psyche, not upon an outrageous fool who is brother to the insupportable Bentley and Wotton. How shall we get above the crowd?—"It being as hard to get quit of *Number* as of Hell" (sec. 1.). Here is the controlling idea of the *Tale:* the problem is likened to the desperation to escape hell; the ego must save itself by escaping "number" and the devil take the hindmost. As with religion, so with other sublimities—learning, glory, philosophy. One is doomed to egotism, to kill off and absorb other egos. The *Tale* is a vast pit (Bedlam Hospital, as it develops) in which desperate figures try to escape over one another's heads. The image and the rigor with which the implications of it are pursued in the whole *Tale* have the intensity of a Bosch drawing of damnation. The psychological nightmare is a secularization of the problem of salvation and for Swift only expressible in his zany's mad style of occult "types and fables." Whenever one of his mad or idiot figures begins to spin fantastic

symbols and allegories, Swift is discovering his own truths. The
guise is the way to freedom for a proper priest.

In the *Tale* the trick of playing the fool to speak otherwise unspeakable truths in the service of an "unacceptable" vision of reality
is certainly an adaptation of Erasmus's *Folly*. But Erasmus is content that the world should be a playhouse of illusions; Swift is
driven wild by the spectacle, though he knows the truth, out of the
mouth of the mad author, that *"unmasking*, which I think, has never
been allowed fair Usage, either in the *World* or the *Play-House"* (sec.
9). One *must* speak through masks. And all the splendid fabrics of
institutions and the noble fabrication of an integral personality with
will and reason go glimmering in the course of the *Tale* among the
"false lights, refracted angles, varnish, and tinsel." Yet despite all
this, against his own evidence and knowledge, Swift makes us feel,
with an irrational hatred of irrationality, that there must be a reason
for reason. Like Pascal's bet on God when he contemplates the
narrow room between nothingness and the infinite, Swift's bet on
reason is a spasm of assertion despite his discovery through the eyes
of madmen of the illusion of reason. The *Tale*, like the *Argument
Against Abolishing Christianity*, the *Modest Proposal*, and *Gulliver*,
ends with a desperately felt need of resolution in a situation whose
very definition precludes resolution. Such anxiety might well have
been, as it was for Pascal, the occasion of religious dedication. It is
not, however, and anxiety is the final reality in Swift's satires.
Without denying Swift's priestly dedication, which was impeccable—he religiously corrected his choir and put back the bricks in
the close wall—I shall try in this essay to account for the emotional
intensity of his flirtation, in the guise of his satiric victims in the
Tale, with a reality entirely different from that prescribed by his
confession.

Why is it, first of all, that a satire whose ostensible subject is the
quarrels of Anglicans and gentlemen with Puritans, Catholics, and
vulgarians, quarrels so antique that they have faded beyond our
ability to recall them without scholarly paraphernalia, is as telling
today as it ever was? A modern Catholic or Presbyterian, or even a
vulgarian, can read it without a thought to his confession, and an
Anglican could appreciate it with no greater gusto than an atheist.
Surely this is so because its mad voices are to be discovered, not in a
scholar's revelation of ancient days, but in the mind of any man.
Indeed, our world now being irrevocably topsy-turvy from Swift's
point of view—atheistic, pluralistic, individualistic, progressivist—

a modern reader, were he to consider only the literal objects of the satire, though admiring of Swift's skill, could not but be indifferent to his attitudes. Even as he wrote the *Tale* (1696–97), Swift must have known that events had passed him by. So quickly had the Williamite toleration evolved, so utterly had men abandoned in a few months' time allegiances they thought the condition of their honor and faith, that neither Jack nor Peter could have been considered a threat when the *Tale* appeared in 1704. Defoe the dissenter, only a few years Swift's senior, remembered as a child copying out the Pentateuch with his family the whole night through against the dawn when King Charles would burn all the Bibles; Anglicans had not forgotten the Puritan's holy text of fire and sword and desolation. But in 1704 such passions were spent, and when Swift appended his "Apology" to the fifth edition (1710), nearly forgotten. Then the dissenter like Defoe was a poor worm and the Catholics for the most part a retiring genteel society. In 1710 Alexander Pope could move in the polite world with little notice, save from Grub Street, of his religion. Although Swift's friends rushed through brutally repressive legislation against dissenters in the last year of Queen Anne's reign, it was an act of political desperation to preserve the Tory ascendancy, to be repealed in the Hanoverian reign. Swift's virulent support of the Test Act in Ireland was an embarrassment rather than a support to successive ministers. The very idea of an integral State-Church at the turn of the century was anomalous and would soon be ludicrous when the Church became scandalously Erastian under the Georges.

It is not, then, in studies of the parochial quarrels of the Restoration that we will find a sufficient account of the evolution of the *Tale*, its success in the early years of the new century and its vitality today, but in an understanding of Swift's radical imagination. Let us begin with the *Tale*'s relations to the gentlemanly notions of his patron, Sir William Temple, for here we can grasp the evolution of Swift's peculiar irony of foolery that pervades the work.

From Snobbery to Subversion

An alien in his own country, at Moor Park a poor provincial, by Sir William's grace an amanuensis, Swift naturally smarted under his patron's cold looks. In a remarkable insight, many years later he attributed his hauteur towards great ministers, his refusal to endure their chills and snubs, to that early residence with Temple when he was so painfully unsure of his place.[9] Posthumous child, separated mysteriously from his mother almost at birth ("kidnapped" according to his strange story), poor relation of a dependent family, cut off from all familiar affections and treacherous to natural allegiances, Swift refused to belong to anyone or anything. He was a kind of psychological "bastard." Naturally such a young man, at once superior and self-hating, would identify with the oppressor, adopt his top-lofty attitude, and displace his hatred upon the vulgar. Sir William's mere whim could save him from the fate of living out his life a toady parson to some brutal squire.[10] Sir William being an attractive and accomplished man—as well as a dangerous one—he could not but mimic his manner. He out-snobbed the snob. (Did he acquire then—from knowledge of himself—his lifelong disgust for the Irish character, by his lights only a servile imitation of the English oppressor?) Swift appropriated, in fact, not only Sir William's manner but the ideas and attitudes in which the retired courtier specialized in his declining years. A dabbler in philosophical ideas, Temple loved to expatiate on the way history runs in cycles, on the low ebb of modern times, on the news other ages and times might have for us about our poor pretensions. In short, a kind of dilettante libertine, collecting in diminished times examples of vulgar errors, and, above all, scornful of the search for knowledge. Gentlemen understood the pageant of human life by reading the classics; they could not but smile at the grubs everywhere, in literature, politics, and science, busily trying to bring about "progress" ("Upon Ancient and Modern Learning"). Yet, if Sir William's airs were, by any historical measure, preposterous, he was a man of real talent and reputation, honored for his service in three reigns, respected for his willingness to relinquish ambition. The respectability of his public career was warrant enough to Swift for chiming his snobberies. All ironists begin as snobs, for irony is a trope whose rhetorical effect depends upon the audience's desire to ally themselves with the elite speaker, lest they be counted among the vulgar. They smile archly to signal that they can straighten out his crooked words which mimic the vulgar. Add to this structure Swift's hatred of *arrivistes* (like himself?), this hatred sublimated into high moral purpose; and his alienation from all natural allegiances, this alienation sublimated into intellectual intolerance of clichés and received opinions, or deepened more often than not to a covert nihilism. Such a satirist is as likely to turn the irony back upon his supposed ally as he is to mock the vulgar.

But to begin with the snob, Swift would defend Sir William's wretched mistakes in the Phalaris controversy by tarring his patron's adversaries, Bentley and Wotton, with the same brush he used for grubby writers of the contemporary scene—party hirelings, pamphleteers, smart critics, pedants, theological quarrellers. While he did not know, apparently, that Sir William was utterly wrong-headed, he might have known—had it occurred to him to inquire. Rather, the important thing was to record in the "Apology" how mortified Sir William was to hear Bentley and Wotton termed his "adversaries," they who had had the effrontery to show up a great gentleman in his scholarly errors. Temple had taken up in his casual, aloof way the quarrel in the French court over the relative genius of ancients and moderns. The French quarrel was at once a matter of aesthetics and of court politics. It being assumed by certain courtiers more given to political realism than others that Louis's greatness in political and military realms would naturally be accompanied by a commensurate superiority in the arts, the elevation of the moderns under the aegis of the *Roi-soleil* followed. If one may be cynical about these motives, nevertheless the quarrel had real substance in aesthetics. The questions of progress in perfecting ancient forms of literature, or of the just supplanting of those forms by equally valid modern ones were important, but Sir William had little interest in such real questions; for him the quarrel was class warfare. Although his cyclical view of history precluded the absolute superiority of one age, ancient or modern, over another, in literature he cast his vote for the ancients on the ground that certain ages might well have a particular genius. And after all, a gentleman's taste was perfected by reading the ancients; Sir William's perfected taste enabled him to observe the excellence of the Phalaris Letters, an excellence impossible to any but an ancient. He had the misfortune to choose a forgery to illustrate his grand thesis, but that hardly mattered, for what exercised him was the pretension of the modern age to any accomplishment at all. Just to glance at several of Temple's egregious opinions is to see how impossible was the position Swift so eagerly embraced. "But what," asked Sir William, "are the sciences wherein we pretend to excel? I know of no new philosophers, that have made their entries upon that noble stage for fifteen hundred years past, unless Descartes and Hobbes should pretend to it. . . . There is nothing new in astronomy, to vie with the ancients, unless it be the Copernican system; not in physic unless Harvey's circulation of the blood. But whether either of these be modern discoveries, or derived from old fountains, is disputed: nay it is so too, whether they are true or no; . . . But if they are true yet these two discoveries have made no change in the conclusions of astronomy, nor in the practice of physic." He wonders what has become of ancient skill in magic or in music that could charm the beasts. Modern music is but fiddling and poetry but rhyming. Though modern discoverers have introduced to our acquaintance vast continents and numberless islands, we have done little with this knowledge compared to what the ancients might have done. How little have we performed in the exploration of the Northwest Passage to Tartary so long and confidently promised? Does the sun or the earth move? Some astronomers think the one, some the other. Nor do we know what motion is. Even our tongue seems to Sir William a poor thing when he remembers his Latin and Greek.

In this olio of an aristocrat's vulgar errors, there is nothing to be admired, but one can wonder at the assurance mere accident of birth could bestow upon a man of Temple's class. But Swift's irony, if it begins in snobbish sarcasm, elevating the urbane traditionalist over the pert modern, ends in tragic irony, separating the despairing realist from the desperate illusionist. Something similar happens with Swift's crass appropriation of certain of Temple's philosophical notions. Slowly, inevitably, they deepen to the most radical conceptions of personality. It is as though a demon came to inhabit Temple's weary mind, pursuing his slight judgments of human insufficiencies until they end in the heart of darkness.

To the bill of indictment drawn here against his silliest postures, Temple would have answered, mildly, that he meant the moderns no injury; it was only that they pretended, with their busy schemes to improve man's lot, to more importance than the inevitable pattern of life would allow. What can we do? Old wood to burn, old wine to drink, old friends to converse with, old books to read— these are what we need to get through this vale of tears. A characteristic metaphor suggests the reality, the chill, the fatigue: "The abilities of man must fall short on one side or other, like too scanty a blanket when you are a-bed: if you pull it upon your shoulders, you leave your feet bare; if you thrust it down upon your feet, your shoulders are uncovered."[11] We are, Temple would say, all of us, the victims of progress; the discoveries of today are the problems of tomorrow. This weary wisdom must be set in its context, the daily pronouncement of the millenarians.

If Temple was not really serious about any of his vagrant libertine ideas, it was on principle. Tolerant, Epicurean, easily ironic, he surveyed philosophies and civilizations, remote and near, to demonstrate the amusing confusions of the reason. Still more amusing, if reason gives man the prerogative over the rest of creation, it also subjects human nature to troubles, disquiets and miseries. It does little more than create passions and wants, above all restlessness from infinite designs and endless pursuits. Born crying, man lives complaining, and dies disappointed—and the great culprit is his fatal inclination to reason on all things. Again and again, this aristocratic disinclination to meddle in the follies of humanity comes down to three grand objects of scorn. These Swift made his own. The radical human debilities, thought Temple, were restlessness, "sufficiency," and universalism. Restlessness, he sighs, is our fate; our reason will ever destroy our quiet by creating illusions and dissatisfactions. The ego is so perfect that it will seldom stop with mere ameliorations or petty remedies but will push on, busily, to universal schemes intended to answer to all pains and puzzles of life. Worse still, it is only ordinary that one should assume one's own resources quite sufficient for such everyday tasks of world-making. Thus "sufficiency." We can hardly hope to escape this fate, but a measure of peace is obtainable if we can but quieten the perplexity of thought by embellishing the scenes of life, making our situation convenient, elegant, and magnificent. This is the Epicurean way. Our game is not to soar after knowledge but to cultivate our garden. And of course this is a literal, not metaphorical, injunction. Temple pays charming tribute to English gardens and the gardener's skill. If philosophers' systems are but jugglers' tricks, we must go a ramble into ancient places where men have built gardens. These are a gentleman's meanderings; the poet's apprehension of the garden, Marvell's or Pope's, is wholly absent. For all its "ease," it is a death-dealing philosophy, for it kills the vital instinct, to know.

How can Swift be so utterly different from his mentor? Did he not appropriate his snobbery and hauteur—including his silliest mistakes; did he not borrow his fundamental ideas? On a superficial level the allegory of the Spider and Bee represents Temple's attitudes— and only slightly below the surface, Swift's idea of himself. Restless, self-sufficient, spinning a universe out of his guts, the Spider is everything Temple could not endure in the modern world. The Bee, the freebooter over all of nature and man's works, is simply a figure for Temple himself. Ranging abroad, sipping but not destroying the flowers, enriching himself and bringing home for others honey and wax, sweetness and light, the Bee comes upon the Spider sitting balefully in the center of his nasty web, spitting and cursing, *"A plague split you, said he, for a giddy Son of a Whore; Is it you, with a Vengeance, that have made this Litter here? Could you not look before you, and be d——n'd? Do you think I have nothing else to do (in the Devil's Name) but to Mend and Repair after your Arse?"* Like Sir William, the Bee is inclined to "droll" and turn back the Spider's venom with urbane quips. *"You boast, indeed, of being obliged to no other Creature, but of drawing, and spinning out all from your self . . . You possess a good plentiful Store of Dirt and Poison in your Breast; And, tho' I would by no means, lessen or disparage your genuine Stock of either, yet, I doubt you are somewhat obliged for an Encrease of both, to a little foreign Assistance."* Doubtless this is how Swift wanted to see himself, a honey bee, like Temple a gentleman ranging above the vulgar, drolling with them, benignly teaching them a thing or two about civilization. But considering that Temple had little light and Swift less sweetness, the allegory is a travesty. How right Arnold was! Poor Bentley and Wotton, so foolhardy as to be right when an aristocrat was wrong, so earnest, pedantic, and shrill, were perfect victims to bloody with borrowed spurs. As *Don Quixote* destroyed love and valor in Spain, said Temple, pedantry will corrupt the commonwealth of learning. What an opportunity for Swift—to exercise his high-mindedness by saving this commonwealth, to exercise his self-hate, by assuming Sir Williams's drollery. But Swift had no drollery; his was a higher destiny. The Bee is only a bit of pretension. To speak in tongues, with the venom and imagination of Spiders, was his genius.

What is remarkable in this vignette is the force and vitality of the Spider's personality, the way in which accent and posture call up a radical individualism, perfect in ego, of demonic energy and endless design. So far as the *Battle of the Books* is concerned, one could put this force and vitality down to the artist's success in picturing forth the object of his satire. Except that, even here, the whole vignette is rather an incongruous intrusion in a weak mock-heroic satiric form, a form that was not congenial to Swift. The reason is not far to search. The mock-heroic form can only picture upstarts as inept flailers at this and that, pert posturers, and that is of course the character of the moderns among the books. But that is Temple's manner, not Swift's. The Spider is neither inept nor pert. In his high blood runs the quickening energy of the race of radical individualists that inhabit Swift's satire from first to last. It is they who inherit the earth. It is in his participation in their imaginations that he knows the truth of human existence and gives up the rationalist game. A strange metamorphosis takes place in Swift's mind. His snobbery nurtured in the school of Moor Park reinforces his talent for mimicry and parody, makes him hawk about for the grubs and busybodies who are his natural victims. At this point the worm turns, the parodied vulgarian becomes the radical individualist; his energy and design are not to be put down. The satirist begins to think in the pattern of his victim whose radical notions of life and personality become his own. The satire—a satire fit for gentlemen—turns from the vulgarian back upon the "Christian humanist" with his smug assumptions of reason and order. The provincial Irishman in England, the psychological bastard triumphs. The nihilist asserts his rights against the imitator of Temple, the present snob, the Establishmentarian apologist to be. Self-hate becomes hate; posture becomes art.

When he adopts the pert idiom and cracked fancy of one of the figures the snob in him despises, when he is free of his gentlemanly decorum ("proper words in proper places"—*Letter to a Young Gentleman*) and can speak in the crazy, catachrestical images and metaphor of the busy vulgarian, then Swift's mind is free and his invention at its height. ("The author was then young, his invention at its height, and his reading fresh in his head"—"Apology"). The vaunted simplicity and clarity of Swift's prose style are apparent only when he speaks in official tones—in the *Sentiments of a Church-of-England Man*, in the *Sermons*, in the *Letter to a Young Gentleman*, for example. In the great satires he is not only cruelly complex but even mysterious. In the *Tale* his invention took the form of a discredited sort of wit, a debased metaphysical style of runaway metaphors, pseudological relations established by puns and quibbles, unexpected authorities, and odd learning. In this discredited sort of wit he could indulge himself in the guise of a parodist. The pleasures and insights of the *Tale*, the wild correspondences that destroy familiar categories and set the mind erring in a wilderness of doubt, are in this sense stolen fruits. As he adopts the extravagances of his enemies, his invention takes fire and he becomes his enemy, working out his own sceptical ideas in the enemy's guise. It is at this point that the problem of irony, the trope supposed to separate the sheep from the goats, becomes hopelessly complex. The critics begin to subtilize: is it a "persona" who speaks? is it Swift the Anglican rationalist? is it Swift the diabolist? is it confusion worse confounded? Parody imperceptibly seems to pass into positive statement of what really goes on in the world, and goes on world without end, what really is true of human psychology. Then the critic, like a traffic policeman, shrilly signals which way to go: *here*, for an instant, Swift shows himself through the mask, or is it *there?* or everywhere? or nowhere? *Hic et ubique*, the old mole, the fellow in the cellarage there, moves about. The obvious examples in the *Tale* are the ways in which the parody of the prostitute writer, the hireling of six and thirty factions, now supposedly employed to get up an inane farrago to divert the wits from Church and State— the ways in which this parody becomes a positive account of the reality that the world is a madhouse. Scarcely has he begun his silly stuff when he enunciates the most fundamental proposition of the *Tale*, the controlling notion of the satire, that it is "as hard to get quit of number, as of hell." Scarcely has he metamorphosed himself into a madman when he utters the most famous of Swiftian ironies: "Last week I saw a Woman flay'd, and you will hardly believe, how much it altered her Person for the worse." The sentence is never quoted as the remark of a madman. If Swift can be at his most philosophical when he is personating a pert Grub Street writer and at his most typically ironic when he is personating a madman, why should he not bring off his most heartfelt exploration of human psychology when he is spinning out the fantastic conceits of clothes and wind in the guise of a maniac Papist, Peter, and a fanatic Puritan, Jack?

Far from resting in the quietism Temple affected to believe man's only relief from pain, Swift, wholly insensitive to his patron's taste for the gardens of Epicurus, has an obsession to follow the implications of various schemes of power or reason or vision to nihilistic conclusions as he imagines their force in human affairs. Thus the characteristic entrapment of the reader in Swift's irony. Led on by the wonderful assurance of his irony towards pedantic fellows like Wotton and Bentley to indulge in the Augustan game of baiting (in Temple's fine phrase) the "wonderful pretension and visions of men possessed with notions of the strange advancement of learning and science", the reader finds himself before long puzzling over pyrrhonistic, paradoxical, and despairing conclusions in which the satiric victim somehow seems to triumph. Thus the madman of the *Tale* seems to prove the truth of his assumption that life is a tale told by an idiot; thus Peter and Jack who are set up at the outset to be satiric butts of Anglican rationalism end by convincing the reader that their corruptions of the religious spirit are universal and inevitable. Thus the corruptions of English society that Gulliver discovers are, before we are quit of the Yahoos, seen to abide forever in the human psyche which is bitterly mocked by the

Houyhnhnm's impossible reason. Augustan hauteur towards irrationality and egotism gives way to deep and troubling questions
(most of them utterly unanswerable) out of the mouths of the assumed satiric victims, and ends with a conviction of their inevitable
triumph. Without any doubt Swift hated pyrrhonism and paradox,
and of course his religion forbade despair, but what he wished
easily to scorn, his imaginative powers made only too real, far more
real than the Augustan myth of order and reason. Thus the great
objects of Temple's gentlemanly scorn, restlessness, self-
sufficiency, and universalist scheming, are equally the objects of
Swift's satire, but strangely, inevitably they become in his thought
radical and overwhelming aspects of the psyche, a kind of genetic
disease—whether manifested as glory, power, or speculative philosophy, always an example of the instinct to kill, of one ego to
absorb another, "For what man, in the natural state or course of
thinking did ever conceive it in his power to reduce the notions of
all mankind exactly to the same length and breadth, and height of
his own?" Swift asks the question, with lip-service to the Augustan
norm of common understanding and common forms, but the answer is that examples of men "in the natural state or course of
thinking" are nowhere to be found. Rather, the world is a
madhouse. Temple would smile serenely at reports of the
madhouse that might filter into his garden—ah, the "sufficiency" of
man, he would sigh. But Swift imagined "sufficiency" in the figure
of the Spider, spinning a poisonous web of a universe out of his
own guts, a universe of which he is the only begetter and the only
denizen. Dryden and Pope love to dilate on the busy-ness of grubs.
"Cool was his kitchen but his brains were hot," Dryden says of
Corah, his Puritan malcontent. Pope sets his dunces frenetically
spinning their cobwebs over the eye of day. Restlessness, it seems,
is a debility of the lower classes, though easily infectious in the
whole society. For Pascal the matter is more awesome, touching on
the existential misery of the race: "All men's misfortunes spring
from the single cause that they cannot rest quietly in one room."
Swift, like Temple and Dryden and Pope, has his snobbery; the
Tale begins with top-lofty scorn of rampant restlessness in Grub
Street and we are to understand that the Wottons and Bentleys
smell of the lamp not because they love learning but because they
cannot stop concocting absurd and pedantic theories. But in Swift
the Augustan snobbery is soon put aside as the examples broaden—
from Louis XIV, ever gloriously nervous to sally forth "to fright
children from their bread and butter," to Descartes, spinning his

"romantick" vortices; from Jack the Puritan to Peter the Catholic; from silly critics and beaux to the pensioners of court and camp and church and city. It is a Hobbesian landscape—every member of the race busily preparing his deadly aggression against his fellow—but a Pascalian overview of the dismal scene, mindful of the desperate office of reason to know the narrow room of dignity. What is unique in Swift is the absolute hatred of pretensions to dignity in busy "scholastic midwifery" that delivers meanings never conceived from "the universal mother," night, which is nothing. Dignity is found in hatred.

The fact is that we should not have Swift at all, his terrible truths, if he were a mere parodist, if his imagination did not work through the psychologies of the outrageous figures he officially hates. Their indecorums, their farfetched metaphors, their absolute egotism free his imagination, defrock the priest, and give us a radical and libertine thinker. The best of Swift is not to be found when he is following his own ideal of "proper words in proper places" or when he is speaking as a priest but when he has forgotten his urbane purview of the hell of lesser creatures, and speaking in their tongues can imagine the world they see. Speaking in the tongues of madmen, he had always the excuse that whatever shocking thoughts were expressed were not after all *in propria persona*. That was exactly his defence of himself when the clear implications of the *Tale*'s indecorous language and subversive thoughts had aroused suspicions of his orthodoxy and resentment of his improprieties. Then he thought it expedient to append an "Apology" of his orthodoxy to the fifth edition of 1710. Did not those exceptionable opinions and manners come plainly in the voices of "illiterate scribblers, prostitute in their reputations, vicious in their lives, and ruin'd in their fortunes, who to the shame of good sense as well as piety, are greedily read, merely upon the strength of bold, false and impious assertions, mixt with unmannerly reflection upon the priesthood, and openly intended against all religion"? This sort of parody was the way to satirize the "corruptions in religion and learning". "Men of taste" would understand that. And why should any Anglican cleryman be angry to see fanaticism and superstition (i.e., Puritanism and Popery) exposed? Even in this sobersided apology, so different in tone from the rest of the book, he cannot quite stay sober but must play the fool. The book is "calculated to live at least as long as our language"; his original intention was to have had four machines for rising above the crowd rather than the three, for that would have been more cabbalistic; the "chasms" in the work (referring to two of the zaniest passages of Section 9, "A Digression on Madness": "THERE is in Mankind a certain * * * *Hic multa desiderantur* * * * And this I take to be a clear Solution of the Matter," and the passage discussed on pages 101–2, below) would have been fewer had not the manuscript got out of his hands. In truth, Swift was nearly incapable of saying anything in *propria persona*. That the *Tale* "celebrates the Church of England as the most perfect of all others in discipline and doctrine" is patently absurd—unless we are to believe that what is *celebrated* is insipid, without force or vitality. No reader's interest is in Martin; every reader's interest is in the psychopathology of religious experience figured in Jack and Peter. Doubtless Dr. Swift was perfectly orthodox and wanted to say the best for his Church; it is only when he is someone else—all the time in the *Tale*—that he says the worst.

In a strange way, Swift's worst instincts led him to his most creative work, or to be fair, he had the glory to turn his worst instincts, snobbery and hatred, to the service of his creative mind. Grinding Sir William Temple's axe (a surrogate for his own), mimicking vulgarian types he fancied an affront to Sir William's aristocratic repose, he imagined, when he began to speak in tongues, the madness of all men; driven by an Anglo-Irishman's hatred of dissenters and Catholics, he imagined the destructiveness of the religious personality. Parody, the satiric device encouraged in Swift by the snobberies of the Temple circle, led him to a sympathy (perhaps largely unconscious, though not entirely so) with the enemy he mocked, so that in the grubby or mad postures he affects he is liberated from the decorums of his class and office. He can be as libertine as he pleases speaking in the crazy metaphysical conceits and ingenuities of the character parodied. Catachresis is a sort of franchise.

Here is the crux of the notorious problem of Swift's irony—whether we are to believe the speaking voice, or invert it, or twist it north-northwest, or throw up our hands.

Rabelais in His Right Mind

The fool Swift sets up for is paradox-crammed; he feeds on air, all the winds that blow. He packs up unconsidered trifles and retails them as the heart of the mystery. If he has a lot of the main-chancing Autolycus in him, peddling modern gew-gaws, he has even more of the occultist, seeking the best in the worst, translating

excrement to ecstasy. Being so disreputable he need not be a re-
specter of persons. Considerations that never trouble the sleep of
the orthodox—that historically Christians have a remarkable record
as maniacs (he would overstate the case and say an impeccable
record), that glorious kings may live to frighten children from their
bread and butter, that many people believe that scholastic reasoning can turn a stale crust of bread into a shoulder of mutton—
suggest to him the truth of his fondest dream, that the world is a
more perfect version of Bedlam hospital. There sit the doctors who
should heal us, raking in their own dung. Suddenly the speaker,
looking in at the grate of a madman's cell, is so giddy he cannot find
words to disclose his secret to the reader. *"Heark in your ear."* A
"chasm" in the manuscript and a footnote, *"I cannot conjecture what
the Author means here, or how this chasm could be fill'd, tho' it is capable of
more than one interpretation."* Left with the chasm—and the stagy
machinery of various voices, postures, and costumes, and a choice
of fantastic conceits of wind and clothes—the reader can try to
make his own paradoxes to fill in the psychology of man, but the
poor, bare, forked animal is not to be discovered—only suits of
clothes or bags of wind, social conditioning or private self-
gratification. Such realities of Swift-the-fool set Swift-the-
rationalist in a rage. If the fool's crazy imagination is fun in its
parody of men's antic dispositions, it is painful, too, in the knowledge it gives us in nerve and bone that here is the reality of the way
men live. Are we in the presence of an aristocratic ironist mimicking egregious idiots or a satanic conjurer calling up the damned
human race?

An obvious and crucial example of Swift's appropriation of the
idiot voice to express his own subversive thoughts is his use of
sexual imagery. Solemnly, clerically, he tells us in the "Apology"
that *"lewd Words, or dangerous Opinions though printed by halves, fill
the Reader's Mind with ill Idea's, and of these the Author cannot be accused.
For the judicious Reader will find that the severest Stroaks of Satyr in his
Book are levelled against the modern Custom of Employing Wit upon those
Topicks, of which there is a remarkable Instance in the 153d. Page, as well
as in several others, to' perhaps once or twice exprest in too free a manner,
excusable only for the Reasons already alledged."* On that page in "A
Digression in Praise of Digressions" (*Works*, 1:92–93) the fool "author" complains that modern wit is running dry, including even the
vogue of deducing similitudes, allusions, and applications from the
pudenda of either sex. The genius of the moderns, like the stature
of Indian pygmies, seems to be proportionate to the length of their

penises. So much for modern wit, condemned out of his own mouth. The only fly in this ointment for fretted sensibilities is that if we eliminate the raw sexual metaphors that define inspiration, the character of Jack, the glory of kings, we have precious little left. In short, Swift, not the salacious modern, is in need of the pudenda of either sex to deduce similitudes, allusions, and applications, simply because he, Swift, sees sexuality as essential to his explanation of psychology. Like literary fools in a long tradition, he is hardly to be judged by his sincerity.

To digress in the midst of digression, to address the universe ("This, O universe! is the adventurous Attempt of me thy Secretary"), to ape solemn impostors, to spin out catachrestical conceits—these are tricks to relieve oneself of the necessity of logic. When Swift wrote as a sober historian of Queen Anne's last years, he wrote with *parti pris* but with the pretense of logic; in the *Tale* and in *Gulliver* history is treated as though it makes no sense at all, except as a case book in abnormal psychology. Psycho-logic deals with strange and unsuspected correspondences. The fool is free to deal in such correspondences where rational explanations break down. Why did a mighty king for thirty years frighten children from their bread and butter, amuse himself to take and lose towns, beat armies and be beaten, lay waste subject and stranger, friend and foe? All the philosophers dispute the causes natural, moral, and political. The truth lies in his bowels, the vapors from which animate his brain and at last conclude in a *fistula in ano*, in that region especially precious, according to Paracelsus, for furnishing perfume. Here is Swift in idiotic guise, mimicking dark authors, availing himself of their freedom from logic to strike out the connection between glorious history and a man's bowels. Louis XIV's glory is "caused" it seems by his narcissim and retentivity. The touch about perfume seems exactly right to describe quite literally the pleasure men find in their own bowels. Such mad correspondences may not impress an historian but in fact Louis's conduct does defy ordinary historical explanations. The historian David Ogg writes ironically of Louis's mysterious attack on Holland in 1672:[12] "Louis was prompted by three motives worthy of a really great King— "religion," glory, and revenge, motives strikingly contrasted with the economic calculations of Colbert and other Europeans. It was if seventeenth-century Europe was suddenly transformed into Old Testament Israel, and at no point in the reign did there seem such brilliant justification for the parallel between Jehovah and Louis XIV." On the birth of the Dauphin, Louis had preached to him a sermon in which he was compared with God and the Dauphin with Jesus Christ. The Dauphin's chief characteristic turned out to be, Ogg writes, an insipid lassitude. As for Louis's wars, after years of amusing slaughter, they left the French nation at the boundaries where it began, but starving, and with Europe united against it.

Because Swift's use of the fool bears resemblance to that of Erasmus and Rabelais, we can understand a good deal about his cast of mind by suggesting the similarities and the crucial differences.

No one who has read both these treatises on delusion, *The Praise of Folly* and the "Digression concerning Madness," can doubt that Swift is deliberately parodying Erasmus. Folly is quite as aware of the dregs of life as Swift—his picture of a decaying whore is nearly as withering as Strephon's discovery of Chloe—yet Erasmus knows that Folly's business is not to wither but encourage life. But Erasmus's genial, humanistic scepticism becomes in Swift's mind the ultimate horror rather than the final wisdom. Self-love, always a delusion, has this to be said for it, says Folly, will he who hates himself love anyone? Swift hates his fool and that fool in himself. By reducing the world to a playhouse and the playhouse to a set of masks that the maskers gladly accept in lieu of their real selves, Erasmus's Folly comes in the end to accept Paul's words: "We are fools for Christ's sake" and "Let him that seems to be wise among you become a fool, that he may be wise." Reality exists only in God and even a peroration, a summing up of our folly, is impossible: "I see that you are expecting a peroration, but you are just too foolish if you suppose that after I have poured out a hodgepodge of words like this I can recall anything I have said. There is an old saying, "I hate a pot-companion with a memory.'" Swift's manner is similar ("I my self, the Author of these momentous Truths, am a Person, whose Imaginations are hard-mouth'd, and exceedingly disposed to run away with his *Reason*"—sec. 9) but crazier, being entirely free of any thread of argument; the device, however, is the same—the whirling mountebank upon the stage itinerant (see Holbein's illustration), the quick, inane changes, the mocking seriousness and serious mockery, the deliberate attempt to make received wisdom fade away like a dream in paradoxes and contradictions. But Swift hates this theater of illusion and wants to make the play come out right in this world, not the next (though with no expectation of success). In a Christian world of Erasmus's sort he would have to be counted a man of little wisdom. He knows that satire is resented by none—the world's posteriors are calloused and every man carries with him a racket to bandy the ball from himself into the crowd.

The satirist is as great a fool as the fanatic preacher who shouts in the public place "that all are gone astray: that there is none that doth good, no not one . . ." And yet Swift hates the Epicurean fool who "creams off nature," who teaches the use of "artificial mediums, false lights, refracted angles, varnish and tinsel." That one must play the fool to whip the dog truth out from its kennel when Lady the brach may stand by the fire and stink, this reality is both a source of energy to Swift the artist and of terrible anguish to Swift the rationalist. From this point of view Erasmus's solution of praising delusion is either an act of faith—or a failure of nerve.

What there is of Rabelais in Swift—and what there isn't—shows up another facet of his personality. The search for the oracle, some occult maggot at the center of life, is a futile chase. Swift as well as Rabelais likes to lead on the reader—Rabelais because he believes the verb *trinquer* conveys a sufficient wisdom, Swift because he wants to afflict his reader with his own anxiety. Swift, especially, likes to bait critics, warning them that there is a "superficial Vein among many Readers of the present Age, who will by no means be persuaded to inspect beyond the Surface and Rind of Things; whereas *Wisdom* is a *Fox*, who, after long hunting, will cost you the Pains to dig out. 'Tis a *Cheese*, which by how much the richer, has the thicker, the homelier, and the coarser Coat; and whereof to a judicious Palate, the Maggots are the best . . . 'tis a *Nut*, which unless you chuse with Judgment, may cost you a Tooth, and pay you with nothing but a *Worm*." (sec. 1) What does this mean? Doubtless it satirizes party hacks and small critics who appear wise by hinting at a meaning, but it recalls very explicitly Rabelais's prologue to the first book. "In imitation of a dog, it becomes you to be wise, to smell, feel, and have in estimation these fair goodly books, stuffed with high conceptions . . . you must break the bone, and suck out the marrow,—that is, my allegorical sense . . . signified by these Pythagorean symbols." If you think such tales as I tell, of codpieces, of bacon, of peas are mere foolery, look deeply for the allegorical and sublime sense, says Rabelais. For Plato's philosophical dog worrying a marrow bone, Swift substitutes a fox, a rotten cheese, a hard but wormy nut—fleering replaces fun. Like Diogenes, Rabelais will thump a tub to make a great pother, as though there were some significance in the thumping. Wasn't Socrates, that Silenus, always playing the fool? But what can you believe of a drunkard? (Prologue, bk. 3). Swift throws out his tub to take off attention from others; his work, like other deep pieces such as *Tom Thumb* or *Tommy Potts* or *The Hind and the Panther*, has its dark Pythagorean meanings. The wisdom of Socrates is to be found in his types and fables. But he is only a hack, threadbare and broken, and (later on) quite mad.

Pope's character of Swift in the *Dunciad*'s invocation—that of a quick-change artist who may choose, among other guises, "to laugh and shake in Rabelais's easy chair"—is less accurate than honorific. Though Swift borrowed much of Rabelais's foolish guise, and often in similar words, he could not have imagined Rabelais's system of strange and exhilarating correspondences that unify and bless life, celebrating scoundrels, pedants, subversives, hobby-horses, and rapists as agents of life, even while informing the whole with a love of humane letters, natural history, and civil law. Rabelais can celebrate, in a sentimental and moving context, the dead Queen Baldebec's acres of *"petit con."* (Contrast Swift's handling of the same image in the vignette of the Brobdingnagian maid of honor's obscene toying with Gulliver.) Gargantua breaks wind so festively that 106,000 little men and women are engendered. (Contrast Swift's handling of the same image in the *Tale*'s description of the communication of spirit among Puritans.) Panurge, tired of amorous flowers of rhetoric, makes an utterly vulgar approach to a grand lady of Paris. Rejected, annoyed by her nice airs, he sprinkles essence of bitch-in-heat over her while she is at prayers and she is assaulted by 600,014 dogs. (Contrast Swift's gruesome story of the Aeolian priests who blow into one another's anuses, thus becoming inspired vessels of the Lord (*Acts* 9:15), and expel wind to teach, for learning puffeth a man up (I *Cor.* 8:1), or convey oracular gusts into the genitals of females, thus refining a carnal into a spiritual ecstasy.) Rabelais plays the fool to create a delicious and gay wish-fulfillment fantasy that escapes all propriety and brings the backsided part of life into its real relation with the sublime. His cruelty is not oppressive because it remains in the comic domain of wish-fulfillment. Swift, on the contrary, is the master of exhibiting, with hatred, the backsided reality of sublime pretensions. Changing the drunkard for the madman, as befits the change from fantastic comedy to reductive satire, Swift has a cruelty that is owing to his desire to show up the "fantastic" quality of actuality. Fantastic metaphors are moved to the edge of literal statement (or slander). Clearly he wants to suggest that, literally, Puritan fanaticism is a perverse sexuality. The fool's manner in the *Tale* (and in other satires) is in large part a covert way of speaking the unspeakable. Panurge's spinning out of the fantasy of monetary debt that binds all men into a universal commonwealth has been taken for a clown's

serious metaphor for the brotherhood of man, under natural and
divine law. Swift's generation of the vast system of clothes to explain the universe and the microcosm of man is a bitter parody,
funny as it is, of man as a creature made in God's image. That the
souls of man are in their clothes is an apparent fantasy that turns
out to be only a slight exaggeration.

Voltaire and Coleridge described in remarkably similar terms the
paradox of Swift's taking into his bitter imagination the festive
manner of Rabelais. For Voltaire, Swift was "*Rabelais dans son bon
sens*," and Coleridge found in Swift "the soul of Rabelais dwelling in
a dry place." Both judgments seem impossible contradictions. Had
Rabelais been "in his right mind," he would have had nothing to
say; had the soul of Rabelais inhabited a dry place, it would have
been a dead soul. And yet both judgments are exactly descriptive of
Swift. Both Rabelais and Swift invent fantastic images, spun out to
the edge of sanity, both play the fool to reduce the sublime to the
thing sublimated, but Swift drives the grotesque and the fantastic
into the actual, i.e., he rationalizes the fantastic. That is his way
with satire, and with life. That is why he can be said to be Rabelais
in his right mind, inhabiting a dry place.

Only in the guise of the fool, inventing some fantastic comic
fiction, was Swift able to reach the frontier of tragedy. Were he
merely a reductive satirist, looking down with Augustan serenity
upon the pageant of folly, we should not feel the anguish that
pervades all his satires. How shall we account for this anguish
except as the tragic conflict of a rationalist personality, seeking
everywhere the leaven of good sense that his Anglican confession,
its assumption of natural law and civil polity, warrants as the condition of a decent life, but finding nowhere anything but radical
egotism, a fatal talent for using the rational faculty for explaining
away in sublime terms ordinary instincts for aggression and self-
gratification? A conviction, moreover, of the operation of the
"spirit" by either social conditioning or necessities of body mechanics, is so overwhelmingly present in every part of the *Tale* that
it amounts to a universalism of the kind the satirist attacks in Lucretius and Descartes, among other systemizers. Although Lucretius
and Descartes are clearly objects of satire, as their pre-eminent
place in the madhouse shows, their mechanistic systems are simply
appropriated to provide the pervasive imagery of sublime perversions. If we read the *Tale* with any regard to what is in the text
rather than with a pre-determination of what it *must* or *ought* to
mean, considering Swift's holy orders, it is obvious that by Swift's

lights the history of Christianity is one of tyranny over mind and body by means of a subtle combination of ingenious rationality and holy mystery (Peter), or of nihilistic and aggressive egotism by means of inner spiritual light and hatred of visible authority. It is obvious as well that this religious judgment is given larger, in fact universal, application to all sublime pretensions in history. We have, then, this paradoxical technique—satire by way of parody, but also a fool's truth about the human condition told in the catachresis and fantasy of the parody. It is useless to try to rationalize these divided aims; they represent a divided soul in Swift. His allegiance to Augustan decorums and to his holy office was never surrendered or betrayed; rather, the undermining of the very assumptions of that decorum and that office is accomplished in such outrageous guises and language that the priest can almost legitimately protest that *he* is innocent of "ill meanings."

The manners of Erasmus and Rabelais afforded him the necessary cover. Like Rabelais he writes about nothing; like Erasmus he forgets what he is saying. One could say that these are Jesuitical subtleties, betraying an hypocrite, were it not for the virulent hate Swift obviously bears the fools through whom he speaks his truth. What he hates is what they know, and, inhabiting them, what he knows. And against what he knows, what he would believe and would have others believe, always a will o' the wisp of an ideal, works to produce his violent irony. This inconsistency is a fault only if one wants doctrine or polemics as the solution to ultimate questions. The inconsistency is, in short, the human fate, as is the self-hatred that animates it. The love of reason is, after all, also a fear of the irrational, and as a sublimation of irrational instincts, naturally subject to all the distortions and perversions Swift is so fond of demonstrating. Although reason in Christian story is subject to various incapacities, according as the believer moves nearer to or further from the pessimism of Augustine and Luther—and Swift in his sermons utters conventional cautions—it nevertheless plays as important a role as in classical thought. For Swift the priest, as for many seventeenth-century Anglicans, reason holds a place only a shade less compelling among the faculties than it does in Arminianism. It is as a fool—the libertine idiot of the *Mechanical Operation of the Spirit* and the madman of the "Digression concerning Madness"—that Swift analyzes the reason in a way other than conventional, in a way that goes to the quick of the living man. The fool confuses the frontiers of true and false, sense and nonsense, good and evil, and in metaphors so indecorous that it might seem that the top-lofty Augustan trained in the school of Temple was merely putting us through our paces as gentlemanly ironists, were it not that the confusions bring us to Swift's fundamental insights in the *Tale*. One of the most startling of the fool's images, exploiting metaphysical catachresis (the technique mastered in parody) but illustrating perfectly the tragedy of psyche in which reason and morality serve egotism and aggression is the famous "bird of paradise" passage (sec. 8). Having got through the scurrilous explanation of female inspiration by way of the genitals, the refining of a carnal into a spiritual ecstasy, the fool explains it all:

> AND, whereas the mind of Man, when he gives the Spur and Bridle to his Thoughts, doth never stop, but naturally sallies out into both extreams, of High and Low, of Good and Evil; His first Flight of Fancy, commonly transports Him to Idea's of what is most perfect, finished, and exalted; till having soared out of his own Reach and Sight, not well perceiving how near the Frontiers of Height and Depth, border upon each other; With the same Course and Wing, he falls down plum into the lowest Bottom of Things; like one who travels the *East* into the *West*, or like a strait Line drawn by its own Length into a Circle. Whether a Tincture of Malice in our Natures, makes us fond of furnishing every bright Idea with its Reverse; Or, whether Reason reflecting upon the Sum of Things, can, like the Sun, serve only to enlighten one half of the Globe, leaving the other half, by Necessity, under Shade and Darkness; Or, whether Fancy, flying up to the imagination of what is Highest and Best, becomes over shot, and spent, and weary, and suddenly falls, like a dead Bird of Paradise, to the Ground. Or, whether, after all these *Metaphysical* Conjectures I have not entirely missed the true Reason.

Cavalier, bird, geometer, astronomer, mythological creature: all these far-fetched metaphysical metaphors, worthy certainly of Donne, represent the mind of man, all develop from the tragic mystery that good and evil border each other: idealism becomes fanaticism; the straight path turns full circle unawares, merely by its indefinite prolongation; an excess of light on one object obscures another; idealism wearies the spirit and kills. All this is poetry, outwardly of the corrupt metaphysical breed and so stuff of comedy (see Johnson on Cowley), but behind the comic mask a moving image of the inescapable anxiety of being a man. Such a perception is close to religious feeling—this, besides its "metaphysical" account of the psychological origin of God and the devil. The zany license of the fool pose allows the unexpected association, the pert jumps of thought, the imaginative generation. Where satire verges on such human mysteries, it is of course "confused"—assurance yields to description, reductive certainly but only apparently fantastic. Incapable of Blake's vision, Swift had something of his understanding, that God and the devil are ordinarily reversed by the pretense of reason.

Evolution of an Image

The "bird of paradise" image is only typical of metaphysical foolery in the *Tale* that becomes serious symbolic expression. It is a kind of gloss on the four central images—"the mad crowd," the wind mechanics of the Aeolists, the clothes religion, and the madhouse. The clothes and wind religions are metaphysical exfoliations of the fundamental proposition of the *Tale*, that to escape the "mad crowd" is a radical need only to be compared with the hunger for salvation, and the "madhouse" is a generalized version of clothes and wind mechanics. To understand the seriousness of this fool's system, it is helpful to try to reconstruct the evolution of the "wind" image in Swift's mind as he appropriated the systems of Lucretius and Descartes to his own purposes. Here we can see how, in the midst of satire of the spider personality in these great universal philosophers, Swift's irony turns back upon the reader his assumption of Augustan superiority and makes of the system that is supposedly the object of contempt the real explanation of human conduct.

How to get quit of number? Room enough overhead but how to reach it? Even Socrates, says the zany, suspended himself in a basket to help contemplation. This slight allusion to Aristophanes's *Clouds* suggests the mad train of thought that, ransacking Lucretius and Descartes, spicing the olio with odd bits from scholastic philosophy and Scripture, yoked illustrations, comparisons, and allusions into the grand conceptual metaphor of wind. The process is exactly as Johnson describes metaphysical wit, only here the occult resemblances are so perverse, the industry so "ant-like" (F. R. Leavis's wonderful epithet for Swift's imaginative processes),[13] that Johnson might well have enjoyed the parody of what he thought in any case an unnatural talent, especially so as the working out of the metaphor concludes with an adaptation of Donne's compass image

that Johnson singles out for special contempt. Swift's joke, however, is that the joke is serious, creating the devastating analysis of
the "inspired" religious personality.

Socrates's great god Vortex is discovered, like the Aeolist's and
Jack the Puritan's inspiration, in the bowels. Every man his own
wind machine, a fart is perfect evidence of Vortex within. Says
Socrates to his pupil Strepsiades (who is practicing farting): "Shalt
thou then a sound so loud and profound from the belly diminutive
send, / And shall not the high and infinite Sky go thundering on
without end? / For both, you will find, on an impulse of wind and
similar causes depend." One must rise to ply the philosopher's
trade. There is no god but Vortex; all rumbles are holy and by
necessity, in the microcosm of the bowels as well as in the macrocosm of the Clouds. Swift would take up the idea of necessity in
inspiration, not merely to carry on Aristophanes's scatological joke
about the urgency of intestinal tract, but to illustrate the compulsion under which the brain works, just when pretensions of sublimity, of will and reason, are most elaborate. And like Socrates's
explanation of the similarity between internal vapors and the
Clouds, the Aeolists have their theory of the microcosm of man and
the macrocosm of universe, for as vapors ascend from the lower
faculties to water the imagination, so mists may arise from a jakes to
form clouds overcasting the face of nature.

The connection of anality with inspiration is so fixed in Swift's
mind that he cannot think of the pretensions of philosophers without thinking of defecation. Orators, he says, climb above the crowd
so as to let their words drop upon the crowd, which obediently lift
up their open mouths in a plane perpendicular to a line from the
zenith to the center of the earth, so that no droppings conveyed by
gravity will be lost. They are so many jakes. Were the image itself
not enough to make clear Swift's idea that the desire to elevate
oneself is a desire to dirty others and that respect for the "elevated"
is a desire to be dirtied, the explanation of this mechanics by an
allusion to Lucretius makes the train of ideas obvious. Sitting in a
citadel, alone, aloof, Lucretius watches from his elevation others
wandering aimlessly, pitting their wits against one another, struggling to gain the pinnacles (De Rerum Natura, 2. 1-61). (The context
of Swift's allusion suggests that he developed his image of the "mad
crowd" and the hellish struggle to get above it from this reading of
Lucretius.) Here Lucretius explains sensation of bodies by the eternal downward stream of atoms, inclined ever so slightly so as to
collide occasionally and coalesce. Swift applies this to words and

then jumps to 4. 26-521, where Lucretius explains sensation by the penetration of the senses by films of atoms from a distant object. Though hearing is the sense involved, the references to jaws and circles and mouths suggest taste. The auditors like to taste the droppings. And then a prurient joke about ladies in the circle of boxes enjoying lewd wit that runs in a line into a circle makes the imagery "complete"—anal, genital, and oral. At the outset of the *Tale*, then, the associations—suggested only by metaphor—by which later on Aeolist inspiration is defined. Lucretian mechanistic theory will be reduced to anal-genital-oral stimulation and this "psychology" will be equated with various sublimities; the indwelling spirit of the Lord, glory in empire, in philsophy, in religion become wind rushing through tubes and orifices.

The exposition of Aeolist religion beings (end of section 6) with an invocation of Lucretius (1. 934) and a parody (sec. 8) of Lucretian cosmology (bk. 5). The accidental concourse of atoms that brought forth land, sea, and sky, stars and sun and the round moon, the vegetables and man himself, must reverse itself and all things perish in an atomic cataclysm. Do not be so superstitious as to think that the gods control this, or that the universe is created for the sake of man. Swift's adaptation (sec. 8) reads, "The Learned *Æolists*, maintain the Original Cause of all Things to be *Wind*, from which Principle this whole Universe was at first produced, and into which it must at last be resolved; that the same Breath which had kindled, and blew *up* the Flame of Nature, should one Day blow it out.

Quod procul à nobis flectat Fortuna gubernans."

Lucretius's prayer to Fortune (5. 107) to spare us this fate is ironic, running contrary to his own principles, since destiny is indifferent to man and it is to inculcate this anti-superstition that he says he writes. Perhaps Swift incorporated the prayer for the same purpose—to mock those who create gods in their own image. To this system he adds a scholastic distinction of the informing form—here, wind—and some word quibbles from hermetic philosophers connecting wind and spirit.

The mock-theology relieves Swift of all decorum and the fool in him, an ingenious modern witling, crazily yokes by force and violence all the possible implications of the metaphor: wind is the material of the universe, spirit, breath of our nostrils, flatulence, farting, belching, prophesying, preaching, the quality of being puffed up by learning (1 Cor. 8: 1), the thirty-two points of the compass rose (of the same importance as the thirty-nine articles), the four corners of the world corresponding to the four winds and equivalent to the four points of the body (anus, mouth, left and right arms), the soaring of the mind, the gasping and panting after fame—and more.

With such mystical correspondences in the universe and the little world of man, and between the two, the Aeolists are ready for mysteries and rites. Here Swift is on his own, Lucretius having provided the general idea of materialistic explanations of the mind and spirit and of atomistic winds. (Words are but wind, says Swift; words are but material particles sent steaming in the air, says Lucretius [bk. 4]). Every rite is some sexual application of wind, variations on the oral, genital, anal imagery. The Aeolists have their Communion: ". . . several Hundreds link'd together in a circular Chain, with every Man a Pair of Bellows applied to his Neighbour's Breech, by which they blew up each other" (sec. 8). When replete they belch or fart into one another's mouths, thus becoming vessels of the Lord (Acts 9:15). Since their gods are the winds, they convey wind into the posteriors of their priests who then belch for their disciples. Female priests of course receive inspiration through "a Receptacle of greater Capacity," thus refining "a Carnal into a Spiritual Extasie."

By resolutely twisting Lucretius's explanation of sensation (bk.4), Swift is able to extend the sexual implications of inspiration to another sublimity, princely glory. I have shown, says Lucretius, how all things are atoms flying through space, how objects are created (by accidental hookings of atoms inclined this way and that), how mind also is a wind of atoms. What now are images of things but a sort of outer skin perpetually peeled off the surface and flying about, wearing the aspect and form of the object from whose body it has emanated. There follows a complete mechanics of these flimsy atomistic images. By collision of images a centaur may be created, or in sleep a mind so disposed by its particular contexture of atoms may receive an image aimlessly floating in the air. It is not, however, the senses that are deceived but the mind, for the mind gives us a false account of the discrepancies between the films and the objects. So heaven's entire firmament may appear in a puddle no bigger than a finger's breadth. Senses are true and do not lie but reason is fallible. Lucretius is not a man for romance: we do not need tales of Pan piping in the haunted woods but only a theory about rebounding atoms of sound. Our organs were not created to help us but the organ having been created by a fortunate conjunction of atoms demands its use.

This sense mechanics being admitted, we have exactly Swift's madman's theory of the imagination: flimsy films "from the superficies of things" are flying about everywhere so that a mind ready to receive particular images, according to its disposition, will find them, and grotesque combinations of them, available in the ambient airs (4.722-822). Now, as to sex, for that instinct most obviously victim of the dangerous prevalence of the imagination, Lucretius has a complete explanation (4.1037-1191). The one stimulus that draws the human seed from the human body is a human form. The seed collecting in the generative organ is ejected in the direction from which the film of a bodily form floats into the mind. Swift (sec.9) refers to Lucretius (4.1048-65). When the film of a (desired) absent human form strikes upon the senses, the seed of generation is dislodged and swells the sexual organs. Hence follows the will to eject it in the direction of one's lust. The body makes for the source from which the mind is pierced by love. The shafts of Venus create a yearning to transmit the substance of one body into another. Though absent, the object of love will haunt one with these images. Keep such images far off by spilling your seed elsewhere. And then Swift's "madman" explains history by reference to this theory of Lucretius (sec.9). A certain prince (Henri IV of France) made mysterious preparations for war, alarming the whole of Europe. Crowns trembled, small politicians made conjectures—was it a scheme for universal monarchy? for pulling down the Pope? for subduing the Turk? All this conjecture is resolved when the prince is stabbed by an assassin, his vapors fly out, and it is discovered that it was all owing to a female "whose Eyes had raised a Protuberancy, and, before Emission, she was removed into an Enemy's Country." The collected semen having nothing but the image to go to, turns adust, converts to choler, goes up the spinal duct to the brain. So the same principle that moves a bully to break the windows of the whore who jilts him causes a great prince to raise armies and dream of battles.

But even in the midst of Venus's toils the mind will receive images of other bodies more compelling than the real one over which the hands roam. Naturally this insatiable appetite is most subject to false appearances. A sallow wench is proclaimed a nut-brown maid, a slattern has sweet disorder, a stringy female is lithe as a gazelle; pendulous-breasted, she is Ceres suckling Bacchus, waspish harridans burn with a gemlike flame. How wearisome this delusion, says Lucretius. Truth is that Venus herself is only a human body, smelly and foul, but perfumed and ornamented. Had one the will, one could know this truth—even though a lady's dressing room is said to be inviolate.

How close is all this to Swift, with his talk of ladies' dressing rooms, of happiness as "a perpetual possession of being well-deceived"! It is from the larger context of Lucretius's explanation of sensation and sex (bk. 4) that Swift has borrowed the central conception of this famous passage of the "Digression on Madness" (sec. 9):

> He that can with *Epicurus* content his Ideas with the *Films* and *Images* that fly off upon his Senses from the *Superficies* of Things; Such a Man truly wise, creams off Nature, leaving the Sower and the Dregs, for Philosophy and Reason to lap up. This is the sublime and refined Point of Felicity, called, *the Possession of being well deceived;* The Serene Peaceful State of being a Fool among Knaves . . . .

A little earlier, he had said:

> The Question is only this . . . . Whether Things, that have Place in the *Imagination*, may not properly be said to exist . . . . How fade and insipid do all Objects accost us that are not convey'd in the Vehicle of *Delusion?* How shrunk is every Thing, as it appears in the Glass of Nature? So that if it were not for the Assistance of Artificial *Mediums*, false Lights, refracted Angles, Varnish, and Tinsel, there would be a mighty Level in the Felicity and Enjoyments of Mortal Men.

How are we to read all this parody of Lucretius? Does he stand for all mad systemizers who strike a pompous and pedantic posture above the crowd? Does the speaking voice that spouts his theories represent modern libertine thought (for the revival of atomic philosophy had made Epicurus "modern")? Certainly Epicurus and Lucretius are exemplars of the academicians of Bedlam because they hoped to reduce the notions of all mankind exactly to the same length and breadth as their own (according to Swift's simplistic notion of them, which ignores their pre-eminent good sense and reasonableness). The caricature of Lucretius would seem to suggest only a vivacious version of the Temple snobbery. The Lucretian picture presented notions of a world made up by accidental collision of atoms, indifferent to man, of mental and spiritual processes no more than a jiggling of the atoms of the nerves, of imagination as only a licentious receptivity to films and images floating in the ambient airs, of will and desire as tissues of delusion—these notions

are certainly hostile to a Christian's faith. And yet, though the
Lucretian picture remains a poetic image, what it symbolizes, a
materialistic reality, runs strongly in Swift's mind. It is after all the
only basis of the satire of the "abuses" in religion and learning, and
those "abuses" are so generalized as to be more properly de-
nominated "the inevitable results of religion and learning." The
Tale does not reassure the reader of the truths of Christianity. On
the contrary, it is a devastatingly convincing attack on the very
sublimities that are essential to Christianity. If dissenters and papists are its ostensible object of attack, we should remember that
these two groups represent the mainstream of Christian experience.
They represent, moreover, something far more important, the two
aspects of religious experience, the inner voice and the authority of
the visible community of the Church. Swift's satire does exactly
what he condemns revolutionists in empire, religion, and philosophy for doing—it universalizes. "I stay awake nights," says Lucretius, "to give you this look into the heart of hidden things"
(4.143). "Since my vein is once opened," says Swift's voice, "I am
content to exhaust it at a running . . . for the universal benefit of
mankind." Such statements, while certainly parodies of the Augustan universalizing inclination, must be seen as expressing a tendency in Swift himself. His development of the sexual origin of
"sublimity" is too pervasive and of too wide an application—both to
various aspects of life and to the range of history—to be anything
but a dark vision of the human condition. His development of the
mechanical operation of the spirit leaves precious little room for
genuine spirituality. Certainly, his explanation of glory in empire,
philosophy, and religion is utterly serious. The satire does not fall
back upon the fool but the fool is the agent by which Swift freed his
imagination and gave vent to his deepest thoughts.

The use of Lucretius is the most pervasive example in the *Tale*—
though as we have argued, there are many others—of the divided
aims of parody on the one hand and of serious vision on the other.
One can hardly repeat too often that Swift's imagination begins in
parody and takes fire from the mad elaborations of metaphor so that
catachresis is not only his liberation from Augustan decorums but
the sluice gate by which his subversive instincts escape repression.
Swift was far too repressive a personality to accept the freedom of a
Blake—and, moreover, his age was not propitious for such freedom—but he could think freely of the reversal in men's hearts of
good and evil once he gave a sop to his snobbery and that of the

class of Temple with which he most wished to identify himself. It is no accident that he became a Churchman "rationally zealous," for the High Church party he chose had the nostalgic authoritarianism of a dispossessed elite and a high-minded disdain of the watery Erastian church then dominant. With this shoring up, this bulwark, he could use the zany characters he parodies to voice his own bitter vision. But it is his unresolved hatred of the realities his fools discover that gives to his satire its tragic overtone.

If Lucretius could set Swift's fantasy going, Descartes would of course be as useful. Swift was not one for fine philosophical discriminations and he deliberately runs together the systems of the ancient and the modern. "*Epicurus* modestly hoped, that one Time or other, a certain Fortuitous Concourse of all Men's Opinions, after perpetual Justlings, the Sharp and the Square, would, by certain *Clinamina*, unite in the Motions of *Atoms* and *Void* . . . *Cartesius* reckoned to see before he died, the Sentiments of all Philosophers, like so many lesser Stars in his *romantick* System wrapped and drawn within his own Vortex" (sec. 9). If this passage suggests that rational systems are really extensions of the ego of the reasoner, it also shows, as do the actual images of mechanistic sublimity, that Swift had a very particular use for these two philosophers, essentially the same use, to provide an account of life as utterly materialistic that would answer to observable facts. What Swift wanted from Descartes was his materialistic cosmogony by vortices, the mechanics of animal (including human) bodies, and his spider personality. Like Lucretius, Descartes is a world-maker of rather pert assurance. Amused by the welter of opinions of his ancient exemplars and present mentors, resolved to seek all knowledge within himself, in his own self-consciousness, he retired, he tells us in the *Method*, to a warm room to build the "romantick system" Swift parodies. While willing to grant God His mysterious ways, Descartes makes it clear that the Deity might have availed Himself of his system of vortices to create the universe, had He wished. Nor does Descartes wish to deprive the human animal of his traditional, God-given spiritual soul, but he is put to such a fantastic expedient to allow the operation of spiritual substance in a materialistic world that he was suspected of being in fact a materialist. The apparatus of the pineal gland as a valve by which spirit acts upon body not only violates, magically, Descartes's system of mechanics but is so bizarre as to seem almost a Swiftian parody. Descartes's notion of the mechanics of the animal body is more plausible. Like Lucretius, he supposes an agitation of the body by the impact upon the senses of external corpuscles of matter. From the nerve ends, animal spirits transmit these impulses by canals inside the nerves to the brain and pineal gland and thence to the motor centers. A shrewd guess at the operation of the heart and the emotions makes the Cartesian mechanics very much available to Swift as a metaphor for the mechanical operation of the spirit, a metaphor that hovers, as he wished it to do, on the edge of actuality. Here again, as with his use of Lucretius, Descartes serves an inherently self-contradictory double purpose—to parody the restless, self-sufficient universalist but also to give voice to Swift's dark vision of the fraud of sublime pretensions, including Christian, in human economy.

Pascal seems again close to Swift's thought. "I cannot forgive Descartes," writes Pascal, "he would gladly have done without God in his philosophy, but he could not spare Him to give [his system of vortices] a little shove to start it going. After that he had no further use for God."[14] Descartes himself observed that life is a war between the infinite will and the finite understanding, which is an exact description of his own predicament and Swift's description of the great ones in empire, religion, and philosophy—in short, the spiders of history. But for Pascal such realities of life were the occasion of spiritual commitment, of a bet born of despair for a desperate hope. For Swift, however, such realities were the occasion only of metaphysical anxiety, being driven as he was to undermine in the guise of a fool the very spiritual pretensions in which officially he placed his faith.

We have only touched on the involutions of thought in the *Tale*, with much emphasis upon its inconsistency, but we have followed through Swift's characteristic imaginative processes. There remains the fantastic metaphor of "clothes," by which Swift defines the corruptions inherent in the religious authority of the visible Church, much as by the metaphor of "wind" he defines the complementary corruptions inherent in the authority of one's inner voice. The allegory of the *Tale*, the development of the personalities of Jack and Peter, the personification of these two corruptions, is a remarakable psychological study. Unless one assumes that the fool speaker represents Swift's most serious thoughts, this entire allegory, these elaborate metaphorical structures of "wind" and "clothes," must be the meaningless patter of an idiot modern. If the argument conducted here is convincing, however, the thought of the *Tale* explores real questions about human pretensions and the answers are not reassuring to the Christian or to the apprentice Augustan rationalist.

"The Self-defeat of Life"

If we listen to the fool and madman as Swift's voice, we cannot but feel the force of the "Digression concerning Madness" as the culmination of Swift's anxiety in the *Tale*, of his satire against pretensions, including his own, that worthies of state and religion and learning can escape the mechanical operation of the spirit. Such a reading is rather different from one in which the in-group joke is that "the author of these momentous truths" is merely a parody of the types Sir William Temple could not abide. The charge levelled by F. R. Leavis,[16] that Swift is wholly negative in this section (and by implication throughout), is at least arguable. The "genius delights in its mastery, in its power to destroy, and negation is felt as self-assertion." This paradoxical vitality, says Leavis, is "the self-defeat of life, life turned against itself." While obviously unsympathetic to Swift's moral attitudes, Leavis was nevertheless the first critic to enter the withering mazes of Swift's irony in the "Digression" and follow faithfully the unpredictable turns of the famous "fool among knaves" passage. Of the secure body of assurances, habits, and assumptions that characterize most ironists he finds nothing at all. Instead the very intensity of the trickery of expectation, the spontaneity, copiousness, and violence of metaphor continually throw the reader off balance and foil his every attempt to get his bearings from some secure vantage.

Great kings are mad—victims (i.e., beneficiaries) of mechanical internal disturbances such as circulating vapors or atomic films of absent females. Philosophers wishing to reduce the notions of all mankind to their own length and breadth, might in this undistinguishing age be confined to Bedlam. Without enthusiasm—vapors that the world calls madness—the world would be deprived of conquests and systems and all mankind unhappily reduced to the same belief in things invisible. As the vapor strikes we may get a Descartes, Jack of Leyden, or an Alexander. "For the brain in its natural position and state of serenity, disposeth its owner to pass his life in the common forms . . . ."

As Leavis points out, all this is perfectly ordinary Augustan doctrine. Presumably if all mankind were reduced by sanity to the same belief in things invisible, they would all be Anglican rationalists, a religion that teaches people to behave themselves and not examine the mysteries over-curiously. (Swift, his sermons show, had something of the sort in mind, at least as an everyday faith.)

One would suppose that if the author really believed, except as an official stance, that such a Houyhnhnm faith had any reality in this world, he would write a satire of a particular rather than general application. For nothing at all in the picture the *Tale* presents of psychology or of history suggests that men are, or were, or will be other than irrational. The metaphor is of the world as madhouse, but Swift's way with metaphors—the more "fantastic" the better— here as elsewhere in his satires, is to show that fantastically reductive metaphors are nearly indistinguishable from literal truth. From this point on, the "Digression" completely obfuscates the rationalist ideal of common forms. Fancy gets astride the reason. To delude oneself is so easy as to be inevitable; to delude others is no more difficult, for happiness is "a perpetual possession of being well deceived." How insipid is everything not seen with the assistance of false lights! The ironic argument has imperceptibly veered from a commendation of the madness of great schemes in empire, religion, and philosophy to a recommendation of silly credulity, lest one be unhappy. Quite a different matter. And Leavis rightly asks whether "credulity" is not perilously close to the acceptance of "common forms," which, we have already been told, no accomplished madman would accept. And now we are told that "curiosity" is a bad thing for madmen and therefore a good thing for sane men. But "curiosity" is not a virtue in polite circles—the "true [i.e., false] critic" is "curious to observe the colour and complexion of [a writer's] ordure"—and even here is presented as pompous pedantry—"that pretended Philosophy which enters into the Depth of Things, and then comes gravely back with Informations and Discoveries, that in the inside they are good for nothing." Does not "reason" tell us that the outside is preferable to the inside? "Last Week I saw a Woman flay'd . . ." And so "reason" may mean "common sense," or "curiosity," or a preference for illusion. "Philosophy" is as dubious. If we do not content ourselves with Epicurean films and images, is the only alternative "to lap up" the Sower and Dregs with Philosophy and Reason? Perhaps this is all quite mad, but if a madman is speaking why should he claim those who accept his advice to be well-deceived fools among knaves? Clearly the speaker is not a clay pigeon set up for the sport of the gentlemanly fowler but Swift's own voice ironically baiting the reader's

serene Augustan assumption that irrationality is only an unfortunate lapse of good taste. Reality is sad and insipid; we do crave
tinsel; to be forever cutting is pompous and officious; to accept films
and images is to be fool among knaves but to rest in common forms
is somehow desirable; curiosity is bad form but credulity is idiocy.

Are these contradictions in action and thought that must puzzle
the will merely "negative" as Leavis complains or do they, like the
"bird of paradise" passage, represent Swift's despair of rationality?
It is after all the mad metaphors that teach us the terrible truths of
the *Tale*. And who are the sane who pass their lives in the "common
forms," never forming parties after their own interest, shaping their
understanding by the pattern of human understanding, serenely
reasonable? Throughout his life Swift raises this Houyhnhnm ideal
only to despair of it. It is in his despair that he reaches interesting
truths about the human condition. It is to his abandonment of the
"common forms" that we owe his fool's voice and his extravagant
fictions. "Now, I would gladly be informed, how it is possible to
account for such Imaginations as these in particular Men, without
Recourse to my *Phænomenon* of *Vapours*, ascending from the lower
Faculties to over-shadow the Brain, and thence distilling into Conceptions, for which the Narrowness of our Mother-Tongue has not
yet assigned any other Name, besides that of *Madness* or *Phrenzy*."
Sometimes Swift's parodies are deeply hidden and seem to represent some inner diabolism, too intimate to question. The passage is
a parody of the annunciation (Luke 1:35): "The Holy Ghost shall
come upon thee; therefore also that holy thing which shall be born
of thee shall be called the Son of God." For Holy Ghost read
Vapor; for Highest, the lower faculties; for conceive (Luke 1:31),
conceptions; for Holy Thing, madness.

What seems to annoy Leavis is that he cannot find a secure
position from which Swift levels his assaults upon the world and
his fellow creatures. The bedeviling irony he traces is certainly
owing to Swift's habit of changing the perspective of his attacks.
The Augustan appeals to simplicity and common sense, the ironist
surveys the burrows of busy grubs, the Anglican bows decently to
his confession's *via media*, but the radical assaults are upon the
sublimities, or as he puts it with such filthy festivity in that out-
house of the *Tale*, *The Mechanical Operation of the Spirit*, the "ways of
ejaculating the soul":

> Too intense a Contemplation is not the Business of Flesh and Blood; it
> must by the necessary Course of Things, in a little Time, let go its
> Hold, and fall into *Matter*. Lovers, for the sake of Celestial Converse,

are but another sort of *Platonicks*, who pretend to see Stars and Heaven in Ladies Eyes, and to look or think no lower; but the same *Pit* is provided for both; and they seem a perfect Moral to the Story of that Philosopher, who, while his Thoughts and Eyes were fixed upon the *Constellations*, found himself seduced by his *lower Parts* into a *Ditch*.

Although the allusion is to a parable by Socrates in the *Theaetetus*, Swift's meaning is entirely his own. Socrates merely wishes to illustrate the silly simplicity of the Philosopher; Swift wishes to say that sublimities are, as we would say today, a sublimation of the lower parts. Such a potpourri of attitudes is hardly possible in sensible discourse, nor was Swift's talent in such discourse. His talent lay in his ear for real voices, his ability to hear in their fragmentary accents the attitudes of a culture and the psychology of men; it lay in a vein of poetic fancy, mad metaphors, so outlandish as to obliterate any question of decorum. A zany patter, parodying grubby, main-chancing attitudes in modern culture, sets the reader up to play the ironic Augustan. But, occasionally at first, and characteristically as the *Tale* develops, the zaniness deepens to fantastic and grotesque conceits discovering radical realities of psychology that wither not only Augustan assumptions of reason and clarity but also the longer tradition of Christian and humanistic glorification of the higher faculties. It is suddenly clear that the fool and madman knows truths that Sir William Temple could never know. As in the initial stage of this irony Swift's playful voice mocks the pompous universalizing of small "philosophers," so in the next stage the grotesque conceits which characterize glory in empire, religion, and philosophy turn back the irony upon the superior reader when it becomes clear that these assaults are not upon particular objects but upon universal pretensions that the sublime faculties can ever be more than sublimations of the lower parts. "The very same Principle that influences a *Bully* to break the Windows of a Whore, who has jilted him, naturally stirs up a Great Prince to raise mighty Armies, and dream of nothing but Sieges, Battles and Victories.—[*cunnus*] *teterimma belli causa* (Horace)" (Another Swiftian misapplication of a classical author.) The last stage of the ironic process of the *Tale* grows out of the universal application of the satire: the fantastic and grotesque conceits are shown to be not in the end so much metaphoric but literally true. Puritan narcissism is not like that of a sexual pervert; it is that of sexual pervert. Great kings are not prone to make mistakes that make them look like inmates of Bedlam; they are mad.

One has only to deal at the end with the question, what is

madness? Clearly Swift answers the question: it is the rock-bottom, universal, and irreducible narcissism and aggression of all men.

It would be an idle work to deny that Swift's politics and religion were for the most part oppressive, and that he himself was a repressive personality, but his salvation as an artist—and sometimes as a politician and Churchman—was his hatred, a hatred like Gulliver's, that compelled him to throw back into men's faces their pompous idealism and pretended rationality and ask them how they liked the smell of it. Faced with their own truth by the bedeviling irony, rational readers are literally created by Swift. His satire is hardly "corrective"—one cannot correct one's being. If "rationis capax" means anything then it means "capable of reasoning if one knows that when one fixes one's eyes on the constellations, one's lower parts will seduce one into a ditch." It is an improbable possibility, this demand for incessant irony in order to be rational. In this sense only is Leavis's charge of negativism, "the self-defeat of life," a true bill. And it is precisely here that Swift's irony becomes tragic.

But Swift's satire is so festively inventive, so raucous in its humor that the reader's experience of its harlequinade is far more euphoric than lugubrious. The Hobbesian "sudden glory" of mastering life in those mad metaphors and parodying voices is a continuing effect. To triumph over vulgarity and yet to adopt the vulgar voice to express one's own truths is a feat of artistic legerdemain that gives great pleasure, and with this pleasure comes the franchise to participate in Swift's reduction of sublime pretensions to their elemental coprology. One cannot read the *Tale* without laughter that gives dominance to the rational faculties. In short, Swift's rationality is of little avail without its aesthetic component. We honor the artist, not the priest.

The problem of Swift's religion, so far as we can deduce it from the *Tale*, can be only briefly touched on here but touch on it we must to understand Swift's cast of mind that plays such tricks with our sensibility in the *Tale*. In choosing the *via media* of Anglicanism Swift was not thinking of the predominant latitudinarian current in the Church represented most respectably by Bishop Burnet. This accomplished if garrulous man Swift libeled and ridiculed as though he were an illiterate. A few years after the publication of the *Tale*, and before his "Apology" in the Fifth Edition, Swift had cast his lot with the Tory lower clergy (and this while still a Whig in politics) and against the Erastian bishops. Such an allegiance does not imply any serious concern for doctrine or spirituality. He was willing that the heathen should be deluded into accepting the faith by suppressing "hard" points in doctrine, points such as the divinity of Christ. (What is shocking in this is not the deception but Swift's ignorance that it would be the mysteries not the rationalities that would convert the primitive. Such ignorance must be the consequence of his disinclination to indulge the spiritual dimension of religion.) He is as willing to recommend hypocrisy as a way to faith—for the hypocrite can withstand no better than other men the force of habit. No man, he thought, was responsible for his doubts as long as he kept them to himself. He could insist upon the imposition of mere forms of religion without regard to the belief of the "practitioner."[17] All this adds up not to hypocrisy in Swift but to an anachronistic commitment to the Church of Hooker, though to the form of it rather than the substance. Though liberal in the interpretation of doctrine and ritual, Hooker was absolute in his insistence upon an integral State-Church in which citizenship in the commonwealth was convertible with membership in the Church. Such a society was one manifestation of God's grace, and unlike a Puritan theocracy, was thought to be a blessing to reasoning men, not a curse upon the depraved. By Swift's day, however, it was the individualistic personality that ruled the roost rather than the collectivistic Anglican of Hooker's stamp. Burnet could recognize a reality. Swift's anachronistic attitudes were, therefore, if noble, dry and without real substance. This anachronism accounts for their repressive odor. How else but by repression could they be made to prevail? But more serious, Swift's radical undermining of reason and will brings into question the fundamental assumption of Hooker's Church, which is that the *societas perfecta* is found on reason and through reason, law, both effects of God's grace. Such a reasonable theory of human life, respecting God and man, admitting the fall, certainly, but insisting upon the goodness of God in preserving in men sufficient reason for establishing a just society and recuperating his own estate. This ideal seemed hardly compelling after the violence of the seventeenth century, and Swift's own insight into the perversion of rational processes, and, indeed, the inevitability of that perversion, makes it untenable. That Swift was sincere in his support of the faith is not in question. He wanted to rebuild churches in the decayed parishes of London, to establish bishops in the New World, to make the Church a reality in the daily lives of his own parishioners, and yet his obsessive probing of psychological realities that bring assumptions of the glory of the rational faculty into question, his hatred of men's pretensions to spirituality, make of his religion more an anxiety than a faith. The *via media* of Swift is not the gracious and pious

way of Herbert. Nothing in the *Tale* makes us believe that the
authority of the visible Church can be brought into harmony with
the inner conviction of justification. Little wonder that Martin is a
manikin when Jack and Peter appear finally not as exceptions to the
rule of life but the rule itself. Had he been a saner man, a Burnet or
an Addison, Swift would have had little news for us from the
frontiers of faith. There, where men ask ultimate questions, the
answers are not clear and the guise of the fool was for this Churchman the only way to report back. We come a long way in the *Tale*
from the purlieus of Sir William Temple. One can almost imagine
that the "fool among knaves" is Temple himself, puttering in the
Gardens of Epicurus. As we have seen, Swift takes Temple's ideas
but changes them utterly—from ironic amusement at the antics of
men to ultimate questions about reason and the will of God. The
change from Temple's feeling for life to Swift's is perhaps represented in the *Tale* by the suppression of any mention of the sweet
reason of Epicurus, mindful of illusions and physical necessities,
but confident of the good life. This true aspect of Epicurus Temple
understood. In the place of this sweet reasonableness of Epicurean
philosophy, Swift gives us a bitter analysis of the mechanical operation of the spirit by borrowing Lucretius's materialistic system.
Instead of representing the truth that Epicurus while describing the
prevalence of films and images in our perception, wanted to provide
the reason with defenses against its own deception, Swift simply
assumes that men will content themselves with films and images.
This change perhaps implies a thoroughgoing criticism of Temple's
Epicurean contentment before the amusing spectacle of lesser
breeds outside the garden. It would seem to suggest as well the
thought processes by which Swift found his own genius after a false
start as Temple's minion in the school of gentlemanly irony. Swift's
irony simply shatters the values of Christian humanism by showing
how they mask the reality of the mechanical operation of the spirit.
Far from leaving us in the secure position of the conventional ironist, he leaves us with the burden of anxiety that is his own.

Notes

1. Review of Ronald Paulson's *Theme and Structure in Swift's "Tale of a Tub,"* *Review of English Studies*, N.S. 12 (1961):300-302.
2. For a thorough discussion of the virulence and inhumanity of Anglican ridicule of Puritans, see W. P. Holden, *Anti-Puritan Satire 1571-1642* (New Haven, Conn.: Yale University Press, 1954).
3. Professor George Sherburn complained thirty years ago about "sensational" critical

treatments of Swift as "tiger." Not Swift's personality but his rhetoric is the interesting thing, said Sherburn; Swift himself was conventional and orthodox. In the past three decades, academic criticism has indeed followed Sherburn's strictures, endeavoring to remove questions of his personality from consideration of Swift's works. This endeavor has had three main streams: abstract considerations of the demands of the genre of satire, background studies, and a combination of the two first in "persona" studies. The most elaborate example of the last is Ronald Paulson's *Theme and Structure in Swift's "Tale of a Tub"*, which presents the "hack" as a consistent satirical device that Swift sets up in the *Tale* to carry all his animus against hermetists. As Paulson sees it, the "hack" has a long history, going back to the early Christian gnostics. The object of the *Tale's* satire is therefore this "hack" as a vessel of hermeticism. Paulson's view makes of the *Tale* a hermetic work in itself, available only to scholars. His treatment of the long history of hermeticism provides, nevertheless, a valuable understanding of *one* of the objects of Swift's contempt, though it does not account for either the complexity or the emotional impact of the *Tale*, and indeed, as Professor Davis (see n.1) has written, imposes a formidable barrier to the reader's intuitive understanding of the work. A more rigorous treatment of satiric techniques is Edward Rosenheim's *Swift and the Satirist's Art*, and a less polemic discussion of the religious background is Phillip Harth's *Swift and Anglican Rationalism*, both valuable works. It is true, however, that Rosenheim's study is so abstract and rigorously formalistic that it ignores Swift's own quality and meaning; and that Harth's study does not pretend to discuss the peculiar use Swift made of his Anglican heritage. We are led back, then, to Swift's personality and the peculiar quality of his mind, and it is the purpose of the present argument to suggest that Swift studies might usefully return to a humanistic criticism, the apprehension of the *unique* mind and art of Swift. The interesting thing is to see a remarkable personality such as Swift's forging from conventions and tradition its unique world-view. It seems aesthetic and philosophical nonsense to expect, as did Sherburn, that a writer's art and mind can be understood apart from his personality. Where else but from the personality can art come? I have listed the three works that seem best to exploit the currents of Swiftian criticism since Sherburn's complaint. (I do not mean to imply that they derive from Sherburn.) A multitude of articles of various worths in these currents—studies of the satiric genre, of background, and of their combination in the "persona" figure—cannot be listed but point towards the three books mentioned. I should like to think that the present discussion will respond to the question, "how does Swift's *Tale* affect the reader?"; such a discussion must transcend, while respecting, abstract considerations of genre and background.

4. The phrase "university lecturer" is Donald Torchiana's in his study, *W. B. Yeats and Georgian Ireland* (Evanston, Ill.: Northwestern University Press, 1966), ch.4. See also Donald Davie's essay reviewing the methods of Quintana and Bullitt, "Academicism and Swift," *Twentieth Century* 154 (1953).

5. In Swift's day, religion was not a matter of theology but of church-going and moral guidance. Swift and his contemporaries were notoriously hostile to theological subtilizing. See n.16, below.

6. "Compromise" is Kathleen Williams's formula for Swift's message in her study, *Jonathan Swift and the Age of Compromise*. My reading of the *Tale* is obviously not in accord with hers, and, indeed, I should say that "compromise" is the most unlikely of messages to attribute to Swift. In my experience his readers *always* respond to him by remarking his violence and uncompromising pursuit of his argument. It is deadening to tell the reader that if he just knew a little more of what a specialist knows, he would see that Swift is only representative of his age or illustrative of a genre. For the truth is that there is not another Swift either in his age or in the history of the genre of satire. When I insist upon his unique aesthetic quality, I am not of course arguing that he was unconversant with the "art of the possible" in the politics of church and state.

7. I have discussed this unresolvable dilemma in my essay "A Voyage to Nowhere with Thomas More and Jonathan Swift," *Sewanee Review* 69 (1961): 534–65.

8. Williams, *Jonathan Swift and the Age of Compromise*.

9. Letter 19, *Journal to Stella*. The editor, Harold Williams, notes that the reference to Temple may be an editorial interpolation, but we have so many stories of Swift's pride before "great ministers" that the reference seems exactly right.

10. In "On the Fates of Clergymen." Swift writes a fable of the fates of a good and a bad clergyman, which are of course the reverse of justice. The good clergyman seems a thinly disguised description of his own character as he saw it. See Swift's letter to Temple, October 6, 1694.

11. "The Gardens of Epicurus."

12. *Europe in the Seventeenth Century*, ch.7, "The Absolutism of Louis XIV."

13. F. R. Leavis, "The Irony of Swift," *The Common Pursuit* (Harmondsworth: Penguin Books, 1962), p.81.

14. *Pensées*, "Misère de l'homme sans dieu," 77. (Brunschvicg edition).

15. I have written on the allegorical implications of the *Tale* and the allegorical habit of mind Swift shows everywhere in "Swift's Allegory: The Yahoo and the Man-of-Mode," *University of Toronto Quarterly* 33 (1963): 1–18.

16. Leavis, "The Irony of Swift," especially pp. 80ff.

17. The best that one can say for Swift so far as his religion is concerned is that he accepted sincerely, by mainstrength of his will, the assumptions of his faith, but one must say his religious sensibility was nearly nonexistent. He was a Churchman and a zealous defender of the non-Erastian foundation of the Church. He was no toady and no time-server. Bishops, he said, could be installed in episcopal palaces by the government by a tight-rope walking contest, if it so pleased the government, but no government could ordain a bishop or perform ecclesiastical functions *(Remarks on Tindall)*. In sum he fought for the dignity of the Church and its place as an integral part of national life. But it requires religious vision to make the Church effectively a part of national life and that Swift did not have. His way was authoritarian. Censorship, spying, religious and moral tests, he thought, might bring about some improvement *(Project for the Advancement of Religion)*. Would this lead to hypocrisy? he asks. Yes, he answers, and a good thing, too, for by being hypocrites under compulsion people fall into a habit and genuinely accept what they are compelled to do. This is astute psychology for social conditioning (and was the practice of all European churches) but hardly religion. (His understanding that "religion" is usually a "Pavlov's dog" reflex is in fact the fundamental idea for the satire of Peter in the *Tale*. It takes one to catch one). In the *Letter to a Young Gentleman, Lately enter'd into Holy Orders*, he suggests that the successful priest should not attempt any explanation of the mysteries—again good advice, but not indicative of theological propensities. *Thoughts on Religion* contains the advice to missionaries to suppress mention of Christ's divinity. Immediately following this thought is one even more interesting, that argument about opinions fundamental to religion is wicked—whether they be true or false. Naturally, therefore, one should conceal one's want of belief. Swift's lifelong bitter defense of the Test Act in a country where not only the vast majority of the population, but the majority of the protestants, were thereby persecuted is eloquent testimony to his sanguine view of false conformity. When we are aware of these real, as opposed to the scholars' imputed, beliefs, we can understand how the *Tale* can be a revelation of evils fundamental to religion rather that a celebration of the perfection of the Church of England.

Swift and English Politics, 1701–14

F. P. LOCK

Swift's single sustained period of active involvement in English politics lasted less than four years, from October 1710 to August 1714. These were among the most important years in his life, for it was then that he came closest to the center of political power and exercised his greatest influence on public events. To understand them, though, it is necessary to trace Swift's earlier, more sporadic, political connections. The complex world of English politics, which Swift entered as an Irish alien, was dominated by the struggle for power between two great parties, the Whigs and the Tories.[1] Swift had the misfortune to be a "natural" Tory who held certain moderate "Whig" intellectual convictions. His classical education and his political apprenticeship in the household of Sir William Temple (which belonged to a rather different political world from the one Swift would enter) led him to adopt certain Whiggish constitutional doctrines. His Irish birth and background gave him divided loyalties: a general commitment to the (naturally Whiggish) Irish protestant establishment, but a more particular attachment to the Church of Ireland. His earliest experience as a clergyman, at Kilroot, gave him an abiding (and most unwhiggish) hatred of the presbyterians. By temperament Swift was a Tory, inclined to pessimism, to a distrust of innovation, and to a nostalgic attachment to the values (including the political values) of the past. Temperament would finally triumph over intellectual conviction.

1

Swift's first political pamphlet has a long and misleading title: *A Discourse of the Contests and Dissentions between the Nobles and the Com-*

mons in Athens and Rome, with the Consequences They Had upon Both Those States (*Works*, 1:195–236; published in 1701).[2] Ostensibly about classical history, it was really a commentary on contemporary political events. Written at a time when Swift was a free agent, it displays his own convictions with less alloy than do his later pamphlets written as a semi-official propagandist. It was published anonymously (as were all his later pamphlets), and contemporaries recognized its quality by attributing it to either of two leading Whig apologists, Bishop Burnet and Lord Somers. As an example of "parallel history" it is brilliant; but its form limited its influence, for only the minority of readers with a sufficient range of classical knowledge would appreciate its allusiveness. All the great pamphlets of Swift's later period would be aimed at a much wider audience. But the elitist assumptions of the *Discourse* are appropriate enough to itself, for it is a defense of aristocratic political domination.

Written at a time when the parties had reversed their traditional roles, when the Tories were the dangerous demagogues and the Whigs the defenders of the royal prerogative, the *Discourse* allowed Swift to champion both a specifically Whig cause and his more deeply held conservative values. For the only moment in his political career, the cause of the Whigs was consistent with his spiritual loyalties. The *Discourse* addresses itself both to the specific issue of the irresponsible impeachments (as Swift saw them) of the four lords (Portland, Orford, Somers, and Halifax) who had been involved in the partition treaties, and to the more general constitutional questions raised by the growing power of the House of Commons. The *Discourse* shows that Swift's conservatism was deeper and more intensely felt than his Whiggism. For he touches very lightly and briefly on the Lockean idea of a *summum imperium* lodged in the people, and then only as a theoretical help to his argument; most of his attention, and almost all his energy, is directed at the follies of the people and at the general ill consequences that attend the exercise of political power by large assemblies. Swift looks backs nostalgically to the time of Romulus, when the commons were convoked only on important occasions and were then subject to the overriding authority of king and nobles. Of parliaments, he would later write that he "adored the wisdom of that Gothic Institution, which made them Annual" (*Works*, 9:32). He made the comment in "A Letter to Mr. Pope" (really a pamphlet in the form of a letter, and dated 1721). It shows the consistency of his basic political ideas (though not of his party loyalties) that twenty years after the *Discourse* he still regarded the proper function of parliament as a check on the executive power, not as a body that either could or should exercise it.

In writing "parallel history," Swift was following the example of (among many others) Sir William Temple, whose *Introduction to the History of England* (1695) contains an indirect defense of William III in its sympathetic account of William I. Swift, however, drew his parallels not from English but from classical history. The classical examples are intended to universalize both the problems and the answers, for Swift believed that what had been true for Greece and Rome would be true also for modern England. This generalizing is helpful to Swift's polemical purpose, for in the *Discourse* and in his later pamphlets (for example, at the beginning of the *Conduct of the Allies*) he is a master of the question-begging statement of principle, the "truth universally acknowledged" that embodies a highly partisan position. The freedom Swift allows himself in the selection (and distortion) of examples shows that he regarded history as a source to draw on at will for illustration and argument. He pays very little regard to historical truth, to anachronism, or to the separation of history from myth; Theseus is as good an example as Themistocles.

Swift begins by arguing in favor of the proper balance of power both within and between states, and stresses that the many (that is, the House of Commons) may be as despotic as any oligarchy or tyrant. He then recounts how the Athenians impeached all their most distinguished leaders. Nothing better illustrates the exuberance of the *Discourse* (a quality that links it, against the later political pamphlets, with *A Tale of a Tub*) than the cornucopia of examples at this point. There were only four lords to defend, but Swift cannot resist citing (among the many more that he tells us he could instance) Miltiades, Aristides, Themistocles, Pericles, Alcibiades, and Phocion. The later political pamphlets are more tightly controlled, rarely giving the impression (as here) of overabundance of material bursting through the seams of the argument. The multiplicity of the examples obliges Swift to provide a summary paragraph in which he spells out the main equations between the Athenian and English leaders (*Works*, 1:210). Swift next turns to Roman history to illustrate the more general constitutional question and to enforce his argument that popular power results in political chaos and decline. He does this through a series of loose parallels between Roman and English history, with less emphasis on personalities. His view that the current danger to political stability in

England came from an excessive growth of "popular" power was in direct opposition to the Tory analysis, which saw the exercise of the royal prerogative as the most immediate threat to constitutional balance. Finally Swift applies his lessons on the dangers of impeachments and the unchecked growth of popular power more closely to the contemporary situation. The *Discourse* compels admiration for its virtuoso manipulation of classical examples and for its mastery of tone and rhetorical temperature. The author is indignant, but it is a controlled indignation. The economy and trenchancy of the *Discourse* (the more remarkable by contrast with the elephantine pamphlets Charles Davenant was writing for the Tories) are qualities that would characterize all Swift's best political writings. For a first effort the *Discourse* is astonishingly good, and Swift was hardly unreasonable in hoping that the writer of such a pamphlet would find his services in demand and rewarded by preferment.

Swift returned to Ireland before the *Discourse* was published, but in April 1702 he was back in London and acknowledged his authorship. His hopes that its services to the Whig lords might lead to his rapid advancement, however, were checked by the Tory revival that had followed the accession of Queen Anne in March 1702. Swift remained at least a nominal Whig, although he published little that was directly political between 1702 and 1710. In 1703 he wrote a pamphlet against the Occasional Conformity Bill, although significantly he did not publish it (*Correspondence*, 1:44). Whatever reservations he must have had about the attitude of the Whigs to the Church, his personal connections remained all on their side. He was on friendly terms with two of the party leaders whom he had defended in the *Discourse*, Somers and Halifax, and with such Whig writers as Addison, Ambrose Philips, Rowe, and Steele. Swift himself, in the Tory pamphlets he wrote after 1710, makes so much of the supposed connection between Whiggism and irreligion that it is easy to forget how many good churchmen (William Wake, Edmund Gibson, for a time Swift himself) were Whigs. Swift certainly did not regard his own connections with the Whigs as being tainted with irreligion, for he tried to use them for the advantage of the Church of Ireland. When he came to England on his first mission to try to secure the remission of the First Fruits (November 1707, to May 1709; the First Fruits were clerical taxes already remitted the Church of England to provide the fund known as "Queen Anne's Bounty"), he planned to exploit his connections with Whig leaders. As late as August 1710, Swift still hoped that

Godolphin might help his search for personal preferment (*Correspondence*, 1:170). In 1708–9 Swift published four political pieces that reveal why he in fact failed to obtain preferment from the Whigs through being "thought to want the Art of being thourow paced in my Party, as all discreet Persons ought to be" (Letter to Charles Ford, 8 March 1709, *Correspondence*, 1:125). Two of the pieces are straightforwardly Whiggish. *A Famous Prediction of Merlin* (*Poems*, 1:101–5; February 1709) is a mock-prophecy in verse with a prose explanation. Several points reveal Swift's current Whig partisanship: the compliment to Marlborough, and the "predictions" of successful campaigns in Flanders and Spain and of the Queen's remarriage.[3] In June 1709 Swift published the third part of Sir William Temple's *Memoirs;* the timing (popular support for the war was flagging) and Swift's own preface amount to an endorsement of the Whig policy of vigorously continuing the war. The *Memoirs* themselves are consistently pro-Dutch and anti-French. They end with a lengthy account of France's expansionist aims and the need for concerted opposition to frustrate them. Swift's preface contains notable compliments to Lord Sunderland, Secretary of State, and to Lord Godolphin, Lord Treasurer (*Works*, 1:268). There was less joy for the Whigs in the other two publications. *A Letter from a Member of the House of Commons in Ireland, to a Member of the House of Commons in England, concerning the Sacramental Test* (*Works*, 2:111–25; dated 1709, but published December 1708) is a warning to the more extreme anticlerical Whigs not to attempt the repeal of the Test Act, which excluded non-Anglicans from public employment. A spirited defense of the right of Ireland to independence and of the Church of Ireland, it reveals the limits to Swift's whiggishness. The fictive author of the *Letter* is an avowed Whig, however, and indeed the pamphlet is an attempt to show that a good Whig can be a good churchman and that most Irish Whigs are in fact good churchmen. The same desire to clear the Whigs from the false (as Swift liked to think) charge of favoring irreligion appears in *A Project for the Advancement of Religion and the Reformation of Manners* (*Works*, 2:43–63; April 1709). It proposes that the Queen should encourage piety and morality by making a good character a prerequisite for public employment. The political message of the pamphlet (addressed to the Whigs as much as to the Queen) is that the Whigs, instead of rewarding irreligious timeservers whose only virtue is their party loyalty, should free the party from the taint of atheism and immorality by promoting deserving men of talent and virtuous Whiggism (men like Swift himself, for example).

2

In May 1709 Swift returned to Ireland, having failed both in his search for personal advancement and in his mission on behalf of the Church. In the summer of 1709 the Whigs missed a favorable opportunity of concluding a peace agreement. On 5 November Henry Sacheverell preached an inflammatory sermon, "The Perils of False Brethren, both in Church and State," intended as a challenge to the Whig government. Sacheverell was impeached, and though convicted, his trial (in February and March 1710) produced a reaction of support for the Church and the Tories and a revulsion against the Whigs and the war. The Queen had been waiting for just such an opportunity to rid herself of the set of Whig ministers that had been forced on her in 1708. Secretly aided by Robert Harley, she begun a piecemeal reconstruction of the government along center-Tory lines. In August Godolphin was dismissed, and it became clear that a new parliament (certain to contain a majority of Tories) would be called. In the midst of this political revolution, Swift arrived in London in September on a second mission to try to secure the First Fruits. Swift did not foresee how these changes would affect him personally (in August he had still been hoping for the patronage of Somers), but it must have seemed that neither he nor the Church could do worse than under the old ministry. Personal factors were not decisive, but they helped. Swift went to see Godolphin; his reception was "altogether short, dry, and morose" (*Correspondence*, 1:173). Harley, by contrast, "received me with the greatest Marks of Kindness and Esteem" (*Correspondence*, 1:184). Swift repaid each minister in kind. On Godolphin he wrote a lampoon, "The Virtues of Sid Hamet the Magician's Rod" (*Poems*, 1:131–35; early October 1710). On 7 October Swift delivered to the printer "A Dialogue between Captain Tom and Sir Henry Dutton Colt," a pro-Tory ballad on the imminent Westminster election.[4] Later the same day, he had dinner with Harley and his first long private talk with the new minister.

Harley not only flattered Swift with respect and promised the long-sought remission on the First Fruits; he engaged him to write for the government. It must have been gratifying to hear, as Swift later put it, "that their great difficulty lay in the want of some good pen, to keep up the spirit raised in the people, to assert the principles, and justify the proceedings of the new ministers" (*Works*, 8:123) and to be asked to take on the task. Swift's first specific assignment was the editorship of the weekly *Examiner*. Although this was in no sense an official position, the understanding was that through government influence Swift would obtain some suitable position in the church as a reward. The first number of the *Examiner* had appeared on 3 August. Its purpose was to counter hostile Whig propaganda by "examining" it and more generally to "examine" the conduct of the outgoing Whig government, or rather to censure its corruptions at home and its misguided conduct of the war abroad. These objectives are set out in the *Letter to the Examiner* written by Henry St. John, who is also credited with having written some of the early numbers, and who in September became Secretary of State (the *Letter*, published in August 1710, is reprinted in Swift's *Works*, 3:221–27). The Whigs took the *Examiner* seriously enough to set up a rival *Whig Examiner*, and when this proved ineffective they replaced it with the more successful *Medley*. There are some individual papers of respectable quality, but the *Examiner* was languishing when Swift took it over with No. 14 (2 November 1710).[5] Swift's hand was soon apparent in the more coherent policy and more commanding tone that he gave the paper. He also reversed the previous policy of "examining" or answering Whig pieces; he took the initiative and left it to the Whigs to answer him. This enabled Swift almost entirely to choose his own ground. One of the difficulties faced by the *Medley* (a skillfully conducted journal) was the constricting format of being an answerer; it was rarely able to strike out on its own path.

By the time that Swift began his series of *Examiner* papers, the *Tatler* had established several usable forms and techniques for the periodical essay. Swift's subject matter was more restricted than the *Tatler*'s, but weekly (rather than the *Tatler*'s tri-weekly) publication meant that, initially at least, this was no problem. Contemporary politics provided a wide enough field, and Swift was easily able to vary his manner to prevent staleness. Some of his papers are straightforward expositions of recent history or of current issues, such as the account of the rise of the moneyed men (No. 13, 2 November 1710) and the discussion of "passive obedience" (No. 33, 22 March 1711). Swift sometimes uses fables, as with the genealogy of merit (No. 30, 1 March 1711) and the fable of faction (No. 31, 8 March 1711). The most distinctive and successful of the papers are those that attack specific targets through some oblique device, such as the classical parallels and allegories characteristic of the *Discourse*. Perhaps the best single paper is the attack on Marlborough in the comparison between British ingratitude and Roman gratitude (No. 16, 23 November 1710). Other notable examples are the attacks on

Marlborough as Crassus (No. 27, 8 February 1711) and on Wharton as Verres (No. 17, 30 November 1710).[6] Also in No. 17 is the simple yet effective allegory of the discarded Whig ministers as a set of dishonest servants, using a reductive technique that Arbuthnot would exploit to the full in *The History of John Bull* (1712).

The *Examiner* was addressed first of all to Tory members of parliament, and more generally to the country gentlemen who elected them. Swift's strategy was to tell these men what they wanted to hear: that the Whigs were a pack of rascals who had prolonged the war for their own benefit, and that the new Tory government would soon bring peace and prosperity and a reduction in taxes. There is a slight change of emphasis during the course of Swift's papers; the later ones are less moderate in tone and more outspokenly and avowedly Tory.[7] In No. 44 (7 June 1711) he reports that "the main Design I had in writing these Papers, is fully executed" (*Works*, 3:171), and certainly the impression given throughout the series is of an uninterrupted course of victories over cunning but contemptible opponents. This is quite misleading, for the *Medley* time and again convicts the *Examiner* (rightly) of error and misrepresentation. But Swift was not writing for the Whig wretches who read the *Medley;* his task was to articulate the prejudices of his own Tory constituency.

While he was engaged in writing the *Examiner*, Swift published the first collected edition of his works. *Miscellanies in Prose and Verse* appeared on 27 February 1711. It included both reprinted pieces (such as the *Discourse*) and others that were here published for the first time. The most important new political piece was *The Sentiments of a Church-of-England Man* (*Works*, 2:11–25), an important statement of Swift's views on government and on the relations between church and state. It begins by denouncing the evils of political parties, but it is soon apparent that if a choice must be made between the Whigs and the Tories (and Swift cites the example of the younger Cato to show that it must), the best choice is the Tories. A bias in favor of Tory ideas and a tenderness to Tory susceptibilities are maintained throughout the tract. This bias is so successfully screened by a rhetoric of moderation that a casual reading of the *Sentiments* leaves the reader with an impression that Swift's position really is near the middle of the road. But this is not so. In the section on religion, Swift condemns "occasional conformity" and any attempt to extend religious toleration. Particularly worth attention is the passage (*Works*, 2:5–6) in which Swift appears to be willing to consider changing the Anglican ceremonial, yet actually supports the clergy's unwillingness to contemplate change except under impossible conditions. Swift's sympathies were with the idea of a "national" church as reestablished in 1662; he refused to recognize that such a church was no longer a possibility or to accept any official recognition of religious pluralism. The Toryism of the section on government is no less apparent, although here Swift does not so much expound Tory doctrine as anticipate and answer more extreme Tory objections to his own "moderate" Toryism. It is thus clear that this tract, like the *Examiner*, was aimed at a Tory audience. In particular, Swift takes up two issues that were real only for the Tories, "passive obedience" and "indefeasible hereditary right." Swift reconciles "passive obedience" with acceptance of the Revolution settlement by transferring the obedience from the monarch to the legislature as a whole. He uses the same argument again in the *Examiner* (No. 33, 22 March 1711; *Works*, 3:113–14). Swift refers the dispute about "indefeasible hereditary right" for settlement by the legislature, as with any other case of disputed property.[8] In the *Miscellanies*, the *Sentiments* is dated 1708, and it has been suggested that it may have been written as early as 1704.[9] Neither date is likely for the work in its present form: the hostility to the dissenters, the argument about "passive obedience," and the attitude towards the parties all point instead to 1710–11. In several respects the *Sentiments* reads like Simon Clement's Harleyite pamphlet, *Faults on Both Sides* (1710).[10] Close inspection of either work reveals most of the faults actually on the Whig side. There is no reason to doubt that Swift wrote a version of the *Sentiments* as early as 1708, when it appears in a list of "Subjects for a Volume,"[11] or possibly earlier still. But it reads too like the political philosophy of the author of the *Examiner* for one to believe that, in its present form, it predates Swift's arrival in London in 1710.

When the first parliamentary session under the new ministry ended in June 1711, Harley could look back with considerable satisfaction. He had established the stability and creditworthiness of his government, he had survived the assassination attempt by Guiscard in March 1711, and he had been raised to the peerage as Earl of Oxford and promoted to Lord Treasurer. Swift's retrospect was by no means so pleasant, for despite his success with the *Examiner* he was still no more than the vicar of Laracor. But at least with the drop in the political temperature he could give up the weekly task of the *Examiner* and enjoy a summer's leisure. The last complete number he wrote was No. 44 (7 June 1711), although he wrote the first part of No. 45 (14 June). His next major assignment would be a pamphlet to prepare the public for the peace that the government had already begun to negotiate with France, *The Conduct of the Allies*. But before turning his energies to this he wrote two shorter pieces, one referring back to the *Examiner* and the other anticipating the concerns of the *Conduct*. Early in 1708, a few weeks before his first (and unsuccessful) attempt to undermine the Godolphin ministry, Harley had suffered a serious loss of credibility when William Gregg, a clerk in his office, was discovered selling secrets to France, tried, and executed for treason. A committee of Whig lords interrogated Gregg, hoping to implicate Harley in his treason. In this they were unsuccessful, though the issue weakened Harley's position. In the *Examiner* (no. 32, 15 March 1711), which gave an account of Guiscard's attempt to murder Harley, Swift compared Guiscard's overt act of hostility with the underhand means to the same end used by the committee that examined Gregg. John Oldmixon came to the defense of the Whig lords in *A Letter to the Seven Lords of the Committee Appointed to Examine Gregg* (reprinted in Swift's *Works*, 3:245–58; published July 1711). Swift defended his insinuations in *Some Remarks upon a Pamphlet, Entitled a Letter* [etc.], published in August as "by the Author of the *Examiner*" (*Works*, 3:187–205). Swift used the occasion to repeat some of his themes from the *Examiner* and he neatly exposes the absurdity of Oldmixon's pretense of despising an opponent that he really fears. But an altogether more sprightly pamphlet is *A New Journey to Paris* (*Works*, 3:208–18; September 1711). Matthew Prior, poet and diplomat, had been dispatched on a secret mission to France in connection with the peace negotiations, but on his return an overzealous official had exposed his disguise and news of the journey had leaked out. Swift's pamphlet is a brief fictionalized account of Prior's mission, supposedly written by a Frenchman who had acted as Prior's servant while in France. It was designed partly to involve the whole episode in an aura of mystery and partly to assure its readers that the terms being negotiated were honorable. This amusing piece anticipates *Gulliver's Travels* in its use of circumstantial detail to create an air of verisimilitude and in making use of an unreliable narrator whom the reader learns partially to distrust, thus contributing to the air of mystery.

The Conduct of the Allies, Swift's single most important and successful work of propaganda for the Tory government, was published on 27 November 1711, timed to precede by a few days the opening of the new session of parliament. Swift had been working on it since September, and he lavished great care on its composition and revision. He had access to official information supplied by the ministers, and both Oxford and St. John read it before publication and offered suggestions. In a famous comment, Dr. Johnson ascribed the pamphlet's success and its considerable influence on opinion inside and outside parliament to "the mere weight of facts, with very little assistance from the hand that produced them."[12] It is a tribute to Swift's rhetoric that so shrewd a reader as Johnson (who would have been happy to convict Swift of lying) should have been taken in. Part of the *Conduct*'s success was due (and this Johnson did recognize) to its telling people what they wanted to hear. But Swift's main achievement in the pamphlet was to transform the natural war-weariness that he exploited into a feeling of righteous indignation against England's ostensible allies, exposed as her real enemies. In the opening pages of the pamphlet, Swift presents an apparently impartial and abstract account of the motives that engage nations in wars. In fact, this section begs all the important questions, for the situations that Swift there "supposes" turn out to be the very ones the *Conduct* is about. Laying down a few self-evident truths about the wars from 1066 to 1688, Swift speaks as though the controversial points he should have attempted to prove were in fact already agreed on all sides. The main body of the pamphlet examines two questions at length, how England arrived at its present deplorable condition, and whether the war should be continued. Swift contends that England should never have been more than an auxiliary power; that naval expeditions should have been used in preference to expensive land operations on the continent; and that the allies have consistently defaulted on all their obligations, leaving England to bear the greatest burden for the least advantage. To explain how all this happened, and why (after so many victories) peace seemed as far away as ever, he advances a "conspiracy thesis." Marlborough, Godolphin, and the sinister "monied men" engaged in and prolonged the war to enrich themselves and their dependents and to keep themselves in power; only those who benefit financially from the war, therefore, can want it to continue. He attacks the Whig slogan of "No Peace without Spain" as both an impracticable and even an undesirable war aim. The reader finishes the pamphlet with two ideas very strongly implanted in his mind: that any peace will be better than a continuation of the war, and that anyone who wants to continue the war must have some selfish personal reason for doing so; must be, in short, a Whig and a plunderer of his country.

Attempts were naturally made to combat so skillfull and persuasive a pamphlet. The longest and least ineffective reply was written by Francis Hare, Marlborough's chaplain and an experienced Whig propagandist. *The Allies and the Late Ministry Defended against France, and the Present Friends of France* (four parts, 1711–12), is several times as long as *The Conduct of the Allies*. On a number of points Hare convicts Swift of particular errors and misrepresentations, without getting the better of the general argument.[13] Hare is diffuse and tedious where Swift is trenchant and pithy. It takes him several pages to get to grips with a paragraph of Swift's multiple innuendos, while many of Swift's most telling points are conveyed through casual asides and unspoken assumptions that are hard to answer at all. Writing for an audience that was emotionally weary of the war, and with enough truth in his case to make a good deal of half-truth look plausible, Swift did not bother trying to convert people like Hare. Conversely, nothing Hare could say was likely to have much impact on Swift's audience; he could only reinforce the opinions of people who already agreed with him.

It seemed at first as though even Swift's rhetoric, which made it seem not only excusable but morally righteous to abandon the allies and seek a separate peace, would be insufficient to secure parliamentary support for the ministry's terms. In the House of Lords, where the government's majority was much less secure than in the Commons, an unholy alliance between the Whigs and the Tory Earl of Nottingham managed to carry an opposition motion for "No Peace without Spain" on 7 December 1711. The Queen was forced to create twelve new peers to ensure the government a majority. Nottingham was both genuinely unhappy about the proposed peace terms and personally piqued against Oxford as a result of his own exclusion from office. Swift took a particularly bitter and uncharitable view of Nottingham's conduct in allying himself with the Whigs. As usual, Swift assumed that his opponents could only be motivated by the basest and most selfish impulses, and in three lampoons over the next few months he reviled Nottingham as a self-seeking opportunist hungry for power and profit and indifferent to principle.[14] In "An Excellent New Song, Being the Intended Speech of a Famous Orator against Peace" (*Poems*, 1:141–45; published 6 December 1711, the day before Nottingham's motion in the Lords), Swift puts into Nottingham's mouth a parody of pompous oratory that exposes the venality and selfishness behind his opposition to the peace. Much more successful is *Toland's Invitation to Dismal, to Dine with the Calves-Head Club* (*Poems*, 1:161–66; June 1712). The "Calves-Head Club" was a gathering of republican

Whigs, perhaps only existing in Tory propaganda and imaginations, to celebrate the execution of Charles I on 30 January. The poem was intended to make Nottingham feel and look uncomfortable with his new friends. Swift obviously enjoyed writing in the guise of John Toland, the well-known deist; most of the poem is a catalogue of the prominent Whigs whom Nottingham can expect to meet at the club, so that the satire extends much further than Nottingham himself. The third lampoon was in prose, "A Hue and Cry after Dismal" (*Works* 6:139–41; July 1712). Written shortly after the British occupation of Dunkirk, it presents Nottingham in the undignified disguise of a chimney-sweeper gone to Dunkirk to incite the inhabitants against the British.[15]

The range and versatility of Swift's political writings, from the *Conduct of the Allies* to *Toland's Invitation to Dismal* are also seen in several lesser works published in 1711–12. There had been variety in the *Examiner*, but its form imposed restrictions of length and tone while the weekly deadline left little leisure for other writing. Once *The Conduct of the Allies* was published, Swift was under less pressure and his natural exuberance found greater play in a variety of literary-political outlets. Written and published for personal as much as political reasons, "The Windsor Prophecy" (*Poems*, 1:145–48; December 1711) is a vicious farrago of scandalous charges against the Duchess of Somerset, the Queen's confidante (though a Whig) and thus a person of political influence. The nominal purpose of the "Prophecy" is to warn the Queen against the Duchess, but it is hard to believe that Swift can have taken this very seriously, and the poem reads more easily as a simple satire against someone Swift believed had blocked his promotion. Its publication was a triumph of wit over prudence, for the Duchess remained with the Queen, who cannot have been gratified by the knowledge that Swift had lampooned her.[16] In a similar vein is "The Fable of Midas" (*Poems*, 1:155–58), a repetition of the old charges of greed and avarice against Marlborough. Swift was, at this time, more successful with humor than with vituperation, for neither of these pieces of character-blackening approaches the success of *Toland's Invitation to Dismal* or of two satirical impersonating letters. In *A Letter from the Pretender to a Whig Lord* (*Works*, 6:145–46; July 1712), Swift deftly transfers the charge of Jacobitism to the Whigs, exposing their factiousness and self-seeking through a letter that purports to be part of their correspondence with the Pretender about who shall have which jobs after his "restoration." Swift borrowed the character of his old enemy Wharton (whom he had lampooned for his corrupt government of Ireland: *Works*, 3:178–84) for *A Letter of Thanks from My Lord Wharton to the Lord Bishop of St. Asaph* (*Works*, 6:151–55; July 1712). The bishop, William Fleetwood, had published a volume of sermons with a militantly Whiggish preface, and the preface had been given wider currency through its reprinting in the *Spectator* (No. 384, 21 May 1712).[17] By having an irreligious scoundrel like Wharton thank the bishop for his service to the Whig cause, Swift neatly impales both bishop and lord; it is the same technique of guilt-by-association as in *Toland's Invitation to Dismal*.

Swift produced these squibs concurrently with more straightforward propaganda pieces. In *Some Remarks on the Barrier Treaty* (*Works*, 6:87–117; February 1712), he expanded on the iniquity of the Whigs in the negotiating of the Barrier Treaty in 1709, a theme to which he had not done full justice in the *Conduct of the Allies*. Two other pamphlets show Swift's skill in addressing himself to a particular group or constituency. Oxford's "moderating" policies exposed his government on occasion to simultaneous attack from both its proper opponents, the Whigs, and its own nominal supporters, the more extreme Tories. Most of Swift's work for Oxford was aimed at the Tories (Oxford employed Defoe and others to write for the Whigs). A group of extreme Tories had formed the "October Club" as a ginger group to press more definitely Tory policies on the government and also to force as many Whigs as possible from the many minor offices they still held.[18] *Some Advice Humbly Offered to the Members of the October Club* (*Works*, 6:71–80; January 1712) is an apology for Harley (as he then was) and his record as prime minister. Swift successfully employs a deliberate darkness of style to sound (remarkably in a published pamphlet) secret and confidential. The reader is given a sense of being on the inside, a sense intended to flatter the club's members into feeling they were part of Harley's deep game and should continue to support him. A rare example of Swift's pamphleteering addressed to the opposition Whigs is *Some Reasons to Prove that No Person Is Obliged by His Principles as a Whig, to Oppose Her Majesty or Her Present Ministry. In a Letter to a Whig Lord* (*Works*, 6:123–36; June 1712). It attempts to win support for Oxford from the more moderate Whigs by exposing the selfish motives of the opposition leaders. This is Swift's constant theme in all these pamphlets, serious and satirical: that the Whigs and their allies are factious, self-seeking, unprincipled opportunists, eager for personal reasons to regain control of the government and resume their plunder of the nation. Swift's appeal, expressed or implied, is that all right-thinking men of good-

will should support the government, which has the real national
interest at heart.

3

The longest and most ambitious of Swift's writings about English politics is *The History of the Four Last Years of the Queen (Works,*
7:1–167), as it is generally known from the title under which it was
first published (long after Swift's death, in 1758). The title is misleading in two ways. The *History* goes no further than the signing of
the Peace of Utrecht in March 1713 and is primarily concerned
with the negotiations leading up to the peace and with their background in the parliamentary events of 1710–13. More important, it
is less a history than a polemical defense of the methods and objectives of the Tory government in negotiating the peace. Swift had
long been ambitious to be an historian, having earlier tried his hand
at a continuation of Temple's *Introduction to the History of England*
(Swift's fragment is in *Works,* 5:11–78). From September 1712 to
May 1713 he put most of his literary efforts and energy into this
new *History,* taking great pains with research and consulting and
abstracting numerous documents.[19] The *History* was intended to
serve an immediate purpose, as well as to inform posterity: Swift
thought it would help secure support for the peace at the next
session of parliament (the opening of this session was several times
delayed; it finally met in April 1713). But both Oxford and St. John
(now Viscount Bolingbroke) hindered rather than helped its progress. It is easy to see why even Oxford, flatteringly portrayed as he
is in the *History,* would not have been very keen on its publication.
There were too many aspects of the negotiations that the ministers
wished to keep in the dark, and Swift's account (which would
certainly have raised a controversy) could only have roused the
opposition without winning over any converts. The parliamentary
session passed, the peace (but not the commercial treaty with
France) was ratified, and the polemical occasion for the *History* had
been missed.

The *History* is too long for a pamphlet, and too polemical for a
history. For once Swift's sense of brevity deserted him, a sacrifice
to his sincere desire to write a serious historical work. The *History*
as a whole is a dull book, though there are some lively passages
(generally the least "historical"). Its strengths and weaknesses are
both seen in its simplistic characterization of the main political

actors. The leading Whig lords are presented (as in the *Examiner*) as
a vile group of self-seeking men whose only motives were ignoble.
Anything openly discreditable in their characters or careers is
seized upon, while any apparent virtues are smeared as hypocritical. The most flagrantly partial is the sketch of Nottingham (*Works*,
7:11–12, 15–16), a masterpiece of character assassination. Swift can
forgive Nottingham for being a narrow-minded bigot, but not for
voting with the Whigs. The Tories, by contrast, are portrayed as a
band of selfless patriots. Oxford's faults, even those Swift complains of in the *Journal to Stella*, are ignored or extenuated. His
failure to anticipate the defeat in the House of Lords on Nottingham's "No Peace without Spain" motion is fantastically ascribed to
his farsighted desire to improve the tone of the Lords through the
creation of new peers (7:19–20). His chronic procrastination is ex-
cused and even praised as a deep reach of policy (7:73–75). Such
passages would have been in place in any of Swift's avowedly
partisan pamphlets, but they do not make credible history, for
there is no mixture of character or motive. Swift's intention, as an
historian, to tell what happened, is submerged by his impulses as a
propagandist to repeat the themes of the *Conduct of the Allies:* the
imperative need for peace, the iniquities of the discarded Whig
ministers, the selfishness of the Dutch and the other allies. Apart
from its vigorous (though hardly historical) character sketches, the
most interesting passages in the *History* are those that expound
Swift's own ideas. The most notable of these are the discussion of
the ideal immigration policy (7:94–95), which reveals a response to
a contemporary problem influenced (as so often with Swift) by
classical ideas, and the arguments in favor of press control and the
best means to effect it (7:103–6).

    After the many setbacks and delays, the Peace of Utrecht, the
major achievement of the Tory government, was signed in March
1713. Swift's own preferment took even longer than the peace. In
April 1713 he was given the deanery of St. Patrick's, Dublin, a
bitter disappointment to his hopes for a settlement in England. In
June he returned to Ireland for the first time since 1710, to be
installed as dean. He spent the summer at his parish of Laracor,
and returned to London in September. There he found that not
only had the peace not inaugurated the golden age of Toryism to
which he had sanguinely looked forward,[20] but the political situation was altered in every respect for the worse. The ministry,
despite the confirmation of its large (nominal, at least) parliamentary majority by the general election held in August and Septem-

ber, was internally divided and hard pressed by its Whig opponents. Swift had been one of the last to perceive the irreconcilable feud between Oxford and Bolingbroke, and he would be one of the last to try to repair it. In the autumn of 1713 he could no longer ignore it, and he would spend much time and energy on his futile attempts to reconcile the warring ministers. The opposition, though still weak in the House of Commons, was strengthened by a propaganda revival on a good issue that would unite the Whigs but split the Tories and even the cabinet: the question of the succession to the throne. On this great issue, Swift himself remained loyal to the Act of Settlement and the Hanoverian succession, though he felt no enthusiasm for the prospect.[21] But both Oxford and Bolingbroke (the latter more seriously) dabbled with the idea of a Jacobite restoration, though without success and without telling Swift. Their failure to evolve a credible policy on the issue (they had offended the future George I, yet they could not come out openly for the Pretender) paralyzed the government. The Queen's health continued to deteriorate, and month by month the succession question became more urgent. But Oxford and Bolingbroke seemed more interested in destroying each other than in preserving the government or the Tory party.

The Whig journalists were not slow to exploit the government's lack of credibility on the succession. As early as June 1713, the defeat in the House of Commons of the commercial clauses of the Utrecht settlement showed that the ministry's large paper majority could disappear on the right (from the Whig point of view) issue. Whig propaganda became stridently francophobe and anti-Catholic, and accused the ministers of plotting to bring in the Pretender. Swift was active in combatting such writings, but he no longer had the relatively easy task of articulating majority opinions. In 1713–14 he was writing from a much weaker position, for it was the Whigs who were able to exploit the perfectly genuine popular distrust of France and hatred of the Pretender.

The most important writings in this last phase of Swift's work for the Tory government are the two pamphlets attacking his former friend, Richard Steele. The topic of their first exchange was Dunkirk. At the Peace of Utrecht, Louis XIV had agreed to prevent its future use as a haven for privateers by demolishing its harbor and fortifications within three months. The Whigs were able to make political capital out of the French failure to carry out the promised demolitions and out of the British government's failure to press the point, interpreted as collusion with France that was likely to lead to the restoration of the Pretender. Steele, who in 1713 was editing the *Guardian*, a successor to the *Spectator*, wrote himself a letter that he duly published in the *Guardian* (No. 128, 7 August 1713). This rather heavy-handed letter reiterated the demand for the immediate demolition of Dunkirk. It was not easy to say why Dunkirk had not been demolished, so Steele's opponents were forced to ridicule his style and attack his presumption rather than answer him. Steele redoubled his attack in a separate pamphlet, *The Importance of Dunkirk Considered* (published September 1713).[22] The pamphlet is little more than a repeat and an expansion of the earlier letter to the *Guardian;* with the flair of the natural journalist Steele filled the required pages by reprinting much previously published material (including his own letter to the *Guardian*) and by making his point repetitively and diffusely. In his riposte, *The Importance of the Guardian Considered* (*Works*, 8:4–25; 2 November 1713), Swift virtually ignores the real issue (the demolition of Dunkirk) in favor of a devastating personal attack on Steele. He mercilessly dissects Steele's character, career, and manner of writing (he will not allow him a "style"). But the success of the ridicule of Steele, which makes the *Importance* one of the most enjoyable of Swift's political pamphlets, cannot quite conceal the inadequacy of the response to Steele's substantive points.

Steele was not the Whigs' only champion. A similar note of rather hysterical alarmism was struck by a Whig of an older generation than Steele, Gilbert Burnet, Bishop of Salisbury, in his *Introduction to the Third Volume of the History of the Reformation of the Church of England*, published in advance of the volume itself (the *Introduction* has 1714 on its title page, but it appeared in November 1713). Swift wrote a *Preface to the Bishop of Sarum's Introduction* (*Works*, 4:55–84; December 1713) in which he mounts a many-fronted attack on Burnet (with whom, as with Steele, he had once been on friendly terms). Burnet is pilloried as a bad writer; as a party hack; as an anticlerical bishop; as a sensational alarmist; above all, as overestimating the danger to the church from popery while ignoring what Swift saw as the far greater menace from those twin supports of Whiggism, atheism and dissent. One aspect of the *Introduction* that Swift touches on surprisingly lightly (in view of its vulnerability) is Burnet's apologies for the haste and inaccuracy of his first two volumes and his excuses for not revising them (at times he sounds like the fictive author of the digressions in *A Tale of a Tub*). Aware of the limited effectiveness of his pamphlet against

Steele, Swift was here careful to put matters of substance rather than style at the center of his attack.

Steele, meanwhile, had dropped the *Guardian* in favor of the more exclusively political *Englishman* (of which the first number appeared on 6 October 1713). He also began to advertise a forthcoming pamphlet, to be called *The Crisis*, and to solicit subscriptions for it at the absurdly low price of a shilling.[23] The puffing continued from October through December, and it became known that Steele was receiving assistance from other Whig writers in the composition of his great party manifesto on the danger to the protestant succession from the present Tory government. At Christmas 1713, Queen Anne was critically ill, and the topic assumed even greater urgency. Early in 1714, Swift tried to puncture the ballooning publicity about Steele's great pamphlet in "The First Ode of the Second Book of Horace Paraphrased" (*Poems*, 1:179–84). Swift is more successful here than in he had been in the earlier lampoons on Nottingham, for humor predominates over vituperation. Steele had a genuinely foolish side that invited ridicule; the huffing and puffing about *The Crisis* was indeed absurd; and in such a poem one does not look for political arguments. It was enough to make Steele look self-important and silly. But no lampoon could prevent the appearance of *The Crisis* later in January 1714. Swift rapidly composed and published a serious reply, *The Publick Spirit of the Whigs* (*Works*, 8:31–68; February 1714). Unlike *The Importance of the Guardian considered*, the *Public Spirit* addresses itself to matters of substance (although Steele's bulking his pamphlet out with redundant reprinted matter does not escape attention). Swift's basic tactic is to expose the Whigs as deliberate whippers-up of a public hysteria intended to serve their own selfish political advantage. If the Hanoverian succession is as strongly supported by both the laws and popular sentiment as Steele affirms it is, then (Swift argues) there can be no cause for alarm. The succession could only be in danger if it were genuinely unpopular; and Steele affirms that it is not. In terms of the logic of the argument, Swift has the better of Steele in this exchange. But in more than one way it proved a hollow victory. However illogical, Whig hysteria about the succession refused to disappear; indeed, as we now know, it was well founded, for both Oxford and Bolingbroke were making overtures to the Pretender. At the time of writing *The Conduct of the Allies* Swift had benefited from the mood of public opinion; now it was increasingly on the side of the Whigs. But the *Publick Spirit* also involved Swift personally in trouble: a price was put on his head. In discussing the terms of the Union with Scotland, he had made some very disparaging remarks about the Scottish nobility (*Works*, 8:49–50). This passage was complained of in the House of Lords, and the government was forced to issue a proclamation (reproduced in *Works*, 8: facing page xxii) offering £300 reward for information about the author of the *Publick Spirit*. Two of Swift's old enemies, Lords Nottingham and Wharton, took prominent parts in the affair.[24] That instead of receiving an English deanery he should be rewarded with such a price on his head, epitomized for Swift the typical fate of a man of integrity in the corrupt world of contemporary politics. The episode marks with an appropriate note of bathos and bitterness the effective close of his pamphleteering for the Tory government. The *Publick Spirit* was the last work he published in defense of the Oxford ministry. About this time he began "A Discourse concerning the Fears from the Pretender" (*Works*, 8:71–72), but it was abandoned and only a fragment is extant. In May 1714, despairing of being able to reconcile Oxford and Bolingbroke and sensing the hopelessness of the political cause of the Tories, he retired to the country, to the parsonage of his friend John Geree at Letcombe Basset. Swift maintained a correspondence with the political world of London, however, and while at Letcombe he even wrote a pamphlet, "Some Free Thoughts upon the Present State of Affairs" (*Works*, 8:77–98). This is an interesting piece, notable for the opening passage in which Swift condemns political refinements and insists on a commonsensical attitude that anticipates the King of Brobdingnag; and for its analysis of the failure of the Oxford ministry. Intended as a warning to the ministers and the Tories to unite in the face of the threat posed by the Whigs and the certainty of the Queen's early death, a series of accidents prevented its publication until it was too late. Oxford was finally dismissed on 27 July, but Bolingbroke's triumph was curtailed by the death of the Queen on 1 August. Later the same month, Swift left for Ireland without revisiting London.

Swift's ambition to be the historian of the important public events he had witnessed, evidenced in *The History of the Four Last Years of the Queen*, was not abandoned when that work failed to achieve publication. As late as April 1714, he prepared a memorial to the Queen, requesting appointment as Historiographer Royal in order to write the truth about her reign (*Works*, 8:200). Denied this opportunity to write as an official historian, Swift nevertheless continued his "historical" writings after the Queen's death, al-

though none were published until many years later and most after
his death. His first attempt (which survives in a manuscript dated 9
August 1714) was "Some Considerations upon the Consequences
Hoped and Feared from the Death of the Queen" (*Works*, 8:101–4),
a fragmentary sketch largely concerned with the change of ministers in 1710. The same events and their background are covered in
greater detail in the "Memoirs, Relating to that Change which
Happened in the Queen's Ministry in the Year 1710" (*Works*,
8:107–28; dated October 1714). These "Memoirs" contain an account of the decline of the Whigs in the Queen's favor and of
Oxford's rise to power; more interestingly, they contain an autobiographical sketch of Swift's own involvement in English politics
from the *Discourse* of 1701 to about March 1711. The defense of
Oxford, begun in these "Memoirs," was continued at greater length
in "An Enquiry into the Behaviour of the Queen's Last Ministry"
(*Works*, 8:131–80), begun in 1715 but not finished until 1719 or
1720.[25] Besides the defense of Oxford, to whom Swift retained a
strong personal loyalty, the "Enquiry" launches an attack on the
new Whig and Hanoverian regime. It was the last of the partisan
pieces that Swift wrote about English politics. He was by 1720
deeply involved in Irish affairs, and by the time he came to write
Gulliver's Travels he was ready to make a more objective commentary on the political follies of mankind.[26]

4

Widely different assessments of Swift's political activities in
these years are possible. Swift himself took different views at different times. In "Part of the Seventh Epistle of the First Book of
Horace Imitated" (*Poems*, 1:169–75; October 1713) he presents an
image of himself as he would have liked to be seen: the disinterested
patriot and wit sought out by a great statesman with whom he
labored for the good of his country. Less cheerful retrospects are
found in two poems written at Letcombe in 1714, although not
published until many years later. In "The Author upon Himself"
(*Poems*, 1:191–96; published 1735), Swift looks back bitterly on the
ingratitude he has received in return for his great services to the
nation. In "Horace Lib. 2, Sat. 6, Part of It Imitated" (*Poems*, 1:197–
202; published 1727), he contrasts the worries and frustrations of
life in politics with the pleasures of retirement at Laracor, a theme
that occurs frequently in the *Journal to Stella*. Swift's enemies natu-

rally drew a very different picture to any of these: they saw an
irreligious priest and venal political turncoat who prostituted his
literary talents to become the willing tool of a corrupt ministry.[27] A
more balanced view would recognize that while Swift in some
respects idealized his involvement in English politics, he genuinely
believed that the Tory government was acting in the nation's best
interests and that his writing for it was an act of disinterested public
service. There can be no doubt, though, that ambition and the
desire for preferment were part of his motives; but a mixture of
motives, in others as well as himself, was something Swift found
hard to understand or accept.

Swift gained from his association with the Oxford ministry his
deanery, with its ample income and dignity; a literary reputation as
a brilliant pamphleteer; and the experience of living close to the
center of political power and influence. This was a kind of experience that he relished at the time and that would later inform the
political satire of *Gulliver's Travels*. What he lost was the chance of
higher preferment in the church: the Irish bishopric that would
probably have come his way had he stayed with the Whigs long
enough to enjoy their triumph in 1714. He could have made this
more certain by publishing conventional sermons, or by taking
Archbishop King's advice to write on some out-of-the way theological topic (letter of 1 September 1711; *Correspondence*, 1:154–55).
Swift, however, knew his own powers better than the archbishop;
he was unlucky in his timing rather than his talents. If Dr. Robert
South had died in 1709' and Halifax had secured for Swift his
valuable prebend and living, or if Dean Graham of Wells had died
just two months earlier than he did, before the publication of the
Windsor Prophecy rather than after, Swift might have been spared his
exile and the bitterness of his old age.[28] But the world would have
lost *Gulliver's Travels*, a product in part of his disillusioning experiences in the political world of the reign of Anne.

Notes

1. Two concise surveys of the period that reflect recent research are in John P. Kenyon,
Stuart England (London: Allen Lane, 1978) and in James Rees Jones, *Country and Court:
England, 1658–1714* (London: Edward Arnold, 1978). The most detailed account of Anne's
reign is George Macaulay Trevelyan, *England under Queen Anne*, 3 vols. (London: Longmans,
1930–34); the best analytical study of its politics is Geoffrey Holmes, *British Politics in the Age
of Anne* (London: Macmillan, 1967). There are several interpretive narratives that treat these
years in larger contexts: Keith Feiling, *A History of the Tory Party, 1640–1714* (Oxford:
Clarendon Press, 1924); John H. Plumb, *The Growth of Political Stability in England, 1675–
1725* (London: Macmillan, 1967); Brian W. Hill, *The Growth of Parliamentary Parties, 1689–*

1742 (London: Allen & Unwin, 1976); and John P. Kenyon, *Revolution Principles: The Politics of Party, 1689–1714* (Cambridge: Cambridge University Press, 1977). Essays on various topics are collected in *Britain after the Glorious Revolution, 1689–1714*, ed. Geoffrey Holmes (London: Macmillan, 1969); the following are especially useful for the background to Swift's writings: G. V. Bennett, "Conflict in the Church"; A. D. MacLachlan, "The Road to Peace, 1710–13"; and Geoffrey Holmes, "Harley, St. John and the Death of the Tory Party." More specialized studies of subjects relevant to Swift are Sheila Biddle, *Bolingbroke and Harley* (New York: Knopf, 1974), and J. A. Downie, *Robert Harley and the Press: Propaganda and Public Opinion in the Age of Swift and Defoe* (Cambridge: Cambridge University Press, 1979). Edward Gregg's *Queen Anne* (London: Routledge, 1980) is a sympathetic biography that emphasizes the Queen's political importance. Other useful biographies of important Whigs and Tories are: John H. Plumb, *Sir Robert Walpole: The Making of a Statesman* (London: Cresset Press, 1956); Harry T. Dickinson, *Bolingbroke* (London: Constable, 1970); G. V. Bennett, *The Tory Crisis in Church and State, 1688–1730: The Career of Francis Atterbury* (Oxford: Clarendon Press, 1975); and William L. Sachse, *Lord Somers: A Political Portrait* (Manchester: Manchester University Press, 1975). The most detailed biography of Swift covering these years is Irvin Ehrenpreis, *Swift: The Man, His Works, and the Age. Volume II, Dr. Swift* (London: Methuen, 1967). Particular aspects of Swift's political writings are the subject of Bertrand A. Goldgar, *The Curse of Party: Swift's Relations with Addison and Steele* (Lincoln: University of Nebraska Press, 1961); and of Richard I. Cook, *Jonathan Swift as a Tory Pamphleteer* (Seattle: University of Washington Press, 1967), which is mainly concerned with rhetorical analysis. There are chapters on Swift's political and historical thought in F. P. Lock, *The Politics of "Gulliver's Travels"* (Oxford: Clarendon Press, 1980).

2. The edition by Frank H. Ellis (Oxford: Clarendon Press, 1967) has a substantial introduction on the historical context, as well as full notes and commentary.

3. By 1709 support for the war (and especially for the war in Spain) came largely from the Whigs. The "prediction" of the queen's remarriage is more obscure and is related to a Whig parliamentary tactic. Queen Anne was very averse to the idea of her successor living in or even visiting England. In 1705 the Tories, to embarrass the government, proposed to invite the dowager Electress Sophia (the heir to the throne) to England. The Whigs countered by passing the Regency Act, which provided for an interim government between the death of the Queen and the arrival of her successor. Early in 1709, the Tories were planning to revive the question of the invitation to the Electress. In an attempt to prevent such a move in parliament, the Whigs passed an address to the Queen (presented on 28 January) urging her to remarry (her husband had died in October 1708) and so provide for the succession through children of her own. On both occasions the Whigs wanted to demonstrate their support for the protestant succession without alienating the Queen.

4. The ballad (which is not in *Poems*) is reprinted in *Poems on Affairs of State*, vol. 7, ed. Frank H. Ellis, (New Haven, Conn.: Yale University Press, 1975), pp. 480–86.

5. When the papers were reprinted in volume form, the original No. 13 was omitted and the following papers renumbered. Swift wrote Nos. 14–45 and the first part of 46; 13–44 and 45 as renumbered. The renumbered sequence is used in *Works*, 3, and I have followed it for all subsequent references.

6. Swift also wrote *A Short Character of His Excellency Thomas Earl of Wharton* (*Works*, 3:179–84; December 1710), more exuberant and scurrilous than anything in the *Examiner*.

7. This would be such a natural development, as the new ministry's position became more secure, that there is no need to suppose that it was because Swift "gradually fell under the influence of St. John" (Downie, *Robert Harley and the Press*, p. 135).

8. It is interesting to note that on both questions Swift's arguments had been anticipated by the "high" (but not extreme) Tory, Archbishop Sharp of York. In his *Sermon Preached before the Lords* on 30 January 1700 (London, 1700), he restrains "passive obedience" within constitutional bounds (pp. 20–21), just as Swift does. In 1702, Sharp wrote to the Earl of Nottingham that he thought that princes "hold their crowns by the same legall right that your Lordship holds your estate . . . and that the legislative is judge in the one case as well as the other" (quoted in Holmes, *British Politics*, p. 88; here slightly normalized). The particular argument against "passive obedience" used by Sharp and Swift came into prominence at the

trial of Sacheverell in 1710 (see Kenyon, *Revolution Principles*, p. 136), which makes it less likely that Swift would have used it before that date.

9. Irvin Ehrenpreis, "The Date of Swift's *Sentiments*," *Review of English Studies*, N.S. 3 (1952): 272–74; and *Swift*, 2:767.

10. *Faults on Both Sides* is reprinted in *A Collection of Scarce and Valuable Tracts* (usually known as the *Somers Tracts*), ed. Walter Scott, vol. 12 (London, 1814), pp. 679–707. For its authorship, see Henry L. Snyder, "The Authorship of *Faults on Both Sides* (1710)," *Philological Quarterly* 56 (1977): 266–72.

11. The list is reprinted in Ehrenpreis, *Swift*, 2:768–69.

12. "Swift," *Lives of the Poets*, ed. George Birkbeck Hill (Oxford, 1903), 3:19.

13. The first part only of Hare's tract is reprinted, with other replies, in *Swiftiana III: On Swift's "Remarks on the Barrier Treaty" and His "Conduct of the Allies," 1711–1712* (New York: Garland, 1974).

14. For a corrective account, see Henry Horwitz, *Revolution Politicks: The Career of Daniel Finch, Second Earl of Nottingham, 1647–1730* (Cambridge: At the University Press, 1968).

15. Swift also wrote some feeble verses, "Peace and Dunkirk" (*Poems*, 1:167–69; July 1712), celebrating the British occupation. On Dunkirk as a recurrent issue and diplomatic counter, see John Robert Moore, "Defoe, Steele, and the Demolition of Dunkirk," *Huntington Library Quarterly* 13 (1950): 279–302.

16. See Philip Roberts, "Swift, Queen Anne, and the *Windsor Prophecy*," *Philological Quarterly* 49 (1970): 254–58. Sir David Hamilton's *Diary*, which provides the main evidence, has since been edited by Roberts (Oxford: Clarendon Press, 1975).

17. Swift also wrote an *Examiner* paper (Vol. 2, No. 34, 24 July 1712; *Works*, 6:159–61) exposing Fleetwood as a turncoat by reprinting an earlier preface in which the bishop had expressed anti-Whig sentiments.

18. See Harry T. Dickinson, "The October Club," *Huntington Library Quarterly* 33 (1970): 155–73.

19. See the Introduction and Appendixes to *Works*, 7, and also such references in the *Journal to Stella* as on 29 October 1712 (2:569).

20. Swift hoped, for example, that his idea for an academy would be acted on after the conclusion of the peace (*Correspondence*, 1:316).

21. Swift was often accused of Jacobitism, for example by Archbishop King in his letter of 22 November 1716 (*Correspondence*, 2:228). Swift's restrained and dignified reply (22 December 1716; *Correspondence*, 2:238) has an air of truth. It is more likely that Swift had been naive and imperceptive in his observations of Oxford and Bolingbroke than that he was lying in his letter to King.

22. *The Importance of Dunkirk Considered* is reprinted in Steele's *Tracts and Pamphlets*, ed. Rae Blanchard (Baltimore, Md.: Johns Hopkins Press, 1944), pp. 87–124. For a general account of Steele in these years, see Calhoun Winton, *Captain Steele: The Early Career of Richard Steele* (Baltimore, Md.: Johns Hopkins Press, 1964).

23. 23. There is an edition of the *Englishman* by Rae Blanchard (Oxford: Clarendon Press, 1955); *The Crisis* is reprinted in *Tracts and Pamphlets*, ed. Blanchard, pp. 129–81.

24. For this episode see Maurice J. Quinlan, "The Prosecution of Swift's *The Public Spirit of the Whigs*", *Texas Studies in Literature and Language* 9 (1967): 167–84.

25. There is a separate edition of the *Enquiry*, with a substantial introduction and full notes, by Irvin Ehrenpreis (Bloomington: Indiana University Press, 1956).

26. There are various current interpretations of the events of Part 1 of *Gulliver's Travels* in terms of the politics of Anne's reign. Lock, *The Politics of "Gulliver's Travels"*, pp. 89–122, argues against them and sees Lilliputian politics as a paradigm rather than an allegory. Swift's political experience did affect *Gulliver's Travels*, but not in the very particular ways that have often been proposed.

27. Two of the most amusing attacks are *A Hue and Cry after Dr. S——t* (London, 1714) and *Dr. S——t's Real Diary* (London, 1715). Both are reprinted in *Swiftiana II: Bickerstaffiana and Other Early Materials on Swift, 1708–15* (New York: Garland, 1975).

28. For these hopes and possibilities of preferment, see *Correspondence*, 1:143, 288.

5

Swift and the Anglo-Irish Tradition

J. C. BECKETT

If we are to understand the significance of Ireland for Swift, and of Swift for Ireland, we must remember that he hardly thought of himself as an Irishman at all, but rather as an Englishman who had, by a kind of unhappy accident, been born in Ireland. Though he defended the rights of Ireland against England and was hailed as an Irish patriot, he never forgot the English background of his family and never ceased to regret his enforced residence in the country of his birth. Towards the end of his life, we find him writing to Lord Oxford, the son of his old friend the lord treasurer of Queen Anne's reign:

> I loved My Lord your father better than any other Man in the World, although I had no obligation to him on the Score of Preferment, having been driven to this wretched Kingdom (to which I was almost a Stranger) by his want of power to keep me in what I ought to call my own Country; though I happened to be dropped here, and was a Year old before I left it, and to my Sorrow did not dye before I came back to it again. (14 June 1737, *Correspondence*, 5:46–47)

No doubt Swift is here minimizing the extent of his connection with Ireland. If he was taken to England as an infant he was brought back a few years later, and his education, both at school and at the university, was entirely Irish. But the biographical facts are less important than Swift's attitude to them. There can be no doubt at all that he regarded himself, and wanted others to regard

A revised and expanded version of a talk broadcast on the B.B.C. Northern Ireland Home Service in November 1967, to mark the tercentenary of Swift's birth. © Copyright J. C. Beckett.

him, as an Englishman. Indeed, according to one contemporary account, he would sometimes assert that he had not been born in Ireland at all, but "was stolen from England when a child, and brought over to Ireland in a band-box."[1] It is not likely that Swift could have intended such an assertion as more than a rather bitter jest, but it provides further evidence, if any were needed, that he took no pride in his birthplace and was insistent on his claim to be an Englishman.

Swift's attitude, however, could not alter the fact that he was Irish by birth and upbringing; and, we may add, by connection also, since several members of the Swift family had settled in Ireland, part of the mid-seventeenth-century stream of recruits to the English colony that had existed for almost five hundred years. It was into this colony that Swift was born: he claimed to be an Englishman; he was really a colonial. He might, perhaps, have accepted this position if Ireland had offered any prospect of a satisfactory career, but he could find no opening that would answer his ambitions; and, once he had removed to England, he tried (as other colonials have tried before and since) to gloss over his colonial origins and to identify himself completely with the home-born citizens of the mother country. He found that it could not be done. Even at the height of his influence in the great world of English politics he was still looked upon as an Irishman. His powerful friends could not or would not provide him with a permanent settlement in what he regarded as his "own country"; and instead of getting what he hoped for—"a fat deanery or a lean bishopric" in England—he finally returned, as dean of St. Patrick's, to "wretched Dublin in miserable Ireland."

Though Ireland was to be Swift's home for the rest of his life, and though he strongly supported the "Irish interest," as against the "English interest," in public affairs, his outlook remained essentially that of a colonial, aggressively determined to hold himself aloof from the despised "natives" and resentful of any assumed superiority on the part of the mother country. In one of his last surviving letters to Alexander Pope, in June 1737, he complains that Pope, in his published correspondence, had failed to distinguish between the two population groups in Ireland—"the savage old Irish," on the one hand, and "the English Gentry of this Kingdom," on the other. He assured Pope that "the English Colonies" in Ireland were "much more civilized than many Counties in England, and speak better English, and are much better bred." On other occasions, we find Swift himself heaping unlimited abuse on "the English Gentry of this Kingdom." But that was, so to speak, inside the family. To the outside world it must be made clear that the colony of which Swift was, however unwillingly, a member, was on the same level of civilization as the mother country. He was even concerned to deny any inferiority in climate: the northern counties of England, he says, "have a more cloudy ungenial air than any part of Ireland" (*Correspondence*, 5:58).

Swift's defense of Irish constitutional rights, though perhaps better founded than his defense of Irish weather, was an expression of the same attitude, the same colonial unwillingness to admit any kind of inferiority. Ireland was not, by the law of nature, condemned to a worse climate than England; Englishmen living in Ireland were not, by the law of nations, condemned to a dependence unknown to Englishmen living in England. "Am I a *Free-man in England*," he asks indignantly in the third of the *Drapier's Letters*, and do I become a *Slave* in six Hours, by crossing the Channel?" (*Works*, 10:31). The use of the first person singular, though a necessary consequence of his literary disguise, has here a peculiar force: it is Swift himself, not the drapier of St. Francis Street, who feels so poignantly the contrast between the political atmosphere of England and that of Ireland. And Swift was a man who found it more difficult than most to separate the private from the public: it was when a grievance touched him personally that he made an issue of it, and his concern for Ireland sprang from the fact that he was compelled to live there. Had he received the English preferment that he hoped for we should have heard nothing from him about the wrongs of Ireland.

To say this is not to imply that Swift's attitude was merely selfish. Injustice aroused his indignation. Poverty and wretchedness moved him to real, if seemingly cynical or half-contemptuous, generosity. But the injustice and poverty must be there for him to see. It is the common characteristic of all his political writings that they arose from the immediate circumstances and dealt with questions to which he felt that an answer must be found at once. He was stimulated by what lay before him, not by abstract principles or remote themes. While he was in England, and could look forward to establishing himself there, the condition and prospects of Ireland made little impression on his mind; he neither saw, nor experienced directly, the effects of English policy on the Irish economy; and he felt no urge to stand out as the champion of Ireland simply because he happened to have been born there. In this respect he presents a sharp contrast to Burke, who, though he

had succeeded where Swift had failed and made a career for himself
in England, retained throughout life an active concern about Irish
affairs.

This account of Swift's attitude is borne out by his first tract on
Anglo-Irish relations, *The Story of the Injured Lady, in a Letter to her
Friend, with his Answer* (*Works*, 9:1–12). It was composed in the early
months of 1707,[2] when Swift had been living in Ireland, with only
one visit to England, for close on three years, his longest period of
residence since he had left Dublin for Leicester in 1689. He could
not help seeing for himself the depressed state of the country; and it
was natural that he should accept the view prevalent among his
Irish acquaintances that this depression was the result of English
legislation, and especially of the restriction recently placed on the
export of Irish woolens. Here was the direct stimulus that moved
him to write; and the contemporary negotiations for a union between England and Scotland dictated the line of argument he followed. The "injured Lady" (Ireland) confesses that she has been
"undone" by her wooer (England), "half by Force, and half by
Consent, after solemn Vows and Protestations of Marriage." But
the "gentleman," having got possession of her person, next obliged
her to place her whole estate under the management of his servants
and has behaved so harshly that both she and her tenants are reduced to dependence and poverty. And now, instead of fulfilling
his promises, he is on the point of concluding a marriage with her
ill-favored "rival" (Scotland). What is she to do? The advice given
in the *Answer* is that she should stand on her legal rights and do no
more than she has formally undertaken, namely "to have the same
Steward, and to regulate your Household by such Methods as you
shall both agree to" (in effect, that Ireland and England should be
governed by the same king). Apart from this, she and her tenants
should disown any dependence on the "gentleman" (England) and,
in particular, should insist on freedom to carry their goods to any
market they chose (i.e., Ireland should assert her right to export her
commodities to any country that would receive them).

Here we have in embryo most of what Swift had to say on
Anglo-Irish relations. He asserts the constitutional independence of
Ireland, upon which England has unjustifiably encroached; he condemns the policy of appointing Englishmen to Irish offices; he
asserts Ireland's right to commercial freedom. Though there is no
direct reference to the policy, which he advocated later, of using
Irish goods to the exclusion of English, this may possibly be implied in the last sentence of the *Answer*, where it is suggested that if

the "gentleman" should refuse reasonable terms, "perhaps I may think of something else that will be more effectual."

But though Swift had thus set down on paper, as early as 1707, the essence of the constitutional doctrine that he was to preach so vigorously in later years, he kept it to himself: *The Story of the Injured Lady* was not published until after his death. Various reasons have been suggested for his failure to publish at once,³ but the simplest and most obvious explanation is that in 1707 Swift still had his eye on a career in England and did not choose to take up publicly a position that might imperil his chances of success. This reluctance contrasts sharply with his attitude to ecclesiastical affairs. When the safety of the church, as he saw it, was involved, he published his views to the world with no regard at all to his own prospects of promotion: *The Sentiments of a Church-of-England Man* (probably written in 1704) and *A Letter Concerning the Sacramental Test* (1709) were little likely to commend him to the whigs, upon whom his hopes still rested. But Swift was committed to the cause of the church, at whatever cost to himself; he did not yet feel that he was committed to the cause of Ireland. It was not until after the political changes of 1714, when all his hopes in England had been shattered and he was permanently settled in Dublin as dean of St. Patrick's, that he was willing to come out openly on the Irish side.

Even then, however, Swift was in no hurry to publish—indeed, as he told Charles Ford in September 1714, his first resolve seems to have been to leave Irish politics alone (*Correspondence*, 2:127)— and it was not until 1720 that he produced his *Proposal for the Universal Use of Irish Manufacture . . . Utterly Rejecting and Renouncing Everything Wearable that Comes from England* (*Works*, 9:13–22). In coming forward at this point Swift may have been influenced by the contemporary controversies over the claim of the British parliament to legislate for Ireland and over the appellate jurisdiction of the Irish house of lords.⁴ But, though he takes occasion to sneer at any assumption that England is superior to Ireland, he sticks pretty closely to the theme announced on the title page. He simply accepts the fact that Irish trade has been placed under serious restrictions and suggests what he considers the best line of action in the circumstances: if Ireland cannot send her goods abroad at least she can consume them at home, and by supplying her own needs do away with the necessity for imports from England. In effect, his main complaint is not against English policy but against the people of Ireland, who have at hand a remedy for their ills if only they would apply it; and he makes a savage attack on the landlords, to whose greed for higher rents he attributes the wretched condition of the countryside.

The argument of the *Proposal* did not turn directly on the constitutional relations between the two kingdoms. But Swift was undoubtedly appealing to popular anti-English sentiment; and he did raise, though only parenthetically, a constitutional issue of fundamental importance: "whether a Law to *bind Men without their own Consent*, be obligatory *in foro Conscientiae*" (*Works*, 9:19). It was a dangerous question to ask at a time when the British parliament had just reasserted its right to legislate for Ireland, and the government was sufficiently alarmed to prosecute the printer, though the prosecution was subsequently dropped, because, as Swift reported to Pope, the cause was "so very odious and unpopular."[5] The government's action was some measure of the pamphlet's success: it "soon spread very fast, being agreeable to the sentiments of the whole nation, except of those gentlemen who had Employments, or were Expectants" (*Correspondence*, 2:367). But this kind of popularity meant little; and, so far as Swift's main purpose was concerned, the *Proposal* was a complete failure. The policy he put forward might seem a simple one, but it called for a degree of organization and self-discipline that Ireland did not possess. Swift himself, though generally so quick-sighted in detecting the weaknesses of humanity, seems to have been genuinely disappointed at the lack of response; and, almost ten years later, the main point in his ironical defense of the *Modest Proposal* (1729) was the utter hopelessness of expecting the people of Ireland to make any honest concerted effort to help themselves.

Disappointment at the lack of response to the *Proposal* of 1720 (and, perhaps, alarm at the violence with which the government had pursued the printer) made Swift reluctant to engage any further in Irish politics; and when a new opportunity offered he was slow to intervene. In July 1722 the king granted a patent to William Wood, a Wolverhampton ironmaster, empowering him to coin copper money for Ireland. There was good precedent for such a patent, and the country was certainly in need of currency, but the circumstances of the grant alarmed and alienated public opinion. Both the amount of the new coinage to be issued and the margin of profit to be allowed were considered excessive, and there had been no prior consultation with Irish officials. The lords justices and the privy council expressed their disapproval; the commissioners of revenue refused to receive the coin; and when parliament met in September 1723 both houses postponed all other business till they had drawn up addresses to the king, declaring that the patent granted to William Wood was prejudicial to the revenue, destructive of trade and dangerous to property.[6] This unwonted unanimity and vigor probably persuaded Swift that public opinion was in earnest; in any case, he now resolved to take an active part in the controversy. But it is worth noting that in the opening paragraphs of his first pamphlet he refers to the reception accorded to the *Proposal*, and comments sourly: "This would be enough to discourage any Man from endeavouring to do you Good" (*Works*, 10:3).

Swift opened his campaign with *A Letter to the Shop-Keepers, Tradesmen, Farmers, and Common-People of Ireland . . . By M. B., Drapier*, which appeared in February 1724. This choice of a Dublin shopkeeper as the *persona* through whom to express his views is admirably suited to the initial appeal, which is directed primarily to the commercial classes; but even when the basis of the argument broadens, as it quickly does in the succeeding letters, the fiction is skillfully maintained. If the Drapier displays any knowledge of law or history that might seem unnatural in one of his position there is always some plausible explanation; and if he wants to illustrate a point he does so in the language of commerce: ". . . if a fierce captain comes to my shop to buy six yards of scarlet cloth." Swift knew the mercantile life of Dublin well, and it no doubt amused him to build up the character of "M.B."; but the maintenance of the fiction, even after the real authorship of the pamphlets was widely known, could serve a more serious purpose. In Ireland, as in England, opposition to government policy among the ruling classes was commonly the result of disappointment, or, more often, a tactical move made in the hope of being bought off; but a Dublin shopkeeper could have no such motive, and it was an essential part of Swift's theme that the opposition to Wood's patent was not merely factious or narrowly self-interested, but represented the national will aroused in defense of the national well-being. The Drapier, with no personal or class interest separable from that of the community in general, could speak for everyone; and his fourth letter, which contains the essential argument of the entire series, is addressed to "the Whole People of Ireland."

The title of this letter raises directly a question that can never be far below the surface in any discussion of Swift and Ireland. To whom was he addressing himself? What, in fact, did he understand by "the Irish nation"? Middleton Murry takes the view that "'The Whole People of Ireland' suggests, and was meant to suggest, Protestants and Papists combined"; and he argues that the explicit disavowal of any such intention in the text of the pamphlet was mere pretense.[7] This argument might be strengthened by the suggestion that Swift was simply guarding himself in advance from a repetition of the charge made against the *Proposal* of 1720 that it had been written in the interest of the pretender and the popish cause. But, even when reinforced in this way, the argument will not stand. From the very beginning the Drapier's appeal was distinctly and deliberately protestant. In the middle of the title page of the first letter, in bold type, stood out the words "Brass Half-Pence"; and to the Irish protestant "brass money" inevitably connoted Stuart tyranny, popish persecution, and French conquest. The reader is not allowed to forget the term, which is repeated over and over again; and, more than once, the significant connection is explicitly brought out: "I will buy Mr. Wood's Money, as my Father did the Brass Money in King *James*'s Time; who could buy *Ten Pound* of it with a *Guinea*" (*Works*, 10:7). This repeated playing upon protestant prejudice is an unmistakable guide to the kind of public the pamphlets were aimed at, and it shows that the open rejection of any reliance on papist support, though possibly intended to disarm government attack, was perfectly genuine.

This protestant exclusiveness reflects Swift's "colonial" view of Anglo-Irish relations. His concern is with the position and prospects of "the true English people of Ireland" (i.e., the protestant population), whose ancestors "reduced this kingdom to the obedience of England." It is they whose natural liberties have been encroached upon: they are governed by laws to which they have not given their consent; the jurisdiction of their house of lords has been taken away; their trade has been ruined; they are excluded from public employments in favor of newcomers from across the Channel, and now they live under "the dread of Wood's halfpence." It is to them, also, that Swift, under the guise of the Drapier, now preaches openly the constitutional doctrine earlier adumbrated in the still unpublished *Story of the Injured Lady*.

The core of this doctrine is to be found in the fourth of the *Drapier's letters*, addressed to "the Whole People of Ireland":

> And this gives me an Opportunity of explaining, to those who are ignorant, another Point, which hath often *swelled in my Breast*. Those who come over hither to us from *England*, and some *weak* People among ourselves, whenever, in Discourse, we make mention of *Liberty* and *Property*, shake their Heads, and tell us, that *Ireland* is a *depending Kingdom*; as if they would seem, by this Phrase, to intend that the People of

Ireland is in some State of Slavery or Dependence, different from those of *England:* Whereas a *depending Kingdom* is a *modern Term of Art;* unknown, as I have heard, to all ancient *Civilians,* and *Writers upon Government;* and *Ireland* is, on the contrary, called in some Statutes an *Imperial Crown,* as held only from God; which is as high a Style, as any Kingdom is capable of receiving. Therefore by this expression, a *depending Kingdom,* there is no more understood, than that by a Statute made here, in the 33rd Year of *Henry VIII, The King and his Successors, are to be Kings Imperial of this Realm, as united and knit to the Imperial Crown of England.* I have looked over all the *English* and *Irish* Statutes, without finding any Law that makes *Ireland depend* upon *England,* any more than *England* doth upon *Ireland.* We have, indeed, obliged ourselves to have the *same King with them;* and consequently they are obliged to have the *same King with us.* For the Law was made by *our own Parliament;* and our Ancestors then were not such *Fools (whatever they were in the preceding Reign)* to bring themselves under I know not what *Dependance,* which is now talked of, without any Ground of *Law, Reason,* or *common Sense.* (*Works,* 10:61–62)

A few paragraphs later, he summarizes the constitutional position in a brief passage, the intrinsic vigor of which is reinforced by a liberal use of capitals:

by the Laws of GOD, of NATURE, of NATIONS, and of your own Country, you ARE and OUGHT to be as FREE a People as your Brethren in *England.* (*Works,* 10:63)

But between these two bold assertions of Irish independence stands another passage, in which Swift, after recounting briefly an earlier controversy over Anglo-Irish relations, describes the actual position in realistic terms:

Indeed, the Arguments on both Sides were invincible. For in *Reason,* all *Government* without the consent of the *Governed,* is the *very Definition of Slavery:* But in *Fact, Eleven Men well armed, will certainly subdue one single Man in his Shirt.* (*Works,* 10:63)

It might seem, at first sight, that this admission made further argument or effort irrelevant. But Swift knew very well that force could not be as simply applied in government as in highway robbery. Ireland might be compelled to submit to British legislation, but the orderly administration of the country required from the people a degree of cooperation, or, at least, of acquiescence, of which external force was a very imperfect guarantee. An actively hostile public opinion was a dangerous inconvenience that the ministry would, sooner or later, be anxious to get rid of, even at the price of some concessions. Swift's immediate purpose was to keep popular indignation alive until that point had been reached. In this he succeeded; and when parliament met in September 1725 the lord lieutenant announced that "an entire end has been put to the patent formerly granted to Mr Wood."

The victory confirmed Swift's popularity and gave him an established place in the succession of Irish patriots, but it brought no real benefit to Ireland. The constitutional position was unchanged; restraints on Irish trade continued; the policy of appointing Englishmen to important posts was even extended, for the government had been frightened at the number of place-holders who had taken the popular side during the controversy. Swift's own view of the position can be judged from a pamphlet that he wrote a couple of years later, *A Short View of the State of Ireland* (*Works*, 12:1–12), published early in 1728. In this, he goes again, though more briefly, over much of the ground covered in the *Drapier's Letters:* the enforcement of legistlation to which the nation had not consented; the restriction of commerce; the exclusion of men of Irish birth from public employments. But the aggressive confidence of the *Drapier's Letters* is gone; the tone is now rather one of disgruntled resignation; and the best comfort he can offer is that, though England is enriching herself at Ireland's expense, this cannot last for ever: "One Thing I know, that *when the Hen is starved to Death, there will be no more Golden Eggs.*" He was already on the edge of the savage despair that was to find expression, a year later, in the *Modest Proposal.*[8]

The essential characteristic of the *Modest Proposal* is indeed despair. The immediate occasion of its writing was the state of the country after a succession of bad seasons:

> As to this country, there have been three terrible years dearth of corn, and every place strowed with beggars; but dearths are common in better climates, and our evils here lie much deeper. Imagine a nation two-thirds of whose revenues are spent out of it, and who are not permitted to trade with the other third, and where the pride of the women will not suffer them to wear their own manufactures even where they excel what come from abroad: This is the true state of Ireland in a very few words. These evils operate more every day, and the kingdom is absolutely undone, as I have been telling it often in print these ten years past. (Swift to Pope, 11 August 1729, *Correspondence*, 3:341)

For Swift, the famine conditions of the period were the outcome of an essentially evil situation, not just the result of a few bad harvests. But his own reaction to the situation has changed. In the *Proposal for the Universal Use of Irish Manufacture* he was urging a plan of action; in the *Drapier's Letters* he was calling for a popular assertion of national rights; even in the *Short View of the State of Ireland* there is, at least by implication, some hint of the possibility of improvement. But in the *Modest Proposal* this possibility is swept away; the only practicable remedy for Ireland's ills is the scheme now put forward.

It is typical of Swift's method that this defensive explanation, with its tone of indignation and resentment, is kept to the end. The proposal itself is introduced and described in calm, businesslike terms, and in the opening paragraphs there is nothing to warn the reader that he has in hand anything other than some charitable scheme for the endowment of schools or the raising of a fund to bind pauper children as apprentices. Ireland, he is told, contains many thousands of beggars, whose offspring have no prospect of improving their position; and even among the population in general the vast majority of parents are too poor to provide for their families. These statements are accompanied by some speciously convincing statistics about the number of children involved and the cost of maintaining them. So far, all is sufficiently commonplace, though the reader might, perhaps, be surprised at the casual way in which stealing is referred to as, apparently, a perfectly natural way of making a living. But even this would hardly prepare him for what follows:

> I have been assured by a very knowing *American* of my Acquaintance in *London:* that a young healthy Child, well nursed, is, at a Year old, a most delicious, nourishing, and wholesome Food; whether *Stewed, Roasted, Baked,* or *Boiled;*; and, I make no doubt, that it will equally serve in a *Fricasie,* or *Ragoust.* (*Works,* 12:111)

In the same matter-of-fact tone the author goes on to develop his proposal that the children of the poor should be eaten by the rich. He considers carefully how many should be reserved annually for breeding; how many will be available for sale; what will be their average weight when they come to market; what arrangements should be made for slaughtering them; what use might be made of the skin; and he explains, in some detail, the advantages, that will be gained, financially and otherwise, by the parents and by the community at large. Only when he has extracted the utmost effect from this pose of calm detachment does Swift allow the bitter indignation that it disguises to break through:

> I desire the Reader will observe, that I calculate my Remedy *for this one individual Kingdom of* IRELAND, *and for no other that ever was, is, or I think ever can be upon Earth.* (*Works*, 12:116)

Then comes the defense that makes the purpose of the *Modest Proposal* explicit. After listing the expedients that he had himself put forward in vain during the previous ten years, Swift continues:

> Therefore I repeat, let no Man talk to me of these and the like Expedients; till he hath, at least, a Glimpse of Hope, that there will ever be some hearty and sincere Attempt to put *them in Practice.*
> But, as to my self; having been wearied out for many Years with offering vain, idle, visionary Thoughts; and at length utterly despairing of Success, I fortunately fell upon this Proposal; which, as it is wholly new, so it hath something *solid* and *real*, of no Expence, and little Trouble, full in our own Power; and whereby we can incur no Danger in *disobliging* ENGLAND: For, this Kind of Commodity will not bear Exportation; the Flesh being of too tender a Consistence, to admit a long Continuance in Salt; *although, perhaps, I could name a Country, which would be glad to eat up our whole Nation without it.* (*Works*, 12:117)

Though he thus returns to the old attack on English policy, his main complaint now is against the selfishness and apathy of the people of Ireland themselves; it is the impossibility of arousing them to effective action, rather than the overriding power of England, that lies at the root of his despair.

On the surface, at least, Swift's main concern in the *Modest Proposal* is for the poverty-stricken masses. It is their condition that forms the theme of the penultimate paragraph:

> I desire those Politicians, who dislike my Overture, and may perhaps be so bold to atempt an Answer, that they will first ask the Parents of these Mortals, Whether they would not, at this Day, think it a great Happiness to have been sold for Food at a Year old, in the Manner I prescribe; and thereby have avoided such a perpetual Scene of Misfortunes, as they have since gone through; by the *Oppression of Landlords;* the Impossibility of paying Rent, without Money or Trade; the Want of common sustenance, with neither House nor Cloaths, to cover them from the Inclemencies of the Weather; and the most inevitable Prospect of intailing the like, or greater Miseries upon their Breed for ever. (*Works*, 12:117–18)

But this pity for their wretched condition is unaccompanied by any sense of community. These are not the fellow-citizens to whom he has, in the past, addressed his vain appeals for cooperation. They are a passive multitude, of no more account politically than the animals whose fate he proposes they should share. Though the language in which he speaks of them is, no doubt, colored by his theme, it is hard not to detect in it the expression of a genuine contempt:

> I do therefore humbly offer it to *publick Consideration*, that of the Hundred and Twenty Thousand Children, already computed. Twenty thousand may be reserved for Breed; whereof only one Fourth Part to be Males; which is more than we allow to *Sheep, black Cattle*, or *Swine;* and my Reason is, that these Children are seldom the Fruits of Marriage, *a Circumstance not much regarded by our Savages;* therefore, *one Male* will be sufficient to serve *four Females.* (*Works*, 12:111)

"Our Savages"—it is a revealing phrase, especially when taken along with "a very knowing *American*" in the immediately preceding paragraph. For Swift, "the savage old Irish" (as he calls them elsewhere) were no more a part of the "Irish nation" than the Iroquois or the Sioux formed part of the British colonies in North America. Their poverty aroused his indignation; but they lay beyond the frontier of his political and cultural world and could have no share in the constitutional claims that he urged so fiercely on behalf of those whose ancestors had "reduced this kingdom to the obedience of England." Swift might stand forward as an Irishman in his resistance to the British parliament's claim to legislate for Ireland, but as against the majority in Ireland itself—the "Popish natives"—he was an Englishman and a protestant.

The dangers and difficulties implicit in this position had existed in one form or another, since the first establishment of the English colony in Ireland, in the twelfth century: "Such in truth is our lot," declared Maurice FitzGerald, one of the first invaders, "that while we are English to the Irish we are Irish to the English."[9] By the eighteenth century the basic division in Irish life had become one of religion rather than of race, but the dominant Anglo-Irish minority—the "Protestant Ascendancy"—found itself precisely in the dilemma described by Maurice FitzGerald. For the time being, however, the dilemma was less obvious and less dangerous than it had been in the past or was to become in the future. The seventeenth-century wars had given the Anglo-Irish such a firm grip on property and influence that they could afford to ignore the sub-

jugated majority, and in asserting their own rights against domination from England they thought and spoke of themselves, without
any sense of incongruity, as the "Irish nation."

Swift's stalwart defense of Irish claims made him one of the
heroes of this national sentiment. His teaching was remembered
even if his advice was neglected; and it was the "Spirit of Swift"
that Grattan invoked when he hailed the dawn of constitutional
independence in 1782. But one may reasonably doubt if Swift was
ever a nationalist after the fashion of Grattan and his supporters.
Though he stood up for the rights of the Irish parliament, he was
fiercely contemptuous of its members; and his private letters to
friends in England contain less about Irish nationality than about
his own sense of living in exile. Other Irish protestants of the
eighteenth century could feel themselves at home in the political
and social life of Ireland, and could express their sense of security
and permanence in the public buildings and the great town and
country houses that are their most enduring visible memorial. But
Swift, exiled from England and restless in Ireland, could not feel at
home anywhere; out of tune with both countries, he could commit
himself fully to neither.

It is this uncommittedness that gives Swift such an important
place in the development of the Anglo-Irish tradition; for it proved
a more enduring characteristic than the nationalism of Grattan and
his contemporaries. The national fervor of that period soon burned
itself out, and in the nineteenth century it became little more than a
memory. The Anglo-Irish could no longer see themselves as "the
Irish nation." Their utter dependence upon England was now fully
exposed. And yet, much as they might resent that dependence,
they dared not counter it by coming to terms with the majority in
their own country, a majority that was now pushing its way towards power and developing a nationalism of its own with which
the Anglo-Irish could have no sympathy. Their circumstances
were different from Swift's, but their dilemma was the same, and
they were exiles in the country of their birth. Even those of them
who abandoned inherited prejudice and took up the cause of the
majority were seldom altogether at home. They could not wholly
escape the sense of isolation, the sense of standing between two
worlds and belonging completely to neither, which is the heritage
of the Anglo-Irish protestant. It need not surprise us that the greatest of Anglo-Irish poets should, in the end, have turned back to
Swift for inspiration. Yeats had moved far from the protestant faith
and the political outlook of his Anglo-Irish background, but the

links were still there, and even across the centuries that divided him from Swift, across the revolutions that had shattered the Ireland Swift knew, he could feel a sense of community with the great archetypal figure of the Anglo-Irish tradition.

Notes

1. Irvin Ehrenpreis, *Swift: The Man, His Works, and the Age. Volume 1: Mr. Swift and His Contemporaries*, (London: Methuen, 1962), p. 31 (quoted Deane Swift, *Essay*).

2. O. Ferguson, *Jonathan Swift and Ireland* (Urbana: University of Illinois Press, 1962), p. 28 and *n*.

3. Ibid., pp. 30–31.

4. W. E. H. Lecky, *History of Ireland in the Eighteenth Century* (London, 1892), 1:447–48; J. C. Beckett, *Making of Modern Ireland* (London: Faber, 1966), p. 164.

5. Swift to Pope, 10 January 1721 (*Correspondence*, 2:368; on the date of this letter, and on its general character, see ibid., 2:366, n. 2).

6. For the controversy over "Wood's Halfpence" see A. Goodwin, "Wood's Halfpence," in *Englsih Historical Review* 51 (1936):647–74; Ferguson, *Jonathan Swift and Ireland*, pp. 83 ff.

7. J. Middleton Murry, *Jonathan Swift* (London: Cape 1954), p. 368.

8. *A Modest Proposal for Preventing the Children of Poor People from being a Burthen to their Parents, or the Country and for Making them Beneficial to the Publick*, in *Works*, 12:107–18.

9. E. Curtis, *A History of Medieval Ireland*, 2d ed (London: Methuen 1938), p. 55.

6

Swift in His Poems: The Range of His Positive Rhetoric

RICHARD FEINGOLD

1

Swift's imagination is always extravagant, and the pleasure we take in it must be an effect of the freedom such extravagance springs from and creates. He is, moreover, always asking us to watch him at his work, as if our fullest response to its energy and freedom depended upon our delighted, amazed, or uneasy perception of his own presence in it. In fact, if there *is* anything that can be called "development" in Swift's poetry, it is in just this: the single step he took when he discarded the forced solemnity of the Cowleyan pindarics and learned how to write himself into a verse whose central display would be his own intense and extravagant playfulness. Once Swift made himself his own central subject— and this happened very early in his career as a verse writer—there was very little change in the range or character of his poetry. Early and late it is dominated by invective, lampoon, burlesque, along with a broadly Horatian, sophisticated, conversational kind of verse whose gentlemanly façade hardly disguises Swift's own extravagant self-promotion, as in the early poems to Harley or the later "Verses on the Death of Dr. Swift." What distinguishes Swift's poems from each other is not any plainly discernible technical development, then, but rather their ethical seriousness or personal intensity. And these Swift conveys more in terms of new matter than new manner. There is certainly in his later Horatian poems a greater tonal diversity and therefore a more pronounced dramatic character than is evident in his earlier work, but again this

is largely a matter of personal urgency and not easily demonstrable
as an effect of richer or more complex technique. The fine caesural
shifts, the supple handling of parenthetical observations, the skill-
ful variations of end-stopped and run-on lines are as much evident
in Swift's earlier poems about himself and Harley as in the later
poems about himself and Stella. Perhaps it is implicit in Swift's
peculiar genius that it could only grow in its intensities, not its
range—a narrow channel whose current is forced into more or less
violent motion but never in a new direction. I say this with an
intent to praise: it is the restrictiveness of Swift's genius that energizes its sublimities, producing the spectacle from which we derive
our pleasure.

His commitment to the Cowleyan high style discarded, Swift's
early poems display his presence not as autobiographical fact but in
stylistic playfulness. Whimsical or abusive, the most energetic of
them—"A Description of a Salamander," the poems on Vanbrugh, the two versions of "Baucis and Philemon," "Sid Hamet's
Rod," "The Fable of Midas," "A Description of a City Shower"—
all are marked by that verbal opacity that seems so central to burlesque or travesty and by means of which we become aware of the
author at work on his text.[1] The reification of words themselves in
an outrageous rhyme, a wildly inappropriate adaptation of some
familiar literary work, or simply some peculiar idea spun out for its
own sake, or *any* idea spun out for its own sake—these are some of
the characteristics of Swift's verse throughout his career, and they
are especially evident in his earlier output. In what must certainly
be the most minor of minor poems, "On the Little House by the
Church Yard of Castleknock," Swift makes an extended joke about
a building so excessively small that it becomes, merely by virtue of
that peculiarity, an inevitable object of attention and finally the
stimulus of an odd kind of wonder. For the reader, the pleasure of
the poem is in Swift's display of his ability to run through a dozen
or so ways of reifying smallness. Here are a few:

> The Vicar once a Week creeps in,
> Sits with his Knees up to his Chin; . . .

> A Traveller, who by did pass,
> Observ'd the Roof behind the Grass;
> On Tiptoe stood and rear'd his Snout,
> And saw the Parson creeping out;
> Was much surpriz'd to see a Crow
> Venture to build his Nest so low.

> *Warburton* took it in his Noddle,
> This Building was designed a Model,
> Or of a Pigeon-house, or Oven,
> To bake one Loaf, and keep one Dove in.
>
> (1:127)[2]

As with riddles or limericks, the reader is immediately aware of and engaged by his commitment to join in the outlandish game, which in this case draws him into a half-dozen still-to-come ways of looking at a tiny structure quickly becoming as fascinating as it is ridiculous. So Stella (here called Mrs. Johnson) supposes the house to be a "Still which wants a Spout." Another suggests "but that it wanted Room/It might have been a Pigmy's Tomb." To a child passing by it seems a toy, and upon her demanding it, her mother asks in "manner mild,"

> Pray reach that Thing here to the Child,
> That Thing, I mean, among the Kale,
> And here's to buy a Pot of Ale.
>
> (1:128)

(This is very fine in its representation of an adult intelligence drawn into the foolery in the very act of voicing its aloofness from it.)[3] The building having thus been diminished from birdhouse to oven to still to (not quite) pygmy's tomb to doll's house to "that Thing," the final view of it is that of the child's nurse:

> Says *Nancy*, I can make for Miss,
> A finer House ten times than this,
> The Dean will give me Willow-Sticks,
> And *Joe* my Apron full of Bricks.
>
> (1:128)

Here the apron full of bricks attracts our delighted attention as Swift's triumphantly tiny "idea" for a smallness so extreme that imagining it is a strangely enriching act. There are not many less "significant" items in Swift's canon than "The Little House," but surely the wit that animates it is not unrelated to the imaginative energy that created Lilliput, particularly such sections as the description of the contents of Gulliver's pockets.

The display of an odd and copious inventiveness is so frequent in Swift's work that it may be considered his signature. The lists in *Gulliver*, the stuttering series of similes the narrator of *A Tale of A Tub* is always as if helplessly urging forth, the compiling of arguments, pro and con, in *An Argument against Abolishing Christianity* and *A Modest Proposal*—these are analogues to the recurring *seriatim* structures in the lampoons. In "Sid Hamet's Rod," Swift discovers about eight witty transformations of Godolphin's staff of office, engaging the reader's playful desire to know just why that staff is unlike Moses' rod but like a witch's broom; why it is like a divining rod and Hermes' wand and a fishing pole but only just barely resembles a conjuror's wand; why it is not at all like Achilles' scepter but very much like the Golden Bough; and why, certainly superior to any hobbyhorse, it is also well suited for use as a jockey's whip.[4] In two of the poems against Vanbrugh, Swift's lampooning takes off from the myth of Amphion, its exuberant fun more in concert with the old story than at the expense of Vanbrugh. Once again, pleasure arises from our sense of Swift's absurd ingenuity in spinning out from the Amphion material such outrageously literal-minded and therefore entirely fanciful notions as these:

> In times of old, when Time was young,
> And Poets their own Verses sung,
> A Song could draw a Stone or Beam,
> That now would overload a Team,
> Lead them a Dance of many a Mile,
> Then rear 'em to a goodly Pile,
> Each Number had its diff'rent Power;
> Heroick Strains could build a Tower;
> Sonnets and Elegyes to Chloris
> Would raise a House about two Storyes;
> A Lyrick Ode would Slate; a Catch
> Would Tile; an Epigram would Thatch.
>
> (1:79)

There is something at work here very much like the imagination of the movie cartoonist, whose simultaneously broad and meticulous visual wit can take an idea and rearrange it almost inexhaustibly. A line like "Lead them a Dance of many a Mile" especially brings to mind the cartoonist's innocently grotesque wit as it animates minerals or makes vegetables of animals.[5] Note too how the second half of the verse paragraph insistently elaborates upon the original visual joke, giving us a richly funny hierarchy of genres, and without malice playing upon the high meaning of the Amphion story. Amphion's power may have asserted the supremacy of imaginative mind over mere materiality, but here the reader's pleasure is in the exposure of the happy absurdity of that assertion, exposure managed in such a way that he can retain a high sense of the myth and also enjoy its silliness. Swift achieves this happy effect by supporting the myth in its plainest terms—that is, by inducing in his reader a delighted interest in that ingenuity of mind that, having asserted it, will then bother to define precisely the power of poetry to build houses, walls, roofs. If heroic strains can build a tower, what then can a sonnet do or an ode or epigram? We move through these lines experiencing the pleasure of surprise at such things as the conjunction of odes and slate, epigrams and thatch, hoping that the poet will go on as long as he can uncovering similar notions.[6] And certainly some part of the fun is in the witty apportionment of the lines so that as we move down the hierarchy of genres (as well as the hierarchy of buildings and building materials, from towers to cottages, slate to thatch), we see the lines themselves becoming bits of matter: a whole one for heroic strains, a couplet to be shared by sonnets and elegies; uneven line segments for odes, catches, and epigrams. Mind has indeed become matter here but at no cost to the honor of either. Swift's own pleasure in his joke was apparently strong enough to cause him to repeat it; in the third version of his lampoon against Vanbrugh, not only does he begin again with the outlandish lines on the Amphion story but also later in the poem he imagines one of Vanbrugh's plays itself building the architect-playwright's home: the prologue builds a wall ("So wide as to encompass all"); the plot (because it "as yet lay deep") a cellar; the five acts then extend the cellarage, build rooms, and add a roof, until finally,

> The Epilogue behind, did frame
> A place not decent here to name.

> (1:108)

The range of verbal wit in Swift's best lampoons can be surprisingly wide. We see it not only in the apparently inexhaustible variations upon an initially wild idea, but also in sometimes strikingly lively rhythmic and visual effects. The poems loosely based on Ovid provide some fine examples, the "transformation" motif offering Swift especially rich opportunities for sheer play, as the Vanbrugh poems demonstrate. In "The Fable of Midas," Swift shares Ovid's own playful delight in elaborating the effects of the golden touch. Both Ovid and Swift quickly run through several instances of Midas's power; and Swift, though he comically expands upon one or two of them, does not lose the effect of sudden and various wonder Ovid so successfully communicates. Thus Midas

> chip't his Bread, the Pieces round
> Glitter'd like Spangles on the Ground . . .
> He call'd for Drink, you saw him Sup
> *Potable Gold* in *Golden Cup* . . . .
> He cock't his Hat, you would have said
> *Mambrino's* Helm adorn'd his Head.

(1:156)

Here the immediate and sudden wonder of the touch of gold is communicated in couplets, the first lines of which are broken by a marked caesura that itself serves the simple syntactical purpose of connecting effect to cause. But, substituting for a stated connective, the stressed pause enacts the suddenness of the metamorphosis and actually quickens the movement of the couplet's first line into its second, which then plays out the idea in a rhythmic rush with barely any medial pause at all. Rolfe Humphries's translation of Ovid has captured something of Swift's effect here:

> It was all true
> He hardly dared to believe it! From an oak tree
> He broke a green twig loose: the twig was golden.
> He picked a stone up from the ground; the stone
> Paled with light golden color. . . .[7]

But Swift's energy is greater, partly an effect of his suggestion of the reader's own amazed presence as a witness. Compare Humphries's

> He mingled water with the wine of Bacchus;
> It was molten gold that trickled through his jaws . . .[8]

with Swift's

> He call'd for Drink, you saw him sup
> *Potable Gold* in *Golden Cup*.

And Swift's energy is evident too in his extravagantly meticulous attention to the body's mechanical and comic actuality, comical even in one whose touch is golden! Do we wonder how Midas might try to swallow his food?

His empty Paunch that he might fill,
He suck't his Vittels thro' a Quill;
Untouch't it pass't between his Grinders,
Or't had been happy for *Gold-finders*.

(1:156)

Nor is gold a fence against dirt. In the ocean,

Against whose torrent while he swims
The Golden Scurf peels off his Limbs . . .

(1:157)

To this Swiftian signature there is no Ovidian analogue.

The whimsy of these lampoons seems to me to subdue their aggressive force. Their objects of attack—Vanbrugh, Godolphin (Sid Hamet), and Marlborough (Midas)—hardly emerge as much more than opportunities for the play of fancy. Only after devoting forty lines to his Midas material, for example, does Swift turn his poem (only eighty-two lines in all) toward Marlborough. In "Sid Hamet's Rod," our attention is too much engaged by, our pleasure too much derived from, the riddling transformations of the scepter for us to be very much concerned with Godolphin. As in political cartoons, in which the caricature itself tends to absorb our attention, in these lampoons the machinery of the joke is itself the central display. And since it is valued as display, the joke may be quite cumbersome—the more cumbersome it is, in fact, the more pleasure it yields—just so long as it is striking or strange enough to hold our attention as it takes its time to complete itself. Swift does not mind taking ten lines, for example, to prepare a pun as his answer to his riddle: why are rich misers bad literary critics?

None e'er did modern *Midas* chuse
Subject or Patron of his Muse,
But found him thus their Merit Scan,
That *Phebus* must give Place to Pan:
He values not the Poet's Praise,
Nor will exchange His *Plumbs* for *Bays*;
To *Pan* alone rich Misers call,
And there's the Jest, for *Pan* is *ALL* . . .

(1:157)

Our attention here is on the gathering of notions that will finally yield the ridiculous conflation of mythology and etymology, Midas and Marlborough. In the process, Marlborough disappears, absorbed by the autonomously pleasurable Midas story.

This softening of abusive effect is by no means characteristic of all of Swift's lampooning—direct and unmitigated abuse is the hallmark of almost every poem in which Walpole appears and of almost all the late poems on Irish politics. But it is an effect of his technique in those poems whose lampooning attacks are managed through extended allusions to myth and fable. There is in these poems an opacity created by the sheer play of word and idea; they are all surface, and the softening of their abusive force is a sign of their resistance to the moral or didactic intention Swift probably had in writing them. Different in tone, then, as it is from these lampoons, Swift's "Description of A City Shower" resembles them in its most interesting effects—its resistance to interpretation. Here the extended allusion to the manner of *The Georgics* seems to invite a reading that sets London against Rome, low against high, mundane against heroic significance. But in fact the poem's most vivid effects are descriptive displays that elude didactic signification.

> Meanwhile the South rising with dabbled Wings,
> A Sable Cloud a-thwart the Welkin flings,
> That swill'd more Liquor than it could contain,
> And like a Drunkard gives it up again.
> Brisk *Susan* whips her Linen from the Rope,
> While the first drizzling Show'r is born aslope,
> Such is that Sprinkling which some careless Quean
> Flirts on you from her Mop, but not so clean.
> You fly, invoke the Gods; then turning, stop
> To rail; she singing, still whirls on her Mop.
>
> (1:137)

Movement and image are the subject as well as the material here; the lines contrast several kinds of movement and also several perspectives. There is the strikingly precise concentration on *how* rain falls ("born aslope") contrasted with the larger and more "literary" account of the darkening sky. Ovidian, Vergilian, and Miltonic resonances are especially identifiable in the first couplet, none at all in the third. But these are in no sense normative. The sudden precision of description in the third couplet, for example, is as poetically active as the almost grand, if less distinct, play with and against a "higher" style in the first two lines. In their yield of pleasure, so to speak, the two kinds of vision, and of style, even out rather than commenting on each other. The strength of the first couplet is in its evocation of ominous movement, indistinct in its details but vigorous in its force, taking place against broad expanses of space: "the South rising . . . A Sable Cloud a'thwart the Welkin flings." It is easy to notice the stylistic incongruity of that final word, along with its emphatic place, the sole verb of the couplet, the final syllable. Yet the "lowness" of the word does not undermine the force, even the grandeur, of the scene: "fling," with its sense of impetuous action and contemptuous gesture, is just right here and in accord also with the double, but not ironic, vision of the South wind's powerful movement on wings that are "dabbled." So too the elaboration of the first couplet in the description of the drunkard, rather than undermining, supports the imaginative conception of the wind and weather as impetuous and ominous energy, dangerously unruly. To its clear primary meaning, the word "swill'd" joins suggestions of excess, of garbage, and of powerful movement—so that in its metamorphosis into the drunkard, the South wind of the first two lines loses none of its ominous force and retains some of its sullied grandeur. (Perhaps the circumlocutory reticence of "gives it up again" checks the plunge toward simple bathos.) From this point on, as the paragraph fixes wholly upon urban detail, sheer activity becomes its central subject. With a single verb and a single participle, the first couplet was able to suggest the gathering of powerful and ominous energy in the sky. Here five verbs and four participles create the play of contrasting actions and gestures that animate these lines:

> You fly, invoke the Gods; then turning, stop
> To rail; she singing, still whirls on her Mop.

>   (1:137)

For all the display of action and gesture, however, the lines are tightly bound; the enjambment of the first is balanced by obvious pauses that divide it into four almost equal parts. Internal assonances (turn, whirl, flirt) bind the two lines to each other, and also to the couplet immediately preceding. As the paragraph moves on toward its conclusion, the little drama played out in gestures between the "careless Quean" and the pedestrian is transformed into a kind of agon between dust and rain, until by the simple act of repetition—in five lines there are three repetitions each of "dust" and of "rain"—the words themselves grow into each other and become the stain on the poet's coat:

And wafted with its Foe by violent Gust,
'Twas doubtful which was Rain, and which was Dust.
Ah! where must needy Poet seek for Aid,
When Dust and Rain at once his Coat invade;
His only Coat, where Dust confus'd with Rain,
Roughen the Nap, and leave a mingled Stain.

(1:137–38)

This exceedingly precise focus is the resting point of a verse paragraph whose initial perspective encompassed the "Welkin." The
effect finally of all this descriptive activity is to subdue the ironic
possibilities suggested by the hints of a high style in the first line.
The dirty wind, the dusty rain, the drunkard, the whirling mop are
at once ugly, threatening, forceful, and delightful, and our responses to them are enhanced but not simply determined by the
Vergilian presence. The poem suggests the high terms in which we
might judge the urban scene, and then makes judgment seem beside the point.[10]

Perhaps the most energetic example of Swift's verbal responsiveness to movement and gesture is his comically admiring tribute
to the Earl of Peterborough, the Mordanto of the following verses.
Swift admired Peterborough—"He is at least sixty, and has more
spirits than any young fellow I know in England"—for his military,
political, and literary activities, and in these lines gives the character of a figure whom Macaulay later was to describe as "the last of
the Knights Errant."[11]

Mordanto fills the Trump of Fame
The Christian World his Deeds proclaim,
And Prints are crowded with his Name.

In Journeys he out-rides the Post,
Sits up till Midnight with his Host,
Talks Politicks, and gives the Toast.

Knows ev'ry prince in *Europe's* Face,
Flies like a Squib from Place to Place,
And travels not, but runs a Race.

From *Paris* Gazette *A-la-main*,
This Day arriv'd without his Train,
Mordanto in a Week from *Spain*.

A Messenger comes all a-reek,
Mordanto at *Madrid* to seek:
He left the Town above a Week.

Next Day the Post-boy winds his Horn,
And rides through *Dover* in the Morn:
Mordanto's landed from *Leghorn*.

Mordanto gallops on alone,
The roads are with his Foll'wers strown,
This breaks a Girth, and that a Bone.

His Body active as his Mind,
Returning sound in Limb and Wind,
Except some Leather lost behind.

A Skeleton in outward Figure,
His meagre Corps, though full of Vigour,
Would halt behind him, were it bigger.

So wonderful his Expedition,
When you have not the least Suspicion,
He's with you like an Apparition. . . .

(2:397–98)

Here in the service of comic, but genuine, celebration, is the same copious wit and rhythmic energy of the lampoons. The subject of these verses is energy itself, and their effect is to suggest physical movement of such forcefulness and celerity that body virtually becomes spirit.[12] The inventiveness here is in the variety of ways Swift finds to enact not only Mordanto's movement, but also the virtual immateriality of his presence. Speed and movement are conveyed by explicit statement supported by a syntax almost entirely composed of verbs, as in stanzas two and three, where the subject stated only once then governs eight verbs in the succeeding six lines. Intensifying our impressions of Mordanto's speed are those of his suddenness; these are conveyed by Swift's witty deployment of the third line of his three-line stanza, as in stanzas five and six, to enact the surprise Mordanto's appearance generates. The first two lines in each of these cases draw attention away from Mordanto; the third line, after a heavy pause, suddenly turns us toward him again, only to reveal his absence where we anticipated his presence; his presence, where we expected his absence. The wonder of Mordanto's comings and goings is finally presented in stanzas nine and ten as an effect of a constitution both ghostlike and physical—an idea expressed in entirely humorous terms, but without undermining the poem's celebrative intention. In fact, it is one of the major triumphs of this very minor masterpiece to have worked out a decorum in which resonances of the comic and the picaresque together create an image of the heroic as charming as it is imposing. That "Mordanto fills the Trump of Fame" is realized in a set of actions and impressions that include a hearty and very physical vigor: "The roads are with his Foll'wers strown/This breaks a Girth, and that a Bone." And, entirely appropriate to Swift's sense of Peterborough's personality and his metabolism, the poem ends in a rhythmic rush, its compliments hyperbolically and quickly asserted in a series of syntactically incomplete phrases, without benefit of grammatical subject, and almost without verb. Swift gives us Peterborough, grand and comic, too full of life almost for his poem to pause to discover the high words and stately rhythms more usual heroes require.

> Shines in all Climates like a Star;
> In Senates bold, and fierce in War,
> A Land-Commander, and a Tarr.

> Heroick Actions early bred in,
> Ne'er to be match't in modern Reading,
> But by his Name-sake Charles of Sweden.
>
> (2:398)

2

Swift reveals his fullest imaginative power in those masterpieces of ironic prose in which his love of verbal play discovers its accord with an intensely ethical purpose. This accord is not easily attained or easily defined, because, as we have come to understand, the play of Swift's irony never allows him or his reader to settle with assurance into direct connection with his real and identifiable didactic purposes or with the positive beliefs that underlie those purposes.[13] It is impossible to read the fourth voyage, or the *Modest Proposal*, without responding simultaneously to Swift's full commitment to an ethical politics or to his love for the dignity of reason—but also to the sudden intrusions of those elements of his moral and imaginative being that elude and even undermine those positives. Allowing so much of his being its expression is the achievement of Swift's irony—the highest form of self-expressive play he attains. The instruction and pleasure we derive from it are from the spectacle of so much freedom discovering so much truth.

The intensity of a protean ironic imagination is not the hallmark of Swift's verse. This is why, despite its often overtly autobiographical substance, the poetry is, with some notable exceptions, not as self-revealing as the great prose satire.[14] In the lampoons I have been discussing, Swift's verbal play is his personal signature certainly, but it disengages him from any deeply felt ethical or didactic purpose, so we miss that much of him. On the other hand, scattered throughout the body of his verse are Swift's plainest assertions of his ethical commitments and the most direct claims for the ethical purposes of art in general. In their directness it is as if such claims and assertions demonstrate an uneasiness on Swift's part with the strikingly intimate, if ethically indistinct, playfulness of his irony. In place of such ironic activity, with its strong charge of self-scrutiny, we often get in the poems a grand theatricality, sometimes masterfully staged to present an image of heroic virtue, boldly displaying itself. The rhetoric of such heroic self-display has this ring:

> True Poets can depress and raise;
> Are Lords of Infamy and Praise:
> They are not scurrilous in Satire,
> Nor will in Panygyrick flatter.
> Unjustly poets we asperse;
> Truth shines the brighter, clad in Verse;
> And all the Fictions they pursue
> Do but insinuate what is true.
>
> (2:729)

Considering this passage against Swift's more characteristically demeaning presentation of the poetic trade—as in *On Poetry: A Rapsody*—the complete absence of indirection is striking. Itself a model of direct statement, the passage develops from an attack on romanticizing poets and stands in direct relationship to that attack; more, it is itself a celebration of the very *possibility* of direct statement. The celebrative and heroic ring results from a rhetoric of assertion: the lines proclaim the actuality of, and the clear distinctions between, such categories as infamy and praise, and they proclaim the actuality of the race of True Poets, seen here not as unacknowledged legislators but as the recognized executives of man's moral government—the Lords of Infamy and Praise. Swift envisions here, moreover, the possibility of satire without scurrility, panegyric without flattery—the possibility of an unblemished rhetoric of praise and blame, a kind of writing that we can imagine has in it no room, and no need, for play.[15] Celebrative, grand, truthful—it would ideally be, at least in its panegyrical vein, like the poems we are told the Houyhnhnms recited. Perhaps this is the inevitable positive fantasy of a mind whose distrust of play, of ingenuity and imagination, was equal to its obsessive display of all these. What but such a mind could have invented the horses as emblems of the dignity of right reason?[16]

Two poems can illustrate Swift's range in unironic expression: the well-known invective against Marlborough on the occasion of his death, and, less familiar, Swift's celebration of Lord Carteret, "The Birth of Manly Virtue." The poem to Carteret is not able to sustain its considerable initial energy: it ends abruptly on a note of exaggerated compliment referring to Carteret's political presence in Ireland. It is a compliment the extravagant terms of which are almost entirely absent in any of Swift's writings, in any form, on any subject (other than himself) connected with Anglo-Irish politics:

> Fame now reports, the western Isle
> Is made his Mansion for a while;
> Whose anxious Natives, Night and Day,
> (Happy beneath his righteous Sway)
> Weary the Gods with ceaseless Prayer,
> To bless him and to keep him there;
> And claim it as a Debt from Fate,
> Too lately found! to lose him late!
>
> (2:387–88)

It is precisely this kind of rhetoric that Swift had in mind in his "Libel on Dr. Delany," where he speaks contemptuously of Delany's own praise of Carteret as mere "sweetening." Yet here in Swift's lines on Carteret there is no ironic intention; the impulse to praise was genuine, and the initial imaginative idea from which the poem springs is brilliantly embodied in verse entirely adequate to Swift's ethical purpose:

> Once on a Time, a righteous Sage,
> Griev'd at the Vices of the Age,
> Apply'd to *Jove* with fervent Prayer;
> "O *Jove*, if Virtue be so fair
> "As it was deem'd in former Days
> "By *Plato*, and by *Socrates*,
> "(Whose Beauties mortal Eyes escape,
> "Only for want of outward Shape)
> "Make thou its real Excellence
> "For once the Theme of human Sense.

"So shall the Eye, by Form confin'd
"Direct, and fix the wand'ring Mind,
"And long-deluded Mortals see,
"With Rapture, what they wont to flee.

(2:383–84)

The verse here is conversational but not low, witty but not subversive, lyrical but not sentimental. The hyperbolical demand that Swift imagines is nothing less than that an Idea be actualized as a body. The passage focuses on and dramtizes the yearning righteousness that stands behind so hyperbolical a demand as this—that the Platonic scheme be "reversed" ("So shall the Eye, by form confin'd,/Direct, and fix the wand'ring Mind"), all in order that it might be substantiated in experience—that body itself be the final confirmation of the reality of spirit! This is an astonishing idea, and its source is in that same Platonic agon between the ideal and the actual that energizes Swift's most profound writings and generates his most complex ironies, as in the fourth voyage, where the ideal and actual are set down as proofs each against the other. The extravagance of the fictional vehicle required to define *that* conflict and generate its ironies has been well described by Ian Watt: "all allowances made for the needs of dramatic heightening, there is surely nothing else in human thought which equals the violence and the starkness of the dichotomy of Yahoo and Houyhnhnm."[17] But if we examine the poem in honor of Carteret, what we can say is that the same Platonic intensities of the fourth voyage are here realized also in extravagant ideas, demands, and claims, but that the extravagances are positive ones, yielding, in the absence of irony, a strongly heroic tonality; this is the sound of Swift's mind, when, eschewing the privileges of irony, he embraces his best beliefs and seeks to assert his own positive connection with them.

The poem to Carteret is elaborate. Beginning with its focus on the idealism of the sage, it presents Carteret's life as an answer to the sage's prayer. It comments, therefore, on Carteret's childhood, his education, his marriage, his early diplomatic achievements, and finally his Irish mission. If it is not uniformly successful, its best moments still demonstrate Swift's moving command of a positive rhetoric, distinctly heroic in tone. The following passage, for example, seems to owe its force both to its intelligent humor and to its plain assertiveness:

Virtue was of this Sex design'd,
In mild Reproof to Woman-kind;

> In manly Form to let them see
> The Loveliness of Modesty,
> The thousand Decencies, that shone
> With lessen'd Lustre in their own;
> Which few had learnt enough to prize,
> And some thought modish to despise.
>
> (2:383)

The character of this language is determined by its amalgam of sophisticated reticence and hyperbole: the focus certainly is upon the "reticent" virtues of modesty and decency; thus, it is only in "mild Reproof" to womankind that these virtues are said to have been embodied in a man. Swift here is quietly humorous in his handling of his fable, but still he does not make light of it. The blend of fable, myth, and drawing-room sophistication never overruns the ethical intention because the praise of virtue is itself unmistakably direct, intentionally hyperbolic. So it is a "thousand" decencies that "shine" in Carteret's behavior; and, in an especially effective line, it is "The Loveliness of Modesty" that Carteret is said to embody. The force of that line is entirely a function of its directness, of the way its positives—loveliness, modesty—boldly occupy its whole space, speaking clearly and confidently to an audience presumed to know what modesty *is*, to see it as lovely, to wish to honor it. The special beauty of this passage, I think, is generated by that central line, which is linked to the feelings of the poem's opening account of the grief and fervor of the "righteous Sage." Speaking as he does here to an audience that is assumed to experience both the knowledge and love of his positives, Swift can allow himself to introduce a satiric note, as in the last couplet of the passage cited above, without undoing the decorum of praise: thus, the criticism of women is simultaneously bantering, reticent, and firm. Note the play against each other of "few" and "some" in the fourth couplet above. The passage as a whole, indeed, beautifully embodies the blend of social grace and ethical integrity that is the point of its deft celebration of Carteret. I think that we can see here the chief features of Swift's positive rhetoric—the blend of sophistication and fervor that makes it possible for him to discover in the language of the drawing-room a vehicle suitable to the expression of moral idealism. The hallmark of this language is its capacity to contain both reticence and assertion, to blend them or to move from one to the other. At its best, this tonal range is ample enough to impart dramatic force to the didactic material of the poetry, as is especially evident in the serious poems to Stella.

It seems to me true, however, that the intended dramatic movement from section to section in the Carteret poem is not thoroughly
realized, and this largely because the focus upon Carteret is finally
inadequate to the intensity of feeling evident in the poem's opening
lines. These are distinctly personal in their charge; the "righteous
Sage" is surely Swift himself, and the force both of his frustration
and of his idealism simply cannot be grafted onto the Carteret
material. The poem is at its best only when its praise of Carteret is
still subordinate to the story of the sage, which is itself too compelling to yield the poem's center to its ostensible subject.

It is in the "Satirical Elegy on the Death of a Late Famous
General" that we can see Swift very near his best in his command
of a heroic rhetoric at once direct and dramatic. It is certainly one of
Swift's most forceful invectives, and like all invective it is essentially without irony, depending as it does upon the speaker's clear
authority and the audience's understanding and acceptance of that
authority. But the wit of this poem is to withhold until the proper
moment Swift's revelation of his own connection to the material of
his poem, whose tonal movement is designed to make that self-
disclosure as striking as possible.

The first of the poem's two major sections opens as if in the midst
of a conversational situation: "His Grace! impossible! what
dead!/Of old age too, and in his bed!/And could that Mighty
Warrior fall?/And so inglorious, after all!" It isn't until this fourth
line that the poem's attitude is established, and when it is, the
judgmental certainty—"And so inglorious"—does not yet undo the
pretense of social chat on the part of a speaker essentially unin-
volved in the event, though responsive to it as a public fact of some
significance: "And could he be indeed so old/As by the newspapers
we're told?" In presenting his attack on Marlborough as the speech
of an essentially disengaged conversationalist, Swift is able to un-
leash considerable invective force in what appears to be a coolly
judgmental form:

> Threescore, I think, is pretty high;
> 'Twas time in conscience he should die.
> This world he cumber'd long enough;
> He burnt his candle to the snuff;
> And that's the reason, some folks think,
> He left behind *so great* a s——*k*.
>
> (1:296)

"I think," "pretty high," "long enough," "some folks think"—the reticence here is as obvious as the extravagance it sanctions: the celebration of Marlborough's death, the mutilation of his memory. It seems to me, however, that the poem is suddenly at an uneasy moment. By the time we have got through the last line above, the poem's pretenses are perfectly clear *as pretenses* and no longer useful to sustain an attack of this virulence. A firm moral basis for the poem's negative intensity must now be asserted, and, wonderfully, this is precisely what Swift provides:

> Behold his funeral appears,
> Nor widow's sighs, nor orphan's tear,
> Wont at such times each heart to pierce,
> Attend the progress of his herse.
> But what of that, his friends may say,
> He had those honours in his day.
> True to his profit and his pride,
> He made them weep before he dy'd.
>
> (1:296)

With these lines the poem's compositional structure is abruptly altered: it is no longer the feigned report of a conversation between disengaged, if harsh, observers. Suddenly asked to observe the Duke's funeral, the reader is in a situation entirely inconsistent with his initial position as the overhearer of the pretended conversation of the first sixteen lines: instead, he is now directly addressed by Swift himself, who imposes upon him this imagined scene of the Duke's funeral, ungraced either with widow's sighs or orphan's tears—"he made them weep before he dy'd."

With its desecration of Marlborough's life—and death—now fully authorized, so to say, the poem's rhetorical play is complete. The emphatic pause between its first and second sections provides the timing for the poised introduction of a new voice:

> Come hither, all ye empty things,
> Ye bubbles rais'd by breath of Kings;
> Who float upon the tide of state,
> Come hither, and behold your fate.
> Let pride be taught by this rebuke,
> How very mean a thing's a Duke;
> From all his ill-got honours flung,
> Turn'd to that dirt from whence he sprung.
>
> (1:296–97)

This is the unambiguous, authoritative, and commanding voice of angry and contemptuous virtue. It is also obviously the voice of the poet, Swift, boldly disclosing himself in all his authority, dismissing, as if with a gesture of contempt, the uneasiness that mere politeness might have felt in the brutality of the denunciation so far uttered. So it is that the poem's most extreme sentiments are reserved finally for the voice of virtue itself, pointing, in the poem's last line, to that "dirt from which he sprung" as final evidence for the lesson: "How very mean a thing's a Duke."

Now, the movement of this grand invective is plainly dramatic. That is, Swift develops his poem so as to present his most intense denunciation of Marlborough as simultaneous with his plainest declaration of his own presence, his own responsibility for that denunciation. The result is a complex tonal amalgam of didactic and heroic assertion, whose plain force is entirely sufficient to overcome the reticences of mere sociability. What has happened is that the vituperations of the "satirical elegy"—a composition at least as repugnant to any decorum as the "ridiculous tragedy" Swift declared life itself to be—have themselves disclosed a truer form of heroism than they have undone: they have disclosed the heroism of the voice of virtue, declaring itself and justifying its extravagances. Here the heroic *is* the didactic, and the moralist and the hero are Swift himself.

3

Strangely, in the very fierceness of its invective, the "Satirical Elegy" is joyous. The poem's "sudden glory" has, however, richer sources than its mere triumph over Marlborough, which is, as I've tried to show, only the final movement of a rhetorical curve shaped to reveal the author in his direct connection with his poem. The hauteur and assertiveness of the second section show the opening conversational gestures to be the pretense necessary to the poem's final dismissal of all pretense in its grand revelation of Swift's own presence both as the composer of his poem and the authority for its ethical lesson. Swift, indeed, does reveal himself here as a lord of infamy and praise, and, in a very real sense, the meaning of the poem and the pleasure it provides are just exactly that heroic self-disclosure. If I am right to say that the poem's final declarative force is joyous, then certainly that is an effect of the freedom Swift displays and communicates in revealing his lesson, his authority, and his passion.

The pleasure of participating in Swift's joyous self-assertion seems central also to the reader's experience of the grander and subtler "Verses on the Death of Dr. Swift." This, perhaps Swift's best-known poem, enacts at its imaginative center a remarkable transformation of a guarded into a direct rhetoric, a potentially introspective into a public and even ceremonial situation. Simply to point to the features of the poem's initial movement is to describe a rhetorical structure of devious complexity: Swift imagines the reception among his friends of the news of his death; these friends he describes as moved by that brand of egoism defined by La Rochefoucauld in his maxim—"In the distresses of our best friends we discover something that doth not displease us." Nor does Swift deny his own share of such egoism. Yet, having imagined himself (though with wit and humor) in this doubly vulnerable position—when dead, unmourned, and when alive, as ungenerous as any—Swift proceeds to shape a triumphantly declarative self-portrait. Remarkably, this portrait is itself a composition of plainly signposted distortions and exaggerations, and these Swift attributes to a figure he describes as impartial and reliable! Yet, for all this ironizing, we still come to accept with pleasure the poem's grand concluding claims for the Dean. Why do we do so?[18]

David Vieth in a recent study has aptly described Swift's triumph in this poem as the effect of a "fantasy which . . . not only competes with 'reality' but maneuvers it aside and takes its place. . . . The concluding panegyric freezes historical events into a tableau with Swift as its focus, like the central figure in Emanuel Leutze's sentimentalized but unforgettable painting *Washington Crossing the Delaware*."[19] Vieth seems very much on target here: the grandly theatrical figure of Swift that comes forth in the concluding movement from the guarded complexity of the poem's body certainly is both sentimentalized and thrilling:

> Fair Liberty was all his Cry
> For her he stood prepar'd to die
> For her he boldly stood alone;
> For her he oft expos'd his own.

(2:566)

Precisely because this heroic image has been generated as a contrast to the poem's initially guarded and ironic sound, it possesses a dramatic appeal difficult to resist. Of course, acceptance of this grand self-assertion is facilitated by our awareness that despite its exaggerations it is not in substance untrue to Swift's career in Irish politics. But it is finally not an act of authorizing critical judgment on our part, but rather our delight in Swift's plain and audacious presence in his poem—managing its transitions, pointing to himself, enlisting us as his privileged confidants—that works to defeat the guardedness generated by the poem's initial ironies. So it is that when Swift risks so obvious a distortion as this one—

> Yet Malice never was his Aim
> He lash'd the Vice but spar'd the Name

—we do not triumph over him for our having detected the inaccuracy, itself plainly indicated at all points in this very poem. Rather, we eagerly accept what we perceive to be a *positive* distortion, something quite clearly more than a mere lie. Swift's arch disavowal of the spirit of malice registers neither as an attempt to deceive nor as self-satire; it is instead a strangely powerful self-assertion, demanding recognition that the malicious and the ethical satirist are one and the same, and stimulating in us a joyous pleasure at the mysterious and unique conjunction of such disparate energies as those that compose the moral and imaginative character of this one only Dean-Devil-Patriot.[20]

But though the moralist-poet's often theatrical self-promotion is a recurring feature of Swift's verse, it is rare for him to achieve such concentrated and sure effect as he does in the "Satirical Elegy" and in the "Verses on the Death of Dr. Swift." Sometimes the self-promotion is only awkward, as in "A Libel on Dr. Delany." Sometimes, as in the more interesting "Panegyric on Dean Swift," a humorous but by no means trivial effort at self-scrutiny complicates the rhetoric, pushing it toward an uneasy irony. In this poem Swift imagines himself as the subject of the wrongheaded praise of one who, his fortune still to make, uncomprehendingly contemplates the model of Swift's own career in politics and poetry. But most readers will, I think, be more struck with the ambiguities in Swift's account of his involvement in both satire and politics than with his claim that the "panegyric" upon him is wrongheaded or misdirected. Setting these sections of the poem against each other can illustrate its tonal uncertainties:

> Could all we little Folks that wait,
> And dance Attendance on the *Great*,
> Obtain such Privilege as you,
> To rail, and go unpunish'd too;
> To treat our *Betters* like our *Slaves*,

And all Mankind as *Fools*, or *Knaves*;
The Pleasure of so large a Grant
Would much compensate all we want.
Mitres, and *Glebes* could scarce do more
To *scratch* our endless *Itch* of Pow'r.
. . . .
No Wonder you should think it *little*
To *lick a Rascal Statesman's Spittle*,
Who have, to shew your great Devotion,
Oft' swallow'd down a stronger Potion,
A Composition more absurd,
Bob's Spittle mix'd with *Harry's* T——.
. . . .
Be this however your Relief,
Whene'er your Pride recals your Grief,
That all the Loss your Purse sustain'd
By that rebuff your *Virtue* gain'd.
For must you not have often *ly'd*,
And griev'd your *righteous Soul* beside,
Th' *Almighty's Orders* to *perform*,
Not to *direct* a *Plague*, or *Storm*,
But 'gainst the Dictates of your Mind,
To *bless*, as now you *curse* Mankind?

(2:493, 495, 496)

The ambiguities of tone and attitude here inhibit the development of either an ironic or a positive rhetoric. Neither grand nor ironic, the sound of the verse is merely coy, as if its inner impulses toward self-assertion and self-scrutiny were interfering with each other out of mutual embarrassment.[21] I want to conclude this essay, then, by exploring a range of expression Swift is capable of when, neither denying the impulse toward self-scrutiny nor realizing it in a sub-verting irony, he is able simultaneously to contemplate and to cele-brate his moral and imaginative commitments, understanding their value and their costs. This effort is largely the subject and sub-stance of the serious poems to Stella, and the powerfully lyric cast of these poems is an effect both of their celebration of Stella's own costly heroisms and of Swift's scrutiny of the price, both to Stella and to himself, of their extravagant commitments to virtue and to each other.

Among his poems to Esther Johnson are the grandest of Swift's verses, as if in writing to and for her, he discovered the only audi-ence from whom he would not withdraw in irony, as he withdraws from his readers in the great prose satires. Certainly one way to define Swift's irony is as an effect of his withdrawal from an audience whom he first approaches in the direct address suitable to a didactic mission. The ironic game of self-concealment and then aggressive self-disclosure that follows—as in *A Modest Proposal*—is a sign that the audience has been perceived to be unteachable, incapable of understanding or responding to the grand clarities of ethical discourse as conducted among rational beings. I do not think that Swift ever lost the sense of ethical discourse as a kind of majestic clarity; this is why in certain rare circumstances his didactic manner is so much a celebrative one, resonant with heroic overtones, as, for example, in the grand simplicity and directness of his address in the *Drapier's Letters*. Here, committed to the fiction or the pretense or the hope that his readership stands on the same ethical and cognitive ground as the writer, he can so address his audience as if to instruct them were only to remind and almost to celebrate. Hence, the grand directness of a language apparently without play: "Brethren, Friends, Countrymen and Fellow Subjects." "I will therefore first tell you the plain Story of the Fact." "But a Word to the Wise is enough." "When once the Kingdom is reduced to such a Condition, I will tell you what must be the End." "There my Friends, stand to it One and All, refuse this Filthy Trash." The conjunction here of the heroic and the didactic is obvious. It speaks to us of the most romantic of Swift's imaginings—that to be good is also to be grand.

It is both the celebration and the exploration of that imagining to which the best of the poems to Stella are devoted. In "To Stella, visiting me in my Sickness," Swift's celebration of his friend develops from his initial didactic intention to deliver a lesson on honor. Quite interestingly, despite its title and despite the concluding rhetorical situation (in which Swift represents himself to be speaking intimately and directly to Stella), the poem proceeds for two-thirds of its more than 120 lines as a generally directed, public declamation, the intention of which is to define for a comprehending audience, and then to illustrate, by Stella's example, the meaning of honor. In league with this audience of good readers, Swift discloses his contempt for a "stupid vicious Age" (line 8), for which, as he supposes, any use of the word "honor" is an occasion merely for the distortions and "wranglings" of a debased sophistication. When Stella enters the poem, it is as the "fair Example" from which the intended lesson on honor can be grandly derived; she is presented as an example of a severe and selfless certainty and thus identified with Socrates, Cato, and Brutus—figures whose stoic severity determines the poem's tone at this point as it rises toward intense denunciation:

> Drive all Objections from your Mind,
> Else you relapse to Human Kind:
> Ambition, Avarice, and Lust,
> And factious Rage, and Breach of Trust,
> And Flatt'ry tipt with nauseous Fleer,
> And guilty Shame, and servile Fear,
> Envy, and Cruelty, and Pride,
> Will in your tainted Heart preside.
>
> (2:724–25)

But though the invective force here is obvious, the feeling behind it is uncertainly charged and uncertainly focused. We are not far from the horrified perceptions of the fourth voyage and the corrosive ironies they generate. Invective anger begins here to curdle into irony upon Swift's assertion that the alternative to honorable thought or action is a "relapse," not into vice but to *humankind*. And with this turn in the poem, it is no wonder that the relationship between speaker and audience becomes indistinct. No longer the reader or listener who had been, since the poem began, sharing the speaker's indignation against and understanding of "a stupid, vicious Age," the addressee is now implicated in its sins, because simply, like all human hearts, his is "tainted" (line 50). We are on the edge here of insights, feelings, and ironies that are in no sense compatible with a rhetoric of celebration and praise. These are the ironies and insights of a satire intending not to reform but to expose the irredeemability of the human situation.

And yet it is precisely a rhetoric of celebration and praise that triumphantly rises from this uncertain moment as the poem refocuses its attention smartly and suddenly upon Stella:

> Heroes and Heroins of old,
> By Honour only were enroll'd
> Among their Brethren of the Skies,
> To which (though late) shall *Stella* rise.
> Ten thousand Oaths upon Record,
> Are not so sacred as her Word:
> The World shall in its Atoms end,
> E'er *Stella* can deceive a Friend.
> By Honour seated in her Breast,
> She still determines what is best:
> What Indignation in her Mind

> Against Enslavers of Mankind!
> Base Kings and Ministers of State,
> Eternal Objects of her Hate.
>
> (2:725)

Here the force of the invective anger that had been yielding to irony
is retained, but its purpose is transformed or, more accurately,
newly discovered. Explicitly identifying Stella with "Heroes and
Heroines of old," Swift converts the angry energy of the preceding
section into heroically colored celebration. We feel this in the powerfully assertive effect of the third, fourth, and fifth couplets above,
two of which are hyperbolic in their particulars ("Ten thousand
Oaths . . . The World shall in its Atoms end") at the same time as
the third generalizes its praise from these extravagances, confident
in Stella's determination of "what is best." In the two concluding
couplets of this section the turn from irony toward celebration is
made complete. The first is an open, plain expression of wonder—

> What Indignation in her Mind
> Against Enslavers of Mankind!
>
> (2:725)

—honoring Stella for the cognitive clarity that defines, and the
righteous *hatred* she directs against, a clearly perceived evil. And as
the final couplet rises to boldly particular denunciation of those
enslavers of mankind as "Base Kings and Ministers of State," so too
does it provide a hyperbolic description of Stella's moral energy as
the capacity to keep before her the "*Eternal* Objects of her Hate"
(my italics). It seems to me that having attributed to Stella the
capacity for righteous hatred, Swift has freed himself of its bur-
dens. He is thus free to value in her a power that in himself would
be corrosive. The opportunity Stella gives him, finally, is the opportunity to celebrate in another—and scrutinize without guardedness—a moral energy that in himself tends to generate the ironies
that undo a rhetoric of heroic praise *or blame*. And because the
Stella of these lines is represented as an indignant, an angry figure,
Swift's movement into heroic praise involves no softening of feelings that more usually draw from him a meaner language. Because
of Stella's presence in the poem, an occasion for irony or meanness
has become available to a grander eloquence, the rhetoric of wonder.[22]

This union of didactic and heroic tonalities is not the poem's
rhetorical end-point. The celebrative sound is sustained in the

poem's final movement but in a very different register. For the poem's final movement is rendered as an account of the intimacies shared by two difficult people in a difficult situation. Swift portrays Stella's selfless care for him in his sickness—ostensibly the least heroic of situations—and in doing so profoundly enhances his earlier portrayal of her as a pattern of stoic severity. There is certainly some affectionate joking in his portrait of her ministrations—

> I see her taste each nauseous Draught,
> And so obligingly am caught:
> I bless the Hand from which they came,
> Nor dare distort my Face for Shame.
>
> (2:726)

—but the joking never threatens to undermine the tribute here intended. Indeed, the joking enhances the tribute by its evocation of intimacies too profound to be shared. Moreover, Stella, earlier portrayed as the very pattern of stoic severity, subordinating personality to character, is now seen as a figure of effective blessedness, whose personality is fully revealed in the very restraints imposed by character—

> Then Stella ran to my Relief
> With chearful Face and inward Grief
>
> (2:726)

—but revealed only to the single sensibility which has known the person behind the pattern. Swift, moved toward a profoundly lyric expressiveness now, discovers the final and full meaning of his grand lesson on honor in the human costs of such virtue as Stella possesses.

> Best Pattern of true Friends, beware;
> You pay too dearly for your Care;
> If, while your Tenderness secures
> My Life, it must endanger yours.
> For such a Fool was never found,
> Who pull'd a Palace to the Ground,
> Only to have the Ruins made
> Materials for an House decay'd.
>
> (2:727)

Here, finally, Swift speaks directly to Stella, imagining her as the recipient rather than the teacher of the lesson, as had been her role

throughout the poem as its pattern of honor. Indeed, Swift uses
that word as he directly addresses her in his thoughts—"Best Pattern of true Friends, beware"—but he can so address her because
the other term that he applies to her in this small, lyric homily, the
term *fool*, declares his poignant awareness of her real selfhood, just
as the entire passage declares his recognition of the cost to that self
of its virtue: "You pay too dearly for your Care." In full coordina-
tion with the poem's didactic material, these last lines complete the
dramatic curve of personal feeling from invective anger to wonder
to elegiac celebration, making the lesson in honor, which had celebrated Stella as pattern, now into a source of lyrical awareness,
yielding the recognition of Stella as a person, vulnerable to her
virtues.[23] The vehicle of this last movement is an almost Aesopian
parable, simple in its didactic character: "For such a Fool was never
found, / Who pull'd a Palace to the Ground." Certainly the didactic
character of this homily is subordinate to the deeply lyrical feeling
that informs the passage: indeed, it helps to create that feeling, as if
Swift were invoking the public manner of the homily the more
fully to demonstrate for his friend how intensely private this emotional moment is. More, the moment is made to carry a charge of
self-revelation, also through the homiletic image Swift applies to
himself: "an House decay'd." The poem completes its emotive
curve in this self-revelation with its elegiac tonalities, fully expressive of the human actuality of the "pattern" of virtue it has celebrated and defined, and of the intensities in the relationship
between two people whose heroic *and* human experience of suffering and sacrifice becomes the poem's final subject, the vehicle for its
fullest demonstration of the meaning of honor, its didactic subject.
As pattern yields to person, honor is shown to be the costly virtue
whose effects are finally known only in suffering and sacrifice.
Swift's scrutiny of his positives has been complete, convincing, and
invulnerable to irony.

The finest, and the last, of Swift's celebrations of Stella marks
the fullest integration he achieves of scrutiny and celebration, of
lyric and didactic expression. "Stella's Birthday, March 13,
1726/7" is a dramatic poem, entirely conceived as a mimesis of an
inner action, and as such dominated throughout by its charge of
lyric feeling. To that feeling the didactic movement is engrafted,
quite unlike the previous poem, which traces its emotive curve
through several stages of public address toward a moment of private self-revelation. Now the private focus and intensity are immediately revealed in the opening lines, which set a scene the
previous poem had worked toward at its conclusion:

> This day, whate'er the Fates decree,
> Shall still be kept with Joy by me:
> This Day then, let us not be told,
> That you are sick, and I grown old
> Nor think on our approaching Ills,
> And talk of Spectacles and Pills;
> To morrow will be Time enough
> To hear such mortifying Stuff.
>
> (2:763)

Explication is hardly necessary here to point out how precisely and plainly the unadorned language defines the intimate privacy of this occasion and also its solemnity. I say solemnity because, although Swift speaks of his intention to mark the occasion with joy, and despite the witty offhandedness of the detail, there is an almost ceremonial decorum to the moment. Stella's day is a day he "keeps," and in just a few lines he will show that "keeping" this day means, among other things, delivering some "serious Lines." Moreover, keeping this day with joy requires that he arrange its circumstances: he will exclude for the proper observance of the occasion all that "the Fates decree"; "let us not be told/That you are sick, and I grown old" is a poignant yet willful self-assertion; a necessary condition for the didactic meditation on virtue that is to compose the poem's body and be the celebrative commemoration of Stella's life. Yet, if we look ahead to the poem's conclusion, we can see that the poise of this first movement will give way to more complex and difficult feelings:[24]

> O then, whatever Heav'n intends,
> Take Pity on your pitying Friends;
> Nor let your Ills affect your Mind,
> To fancy they can be unkind.
> Me, surely me, you ought to spare,
> Who gladly would your Suff-rings share;
> Or give my Scrap of Life to you,
> And think it far beneath you Due;
> You, to whose Care so oft I owe,
> That I'm alive to tell you so.
>
> (2:766)

The plaintive urgency of these final lines, in language as unadorned as the poem's opening, clearly reveals the difficulty of maintaining the ceremonial poise of that opening, and what had begun in poise ends in pleading. In the distinctly different tonal coloring of these framing sections of the poem we can sense the direction of the poem's movement, the inner emotional action it imitates.

The final lines, perhaps the most personal Swift ever wrote, are addressed to a difficult woman. Swift joins their personal urgency—"Me, surely me, you ought to spare"—to an elegiac acknowledgment of that woman's lifelong virtue—"You to whose Care so oft I owe,/That I'm alive to tell you so." The extravagant plea these lines make is that Stella demonstrate, now when such a test is most difficult, that her life of virtue is not vitiated by the strain of her final crisis. As such it is a plea that the authenticity of her life, and of the poetry that has regularly celebrated it, be proved out. The personal urgency of the poem's conclusion expresses not only a poignant and realistic description of Stella's impatience now toward the beneficiary of her former selflessness but also, I think, Swift's full awareness that the authenticity of his celebration of her, and of Virtue, is at the stake. This poem is as much a test of what he has written about Stella as it is of her, and it is no surprise that in its final lines it should record his sense that his life is an adjunct of hers. It is the value of his own life that he pleads for here.

Of the results of that plea we can know nothing. The tact in this refusal to conclude and to assert is itself a moving acknowledgment of Stella's plain actuality, indeed of her physical being, now in its last painful illness. This final scene of Swift's final poem for Stella is brutally realistic in its presentation of a strained experience charged with retrospective significance, demanding of the sufferer that she prove out in her suffering the force of that virtue Swift had attributed to her throughout her life, the life that has provided the measure of the value of Swift's own. And yet the poem is in no significant sense inconclusive. This intensely elegiac final movement, for all its contrast with the more poised and assertive opening, still develops naturally from the poem's body, that is, from those "serious Lines" which Swift delivers as his birthday gift, the sign of the joy with which he means to keep this day.

Those earlier lines are a didactic meditation of the efficacy of virtue, offered to Stella now as support for her effort to endure her present crisis, and their argument, simply, is that a life of Virtue should "leave behind/Some lasting pleasure in the Mind,/Which by Remembrance will assuage,/Grief, Sickness, Poverty, and Age." Swift announces this as a wisdom in keeping with his station: "From not the gravest of Divines/Accept for once some serious Lines?" (2:13–14). We should notice how he invokes his station here as against Stella's more intimate knowledge of his personality, his identity as "not the gravest of Divines," and perhaps as the most corrosive of ironists. The delivery of the doctrine that is to follow, then, is a special effort to realize for Stella the force of his character as against the more private energies of a personality that pulls against it. To be adequate to Stella now means to realize the positive identity he most fully experiences as her poet.

What, then, is the quality of the didactic movement that follows? Its substance, as I have said, is that Virtue's force will sustain in the mind the moral identity now being challenged by grief, sickness, poverty, old age.

> Were future Happiness and Pain,
> A mere Contrivance of the Brain,
> As Atheists argue, to entice,
> And fit their Proselytes for Vice;
> (The only Comfort they propose,
> To have Companions in their Woes.)
> Grant this the Case, yet sure 'tis hard,
> That Virtue, stil'd its own Reward,
> And by all Sages understood
> To be the chief of human Good,
> Should acting, die, nor leave behind
> Some lasting Pleasure in the Mind,
> Which by Remembrance will assuage,
> Grief, Sickness, Poverty, and Age;
> And strongly shoot a radiant Dart,
> To shine through Life's declining Part.
>
> (2:764)

What we must not miss here is the blend of assertion and tentativeness, the organization of the lesson as a concession first to the other party, imagined here as "Atheists," and then as a response to them. But this response is muted in its strictly argumentative character. That is, it arises not from personal certainty but from personal need. Grant the atheists their rejection of future happiness and pain, "yet sure 'tis hard, / That Virtue, stil'd its own Reward . . . Should acting, die." The word "stil'd"—i.e., "written" and hence "said to be"—is peculiarly active here; it contributes to the passage's argumentative tentativeness and seems a choice appropriate to the special impetus of the thought, the feeling that the other alternative—Virtue as ineffective—were "hard" (not, we should note, "untrue").

Swift had earlier introduced these "serious lines" as "A better and more pleasing Thought" (line 10). This better thought, however, he develops with a full sense of its willed character, its responsiveness to a compelling need, not its doctrinal certainty. It is an effect of that rational will that seeks to be adequate to the plain experience of such moral beauty as Stella's life has demonstrated. The didactic body of this poem, in fact, develops its "argument" in accord with this prompting of the rational will, and the lyric intensity toward which the poem builds is in great part created by our sense that the didactic argument is wholly shaped and tested by the subjective knowledge of Stella's worth that Swift brings to the occasion. His lesson, as lesson, then, seeks to activate Stella's own moral being to fit itself to what Swift imagines, or hopes, are similar inner promptings. "Say, Stella, feel you no Content,/Reflecting on a Life well spent?" (2:35–36).

Organizing the poem's didactic matter in this way opens an opportunity for celebration, and the next movement is emphatically celebrative, a rehearsal of Stella's conduct (2:37–50). But this celebrative movement is, after all, introduced by the question just put to Stella, the answer to which we never do hear. And it leads to the next step in the meditation, in which the personal urgency and lyric intensity become unmistakable:

> Must these like empty Shadows pass,
> Or Forms reflected from a Glass?
> Or mere Chimaera's in the Mind,
> That fly and leave no Marks behind?
> Does not the Body thrive and grow
> By Food of twenty Years ago?
> And, had it not been still supply'd
> It must be a thousand Times have dy'd.
> Then, who with Reason can maintain,
> That no Effects of Food remain?
> And, is not Virtue in Mankind
> The Nutriment that feeds the Mind?
> Upheld by each good Action past,
> And still continued by the last:
> Then, who with Reason can pretend,
> That all Effects of Virtue end?
>
> (2:765)

Note again the unadorned language in which this poem is delivered. In this passage the plainest homiletic similes are the vehicle of its didactic movement: shadows, forms reflected in a glass, the body and its food of twenty years ago. These may be said to be the rhetorical adornment of the lesson. But the poetry here is not in such adornment; it is to be found and felt in the form of the statements, all of which are presented as questions. Rhetorically an argument is presented and illustrated; poetically that argument is vindicated. For the poetic meaning of the passage is not that the argument is true, but that the rational will requires that the argument be made, and be insisted upon, even as its certainty is left in doubt, doubt acknowledged by the very questions in the form of which the argument is advanced. Poetically, however, the passage imitates the intensifying force of the speaker's need for this doctrine, and this we can feel only in the rhythms and repetitions of the questions within which it is shaped. The reader feels these insistent rhythms built into the progress from the "medial" summary ("Then, who with Reason can maintain . . .") toward the conclusion ("Then, who with Reason can pretend . . ."), the shift from "maintain" to "pretend" reflecting the intensification of Swift's inner commitment to a doctrine whose truth he feels as rational need, not rational certainty.[25]

This delicate blend of assertion and skepticism, of belief and doubt, is sufficiently forceful to sustain the lesson's application as the poem returns its attention to the difficult woman whose pain and impatience are its final subject. We hear this in the address of the next section—"Believe me, Stella"—and the next—"then, whatever Heav'n intends." But by this time we have come to understand this assertiveness as an expression of need and love, of the fully charged rational will, which is all this poem will vindicate. Furthermore, we can recognize this strained style of assertion as entirely appropriate to the emotional character of the poem's conclusion—that is, its character as Swift's plea to Stella that she find her substantial identity and acknowledge his in his words to her, in his need for her. If we feel in this poem the lyric intensity I have claimed for it, we feel it in its union of didactic content and personal urgency, which come together in a poetic mimesis of the inner movement of the rational will seeking to realize itself, in the most difficult of circumstances, with reference to its best beliefs. In expressing fully the forces against which that will must strive, and the resources it possesses, the poem provides Swift the opportunity for self-revelation and self-scrutiny that make his embrace of his own positives a lyric occasion.

In Swift's poems for his friend we see the opportunities for self-disclosure inherent in a rhetoric without irony, the opportunities for self-scrutiny inherent in the fulfillment of a public charge. I have sought to account for the intensely moving success Swift

achieves in this respect when we consider his poems to Stella over
against the manner of his satire. There the didactic stance is the
platform for attack, the occasion for irony, for the feigned commitment to beliefs and to an audience from which he subsequently
withdraws into the subversive experience of a personality whose
energies cannot be contained by the commitment to culture presup-
posed in the purposes of a moralist. But in Swift's poems to Stella
he succeeds in realizing those purposes, and in a manner fully
responsive, though not vulnerable to, the impulses of his anarchic
energy. The characteristic movement of these poems is from public
toward intimate address, tracing a curve of feeling expressive of the
inner experience of the moralist as he strives to understand and to
value his positive commitments. This curve of feeling creates the
lyric charge of the poetry; it is the sign of the poetry's developing
adequacy as a mimetic representation of the inner meaning of its
initial didactic commitment. As the poetry intensifies, the reader,
responsive to its emotive line, is no longer the object of its public
address, but the overhearer of its inner melodies. He reads a lyric
poem.

What he overhears is the poignant melody that sustains and ac-
companies the speaker's commitment to his high positives. In that
poignancy the reader discovers a language whose oblique dignity,
whose truth to the love and to the strain Swift's best beliefs
generated within him, still survives the anarchic energy he elsewhere directed against those beliefs. The oblique dignity of this
language mirrors the manner in which the great Augustans experienced their best beliefs: with reverence and with doubt. It is striking that, in a few places in his poetry, Swift, whose ironic and
subversive imagination sets him apart from the decorums of Augustan culture, should have discovered a rhetoric through which he
rejoins that culture. It is more striking that in doing so he displays
imaginative inclinations that can justly be described as romantic
and heroic, so that even in discovering an accord between his own
being and the grand positives of his age, he demonstrates how
strenuous an effort of mind and feeling those positives required for
their authentic realization. Dr. Johnson, the most responsible
spokesman for Augustan culture, was, of course, notoriously unsympathetic to Swift and unsure about him. Was not Swift guilty,
after all, of some unsettlingly compelling indecorum of mind and
temperament—producing as he did a language especially suitable
for the "safe and easy conveyance of meaning" at the same time as
by some peculiar "depravity of intellect he took delight in revolving

ideas, from which almost every other mind shrinks with disgust. . .?[26] Yet it was Dr. Johnson who, near the end of his life, composed a prayer that, in its own adequacy to both reverence and doubt, approaches more closely than any other piece I know the thought and feeling of Swift's celebrations of Stella. ". . . [G]ive me Grace always to remember," Johnson wrote, "that thy thoughts are not my thoughts, nor thy ways my ways. And while it shall please thee to continue me in this world where much is to be done and little is to be known, teach me by thy Holy Spirit to withdraw my mind from unprofitable and dangerous enquiries, from difficulties vainly curious, and doubts impossible to be solved."[27] The Swift who wrote heroic and didactic lyrics to Esther Johnson merited, though he did not receive, the praise of the moralist who could compose—but not resolve—his own reverence and doubt into the poise of such a prayer.

Notes

1. In her recent study of Scarron, for example, Joan DeJean comments on that writer's outrageous rhyming practice in his *Virgile travesti:* "Scarron will rhyme any word with any other, even at the risk of creating a nonsense line. In the event that his trick has gone unnoticed, he then usually begins a digression to comment on it": *Scarron's "Roman Comique": A Comedy of the Novel, A Novel of Comedy* (Berne: H. Lang, 1977), p. 28. And W. K. Wimsatt, citing Longinus's advice that "those hyperboles are best, in which the very fact that they are hyperboles escapes attention," remarks: "But Swift's way was to invert all those rules enunciated by classical authorities on the heroic or sublime. His finesses came by extravagance—inventive extravagance. It takes a genius to go so joyfully wrong. This is the open door into the sunlight of laughter which Swift discovered when he moved from the murky constraints of his pentameter metaphysics on the illness of Temple into the abandoned fun of the *Lady's Ivory Table Book*": "Rhetoric and Poems: The Example of Swift," *The Author in his Work: Essays on a Problem in Criticism*, ed. Louis L. Martz and Aubrey Williams (New Haven, Conn.: Yale University Press, 1978), p. 243.

2. All citations of Swift's verse are from *The Poems of Jonathan Swift*, ed. Harold Williams, 2d. ed., 3 vols. (Oxford: Clarendon Press, 1958). Excerpts are identified in the text by volume and page number. Unless otherwise indicated, all italics (and all oddities of typography, orthography, and punctuation) follow Williams's text.

3. Nora C. Jaffe has commented nicely on the "half-peremptory, half-condescending attitude of Madam" in these lines, but seems to me very wide of the mark in saying that in this small poem a "major purpose of Swift's . . . is to parody the Renaissance 'house' poem that Pope refurbished for the Augustans": *The Poet Swift* (Hanover, N.H.: University Press of New England, 1977), pp. 137–38.

4. Irvin Ehrenpreis has pointed to the similarly riddling wit in Swift's "Baucis and Philemon": "Throughout his career as a poet, Swift liked to design his works . . . around systematic analogues between a situation immediately presented and a remote parallel drawn from mythology or nature. The bridge between the real and figurative aspects of the analogy is usually a play on words. . . . In 'Baucis and Philemon' he brings the two aspects of the analogy together as though answering a riddle—'How is a cottage like a church' ": *Swift: The Man, his Works, and the Age, vol. 2: Dr. Swift* (London: Methuen, 1967), p. 246.

5. For a discussion of the connections between the grotesque in painting and the burlesque in literature, see DeJean, *Scarron's "Roman Comique,"* p. 31.

6. Readers may wish to consult John Irwin Fischer's far more elaborate and solemn account of the Vanbrugh poems in his *On Swift's Poetry* (Gainesville: University of Florida Press, 1978), pp. 72–95.

7. *Ovid: Metamorphoses*, trans. Rolfe Humphries, (Bloomington: Indiana University Press, 1957), p. 262.

8. Ibid., p. 283.

9. See Fischer, *On Swift's Poetry*, pp. 98–99 and Brendan O'Hehir, "Meaning in Swift's 'Description of a City Shower'," *ELH* 27 (1960):194–207.

10. Most accounts of this poem in some way acknowledge the primacy of its descriptive over its didactic effect. Even Fischer, who was able to discover intense didactic and moral force in the lampoons against Vanbrugh, remarks, in response to the sheer variety of effect and *possible* meanings in the "City Shower," that "Swift's consciousness, as it is reflected in this poem, gives us no proofs at all but only paradoxes for us to wonder at" (*On the Poetry of Swift*, p. 107). Jaffe, noting that "the reader will find upon examination that the classical allusions do not provide a negative commentary on city life," considers this a sign of the poem's attitudinal incoherence (*The Poet Swift*, pp. 78–81). Ehrenpreis is least solemn and most cogent; all the ugly details, he writes, "add up not to an indictment but to a cheerful acceptance of the urban scene. It is as if Swift were declaring that he knows all these nuisances exist but he loves the structure of energy, change, potentiality, that underpin them": *Swift: The Man, his Works and the Age*, 2:386. Peter J. Schakel echoes this view in a sensible outline of the poem in his *The Poetry of Jonathan Swift: Allusion and the Development of a Poetic Style* (Madison: University of Wisconsin Press, 1978), pp. 57–60.

11. Cited by Harold Williams in his headnote to the verses in *Poems*, 2:397.

12. W. K. Wimsatt has commented on the suitability of Swift's tetrameter couplet for the representation of speedy movement. But these verses on Peterborough certainly display Swift's deployment of the three-line, triple-rhymed stanza to achieve a similar effect. See *The Author in his Work*, p. 240.

13. C. J. Rawson, for example, has argued that even such a representative of Swift's positives as the spokesman for the establishment in *The Sentiments of a Church-of-England Man*, a figure presented in "an unusually sustained portrait of virtuous moderation . . . becomes at moments which are kindled by a real Swiftian intensity . . . faintly unreal. . . . And Swift's most powerfully realized moderates are not virtuous, but calm upholders of the world's wickedness, modestly proposing a nominal Christianity, or mass murder. Behind them stands a Swift whose more absolute moral denunciations . . . turn indistinct under strange pressures of self-implication and self-concealment." Moreover, Rawson argues, "for every Whig or Tory exterminator and every modest proposer that Swift invents and exposes, there is counterbalancing evidence of a primary Swiftian feeling which is unsettlingly similar, a Kurtz-like underside . . . wishing extermination, now of 'all the brutes,' now of selected types": *Henry Fielding and the Augustan Ideal Under Stress* (London and Boston: Routledge and Kegan Paul, 1972), pp. 45, 48. And John Traugott has written that in the "high blood" of the figure of the Spider, Swift's ostensible target in the *Battle of the Books*, "runs the quickening energy of the race of radical individualists that inhabit Swift's satire from first to last. It is they who inhabit the earth. It is in his participation in their imaginations that he knows the truth of human existence and gives up the rationalist game. . . . When he adopts the pert idiom and cracked fancy of one of the figures the snob in him despises, when he is free of his gentlemanly decorum . . . and can speak in the crazy, catachrestical images and metaphor of the busy vulgarian, then Swift's mind is free and his invention at its height." See above, pp. 95–96.

14. "The fact that Swift's presence remains felt [in the ironic prose satires] despite the formal self-dissociation creates between the reader and Swift an either/or relation whose very indefiniteness entails more, not less, intimacy": C. J. Rawson, *Gulliver and the Gentle Reader* (London and Boston: Routledge and Kegan Paul, 1973), p. 52.

15. Edward Said, in a fascinating discussion, has argued that Swift's intentionally "liter-

ary" writing (i.e., his ironic satire) was less significant to him than the work he did in service to the Tory ministry. Said writes of Swift's intentionally literary art as "indicting itself in his mind for being [merely] an appendage to reality. . . . Correct writing for Swift did not merely conform to reality. It was reality . . . an event necessitated by other events. . . . The Tory policy Swift supported and wrote about was policy in the world of actuality: the Whig opposition was projection, mere scribbling. . . . After 1714, Swift occupied no place except as outsider. . . . He had become the scribbler and projector he had once impersonated and attacked": "Swift's Tory Anarchy," *Eighteenth-Century Studies* 3 (Fall 1969): 48, 54, 56–57.

16. The note of contempt that so consistently marks Swift's satire of poets and poetry seems to reflect an intense distaste not merely for bad writing but for the energies of imagination itself, the character of which Swift often represents as meanly hyperactive, aggressive, restless—rather like the behavior of the Yahoos. This is most apparent in "On Poetry: A Rapsody," in which Swift reverses Hobbes to assert that, among poets, the war of all against all is dominated not by the large and powerful, but by the insidious, the tiny, the stinging:

> So, Nat'ralists observe, a Flea
> Hath smaller Fleas that on him Prey,
> And these have smaller Fleas to bite 'em,
> And so proceed *ad infinitum:*
> Thus ev'ry Poet in his kind,
> Is bit by him that comes behind;
> Who, tho' too little to be seen,
> Can teaze, and gall, and give the Spleen. . . .
>
> (2:651)

See also "To Doctor D[elan]y, on the Libels Writ against him," especially ll. 115–58 (*Poems*, 2:504–5).

17. "The Ironic Tradition in Augustan Prose from Swift to Johnson," see below p. 319.

18. Needless to say, not everybody does respond with pleasure and approval to Swift's bold self-promotion in the "Verses on the Death," and critical discussion of the poem has been dominated by the issue of Swift's ironic intention or the lack of it. The plainest reading of the poem as an exercise in ironic self-mockery is offered by Barry Slepian in "The Ironic Intention of Swift's Verses on his own Death," *Review of English Studies*, N.S. 14 (1963): 249–56. But readers who have seen no evidence of ironic self-scrutiny in the poem, or have had no inclination to save Swift from the risks he chose to take in speaking his own praise so plainly, have not necessarily responded positively to Swift's self-promotion. Thus, Irvin Ehrenpreis convincingly rejects Slepian's reading but asserts that Swift, in "acting as his own flatterer" in the final third of the poem, "disgusts his reader" and falls short of the artistry evident in the ironic rhetoric of its earlier sections (*Literary Meaning and Augustan Values* [Charlottesville: University Press of Virginia, 1974], pp. 36–37).

19. David Vieth, "The Mystery of Personal Identity: Swift's Verses on his own Death," in *The Author in his Work: Essays on a Problem in Criticism*, ed. Louis L. Martz and Aubrey Williams (New Haven, Conn.: Yale University Press, 1978), p. 258.

20. Vieth argues that because of its hyperbolic, sentimentalized and melodramatic character, the panegyric Swift constructs for himself must be considered ironic, but that its ironies are not intended to be undercutting. Detailing the many departures from strict historical fact in Swift's self-panegyric, Vieth argues, correctly I think, that the self-praise "gains our assent so far as it fits our preconceived notions of Swift's identity. Above all, this is Swift the national hero, the 'Swift' of Yeats, Joyce, and Beckett" ("The Mystery of Personal Identity," pp. 256–57).

21. The "Panegyric" is a poem of doubtful authorship, and recent students have reaffirmed an early attribution to James Arbuckle. But if the poem is by Swift, its uncertain tonalities in these verses recall the instabilities of the more sensational of the

"scatological" poems, particularly "The Lady's Dressing Room" and "Strephon and Chloe"; there as here Swift is both extravagant and coy, as if his primary intention to shock were struggling against an embarrassed restraint, itself generated by the obsessive intensities the verses both display and mock. This tension between display and disavowal bespeaks an uneasy effort at self-scrutiny on Swift's part—as if the moralist in him were seeking an accord with that violence of mind plainly implicated in but not clearly compatible with his ethical commitments and idealisms. A recent discussion of the scatological poems emphasizing their uncertainties of tone and attitude is Peter J. Schakel's *The Poetry of Jonathan Swift*, pp. 106–19. "Swift," Schakel comments, "himself is in some degree offended by what he satirizes his characters for being offended by" (p. 119).

22. Commenting on Swift's use of hyperbole in his celebrations of Stella here and elsewhere, C. J. Rawson observes that "all impulse to parody is waived, or transcended. The fact that the potential, or the raw material, for parody is so freely preferred suggests the extent of Swift's readiness, where Stella is concerned, to drop his ironic guard" ("The Nightmares of Strephon: Nymphs of the City in the Poems of Swift, Baudelaire, Eliot," in *English Literature in the Age of Disguise*, ed. Maximillian E. Novak [Berkeley: University of California Press, 1977], p. 88).

23. John Irwin Fischer writes movingly of Swift's account of Stella's care for him: "Pained by his pain she accepts her pain and turns it to good. . . . [In her ministering to Swift] she catches entire that 'True Honour' which comprehends all virtues and which, amidst man's allotted pain and frailties, both gives and receives blessings": *On Swift's Poetry*, pp. 143–44. But Fischer dismisses the severe didacticism of the poem's first half as both "silly" and "unfortunate" (p. 142), missing, I think, its crucial importance within the poem's dramatic and lyric *development* of its didactic material. See note 25, below.

24. Fischer, *On Swift's Poetry*, p. 146.

25. Robert Uphaus has pointed to this poem as an example of Swift's capacity for a "poetry of approval": Uphaus sees the poem as a "reaffirmation of the stability of friendship and proof of the invulnerable wholeness of a virtuous life": "Swift's Poetry: The Making of Meaning," *Eighteenth-Century Studies* 5 (Summer 1972): 576, 578. It seems to me that *approval* is a term inadequate to the intensity, and *proof* and *invulnerable* are terms inadequate to the strain, with which Swift experiences and expresses his affirmations—his *need* for affirmation is more accurate—in this beautiful and trying poem. Similarly, Fisher speaks of Swift's "assertion of belief" and of his presentation to Stella of her own acts of virtue as "the evidence of her immortality and future reward": (*On Swift's Poetry*, p. 151). But Fisher is thinking of the poem too much in terms of its argumentation and not at all in terms of its dramatic and lyric movement.

26. Samuel Johnson, *The Lives of the Poets*, ed. G. B. Hill, 3 vols. (Oxford: Clarendon Press, 1905), 3:52, 62.

27. Samuel Johnson, *Diaries, Prayers, and Annals*, ed. E. L. McAdam, Jr., with Donald and Mary Hyde, Yale Edition of the Works of Samuel Johnson, 11 vols. to date (New Haven, Conn.: Yale University Press, 1958–), 1:383–84 (12 August 1784).

7

Swift and the Reanimation of Cliché

PAT ROGERS

1

That it is possible to distinguish between cliché and catchphrase is shown by the fact that the late Eric Partridge was able to compile a dictionary of each. But in ordinary speech we do not generally make very fine distinctions in this area, and even that hallowed form of cliché that is called a proverb belongs to the same scarcely differentiated corner of our lexicon. It is with these various modes of "stale" language, as utilized by Swift, that I shall be concerned here. Most readers know that Swift was fond of language games, that he played Joycean tricks with the form and sound of words (in his "Anglo-Latine," for instance, or in his punning contests with his friend Sheridan)—in short, that he was adept in the literary manipulation of individual units of the language—*mot* rather than *parole*.[1] The aspect of Swift's use of language considered here—the exploitation of stock expressions for comic or disconcerting effect—is different, however.

There is, so far as I know, no term in ancient or modern rhetoric that exactly covers this device. It could be called the restoration, or the revival, of cliché, or cant, or dead metaphor. Christopher Ricks has described the essential property of cliché as residing in the fact that it is "dead but will not lie down." Yet such vitalization of moribund colloquial formulae is a widely active technique in literature. To confine ourselves to English alone, we could think of hundreds of examples in writers as varied in style and outlook as Shakespeare, Sterne, and Byron. In the case of Swift, a broadly comic use of the technique predominates, but we could find in

Kipling the sonorous and stately reapplication of timeworn phrases.

In Swift, the deliberate manipulation of cliché serves a number of purposes. Sometimes, most often in his poetry, he employs the device to mimic social chat: the point is not just to reproduce speech habits but to freeze conventional attitudes along with them. Jargon can itself characterize a speaker or a point of view. At other times Swift appears mockingly to accept the truth of the world's conventional wisdom: by adopting the formulae of polite society, he subjects the familiar maxims by which we live to oblique scrutiny. A more specialized variant is the planting of a familiar tag in an unexpected context.

It is important to grasp the distinction between this sort of catchphrase and an allusion. With a literary reference we are meant to identify a single source and hold on to that. When Byron writes in *Don Juan* (13. 85)

> There was the Duke of Dash, who was a—duke,
> 'Aye, every inch a' duke . . .

the inverted commas nudge us towards a recognition of the borrowing from *King Lear*. Swift does use this kind of allusion, but his more characteristic technique involves the mere retrieval of a commonplace expression. If you know the origin of such a phrase, then you are supposed to forget it. The essence of the game is to appeal to a certain impersonal familiarity. Proverbs are a good example: sometimes they have specific literary sources, which someone like Swift would know: but he is interested in them mainly on account of their apparent agentless, timeless status.[2]

This can be illustrated from one of Swift's poems in which his fondness for reanimating cliché is most evident. The passage occurs in his poem on the South Sea episode entitled *The Bubble* (1720):

> Then, like the Dogs of *Nile* be wise,
> Who taught by Instinct how to shun
> The Crocodile that lurking lyes,
> Run as they drink and drink and run.
> (Ll. 177–80, *Poems*, 1:257)

There is, arguably, a literary allusion here, though it is not signalized in Williams's edition. The stanza paraphrases Phaedrus, the Latin fabulist: "Canes currentes bibere in Nilo flumine, / A crocodilis ne rapiantur, traditum est" (*Fables*, 1. 25. 3–4). The story

occurs in Pliny's *Natural History* (8:149), which is a source closer to
Swift's reading habits. But a proverb evolved, first in Latin as *"ut
canis e nilo,"* found in the *Adages* of Erasmus, and subsequently in
English. The *Oxford Dictionary of English Proverbs* provides an entry
for the phrase "Like a dog at the Nile."[3] Swift's manipulation of the
idea makes it perfectly clear that he knew the classical
"justification" for the cant expression. But he appeals to the extended proverb as a source of common sense and as a prudential
maxim. His obsession with "dog" proverbs (to which I shall return)
leads him to reenergize the saying with an anecdotal support, not to
underpin a literary allusion with proverbial connotations.

Richard Usborne has written of P. G. Wodehouse's *Sunset at
Blandings* in these terms:

> Wodehouse's trained mind was a fat thesaurus of quotations, jargons
> and images: clichés in their proper contexts but, misapplied and mis-
> mated by him, jewels.

It partly depends, of course, on what you consider "proper contexts" to be, and Swift is particularly skilled in his way of inserting
what seems to be an appropriate form of words, which subsequently proves to be maladroit, subversive, or ridiculous. He is one
of the first writers to have perceived the resonance in high literature
of these routine gestures of ordinary speech. In the nineteenth-
century novel, a form of licensed cliché became common, often
used in chapter titles for the purpose of authorial commentary or
ironic suggestion behind the back of the narrative. There are examples in Charlotte Brontë's *Shirley*, where chapter headings such as
"Further Communications on Business," "The West Wind Blows"
and—most notably—"Case of Domestic Persecution—Remarkable
Instance of Pious Perseverance in the Discharge of Religious
Duties" signal to us a meaning dependent on their journalese or
commonplace quality. Similarly in *Vanity Fair* there are chapters
called "Private and Confidential," "Full of Business and Pleasure,"
and (the last of all) "Which contains Births, Marriages and Deaths."
Thackeray had less need than Brontë for a secret method of
semaphoring to the reader, but even so there are things the cum-
brous stock phrases tell us that the main narrative makes less than
explicit.

The characteristic feature of Swift's use of cliché is that he makes
the shopsoiled expression "fit" in its context while allowing its
subversive charge to set off a little local explosion. The very familiarity of a phrase lures us into accepting it at its accustomed face

value, but then some buried meaning will suddenly assert itself. An example of the kind of phrase Swift finds convenient to his purposes is "trial and error." As we normally pronounce those words, *error* means not much more than vaguely unsuccessful attempts, nonhits rather than bad misses. If we introduced it into discourse just after witnessing some hopelessly botched experiments by an incompetent chemist, say—or a sorcerer's apprentice—then the sense of *error* as disastrous failure would be much more readily present to our minds. Swift has a way of making these disruptive overtones reemerge from a familiar set of words.

2

As is well known, Swift spent many years assembling his elaborate anthology of *idées reçues*, which was eventually published as *Polite Conversation* in 1738, or more strictly under this fuller title: *A Complete Collection of Genteel and Ingenious Conversation, According to the Most Polite Mode and Method now used at Court, and in the Best Companies of England*. There is a hint of the conduct book: Samuel Richardson's *Letters to and for Particular Friends, Directing the Requisite Style and Forms to be Observed in Writing Familiar Letters* were to enter the world only three years later. The work is set out "in three Dialogues," a mode appropriate to pedagogy and self-improvement. The author is named as "Simon Wagstaff, Esq"; the affectation of a squirearchic suffix would have amused contemporaries, who knew title-page decorum more inwardly than we do. There follows a ponderously conceited introduction that occupies a quarter of the volume. This contains many sharp hits, as in the apology for not including oaths in the text (*Works*, 4:110–11), but the "practical" examples of mindless speech outdo anything in the prolegomena of Wagstaff.

Swift's guns sweep a wide range of moral targets. A single example may help to make the point: in his introduction, Simon Wagstaff claims that his work was aimed principally

> to the Maids of Honour, of whom I have been personally acquainted with two and twenty Setts, all excelling in this noble Endowment; until some Years past, I know not how, they came to degenerate into selling of Bargains, and Free-Thinking, not, that I am against either of these Entertainments at proper Seasons, in Complyance with Company. . . . However, no Man will pretend to affirm, that either Bargains or Blasphemy, which are the principal Ornaments of Free-Thinking, are so

good a Fund of polite Discourse, as what is to be met with in my Collection. For, as to Bargains; few of them seem to be excellent in their Kind, and have not much Variety, because they all terminate in one single Point; and, to multiply them would require more Invention than People have to spare. (*Works*, 4:108)

Later on, Wagstaff tells us that he has "likewise made some few Essays, towards selling of Bargains, as well for instructing those who delight in that Accomplishment, as in Compliance with my Female Friends at Court." However, since he cannot admit this accomplishment "to pass properly for a Branch of that perfect polite Conversation, which makes the constituent Subject of my Treatise," he has not taken this very far (*Works*, 4:117–18).

Eric Partridge glosses the word *bargains* as follows (*Polite Conversation* [London: Deutsch 1963], p. 44):

To *sell* (someone) *a bargain* is to make a fool of him in conversation, to "catch" him. (Originated by Shakespeare.) In Swift, especially a coarse reply to a question or a coarse comment on a reply.

Swift tends to use the phrase even more narrowly than this would suggest. It occurs three times in his poetry, and always with the strong sense of an obscene answer to an innocent question, rather as with the modern bishop and actress. Specifically, it came to be used of a jest naming "the Parts behind" (Grose's *Dictionary of the Vulgar Tongue*, quoted in *Poems*, 2:590). So we find the conjunction of "Bargains sold, or meanings double" in *Directions for a Birth-day Song*, l. 274, and the passage in *Strephon and Chloe*, ll. 215–18:

> No Maid at Court is less asham'd,
> Howe'er for selling Bargains fam'd,
> Than she, to name her Parts behind,
> Or when a-bed, to let out Wind.
>
> (*Poems*, 2:469, 590)

The anatomy of this tasteless activity goes back to the "Digression in Praise of Digressions" in *A Tale of a Tub*:

What I mean, is that highly celebrated Talent among *Modern* Wits, of deducing Similitudes, Allusions, and Applications, very Surprizing, Agreeable, and Apposite, from the *Pudenda* of either Sex, together with *their proper Uses*.

The tale-teller agrees with Wagstaff that this branch of wit shows signs of depletions, and that a new *"Fonde"* of amusement needs to be sought.

What Swift is doing when he links selling bargains with blasphemy is fighting a contemporary linguistic trend. The separation between *libertine* = "atheist" and *libertine* = "dissolute sensualist" was growing wider, and it would seem soon as if only a pun joined these two usages. "Free-thinker," which was quite a new word (see *OED*), loaded the scales in favor of the atheistic connotations. Canutelike, Swift seeks to show how "polite" manners not merely permit but encourage a debasement of morals, and how colloquial byplay might act out larger social tendencies.

The fashionable repartee in *Polite Conversation* is always suggesting the effect on people produced by their addiction to conventional tags—that is, literally "thinking in clichés":

> *Mr Neverout.* Miss, Never fear: You have the old Proverb on your Side; naught's never in Danger.
> *Colonel Atwit.* Why, Miss, let *Tom Neverout* wait on you, and then I warrant you will be as safe as a Thief in a Mill; for you know, he that is born to be hang'd, will never be drown'd.
> *Nev.* Thank ye, Colonel, for your good Word; but faith, if ever I hang, it shall be about a fair Lady's Neck.
> *Lady Smart.* Who's there? Bid the Children be quiet, and not laugh so loud.
> *Lady Answerall.* O, Madam, let 'em laugh; they'll ne'er laugh younger.
> *Nev.* Miss, I'll tell you a Secret, if you'll promise never to tell it again.
> *Miss Notable.* No, to be sure, I'll tell it to no Body but Friends and Strangers.
> *Nev.* Why then, here's some Dirt in my Tea-Cup.
> *Miss.* Come, come, the more there's in't, the more there's on't.
> *Lady Answ.* Poh, you must eat a Peck of Dirt before you dye.
> *Col.* Ay, ay, it all goes one Way.
> *Nev.* Pray, Miss, what's o'clock?
> *Miss.* Why, you must know 'tis a Thing like a Bell; and you're a Fool that can't tell.
> *Nev.* [*to Lady* Answ.] Pray Madam do you tell me, for I let my Watch run down.
> *Lady Answ.* Why, 'tis half an Hour past Hanging Time.
>
> (*Works*, 4:147)

And so on. The demented farce has something to do with the inexhaustible flow of stale expressions; the rhyming jingles and folk wisdom; the regular rhythms that bespeak gusto and energy among the participants. But several of Swift's obsessive concerns are visible, too. I shall return to the hanging proverbs: it is worth noting that Partridge is reduced to glossing some of the turns of phrase with notes like, "a lost saying—perhaps a proverb, perhaps a catch-phrase." What mattered for Swift was that the idiom was already imprinted strongly on to the surface of conversational speech. The slight Wildean quality of the exchanges is here reinforced by the joust between Neverout and Miss on the subject of secrets: we recall, "a secret is something you tell only one person at a time," and similar *bons mots*. The participants would probably assert that the old jokes are the best, and in their "witty" fencing one with another they easily confuse reach-me-down proverbs with genuine experential wisdom. They know what their word-hoard tells them.

There has been some debate as to the precise manner in which Swift collected his set phrases. One scholar has argued that he ransacked published collections of proverbs, such as John Ray's: another has as vigorously contended he did not.[4] For present purposes this dispute about sources does not matter very much. A more suggestive fact, not previously noted, is that Swift uses sixty or more of the clichés exposed to view in *Polite Conversation* during the course of his poetic career. These expressions fall into certain marked categories, and it is possible to identify distinct emphases on particular corners of life. Swift did not simply pick up catch-phrases at random: he went, again and again, to the existing stock of language for special purposes, and drew out the same kind of cliché, relating to the same area of experience. Where *Polite Conversation* simply piles one usage on top of another, elsewhere Swift makes dexterous raids on the cliché-bank, depending on his immediate rhetorical needs. This can be seen in the *Journal to Stella* and in his letters; but it is most clearly apparent in his poetry.

3

The range of familiar expressions encountered in the poems is astounding. Here is a brief selection of the catchphrases to be found:

Neither rhyme nor reason
Cannot see the wood for the trees
No chicken
Look high and low
A cat's nine lives

All Greek to me
Don't play with edged tools
Anything for a quiet life
A rod in pickle
Stick together like glue
My bread and butter
Flesh and blood
As rude as a bear
Heart of oak
At sixes and sevens
Curtain lecture
Kiss and be friends
Your swans are all geese
Dead men's shoes

The list could be greatly extended. Some of these phrases turn up in bent or adapted forms, or as a variant ("all heathen Greek"), but most occur in their accustomed modern guise. In certain cases the idiom supplies the basic idea of an entire poem, as with *A Quiet Life, and a Good Name* (*Poems*, 1:219–21). It might be added that the puzzling *Fable of the Bitches* (1715), if it is indeed Swift's work, is organized around an *unstated* Scottish proverb, "Bourd not with Bawty, lest he bite you" (Tilley B571), yet one more of the dog expressions. Mere tabulation of such instances does not, of course, take us very far. What is important for the literary understanding of Swift is the way in which the clichés are tailored to rhetorical size, made to cohere in the linguistic universe of the poem, and made to support other aspects of its workings.

The most extreme example of Swift putting stock expressions to unwonted work occurs in a poem concerning the arrest of his friend Atterbury in 1722. This treats the alleged Jacobite plot under investigation (disingenuously) as mere fantasy, and foreshadows a passage in *Gulliver's Travels* (3:6) that satirizes plots, informers, and code-breaking. In the light of modern research it cannot be doubted that Atterbury was substantially guilty: he had been in regular contact with the Pretender for several years, and the slightly comic way in which Walpole's ministry were able to clinch the accusation does not affect that issue. Swift's poem takes its departure from the use of a small spotted dog to help break coded references in letters to the Bishop: hence its title *Upon the Horrid Plot Discovered by Harlequin the Bishop of Rochester's French Dog*. The very phrase "upon the horrid plot" mimics the accents of a righteous Hanoverian press. During the Commons proceedings that took place prior to the full hearing before the House of Lords, William Pulteney had spoken of "a horrid and detestable conspiracy."⁵ The title thus has some of the insincere ring encountered in Charlotte Brontë's use of a headline style in *Shirley*.

The text proper reveals a remarkable and sustained application to proverbial language. A whole series of stock phrases is twined together, like a necklace or a string of sausages.⁶ Most of these belong to the canine area mentioned before. In its seventy-six lines, the poem uses the actual word *dog(s)* on twenty occasions, apart from the appearance of *hound*, *cur*, *puppy*, *bitch* and the like. Several well-known expressions involving dogs turn up, including "to a help a lame dog over a stile" (l. 14: Tilley D479), which predictably does duty in *Polite Converstion* (*Works*, 4:155). A dense cluster is formed around the middle of the poem:

> You pay them well; the *Dogs* have got
> Their *Dogs-heads in a Porridge-pot*:
> And 'twas but just; for, wise Men say,
> That, *every Dog must have his Day*.
> *Dog* W[alpole] laid a Quart of *Nog* on't,
> He'd either *make a Hog or Dog on't*,
> And look't since he has got his Wish,
> As if he had *thrown down a Dish*.
> Yet, this I dare foretel you from it,
> He'll soon *return to his own Vomit*. . . .
> Why then the Proverb is not right,
> Since you can teach *dead Dogs to bite*.
>
> (Ll. 27–36, 39–40)

In these twelve lines the interlocutor named "Tory" has recourse to half-a-dozen proverbial sayings: see Tilley H491, D464, H496, D455, D448. There is more overlap with *Polite Conversation*, and some with Swift's letters. We might observe two further aspects of the technique. The first is the easy way in which Swift moves in and out of the scriptural Book of Proverbs at l. 36.⁷ The second is the suggestion of a reversed proverb at the end. This is highly characteristic. It aligns itself naturally with Swift's little essay *Maxims Controlled in Ireland* (c. 1718); or a passage in his letter to Charles Ford of 16 February 1719, wondering whether it is possible to "reverse" the proverb (perhaps "As honest as any man when the kings are out"); or, in a lighter vein, with the reference in a letter to Knightley Chetwode to a groom who "offended against the very letter of a proverb, and stacked [hay] in a rainy day, so it is now smoking like a chimney" (*Correspondence*, 2:135, 312).[8] Swift habitually tested the reality behind familiar maxims, and his letters are full of references to their reliability or otherwise as guides to conduct.[9] In his own writing he makes the context apply this probationary force.

Early on in *The Horrid Plot*, Tory refers to the use of the word *Dog* to denote informers, perjurers and the like. The dynamics of the poem are controlled so as to deflect the term from courtroom pawns towards the key figures of state, headed by the King himself and Walpole. Subliminally the poem asserts, "You have used a small dog to implicate Atterbury: but the real dirty dogs in the affair are you great ministers." Late on occurs the line, "For Statesmen never want *Dog-tricks*" (see Tilley D546): the accumulated energies of the poem make the opprobrium fall back on Atterbury's accusers. It is therefore important that, in the longer passage quoted, Swift should have used the form of words, "wise Men say." His aim is to make the language of customary speech appear to convict the Walpole administration, as it were, without the author's connivance. The charge is switched from defendant to prosecution, seemingly not by direct intervention on Swift's part, but out of the facts as filtered through proverbial (hence impartial) wisdom.

The same trick is evident in another poem of more or less the same period. *The Bubble* (*Poems*, 1:248–59) uses a wide range of poetic devices, including allegory, allusion, biblical parallel, classical myth, epic simile and much else. However, a leading part is again taken by cliché revived. This emerges plainly in the sixth stanza:

> Thus the deluded Bankrupt raves,
> Puts all upon a desp'rate Bett,
> Then plunges in the *Southern* Waves,
> Dipt over head and Ears—in Debt.
> (Ll. 21–24, *Poems*, 1:251)

This is a sort of pun, but a special sort. The stock metaphor "over head and ears" (Tilley H268) was frequently applied to debt, but here Swift literalizes the figurative expression and makes it physically, as well as morally, accurate. (For similar playful literalization of "over head and ears in love," see *Tristram Shandy*, 6:37). Almost the same thing occurs later in the poem, with the expression "Castles in the Air" (Tilley C126: see ll. 165–72). In *The Bubble* Swift turns the City of London into a rocky and perilous coastline, where the unwary investor may land up on "Garr'way Clifts" (l. 152). Behind all this lies a reanimation of the key expression of the moment: "South Sea" is divested of its protective garb—the impersonality of a financial company, which was not even seriously engaged in overseas trade, but acted as an arm of government monetary policy—and is made to reassume its geographic sense—a deep and treacherous sheet of water. Throughout *The Bubble*, Swift constantly makes the language suggest that the whole sorry affair could have been foretold: we need only have listened to homely idiom:

> The Sea is richer than the Land,
> I heard it from my Grannam's Mouth,
> Which now I clearly understand,
> For by the Sea she meant the *South*.
>
> (Ll. 97–100)

A typical Swiftian way of thinking surfaces a few stanzas later:

> *Directors;* for tis you I warn,
> By long Experience we have found
> What Planet rul'd when you were born;
> We see you never can be drown'd.
>
> (Ll. 189–92)

The planet must be Mercury, which was the presiding influence over thieves and was the most volatile of planetary bodies. Now the opposition implied is with hanging: a contrast drawn in many works familiar to Swift's readers. There is Gonzalo's remark at the start of *The Tempest:* "I have great comfort from this fellow: methinks he hath no drowning mark upon him; his complexion is perfect gallows." This notion was expressed in a wide range of proverbs: *ODEP* quotes Ned Ward, "A man on Board cannot but be thoughtful on two Destinies, *viz.* Hanging and Drowning. . . . It often put me in mind of the old Proverb, *The Sea and the Gallows refuses none." Polite Conversation* offers different versions of the same binary conception: "he that is born to be hanged . . ." has already been quoted (p. 208 above), and we also find the jingle "If he be hang'd, he'll come hopping, and if he be drown'd, he'll come dropping" (*Works*, 4:144). The underlying sense of *The Bubble* might be expressed within the terms of this idiom: "The people who caused the nation to become engulfed in the Bubble deserve to be hanged, since they alone will not be drowned in debt."

The two poems just discussed repeatedly touch on a congeries of proverbial lore that involves first, hanging and second, dogs. *Polite Conversation* draws further on this body of language: "If I had a Dog with no more Wit, I would hang him" (*Works*, 4:156). There are, incidentally, at least twenty more dog idioms in the three dialogues of this work. The covert effect of this state of linguistic affairs is to make possible a number of insinuations that are likely to be missed by the modern reader. Thus, the final line of *The Horrid Plot*,

> Your *B*[ishop]*s* are all *D—gs* indeed
>
> (*Poems*, 1:301)

following as it does so much concentrated allusion to popular speech, carries the unspoken message "The Whig bench of bishops deserve to be hanged, one and all." *The Bubble*, with its references to the dogs of Nile and the influence of Mercury, makes a similar connection.

The link-word in this connection is obviously "hangdog." *OED* supplies a primary definition: "A despicable or degraded fellow fit only to hang a dog, or to be hanged like a dog." This muddling of active and passive senses is found with a number of expressions in English connected with "hanging." In *Measure for Measure* Pompey plays on the ambiguity when he says to the executioner, "You have a hanging look" (4:2.35). Modern usage makes the transitive sense predominate in "a hanging judge," although *OED* cites no example earlier than *Vanity Fair*. Swift refers in *The Horrid Plot* to the "hanging Ears" of the key prosecution witness, the dog Harlequin. Here the literal sense is "pendulous," but it is also implied that the dog will be the death of Atterbury, or of any victim of Walpole's machine. For, whether or not one accepts E. P. Thompson's view of a police-state England in the 1720s, Swift's rhetoric often implies as much. In this connection, it is worth remarking allied turns of phrase in Swift's letters: from December 1715 we find "All of different parties are used like Jacobites and dogs," while in October 1722, very close to the time of *The Horrid Plot*, we have this: "The government, in consideration of the many favours they have shewn me, would fain have me give *St. Bride*'s to some one of their hangdogs" (*Correspondence*, 2:191, 434). And this by no means exhausts the references either to dogs or to "hanging matters," which are dotted through his letters at all periods.[10]

Scarcely any of Swift's poems on public themes, when he reemerged as a directly political poet in the early 1720s, are without their share of allusion to this buried treasure within the language.

An Excellent New Song (1720, *Poems*, 1:236–38) has a citation at line 13 of the saw from Ecclesiastes, "A living dog is better than a dead lion" (long proverbial in English: Tilley D495), and puns in its concluding stanza on several terms associated with hanging. From the same year comes *The Run upon the Bankers* (*Poems*, 1:238–41), which ends with an apocalyptic vision of the last judgment and a reference to the Book of Daniel:

> When Other Hands the Scales shall hold,
> And They in Men and Angels Sight
> Produc'd with all their Bills and Gold,
> Weigh'd in the Ballance, and found Light.
>
> (Ll. 61–64)

We have already learned that "few Bankers will to Heav'n be Mounters" (l. 58), and the principal idea is clearly of the moneyed men cast down to hell at the behest of the recording angel. However, there may well be a secondary idea of guilty men arraigned by secular justice, and possibly strung up on a gibbet. *A Quibbling Elegy on the Worshipful Judge Boat* (1721: *Poems*, 1:284–86) similarly ends with a punning reference to Boate's trade "in hanging People as a Judge" (see ll. 32–36): Cerberus also figures. *The Storm* (1722: *Poems*, 1:301–6) draws arabesques around drowning and hanging: Bishop Hort, designed for the former fate, is spared so as to be eligible for the latter.

It is, however, in one of the poems that concern the Drapier's affair that the habit grows most marked. *A Serious Poem upon William Wood* (*Poems*, 1:334–38) builds up steadily to the hope that Wood should "Dye by a *Drop*" (l. 110). Most of the wordplay centers on wood, trees, and the like, and there is one curious and rather opaque passage:

> But I'll tell you a Secret, and pray do not Blab,
> He is an old *Stump* cut out of a *Crab*,
> And *England* has put this *Crab* to hard Use,
> To Cudgel our Bones, and for Drink give us *Verjuice;*
> And therefore his *Witnesses* justly may boast
> That none are more properly Knights of the POST.
>
> (Ll. 35–40)

A modern reader may have come across elsewhere the expression "knight of the post" (Tilley K164), meaning a professional perjurer. But the reference to "verjuice" is likely to set up few echoes in our

minds. One resonance certainly present to a contemporary would
be the saying "Hang a dog on a crab-tree, and he'll never love
verjuice" (Tilley D473). *ODEP* quotes John Ray's explanation:
"Generally men and beasts shun those things, by or for which they
have smarted." Elsewhere in this poem, Swift displays his customary attitude towards stock phrases, as something to be stripped
down to their ultimate meaning:

> 'Tis a *Metaphor* known to ev'ry plain Thinker.
> Just as when we say, *the Devil's a Tinker*
> Which cannot in Literal Sense by made Good,
> Unless by the *Devil* we mean Mr. WOOD.
>
>   (Ll. 53–56)

(Wood is commonly styled a "tinker" by Swift.) Later on, the poem
plays around variants of the idea "Love in a Wood / Maze / Million":
Swift moves from Etherege's title *Love in a Tub* and Wycherley's
Love in a Wood to popular sayings. (The phrase *in a wood* meant "in a
state of bewilderment". Tilley W732). Right at the end he quotes
the tag "Metal on metal is false heraldry" (M906), and perverts it to
his own needs:

> Why that may be true, yet WOOD upon WOOD,
> I'll maintain with my Life, is *Heraldry* Good.
>
>   (Ll. 121–22)

The body of Wood hanging upon the wooden gallows, that is.
Again we see in Swift's technique the capacity to turn familiar
forms to unexpected (often subversive or highly aggressive) purposes. Most of the cases cited involve punning, which is a device we
still recognize without too much trouble. What may escape us is the
wealth of popular idiom that the poetry dismantles and reassem-
bles.

It would be possible to go right through Swift's verse, uncovering a hidden layer of allusion along these lines. Sometimes the
routine expression is varied or concealed: *Dr. Swift's Answer to Doctor Sheridan* (1719: *Poems*, 3:1017) has, referring to some rhymes by
his friend,

> I nicely examind them every Line
> And the worst of them all like a barn door did shine.
>
>   (Ll. 5–6)

The more familiar version in everyday parlance is given in *Polite Conversation:*

Nev. Why, Miss you shine this Morning like a sh—— Barn-Door.
(*Works*, 4:149)

The trifles that passed between Swift and Sheridan are full of an affectionate repartee which draws naturally on homely and some-times even coarse expressions. With the poems to Stella, a different note is heard. The stock idioms appear, but they are touched by a slight air of tender mockery or gentle scepticism:

> As when a beauteous Nymph decays
> We say, she's past her Dancing Days;
> So, Poets lose their Feet by Time,
> And can no longer dance in Rhyme.
>
> (*Poems*, 2:756)

Compare the more heartless exchange in *Polite Conversation:*

Lord Sparkish. . . . But, pray Madam, was my Lady *Dimple* there? They say she is extreamly handsome.
Lady Sm. They must not see with my Eyes that think so.
Nev. She may pass Muster, and that's all.
Lady Ans. Pray how old do you take her to be?
Col. Why, about five or six and twenty.
Miss. I swear she's no Chicken, she's on the wrong side of thirty, if she be a Day.
Lady Ans. Depend upon't, she'll never see five and thirty, and a Bit to spare. . . . She looks as if Butter would not melt in her Mouth; but I warrant Cheese won't choak her. . . .
Col. They say she dances very fine.
Lady Ans. She did; but I doubt her dancing Days are over.
(*Works*, 4:145)

The bleak finality of this retort is very different from the poem's oblique introduction of the cliché (Tilley D118). (One might add that "no chicken" turns up in an earlier birthday poem.) The sharp and malicious ring of *Polite Conversation* is paralleled more closely in *Cadenus and Vanessa*, especially in the passages that describe the reaction of the "glitt'ring Dames" to Vanessa on her arrival in town. "Thirty and a Bit to spare" duly figures (l. 389), as does "That Gown was made for Old Queen *Bess*" (l. 397), another expression beloved of Lady Smart.

Such mimicry of feminine foibles takes us towards direct characterization through tics of speech. Entire poems are built around this plan, notably *The Journal of a Modern Lady* and *The Furniture of a Woman's Mind*. The linguistic field of the former is identical for long stretches with that of *Polite Conversation*, but the poem is more effective in evoking a mental state rather than just a milieu. Compare these two passages:

> [*The Colonel, Mr.* Neverout, *Lady* Smart, *and Miss, go to* Quadrille, *and sit 'till Three in the Morning.*] [*They rise from Cards.*]
> *Lady Sm.* Well, Miss, you'll have a sad Husband, you have such good Luck at Cards.
> *Nev.* Indeed, Miss, you dealt me sad Cards; if you deal so ill by your Friends, what will you do with your Enemies?
> *Lady Ans.* I'm sure, 'til Time for all honest Folks to go to Bed.
> *Miss.* Indeed, my Eyes draw Straws. [*She's almost asleep.*]
> *Nev.* Why, Miss, if you fall asleep, some Body may get a Pair of Gloves.
> *Col.* I'm going to the Land of Nod.
> *Nev.* Faith, I'm for *Bedfordshire*.
> *Lady Sm.* I'm sure, I shall sleep without rocking. . . .
> *Col.* [*To Miss.*] Madam, I shall have the Honour to escorte you.
> *Miss.* No, Colonel, I thank you. My Mama, has sent her Chair and Footmen. Well, my Lady *Smart*, I'll give you Revenge whenever you please.
>
> (*Works*, 4:200–21)

And now this:

> "Nay, Madam, give me leave to say
> "Twas you that threw the Game away;
> "When Lady *Tricksy* play'd a Four,
> "You took it with a Matadore;
> "I saw you touch your Wedding-Ring
> "Before my Lady call'd a King.
> "You spoke a Word began with H,
> "And I know whom you mean to teach,
> "Because you held the King of Hearts:
> "Fie, Madam, leave these little Arts. . . .
> And truly, Madam, I know when
> Instead of Five you scor'd me Ten.
> *Spadillo* here has got a Mark,
> A Child may know it in the Dark:
> I guess the Hand, it seldom fails,
> I wish some Folks would pare their Nails.

While thus they rail, and scold, and storm,
It passes but for common Form;
Most conscious that they all speak true,
And give each other but their Due;
It never interrupts the Game,
Or makes 'em sensible of Shame.
The Time too precious now to waste,
And Supper gobbled up in haste,
Again a-fresh to Cards they run,
As if they had but just begun.
Yet shall I not again repeat
How oft they squabble, snarl and Cheat:
At last they hear the Watchman knock,
A frosty Morn—Past Four a-Clock.
The Chair-Men are not to be found,
"Come, let us play the t'other Round.
　Now, all in haste they huddle on
Their Hoods, their Cloaks, and get them gone:
But first, the Winner must invite
The Company to-morrow Night.

(Ll. 248–57, 264–89: *Poems* 2:452–53)

It is not just that the poem supplies a fuller narrative. The difference is partly the freer handling of the scene made possible by a
nondramatic presentation: Swift is able to "foreground" the clichés
in verse, while in the prose conversation they follow with an inevitable sequentiality—no individual phrase is made salient. Again,
the use of rhyme and meter permit Swift to emphasise the banality
of particular turns of phrase: the "common Form" of a shared language, used among intimates, is beautifully registered in the ca-
dence and flat rhyme of the couplet,

Spadillo here has got a Mark,
A Child may know it in the Dark.

Swift's technique here is more than simple ventriloquial skill. The
phrases he picks up *are* banal in themselves, but they are made to
proclaim their banality by the pat form in which they are set out in
verse.

　It scarcely needs emphasis that *Verses on the Death of Dr. Swift*
makes magnificent parodic use of "polite conversation," though it is
a less familiar fact that the poem is studded with set forms of
speech, many of them now obsolete. Among numerous instances,
we might note line 191, "Why, is he dead without his Shoes?" This

rests on a slang phrase meaning "to be hanged": Tilley S381: *ODEP* quotes its use in a poem by Gay (1725).[11] Similarly at lines 293–94, of the deist Woolston:

> He shews, as sure as God's in *Gloc'ster*,
> That *Jesus* was a Grand Impostor.
>
> (*Poems*, 2:564)

The simile used in the first line (Tilley G174) was a well-established phrase: according to Fuller, it derived from the fact that "of all counties. . . . Gloucestershire was most pestered with monks." The proverb is signally out of place in this context, emphasizing the vulgar insensitivity of the freethinkers (and their abettors, such as the speaker at this point, Lintot). It is the harder nowadays to recognize such bywords because Swift is very skilled in inventing proverblike formulae, which might easily pass for antiquated catchphrases:

> He's older than he would be reckon'd,
> And well remembers *Charles* the Second.
>
> (Ll. 107–8: *Poems*, 2:556)

What we have is more than an isolated trick of style, a particular resource that enables the writer to import some "rich" folk coloring into this language. Swift always works with the grain of popular speech. He uses set forms, but he also invents aphoristic or sententious phrases that happen not to exist up to the moment of composition. The vivacity of *Verses on the Death of Dr. Swift* derives from Swift's unrivaled ability to scurry in and out of the crannies of familiar diction. It is a poem in which the most commonplace words may suddenly be shocked out of their indolence: consider "Flesh and Blood" (l. 164) or "spick and span" (l. 268). Or the way in which a tired platitude (Tilley F733) is made to dramatize a whole world of complacence and unfeeling inanity:

> But dearest Friends, they say, must part.
> His Time was come, he ran his Race,
> We hope he's in a better Place.
>
> (Ll. 239–41: *Poems*, 2:562)

Other poems, less well known, illustrate this ability to energize the mundane: for example, the amusing and too-little-known Market Hill item entitled *The Grand Question Debated* (*Poems*, 3:863–73).

"Grand question" is itself a moribund cliché, meaning "main point at issue." It is perhaps the poem nearest in spirit, as well as vocabulary, to *Polite Conversation*. But for real density of proverbial allusion, one must go back to a poem of 1710, only recently identified as Swift's.[12] These are the concluding lines of *A Dialogue between Captain Tom and Sir Henry Dutton Colt:*

> When the Captain had finish'd, away went old *Numps:*
> He had got a *Bad Game*, and could not turn up *Trumps.*
> His Eggs they are addle, and Dough was his Cake;
> So fairly he left them to *Brew* as they *Bake.*
>
> (Ll. 37–40)

This is the culmination of a quickfire display of verbal skill, involving some outrageous puns. Within these two couplets we have a series of catchphrases rapidly called up and as rapidly dismissed. *"Bad Game,"* meaning a poor hand, connects up with a number of references to cardplaying in the previous lines. Just one day prior to the ballad's composition, Swift had written to his Irish friends: "Why, the reason you lost four and eight-pence last night but one at Manley's, was because you played bad games"—that is, at the fashionable ombre (*Journal to Stella*, 1:43). "Turn up *Trumps*" is a cliché for once still current (Tilley T544): there is the air in Swift's use of the phrase as if the metaphor were still alive, whereas today the cardgame sense is not strongly present in our minds. The penultimate line recalls the proverb "You come with your five eggs a penny, and four of them addle" (Tilley E92). We can be fairly positive about this, since the expression duly occurs in *Polite Conversation* (*Works*, 4:142). Moreover, it is found in the contemporaneous *Journal to Stella* several times: see in particular the entry for 14 October 1710, the very week in which the ballad must have been published (*Journal to Stella*, 1:58: compare 2:447). The last part of the line alludes to another proverbial phrase (Tilley C12): the usual form of the expression, as found in Shakespeare, follows the order "Cake is dough." Swift's inversion permits the rhyme and also suggests a kind of symmetry with the concluding proverb. This is a saying with the idea "let them reap what they have sown" (Tilley B654): its aptness here derives from the fact that one of the candidates opposing Colt in the hotly contested Westminster election, occasioning this ballad, was a brewer named Cross. Swift alerted his friends in Ireland to the fact that the poem was "full of puns"; he added, "it runs, though it be good for nothing" (*Journal to Stella*, 1:65). In fact, the *Dialogue*, if not among Swift's greatest, is among

his most characteristic productions in verse. It is constantly bur-
rowing beneath the surface of humdrum conversational language,
so as to bring up amusing or damaging implications unsuspected in
normal usage.

Mention of the *Journal* might remind us that the language games
of this intensely creative series of letters go beyond the invention of
childish word forms. While clichés are less thickly strewn about the
text than is the case with the poetry, they are by no means totally
absent. Apart from the instance already mentioned, there are cases
such as the following: "O yes, you are great walkers: but I have
heard them say, Much talkers, Little walkers: and I believe I may
apply the old proverb to you; If you talkt no more than you walkt,
Those that think you wits would be baulkt' (*Journal*, 1:255). I cannot trace the saying in this form, although *ODEP* gives "The greatest talkers are always the least doers" and "Walk groundly, talk
profoundly." Swift may have invented the form of words used in
the *Journal*, or he may unconsciously have adapted a slightly different expression. What shows through clearly is his way of thinking
out the "wisdom" of common speech, as though familiarity might
blunt our perceptions of what is being said. Another personalized
version occurs later in the *Journal*, when Swift remarks, "I must
keep my Breath to cool my Lenten Porridge" (*Journal*, 2:505). The
more usual form appears in *Polite Conversation:*

> *Miss.* Pray, Mr. *Neverout*, keep your Breath to cool your Porridge.
> (*Works*, 4:167)

The insertion of the word "Lenten" suggests a different current of
idiom ("Lenten Diet," for instance, which is found in one of the
trifles: *Poems*, 2:373). The day's entry is principally concerned with
Lent and includes literal references to Swift's eating habits during
this season of the year. Nevertheless, one is struck by the facility
with which Swift locates an apt piece of proverbial lore and converts it to his purposes.

Other examples could be cited and analyzed in the same way: for
example, "Is not this vexatious? and is there so much in the proverb
of proffered service?" (*Journal*, 1:68: this is "Proffered service
stinks," Tilley S252). In addition, there are hackneyed phrases not
precisely proverbial in character, but capable of being opened up in
the Swiftian manner: "He has appointed me an hour on Saturday at
four, when I will open my business to him; which expression I
would not use if I were a woman" (*Journal*, 1:41: for the obscene

overtones, see *OED*, "business," 19*b*). One method of avoiding solecisms in language is not to use tired or cast-off expressions drawn from popular speech: Swift takes the opposite course, which may be either more or less fastidious, depending on how one regards it—he draws freely on colloquial language, but refines it in use, chiefly by restoring a forgotten literal meaning in a figurative expression.

4

To regenerate some hereditary dullness, back to quickness and activity of primal utterance, is surely one of the great deeds of life that creative literature can perform. The poet who learned most from Swift was perhaps Byron, and *Don Juan* many times witnesses to this power of regeneration:

> This was Don Juan's earliest scrape; whether
> I shall proceed with his adventures is
> Dependent on the public altogether.
> We'll see, however, what they say to this;
> Their favour's in an author's cap's a feather,
> And no great mischief's done by their caprice . . .
>
> (1:199)

"A feather in one's cap" (Tilley F157) is the sort of stock locution where we have more or less lost sight of the strange metaphoric base. Byron makes us aware of the matter by a number of devices: the inversion, bringing "feather" to the opposite end of the statement; the rhyme already building up aural expectations; and the curious syntax that heaps one possessive form upon another elision. A kind of scepticism is built into the whole linguistic operation. The subliminal message might be decoded as something like this: "praise from the critics is only a silly little toy to please one's vanity."

This is a brief local effect. Swift seems to me so *habitually* close to popular idiom that he is able to set in motion a complex interplay of linked ideas. This happens with terms of cardplay and gambling in the *Dialogue between Captain Tom and Sir Henry Dutton Colt*. It happens with ideas of drowning, shipwreck, and the perils of the sea in *The Bubble*. Most obviously of all, it occurs as a sustained commentary or subtext in *The Horrid Plot*. One cannot open a work of reference such as *The Penguin Dictionary of Historical Slang* and leaf through the "dog" entries without getting a fresh perspective on the words and feelings of the poem. I suggested that the underlying drift of the poem might be paraphrased as something like "The real dirty dogs are Walpole and his ministers." The central passage, quoted on p. 211 above, plays around an area of folklore expressed in such sayings as "scornful dogs will eat dirty puddings" (Tilley D538, as "hungry": I quote the form used by Mr. Neverout, *Works*, 4:140). Or again the phrase "Give a dog an ill name and hang him" (Tilley N25): Swift's poem implies that the prosecution has used not just the toy dog Harlequin but miserable informers ("Curr *Plunket* Whelp *Skean . . . Mason* that abandon'd Bitch") in order to trap Atterbury. Wanting to rid themselves of the Bishop, they tarred his reputation through the instrument of such low animals. It is worth recalling that "dogged" derives from the word *dog*, and that in Swift's day it meant not "obstinate, persistent" but, on the contrary, currish, malicious, surly or even cruel (see *OED*, "dogged," 2.) The wealth of popular idiom in this area reinforces the critique that Swift mounts in the poem against the methods of prosecution, used by Walpole to obtain a conviction when the ordinary processes of law would have been insufficient to establish Atterbury's guilt. It is an historical irony that Walpole should have become associated in the popular mind with the maxim *quieta non movere*, for the English version is, of course, "let sleeping dogs lie" (Tilley, W7).

It is beyond the scope of an essay in a volume such as this to inquire into the wider cultural ramifications of the literary technique I have explored. One could relate it to the popularity of collections of proverbs, to which writers as distinguished as George Herbert contributed. Or to the influence of Erasmus's *Adages* and the continuing tradition of maxims, *pensées*, and detached wisdom that runs from Pascal and La Rochefoucauld (who of course supplied the germ of *Verses on the Death of Dr. Swift*) to Lichtenberg. In America, Benjamin Franklin was at work in Swift's lifetime on *Poor Richard's Almanac*, that most popular collection of wise saws. Other literary modes, not composed directly of aphorisms, enlisted curt and sententious statements much more frequently than is the case in modern writing: one thinks of Bacon's essays, the character writers, even the *Spectator* papers and the novels of Fielding. Moreover, vernacular literature was often subjected to the same sort of marginal homily to which we are accustomed in divine texts: when James Mabbe translated the picaresque novel *Guzmán de Al-*

farache in 1622, he supplied the reader with glosses, explanations, and even handy maxims of his own. Finally, one observes an increasing tendency in the early eighteenth century to use catchphrases as titles of books. The habit was not totally new, for Elizabethan and Jacobean dramatists had displayed the same fondness for clichés on the title page. But it was certainly developed, as such instances as *A Tale of a Tub, Law is a Bottomless Pit*, and *It Cannot Rain but it Pours* illustrate. Defoe is particularly noteworthy here: one thinks of titles such as *The Shortest Way, Rogues on both Sides, Plain English, The Remedy worse than the Disease, Strike while the Iron is Hot, Fair Payment no Spunge*, and very many more.[13]

But these are historical issues, and they must be left aside. What matters is our sense as readers of what Swift is up to, and how he puts to searing effect the words that others reject as contemptibly worn out by use. For this, the explanation lies not in history but in Swift himself—in his peculiar passion for the inflections and oddities of our ordinary speech. *Polite Conversation* is the record of an obsession more pervasively at work, which contributed to Swift's creative power in every department of his art. Although he may have found that experience commonly "controuled" (or negated) handy maxims, he never ceased to test, reapply, and think out afresh the proverbial wisdom of his day. Sceptical with regard to easy generalizations, Swift nevertheless retained in his mind a store of pithy *sententiae*, one might say a fund of molten cliché that had not quite hardened into the totally useless or inane.

His friend Anthony Henley wrote to him shortly after the Union of Parliaments:

> As Proverbs are the Wisdom of a Nation, soe I take the Naturalizing such a Quantity of very Expressive ones as we did by the Act of Union, to be one of the Considerablest Advantages wee shall reap from it: And I doe not Question but the Nation will be the Wiser for the future. (*Correspondence*, 1:147)

Beneath the irony lies a truth Swift would have abundantly appreciated.

Notes

1. For the invented languages, see George P. Mayhew, *Rage or Raillery: The Swift Manuscripts at the Huntington Library* (San Marino, Calif.: Huntington Library, 1967). For puns, see David Nokes, "Hack at Tom Poley's," *The Art of Jonathan Swift*, ed. Clive T. Probyn (London: Vision Press Ltd., 1978), pp. 43–56.

2. I do not make any sharp distinction between proverbs and other modes of stock expression, since their effect is very much the same in the contexts I shall be exploring. It is true that Simon Wagstaff, in the introduction to *Polite Conversation*, claims that "the Reader must learn by all Means to distinguish between Proverbs, and those polite Speeches which beautify Conversation: For, as to the former, I utterly reject them out of all ingenious Discourse" (*Works*, 4:102). In fact, the dialogues are stuffed with the hoariest of proverbs.

3. *The Oxford Dictionary of English Proverbs*, comp. W. G. Smith, ed. F. P. Wilson, 3d ed. (Oxford: Clarendon Press, 1970), p. 194. Abbreviated in the text as *ODEP*. The other main reference work used is Morris P. Tilley, *A Dictionary of the Proverbs in the Sixteenth and Seventeenth Centuries*, Ann Arbor: University of Michigan Press, 1950: items are indicated by their key number, thus: Tilley B555.

4. See Mackie L. Jarrell, "The Proverbs in Swift's *Polite Conversation*," *Huntington Library Quarterly*, 20 (1956):15–38: and David Hamilton, "Swift, Wagstaff, and the Composition of *Polite Conversation*," *Huntington Library Quarterly*, 30 (1967):281–95.

5. *The Parliamentary Diary of Sir Edward Knatchbull 1722–1730*, ed. A. N. Newman (London: 1963), p. 15.

6. For a more detailed analysis of this technique, see my forthcoming book, *Eighteenth-Century Encounters*

7. Compare the passage: "My Lord; I will as a Divine, quote Scripture. Although the Childrens meat must not be given to Dogs; yet the Dogs eat the Scraps that fall from the Childrens tables" (*Correspondence*, 4:450). The allusion is to Matthew 15:26–27 or Mark 7:27–28.

8. See also Archbishop King to Swift in 1712: "Pray make hay while the sun shines—*post est occasio salva*—and be sure do not call these quotations pedantry for they are grave wise sentences and nobody can say the thing better" (*Correspondence*, 1:318). These are the very accents of Swift himself: his correspondents knew his preferences in both language and morals.

9. See for example a letter to Ambrose Philips: "And thus I have luckily found out the reason of the Proverb, to have Guts in one's Brain, that is what a wise man eats and drinks rises upwards, and is the nourishment of his head where all is digested, and, consequently, a Fool's Brains are in his guts, where his Beef, and Thoughts, and Ale descend" (*Correspondence*, 1:91: for two further examples, see 1:141). The expression cited is Tilley G484: it reappears in *Polite Conversation* (*Works*, 4:157).

10. For "hangdog," see *Correspondence*, 1:268, 311.

11. This is *Newgate's Garland*, sometimes attributed to Swift: *Poems*, 3:1111–15. See also *John Gay: Poetry and Prose*, ed. V. A. Dearing and C. E. Beckwith, Oxford: Clarendon Press 1975, 2:613–14. It may be significant that the poem makes play with a proverb, "Charity begins at home" (ll. 48–49). Another relevant saying was "to die like a dog" (to be hanged): Tilley D509. Swift makes the criminal Ebenezor Elliston conclude his gallows oration with the words "I hope you shall see me die like a Man, the Death of a Dog" (*Works*, 9:41).

12. Quoted from *Poems on Affairs of State*, vol. 7 ed. F. H. Ellis (New Haven, Conn.: Yale University Press, 1975), pp. 480–86. Ellis provides useful notes with, for once, proper attention to the proverbial layer in the text.

13. The importance of tags in education (especially the teaching of law, logic, and grammar) should also be considered.

8

Swift's Letters

IRVIN EHRENPREIS

The fascination of modern readers with the familiar letters of eighteenth-century authors has a special significance that seems both literary and distinctive of the kind. One often regrets the lack of a vocabulary for analyzing this genre, because the eighteenth century is peculiarly crowded with works that are not drama, verse, or narrative prose, and for which, therefore, the usual terms of literary criticism are not really suitable. Letters are only one such genre. The greatest intellects of that century devoted themselves to elegant philosophical or historical works, while other great writers produced biography, political argument, and economic theory. To the extent that we bound our thinking by the so-called imaginative genres canonized in nineteenth-century criticism, we are cut off from a proper judgment of the so-called nonimaginative masterpieces. We neglect Gibbon for Goldsmith. Not our taste but our narrow critical method has sealed us in; and many who must be academic critics condemn themselves to the minute examination of tedious novels, motionless tragedies, icy pentameters, and frivolous essays sooner than confront the fascination of a Walpole or a Hume.

In such a climate Swift survives as the author of half a dozen prose satires and a few humorous or complimentary poems. Who reads more? His *Journal to Stella* and the five volumes of his general correspondence attract specialists but hardly anyone else. As a reader who prefers Swift's letters to the bulk of his other works, whether for their style, their life, or their literary design, I should like to defend my judgment.

In a period like our own, when free-standing forms, independent of history and biography, are the source of literary taste, the familiar letter offers extraordinary difficulties not to readers but to critics. Letters must of course depend for their life upon both history and biography. We cannot begin to judge their art until we recover the razed, built-over world to which they refer, and some essential attributes of their creator. Such explorations of background must remain preliminary, however, if one claims for letters the dignity normally assumed by forms like tragedy and epic. Not only general qualities of style but also particular features of structure must receive close attention.

Yet even the admirers of the epistolary genre seldom deal with it in terms of structural differentia. Though accepting the need for headnotes and footnotes, they tend to leap at once upon the question of prose style, ignoring the existence of subordinate genres and rhetorical patterns. To analyze style within the limits of the paragraph, considering the shape of the sentences, the use of figures, the rhythm of phrases, and the choice of words is necessary and fruitful. But this sort of analysis can hardly distinguish the specific features of the letter. I hope we can relate stylistic elements to larger aspects intermediate between the character of the writer and the matter of his writing.

Fundamental, surely, are the relation of the two correspondents and their acceptance of a common world that they see from different points of view. A great letter-writer must manipulate certain essentials: his private character, his attitude or relation to the addressee, and the world of his own experience that he interprets to the original recipient of the letter. On such materials the modern reader imposes one's normal expectations of the subordinate kind to which a particular piece belongs: the letter of courtship, of compliment, of insult, or—what is most common—the letter of personal history, going over recent events in the writer's life and incorporating anecdotes about the people named.

To some extent we may define the problem of a good letter-writer as using the large features of a form so as to let his unique powers of style, narrative, and persuasion work. For this purpose two elements are especially valuable, the relation between the writer and correspondent, and the nature of the subordinate genre. First, the attitude of the writer toward his addressee can be noticed: whether he feels friendly, indifferent, or angry, whether the two men are strangers or old acquaintance, how regularly they exchange messages. Swift loves to play with this relationship and

switch from mock-anger to open friendship, from teasing to preaching. Secondly, we can tell whether the letter is of a recognizable
kind. Here Swift is usually clear, making his purpose plain and
suiting his manner to it.

In dwelling on such principles, I do not mean to ignore older
doctrine, such as the comparison of a fine letter to good talk. To
make friendly conversation the model of epistolary style—"familiar
speech of the absent," in an Elizabethan phrase[1]—is a principle as
ancient as letter-writing. I shall not refer so far back as Demetrius
Phalereus, or even Cicero and Seneca. But Erasmus can serve as a
locus classicus of this as of so many commonplaces of literary study
(De ratione conscribendi epistolas). In the Renaissance, however, the
kind of speech that the analysts of style actually drew their terms
from was the public oration; and detailed criticism of letters (such
as it was) then derived ultimately from the rhetorics or Aristotle,
Cicero, and Quintilian. England went the way of the world; so the
early manuals of letter-writing in English referred to classical or
Italian models of the subordinate kinds, categorizing them by the
ancient rules of oratory.[2]

When the conversation of intimates really became an ideal of
refined English letter-writers, the manner imitated was French.
During the first half of the seventeenth century the colloquial language of polite French gentlemen was purified by an alliance of
courtiers and grammarians founded in the Hotel de Rambouillet.[3]
In England, Swift's master, Temple, was quick to digest their
lessons without losing his own spontaneity.

Swift himself arrived too late on the scene to be merely precious.
As a letter-writer he belongs to the generation following that which
submitted to the French patterns of *préciosité*—Vincent Voiture and
Guez de Balzac. But neither did he turn against them. Purity of
diction, harmony of phrase, facility and aptness of metaphor—
these are the virtues such ideals promoted[4], and in Swift they linger
pervasively. He particularly admired Voiture. Since compliment is
the normal mode of *lettres galantes*, flattery is their vice. But ironic
raillery, the use of ingenious mock-insults for praise, redeems the
hyperboles of Voiture. Swift keeps some of the egregious features
of this style for letters of compliment addressed to great men. He
also employs the style in letters of gallantry addressed to ladies.
Otherwise, he pretty much abandons it after his mid-thirties. Here
is a flatulent sample from his only surviving love letter (*not* addressed to Esther Johnson):

Why was I so foolish to put my hopes and fears into the power or management of another? Liberty is doubtless the most valuable blessing of life; yet we are fond to fling it away on those who have been these 5000 years using us ill. Philosophy advises to keep our desires and prospects of happiness as much as we can in our own breasts, and independent of anything without. He that sends them abroad is likely to have as little quiet as a merchant whose stock depends upon winds, and waves, and pirates, or upon the words and faith of creditors, every whit as dangerous and inconstant as the other.

I am a villain if I have not been poring this half hour over the paper merely for want of something to say to you. (To Jane Waring, 29 April 1696, *Correspondence*, 1:20)

Surely it is fair to say that the young lover shows little insight into his own nature, that the view he has of his experience lacks coherence, that he needs a much sharper conception of what is going on between himself and the addressee. Finally, if one expects a love letter to convey deep, fresh emotion, this script cannot receive a high mark. The style fails, it seems to me, within these limits. To call it hollow, imitative, and fatuous is to be accurate, but the demands of the epistolary form aggravate these defects.

Characteristically, Swift does not fail, partly because he does not characteristically write *billets doux*. So long as courtship was out of the question, he could be counted on to write splendidly to ladies he liked, especially to young and attractive ladies, whom he enjoyed teasing and charming by post. Besides, he accepted the commonplaces of his age as to the qualities of a good letter. However hard he worked at one, he made believe that the writing was effortless. An air of ease and spontaneity arising, in appearance, from openness of mind and heart, recurs in eighteenth-century criticism as the universal desideratum of the familiar letter. Even a sensibility so artful as Richardson's responded to the dogma. With his usual complacency Richardson practically boasted of his own lack of elegance, saying he had "nothing but *heart*" to recommend him, and that he wrote whatever came uppermost, "trusting to that heart, and regarding not the head." Like Pope, Walpole, and the rest, he thought the ideal epistolary style should follow the negligent ease of well-bred conversation among intimates. Almost alone, Dr. Johnson stood out against the undertow of critical fashion when he recognized what impassable barriers to self-exposure the process of letter-writing raised. Stubbornly, Johnson argued that no transaction "offers stronger temptations to fallacy and sophistication than epistolary intercourse." The impulse to present oneself favorably takes many shapes: "A letter is addressed to a single mind of which the prejudices and partialities are known, and must therefore please, if not by favouring them, by forbearing to oppose them."[5]

Johnson's epistolary style is in keeping with his principles, obviously premeditated and unlike Swift's. But what counts for a reader today is surely not the real presence of sincerity and *spezzatura* in a writer's nature but the perfection of their enactment. On the level of style, the writer must *in fact* choose words with care, turn his phrases elegantly, find neat similes, and so forth, but I still think that in accomplishing all this, he must avoid signs of strain or forethought. Here Swift's achievement is unmatched. Years before writing the passage I have ridiculed, he could handle the subject of courtship with the most elegant detachment, but he was then addressing an inquisitive cousin and not an eligible coquette—and the female under scrutiny was still not Esther Johnson. Here, then, is a sentence composed when he was not yet twenty-five, taken from one of the earliest pieces of Swift's prose now extant, a letter of 11 February 1691–92 to the Rev. John Kendall:

> I shall speak plainly to you, that the very ordinary observations I made with going Half a mile beyond the University, have taught me experience enough not to think of marriage, till I settle my fortune in the world, which I am sure, will not be in some years, and even then my self I am so hard to please that I suppose I shall put it off to the other world. (*Correspondence*, 1:3)

Can we describe this specimen? The peculiar confidence of his attitude toward the recipient is a mark of Swift's letters in general. The asymmetry of structure, conciseness of phrase, and elegance of transition are normal qualities of his prose, and will be found throughout the long letter from which I have taken this sentence. In substance the entire composition has the air of candor and unaffected revelation of thought found in his good letters.

So I suggest as the features of Swift's finest epistolary prose his use of an intimate manner with the recipient and a detached tone toward the people or events discussed—including himself. The style fits the genre. If his phrasing avoids periodic structure, one reason seems to be that periodicity implies formal deliberation, an effect opposed to the spontaneous expression of thoughts growing steadily out of one another; for this unaffected disclosure of inner process in a manner Swift normally tries to convey. At the same time, the inner process itself, though fast, is surprisingly nimble and alert—even deliberate. As the reader, therefore, strives to reconcile the warm intimacy and confidence in one direction with the cool detachment and impersonality in the other, Swift achieves an intensity that gives his letters their broadcast appeal. The modern reader feels that something is happening continually while he goes over them.

What else do we find in the sentence quoted? The substantive nature of Swift's message is characteristic of the other epistolary talents that flourished during his century. I mean the informativeness or factuality of authors like Lady Mary Wortley Montagu and Horace Walpole. Of course, they can be self-centered. But even when exhibiting themselves, the best writers avoid mere effusion, moralizing, or evocation of mood. The ego becomes the object of a lively examination. And what is far commoner than such auto-analysis is their concentration on deeds or matters of general concern, the fruits of observation or experience. From induction, in turn, springs aphorism, the memorable epigrams and reflections we constantly quote from these writers. Swift, like the rest, loved to be the conveyor of news in an age when newspapers rarely carried the important but unofficial details of public events. His private ear was often at the service of his friends' curiosity. There is a famous correspondence of this nature between Swift and his ecclesiastical foreman, William King, Archbishop of Dublin. Here is a passage from one of the letters written in 1708 (12 February). It deals with the resignation of Robert Harley as Secretary of State, after Harley's failure to dislodge the head of his own government, who was then the Earl of Godolphin, Lord Treasurer:

> On Sunday evening last, the Lord Treasurer and Duke of Marlborough went out of the Council; and Harley delivered a memorial to the Queen, relating to the Emperor and the war. Upon which the Duke of Somerset rose, and said, if her Majesty suffered that fellow (pointing to Harley), to treat affairs of the war without advice of the General, he could not serve her; and so left the Council. The Earl of Pembroke, though in milder words, spoke to the same purpose; so did most of the Lords: and the next day the Queen was prevailed upon to turn him out, though the seals were not delivered till yesterday. It was likewise said, that Mrs. Masham is forbid the Court; but this I have no assurance of. . . . All this business has been much fomented by a Lord whom Harley had been chiefly instrumental in impeaching some years ago. The Secretary always dreaded him, and made all imaginable advances to be reconciled, but could never prevail; which made him say yesterday to some who told it to me, that he had laid his neck under their feet, and they trod upon it. (*Correspondence*, 1:70)

Swift and Archbishop King shared a compulsive preoccupation
with the world of British politics. Swift liked to be early and abundant with the facts he gathered. The Archbishop was weighty and
cautious. Accommodating his own view to the Archbishop's
character, Swift produces an agreeable equilibrium between a congenital impulse to tell all and the requirement of discretion.

Many literary genres are endoskeletal. We define them by the
internal relation of their elements. But I have suggested that the
familiar letter has a form derived from its framework, leaving the
internal order of its parts associative and free. Epistolary anecdotes
are framed in two ways: the writer has his knowledge of an incident, but—as Johnson says—he reduces that knowledge to the details he thinks appropriate to the recipient of his letter. When the
modern literary reader enters the situation, he comes upon a message not directed to himself and enjoys a mild excitement derived
from the act of espionage. Usually, he has the futher excitement of
hearing directly about an interesting but more or less concealed
incident. If the action is trifling, the writer cautious, and the recipient solemn, the product can become so elaborately framed and
"distanced" that it bores even the expert scholar. If the action is
important, the writer outspoken, and the recipient a man of the
world, the product can, as with Swift on Harley, gain force and
coherence from the double frame.

Besides, a writer seldom leaves an anecdote without comment;
and if this secondary material is witty or penetrating, the effect of
the anecdote will be transformed. Often, the aphorism giveth life.
Sometimes, Swift delivers his comment not as such but through the
addition of a further, brief story illuminating the first: he gives us a
fresh, closeup view, with a stereoscopic result. This is what he has
done with the report of Harley's fall. The incident gains a sudden,
dramatic roundness from the remark of the prostrate Harley. When
Swift moralizes about an event, he avoid heaviness. In fact, the
relation of anecdote to commentary is reciprocal: if Swift intends
the comment to carry the power, he may reduce the narrative to a
thin summary, merely leading up to a reflection—as in the following bitter passage in a letter from Ireland of 28 August 1730 addressed to the Earl of Oxford in England. The subject is the Dean
of Ferns, an English priest who had accepted a preferment in the
Church of Ireland:

> There is a fellow here from England one Sawbridge, he was last term
> indited for a Rape. The Plea he intended was his being drunk when he
> forced the woman; but he bought her off. He is a Dean and I name him

to your Lordship, because I am confident you will hear of his being a
Bishop. (*Correspondence*, 3:405)

To appreciate the lacerating wit of this passage, one must know
enough history to realize that the British government, as a matter of
policy, was filling Irish offices with trustworthy men sent out from
England, and that consequently the lower clergy of Ireland were
normally native-born but the bishops tended to be imported
Whigs. Swift detested the policy and the bishops. With so much
history and biography in mind, we can see the delicacy of his
delivering such remarks to a member of the British House of Lords,
a man whom Swift honored and trusted but knew to be indifferent
to the fate of Ireland.

I can also indicate how not to do this sort of thing. Here is John
Gay, spoiling the material for a superb anecdote. Until you reach
the comments, things go well enough. But owing to his ex-
plicitness, verbosity, and lack of irony or aphorism, Gay then reduces the tale to the level of a talkative schoolmaster's
reminiscences. Adjusting his report to the scope of the Countess of
Burlington's imagination, Gay spreads it far too thin for us. He is
telling her ladyship of a visit to the paintings of Sir James Thornhill
in the Royal Hospital, Greenwich, where the illiterate guide led the
viewers steadily astray. Gay begins with Thornhill's picture of
William III accompanied by personifications of the four cardinal
virtues:

> For my own part, I was in concern that the show-man did Sir James
> Cornhill (as he call'd him) so much injustice for he pointed out to us
> Four Cardinals near King William, which he called the four Cardinals
> of Virtue. Which seem'd to me to include some absurditys; in the first
> place, that there should be four Cardinals of Virtue in being; & that
> there should be four Cardinals attending a Protestant Prince, I inform'd
> the man that his account tended much to the prejudice of Sir James,
> that though they might appear four Cardinals to him, the Painter cer-
> tainly meant them to express the four Cardinal Virtues. He then
> show'd us the Princess of Savoy, and the Queen of Persia. Here again I
> interrupted him, by telling him, that they might indeed be more like
> those two Ladys, but that certainly Sir James meant them for the
> Princess Sophia and the Queen of Prussia. This a proof that a fine
> puppet-show may be spoild and depreciated by an ignorant interpre-
> ter.[6]

Swift would never have corrected the guide. Rather he would have drawn the man out, asking him whether the cardinals were Italian or French, and suggesting that this Princess of Savoy was Prince Eugene's daughter. He would then have delivered the whole account, with a straight face and no comment, to a deserving friend.

There is a reciprocal relation between the historical or public importance of anecdotes and the elaboration of their framework. The more general the interest, the less complex the structure; for the letter-writer approaches the role of a journalist as his news approaches the level of headline material. Telling Harley's story, Swift almost effaces himself as a literary artist until he reaches the stage of commentary. But when anecdotes have, like Gay's, an appeal independent of history, art matters most. In Swift at this point a unique talent for impersonation takes over. Here is a sample that could hardly be distinguished from pure fiction. Swift writes from London on 18 November 1710, during the War of the Spanish Succession, to his beloved Ester Johnson in Ireland:

> Coming home at seven, a gentleman unknown stopt me in the Pall-mall, and askt my advice; said he had been to see the queen (who was just come to town) and the people in waiting would not let him see her; that he had two hundred thousand men ready to serve her in the war; that he knew the queen perfectly well, and had an apartment at Court, and if she heard he was there, she would send for him immediately; that she owed him two hundred thousand pounds, &c. and he desired my opinion whether he should go try again whether he could see her; or, because, perhaps, she was weary after her journey, whether he had not better stay till to-morrow. I had a mind to get rid of my companion, and begged him of all love to go and wait on her imemdiately; for that, to my knowledge, the queen would admit him; that this was an affair of great importance, and required dispatch: and I instructed him to let me know the success of his business, and come to the Smyrna Coffee-house, where I would wait for him till midnight. (*Works*, 15:98)

There is no comment here: the episode is entertaining, not edifying, and Swift's instinctive hoax is what has unfolded itself. This tale is detachable. It would lose little in isolation. But one reason is that the writer relies on the beloved recipient to know his fondness for acting a part; hence the open, confidential tone. The attitude toward the lunatic is dry and detached, a life-giving contrast to the absurd substance of the anecdote. We notice again Swift's habit of shifting quickly to a fresh view, with the effect of a close-up. Thus telling the time and place in two phrases, he organizes the rest of the account as a pair of speeches, with his own unexpectedly start-

ing from the madman's premise and developing even less predictably through the series of concrete arrangements that leave Swift
squarely in the centre of the stage at the imaginary rendezvous.
This is the Swift who adored April Fool jokes and often tried to
carry them out by letters.

Narrative is only one of Swift's epistolary talents; moral instruction is pervasive. Yoked with the clown in Swift there is always the
preacher. In didactic pieces, however, the framework counts even
more heavily than in narrative. Brevity, for example, will imply
intimacy; length implies that the reader cannot know you well
enough to fill out the details of your general instruction. If the
periodical essayist of the eighteenth century loved to dilate on subjects like the dangers of coquetry and the pleasures of benevolence,
it was because he wrote for a miscellaneous public who looked for
expansive geniality. But the moralizing letter-writer, addressing a
man who was or might become his friend, could hardly afford such
relaxation. He risked a tone of condescension unless he inclined to
be terse or witty.

Though Swift was a priest, he carefully adjusted the angle of his
exhortations to suit the condition of the recipient. Consoling a titled
lady for the death of her great patron the Queen, he is grave, brief,
and profoundly respectful:

> I cannot go about to comfort your Ladyship in your great affliction,
> otherwise than by begging you to make use of your own piety, and
> your own wisdom, of both which you have so great a share. You are no
> longer a servant, but you are still a wife, a mother, and a friend; and
> you are bound in conscience to take care of your health, in order to
> acquit yourself of these duties, as well as you did of the other, which is
> now at an end. (To Lady Masham, 7 August 1714, *Correspondence*, 2.
> 109)

When Swift gives advice to John Gay—a younger friend, of a
humbler level—he shows his affection by the scolding, abrupt a-
vuncularity of his speech:

> I find by the whole cast of your letter that you are as giddy and as
> volatile as ever; just the reverse of Mr. Pope, who hath always loved a
> domestick life from his youth. I was going to wish you had some little
> place that you could call your own, but I profess I do not know you
> well enough to contrive any one System of life that would please you,
> You pretend to preach up riding and walking to the Dutchess, yet from
> my knowledge of you after twenty years, you allways Joyned a violent

desire of perpetually shifting places and company, with a rooted Lazyness, and an utter impatience of fatigue. A coach and six horses is the utmost exercise you can bear, and this onely when you can fill it with such company as is best suited to your tast, and how glad would you be if it could waft you in the air to avoyd jolting; while I who am so much later in life can or at least would ride 500 miles on a trotting horse, You mortaly hate writing onely because it is the thing you chiefly ought to do as well to keep up the vogue you have in the world, as to make you easy in your fortune; you are mercifull to every thing but money, your best friend, whom you treat with inhumanity. (4 May 1732, *Correspondence*, 4:15)

These artful adaptations of language to listener do not only please the first reader. For the later, literary reader they create a kind of drama. He hears one distinctly characterized figure persuasively addressing another in a situation uncomfortable enough to provoke advice. Even when the lessons taught seem commonplace, their appropriateness to the individual keeps us interested. All good letter-writers reach for such devices, but Swift adds a mark of his own. Normally, he reveals an acute foreboding of the probable ineffectuality of his teachings; and this self-consciousness has a drily ironic link with the traditional nature of his doctrine. It implies what he sometimes declares explicitly, viz., that the principles of right conduct have always been obvious, and that if earlier teachers or admonitions have not altered human nature, his present effort is comically unsure of success. *A Modest Proposal* represents the strongest application of this insight. When writing political essays, Swift often suppresses any admission that his argument may fail; in letters this tendency is reversed.

Another of Swift's practices can be seen in the supreme epistolary moralist, Johnson. To make his instruction persuasive and to keep it from sounding officious, Johnson anchors it in a deeply sympathetic relation between himself and his correspondent. Like Swift, he is always in touch. Constantly, he takes on—with dignity or with humor—the afflictions and joys of his immediate reader, so that the general principles brought to bear will seem no more applicable to him than to Johnson. When he congratulates an old friend on the pleasures of making a long foreign tour with a favorite daughter, the glow of Johnson's sympathy removes any hint of preachiness from his didactic reflections:

You have travelled with this felicity, almost peculiar to yourself, that your companion is not to part from you at your journey's end; but you

are to live on together, to help each other's recollection, and to supply
each other's omissions. The world has few greater pleasures than that
which two friends enjoy, in tracing back, at some distant time, those
transactions and events through which they have passed together. One
of the old man's miseries is, that he cannot easily find a companion able
to partake with him of the past. You and your fellow-traveller have this
comfort in store, that your conversation will be not easily exhausted;
one will always be glad to say what the other will always be willing to
hear.[7]

Pope's habit of offering quasi-philosophical sermons that are
neither fresh nor pertinent makes many of his letters hard to digest.
By contrast, here is Swift in England, addressing James Stopford, a
friend much his junior, and trying to console not his correspondent
but himself for the probable death of his own beloved Esther Johnson:

> I fear I shall have more than ordinary reasons to wish you a near
> neighbour to me in Ireland; and that your company will be more neces-
> sary than ever, when I tell you that I never was in so great a dejection of
> spirits. For I lately received a letter from Mr. Worrall, that one of the
> two oldest and dearest friends I have in the world is in so desperate a
> condition of health, as makes me expect every post to hear of her death.
> It is the younger of the two, with whom I have lived in the greatest
> friendship for thirty-three years. I know you will share in my trouble,
> because there are few persons whom I believe you more esteemed. For
> my part, as I value life very little, so the poor casual remains of it, after
> such a loss, would be a burden that I must heartily beg God Almighty
> to enable me to bear; and I think there is not a greater folly than that of
> entering into too strict and particular a friendship, with the loss of
> which a man must be absolutely miserable; but especially at an age
> when it is too late to engage in a new friendship. Besides, this was a
> person of my own rearing and instructing, from childhood, who ex-
> celled in every good quality that can possibly accomplish a human
> crature.—They have hitherto writ me deceiving letters, but Mr. Wor-
> rall has been so just and prudent as to tell me the truth; which, however
> racking, is better than to be struck on the sudden.—Dear Jim, pardon
> me, I know not what I am saying; but believe me that violent friendship
> is much more lasting, and as much engaging, as violent love. Adieu. (20
> July 1726, *Correspondence*, 3:145)

The sudden close-up, switching the point of view in the last sentence of this passage, makes the letter one of the most pathetic
Swift ever wrote. I might also call attention to the combination of
intimacy with Stopford and impersonality concerning the subject,

which turns out finally to be Swift himself. The common world of the two men is, for the younger, newly and permanently colored by the overwhelming emotion under which Swift presents it.

If a central appeal of letters is our pleasure in eavesdropping, it follows that the more a writer seems to expect general distribution or publication—multiple readership, to use an ugly phrase—the weaker the form becomes. Walpole said of Pope's letters that "as they were written to everybody, they do not look as if they had been written to anybody."[8] An extreme case is the pamphlet designed as a familiar letter. Here the form has a clear sense. It means that the writer claims to be telling everyone his honest views as he would freely deliver them in confidence to a discreet friend. Swift, like hundreds of his contemporaries, loved to give this frame to his pamphlets; and he thereby showed the vigor of his passion for seeming candid. That his private and public declarations were always congruent is of course untrue. But he intensely desired people to think they were, and his intensity often deceived himself.

Such an attitude easily produces its opposite, the hoax. Impersonation is the underside of a furious honesty. In Swift's writing, private hoaxes are not so frequent as public, but the more he loved and trusted a friend, the more tricks he played on him. For the modern, literary audience, the effect may be a distillation of the dramatic irony that hindsight bestows on all historical documents. To those who know that Robert Harley was to become Swift's hero, and to be described as "the greatest, the wisest, and most uncorrupt Minister, I ever conversed with" (*Works*, 10:102), the sneering anecdote of Harley's dismissal—which I quoted from Swift's letter to Archbishop King—must reverberate with such irony. But the hoax letter is more resonant. Similing sympathetically, we can stand beside the original recipient, watch his puzzled amusement, and employ our limited knowledge to unwind the riddle with him, because we are very nearly in his position. For hoax letters to work humorously, they must rise out of an obviously conventional structure; otherwise, the reader has no points of reference to direct his interpretation. The writer starts with an invitation, a letter of congratulation, a message of gratitude for a present received. Then he invents a setting that reverses the normal expectation. The recipient must consider the true character of his friend and from that infer the true message. Here, for example, is Swift's invitation to a party at the deanery. The recipient, Esther Johnson, and her companion, Mrs. Dingley, are asked to come and provide dinner; Swift will supply the wine. John Grattan, Dr.

Delany, and Dr. Sheridan will be the other guests. Swift writes as though he has received a message on the subject from Mrs. Johnson; but of course she has sent none, and his cryptic sentences are the first hint she will have of the engagement:

> *Jack Grattan* said nothing to me of it till last night; 'tis none of my fault: how did I know but you were to dine abroad? You should have sent your messenger sooner; yes, I think the dinner you provided for yourselves may do well enough here, but pray send it soon. I wish you would give a body more early warning; but you must blame yourselves. *Delany* says he will come in the evening; and for aught I know *Sheridan* may be here at dinner: which of you was it that undertook this frolick? Your letter hardly explained your meaning, but at last I found it. Pray don't serve me these tricks often. You may be sure, if there be a good bottle you shall have it. I am sure I never refused you, and therefore that reflection might have been spared. Pray be more positive in your answer to this. (30 April 1721, *Correspondence*, 2:385)

Just as true intimacy makes a humorous hoax possible, so the presense of intimacy where it does not exist makes humor dangerous and opens the tap of preciosity. In no letters does this affectation lour more darkly than the compliments Swift wrote to further his search for advancement. The relation of protégé to patron never suits him. When forced to accept it, he cannot reckon with his native pride but reacts too clumsily in the opposite direction. Rather than take for granted the world of rivals starving for a limited supply of promotions, he pretends to be above it. Here is a sample from a letter addressed on 13 November 1709 to Lord Halifax, whom Swift was hoping to flatter into making him a bishop. Writing from Ireland, Swift says,

> I retire into my self with great Satisfaction, and remembering I have had the Honor to converse with Your Lordship, I say as Horace did when he meant Your Predecessor; Cum magnis vixisse invita fatebitur usque invidia. Yet for all this, if I had a mind to be malicious, I could make a Vanity at your Lordships Expence, by letting People here know that I have some Share in Your Esteem. For I must inform You to Your great Mortification; that Your Lordship is universally admired by this tastless People. But not to humble You too much, I find it is for no other Reason, than that for which Women are so fond of those they call the Witts, meerly for their Reputation. They have heard wonderful Things of Your Lordship, and they presently imagine You to possess those Qualityes they most esteem in themselves, as the Asses did when

they discoursed about Socrates. For if Your Lordship were here in disguise, perhaps it would be just as if you sent your Pictures and Statues to a Country Fair; where One would offer half a crown for a Piece of Titian to stick on a Sign-post, Another a shilling for a Grecian Statue to fright away the Crows. (*Correspondence*, 1:158–59)

These are flowers out of Voiture's garden; and whoever quotes them is bound to subjoin what Swift wrote elsewhere about the same Lord Halifax: "I never heard him say one good thing" (*Works*, 5:258).

I hope this extract will not corroborate the widespread misapprehension that the mode of insult suits Swift better than that of eulogy. If anyone needs evidence of his genius for delicate and decorous praise, he may look at Swift's messages to Dr. Arbuthnot, the Earl of Oxford, Vanessa, and the Duchess of Ormonde. In fact, the examples of satirical insult are scarce though well known. I shall not draw on the fiery challenges delivered to Richard Steele. For those who prefer an independent composition, the violence of which can be felt across the quarter-millenium since its writing, the best example is probably the frontal attack on a delinquent Irish squire, heir of an old, covetous parishioner of Swift's. The victim addressed, though a Member of Parliament, had refused to pay his full tithes on the pretext that Swift was in irregular possession of an island (or detached piece of woodland) leased to Swift by his father.

This letter once more illustrates Swift's usual methods. He makes his immediate presence felt, though in purely moral terms, and deals with the recipient as a person intimately though hatefully familiar. Introducing the physical details of the occasion, he also brings in an observer, and nameless "worthy friend" who watches him read the squire's letter, and thus provides that detached tone that the cool insult demands. We can easily seat ourselves in this friend's place and assume the role of witnesses. Unlike Gay, Swift does not add comments that would obtrude upon the action; and the action in turn only frames the message. Instead of lingering on his emotion as such, Swift invents analogies and ironies channeling and expressing that emotion till it seems impersonal. Similarly, his character receives no such analysis as the squire's. Rather we sense the emanations of his confidence and pride through his language. By providing the friend, the stage setting, and the recapitulatory facts (the "historical background"), Swift hardly softens the literary effect of his anger. Instead, he permits us to enjoy it as a contemplative experience. The elaborate but inconspicuous frame keeps us

comfortable in the face of an extreme emotion. It gives artful form
to what might have appeared a frantic outburst.

Seeing your frank on the outside, and the address in the same hand, it
was obvious who was the writer, and before I opened it, a worthy
friend being with me, I told him the subject of the difference between
us: That your Tythes being generally worth 5 or 6ll. a year, and by the
terror of your Squireship frighting my Agent, to take what you gra-
ciously thought fit to give, you wronged me of half my due every year.
That having held from your father an Island worth three pence a year,
which I planted, and payd two Shillings annually for, and being out of
possession of the said Island seven or eight years, there could not
possibly be above 4s. due to you; for which you have thought fit to stop
3 or 4 years of Tyth at your own rate of 2ll. 5s. a year (as I remember)
and still continue to stop it, on pretence that the said Island was not
surrendered to you in form; although you have cutt down more Planta-
tions of Willow and Abeilles than would purchase a dozen such Islands.
I told my friend, that this talent of Squires formerly prevayled very
much in the County of Meath; that as to your self, from the badness of
your Education against all my advice and endeavors, and from the cast
of your Nature, as well as another circumstance which I shall not
mention, I expected nothing from you that became a Gentleman. That
I had expostulated this scurvy matter very gently with you, that I
conceived this letter was an answer: that from the prerogative of a good
estate, the practice of lording over a few Irish wretches, and from the
naturall want of better thinking, I was sure your answer would be
extremely rude and stupid, full of very bad language in all senses: That
a Bear in a wilderness will as soon fix on a Philosopher as on a Cottager;
and a Man wholly voyd of education, judgment, or distinction of person has no regard in his insolence but to the passion of fear; and how
heartily I wished, that to make you shew your humility, your quarrell
had been rather with a Captain of Dragoons than the Dean of St Pat-
ricks. . . .
    I took some pains in providing and advising about your Education,
but since you have made so ill use of my rules; I cannot deny according
to your own Principles that your usage of me is just. You are wholly out
of my danger; the weapons I use will do you no hurt, and to that which
would keep a nicer man in aw, you are insensible. A needle against a
stone wall can make no impression. Your faculty lyes in making bargains: stick to that; leave your Children a better estate than your father
left you; as he left you much more than your Grandfather left him.
Your father and you are much wiser than I, who gave amongst you fifty
years purchase for land, for which I am not to see one farthing. This
was intended as an Encouragement for a Clergyman to reside among
you, whenever any of your posterity shall be able to distinguish a Man
from a Beast. One thing I desire you will be set right in; I do not despise

All Squires. It is true I despise the bulk of them. But, pray take notice, that a Squire must have some merit before I shall honor him with my contempt. For, I do not despise a Fly, a Maggot, or a Mite. (To Robert Percival, 3 January 1730, *Correspondence*, 3:366–68)

The world in which Irish landlords greedily infringed on the rights of their own minority church becomes distinct through Swift's indirect representation. His own relation as an ineffectual but dignified priest to a presumptuous, bullying parishioner is carefully handled so that the pride of the dean overmatches the insolence of the squire. By shifting midway from the third-person mode of giving a friend a summary of the background, to the second-person mode of directly assaulting the landlord, Swift provides a dramatic leap of intensification (his "close-up" effect) for the latter half of his message. The writer has a manifest knowledge of his own place, character, and moral strength. He understands that a letter of insult must establish a visibly higher moral status for the writer than the recipient. It is within this set of epistolary and rhetorical designs that Swift's prose style makes its power felt. No literary form, I think, allowed that great style so many opportunities as the familiar letter.

Yet it is also one of the paradoxes of Swift's career that if he had written worse letters, he would possess a higher reputation. Even when he was young and unknown, correspondents held on to what he sent them. Swift rarely saved their messages unless he wished to keep the facts—or, I'm afraid, unless the authors were celebrated men and he wished to preserve the evidence of his intimacy with them. Besides being widely and quickly collected, the letters were published early, in a series of volumes that began to appear during Swift's own lifetime. Within some decades of his death the correspondence with Vanessa and the ineptly-named *Journal to Stella* were out. Consequently, the indiscretions and faults that prudent men suppress have been freely available to biographers and scandal-mongers. On the one hand, Swift's epistolary works were constantly quoted for the purity of their style; on the other hand, they seemed evidence to Walpole that he had slept with Vanessa, or to Thackeray that he had abused Esther Johnson. Historians know Swift's political allies misled him. Scholars know Swift's private thoughts often contradicted his public declarations. I should like to plead that many of these documents be now elevated from the class of evidence to the class of literature. They are more amusing than Defoe's novels, better polished than Steele's essays, a deeper revelation of the mind of the age than Rowe's tragedies. So I recommend

them as still deserving the extraordinary attention they received
when the first printed texts of Swift's correspondence excited the
literary world two centuries ago.

Notes

1. Katherine G. Hornbeak, *The Complete Letter Writer in English, 1568–1800* (Northampton, Mass.: Smith College Studies in Modern Languages, 1934), 15:20.

2. Ibid., pp. 8–32.

3. Ibid., p. 51.

4. Ibid., pp. 51–52.

5. In this paragraph I have condensed some remarks from John Carroll's introduction to his edition of *Selected Letters of Samuel Richardson* (Oxford: Clarendon Press, 1964), pp. 31–35. For the quotations from Johnson see the *Lives of the Poets*, ed. G. B. Hill (Oxford, 1905), 3:207 (life of Pope). See also Johnson's ridicule of the dogma of epistolary spontaneity in *Rambler* no. 152 and in his letter of 27 October 1777 to Mrs. Thrale. (The dogma remains a commonplace today).

6. Gay, *Letters*, ed. C. F. Burgess (Oxford: Clarendon Press, 1966), pp. 53–54.

7. *Letters*, ed. R. W. Chapman (Oxford: Clarendon Press, 1952), 2:242.

8. Letter to William Mason, 13 March 1777.

9

Swift's Praise of Gulliver: Some Renaissance Background to the *Travels*

JENNY MEZCIEMS

Now tell me: can a man love anyone who hates himself? Can he be in harmony with someone else if he's divided in himself, or bring anyone pleasure if he's only a disagreeable nuisance to himself? No one, I fancy, would say he can unless there's someone more foolish than Folly. Remove me, and no one could put up with his neighbour, indeed, he'd stink in his own nostrils, find everything about himself loathsome and disgusting.

Erasmus, *Praise of Folly*

1

The praise of Folly or of Gulliver must be a matter of fairly complicated inversions, and there is of course no simple equation whereby the relationship between Gulliver and his author may be compared with that between Folly and Erasmus. Neither Swift nor Gulliver claims to conduct an encomiastic exercise until we reach the Houyhnhnms, and there the problem, as with Erasmus, is in deciding what is mockery and what is for real. Parallels between these two works are not immediately evident in form or style but are nevertheless to be found in a shared concern with language and patterns of discourse as well as in the basic satirical intentions of the two authors, in the matters of which both treat, and in their respective attitudes (not identical but with much common ground) to civilized human society. Most of all they are to be found in methods of presentation that demand a particularly strenuous engagement on the reader's part with a narrator who attracts and repels, per-

245

suades and fails to persuade, is at once teacher and stooge, preacher and clown, in part his author's spokesman and in part a facsimile of the reader.[1] The wary relationships between author, narrator, and reader are a difficult and central feature of the link between Erasmus and Swift in these works and the suggestion that Swift in any way "praises" Gulliver as Erasmus "praises" Folly[2] is best approached by way of more familiar connections between Swift and some other writers, not in order to suggest unexpected influences but to fill out a pattern which is already recognized.

Swift acknowledges no direct debts and Gulliver makes no allusions, within the narrative, to works that have nevertheless been compared by readers during and since Swift's time as representative of a tradition. The handful most commonly mentioned with *Gulliver's Travels*, claiming its membership of a genre (but leaving out many travel narratives, many utopian fictions, and many satires), are Lucian's *True Story*, More's *Utopia*, and the works of Rabelais. More peripheral references are made to Plato as source of the utopian idea and to Cyrano de Bergerac for the provision of more nearly contemporary formal models of the imaginary voyage satire. The tradition becomes self-conscious during the Renaissance among the humanists, and a descriptive identification made by C. S. Lewis in an essay on Addison is worth quoting for its emphasis on a kind of narrowness in writers whom one associates more easily with openness and breadth of learning; a similar narrowness or selectivity perhaps is needed to pick out the essential connections:

> Learning to them meant the knowledge and imitation of a few rather arbitrarily selected Latin authors and some even fewer Greek authors. They despised metaphysics and natural science; and they despised all the past outside the favoured periods. They were dominated by a narrowly ethical purpose . . . in Erasmus, in Rabelais, in the *Utopia* one recognizes the very accent of the angry *belle-lettrist* railing, as he rails in all ages, at "jargon" and "straw-splitting." On this side Pope and Swift are true inheritors of the Humanist tradition.[3]

This is meant to be reductive, but the humanists mentioned would have recognized as virtues the limitations attributed to them, and would have claimed that their taste and judgment enabled them to reject all but the highest and purest standards and were more important than wide experience or even deep learning. Their élitism did not require them to shut themselves off from all that they despised, nor did it hinder them from exploring it with a fascinated involvement that has made their imitation of the worst, not the best, a memorable parodic trademark.

The tradition has sometimes been ignored, however, or treated as irrelevant in discussions of Swift's work, which at the time was mostly judged, as it was written, for its practical effectiveness as argument in some local and immediate issue.[4] Thus Swift has sometimes been attacked and sometimes praised for being either remote from everyday life or closely involved with it. The separate contexts are in fact not mutually exclusive or incompatible but interdependent and mutually enriching. *Gulliver's Travels* is obviously in part a satire of local and particular application so that some of its allusions are lost or have to be rediscovered by historians of literature, and equally obviously a work that stands outside its own time with recognized affinities and antecedents in a literary tradition not centered on England or Ireland. The association with Erasmus is not commonly made until well into the present century, as in the quotation from Lewis; even then, the *Praise of Folly* is more usually linked with *A Tale of a Tub* than with *Gulliver's Travels*. Swift himself rarely mentions Erasmus, though he possessed some of his works, including the *Praise of Folly*. William King, however, inviting Swift to visit him at Saint Mary's Hall in 1737, compliments him in phrasing borrowed from Gulliver with the notion of "a triumvirate, that is not to be matched in any part of the learned world, Sir *Thomas More*, Erasmus and the *Drapier*" (*Correspondence*, 5:54). Swift's references to Rabelais are more frequent, mostly in the form of narrative episodes recalled in letters between Swift and Arbuthnot, for instance, assuming appreciative familiarity on the part of the reader.[5] Among his mischievous marginal comments to Addison's *The Freeholder* (1715–16), Swift sums up an unconvincing panegyric on the king as "most undeniable Truth, as any in Rabelais" (*Works*, 5:254).[6] He owned and annotated an early French edition and might also have known the Urquhart/Motteux translation of the 1690s.

A paucity of reference to writers he admired or imitated is not surprising; on the one hand, Swift did not waste many words on literary criticism, and on the other it is a feature of humanist élitism to assume that one's readers are familiar with works from an accepted canon and do not need to have allusions spelled out. There are plenty of references to Plato, predictably for the sake of political attitudes, none to Lucian beyond the record of having bought a three-volume French translation for Stella, a number of passing references to Cervantes (including one in which he and Rabelais are

cited as representatives of "true Humour" (*Works*, 12:32)), and some
references to Thomas More that are of a rather different kind. It
seems odd that the sale catalogue of Swift's library lists no copy of
the *Utopia*.[7] Swift greatly admired More; in one marginal comment
to another work he described him as "the only Man of true Virtue
that ever Engl[a]nd produced" (*Works*, 5:247) and even Gulliver,
who acknowledges as few heroes as Swift does, places him as the
only modern in that "*Sextumvirate* to which all the Ages of the
World cannot add a Seventh" (p. 196). But it is not as an author that
More is upheld and his own writing is mostly as polemical and
occasional as Swift's, though less secular.

Whatever *Gulliver's Travels* owes to *Utopia*, Swift hardly mentions it. But nor for that matter does he ever admit to having read
Robinson Crusoe, though close comparisons between these two contemporary travel fictions have been made from an early date. Some
readers did assume incautiously that the two authors were writing
similar books with similar aims, and weighed one against the other
as though ingenuity, credibility, and an acceptable human image in
the narrator were competitive claims to merit.[8] *Robinson Crusoe*,
published seven years earlier and widely praised, supplies such an
obvious model that Swift's silence seems provocative. His mocking
exploitation of the taste of readers who are susceptible to fiction
dressed as fact gains parodic force from Defoe's popularity, and his
ignoring the existence of the earlier book (which appeared just prior
to the time Swift probably began his own fiction) has the air of a
characteristic disingenuousness. Swift referred disdainfully to his
own voracious reading of "Trash" (and of many travel books) while
he was composing *Gulliver's Travels*, during a period when he was
much given to expressing the spleen of a wasted talent in exile and
might pointedly have imitated a "hack" writer whose work he considered unworthy of acknowledgement in proportion to its success.

Gulliver makes a joke about the association of Houyhnhnmland
with Utopia or *Utopia* in the "Letter to Sympson" that was prefixed
to the 1735 edition: "Some [readers] are so bold as to think my Book
of Travels a meer Fiction out of mine own Brain; and have gone so
far as to drop Hints, that the *Houyhnhnms* and *Yahoos* have no more
existence than the Inhabitants of *Utopia*" (p. 8). He has it both
ways: it is insulting to be told he made it all up, and more insulting
to have it linked with *Utopia*, which even Gulliver knows is a
fiction. Gulliver wants his book to be taken for original fact—but
there is an underlying claim that as fiction it should not stand alone
and that Swift wants it to be seen as imitative of More's work.[9]

Gulliver can afford to acknowledge his factual cousin Dampier (whom he claims to have helped on matters of style) but not his fictional cousin Crusoe. His text has in any case achieved a falsifying fictional autonomy that worries him, since the printer has according to him misspelled "Brobdingrag" throughout and has confused some of the dates (pp. 7–8);[10] Dampier, in a line of stolid Englishmen who want to get their facts right and have no moralizing intent, made similar apologies for similar small inaccuracies. Swift's parodies may range from emulation to mockery or even disgust but the criteria for deciding which is which, and how one allusion is played off against another, are left unspoken; the reader whose literary and moral values are uncertain or wrong (that is, different from Swift's) is left in confusion outside the pale.

Critics who have failed (or felt no need) to link *Gulliver's Travels* with the Renaissance humanist writers naturally include some among Swift's contemporaries who looked primarily for topical truths or distortions. It is interesting, however, that those critics in any period who have most attacked the book have also been the most inclined to treat it in isolation from other works, holding up its author as a uniquely misanthropic monster, denying him any place in a tradition that they usually ignored if they recognized it at all. Many saw that Swift's portrayal of man was subversive, and if they had further recognized what illusions were being subverted might have claimed with some justice that some illusions are socially desirable (as Swift did in rather different contexts). Among Swift's early biographers Lord Orrery and Patrick Delany were both much concerned to defend mankind against Swift's attacks in the *Travels*, but his cousin Deane Swift, protesting at their misinterpretations, significantly quotes freely from the Bible rather than from secular literary authority in Swift's support.[11] Augustan taste, even in the Augustan Age, was a minority culture and it is understandable that the "moderns" in their growing confidence in a less pessimistic view of man should make judgments without reference to irrelevant figures from the past, believing in the competence and authority of their own times.

Pope, in a dedicatory passage in the *Dunciad* (1728), could associate Swift easily and naturally with antecedents in a line of satiric wit:

> Whether thou chuse Cervantes' serious air,
> Or laugh and shake in Rab'lais' easy chair.

> (ll. 19–20)

Pope's allusions compliment Swift by recognizing his use of sources and models, suggesting that it is right to make comparisons and that Swift would welcome the procedure. It is a matter of pointing out not simply that Swift is on a par with other great writers but that associations are invited and are essential to his meaning. To catalogue specific borrowings in detail would be tedious and irrelevant after such labors as those of William Eddy in *Gulliver's Travels: A Critical Study* (Princeton, N.J.: Princeton University Press, 1923). More interesting to a reader sixty years later are questions of why Swift chose certain models and what uses he made of them beyond narrative detail. Swift never emulated in earnest a high style or mode, as Pope did, for the sake of contrast with inferior substance. Instead he chose weapons to suit his target, and if the target was a lowly and unlovely object, then so would be his offering to match or exceed it, casting sour home-grown acorns before swine. If he looked back in admiration at the ideals of Plato and Erasmus and Thomas More he saw also that Lucian and Erasmus and Rabelais could express the remoteness of those ideals through exuberant nonsense. He imitated the adoption of terms from a world that abused or denied or replaced ideals and had made them so ludicrously inappropriate that they could be handled only through mockery and apparent irreverence.

2

Since Swift's own ideals did not readily display themselves in positive formulations or in heroic personifications we have to consider the features, personal as well as literary, of those whose habits of thought and writing he admired and found sympathetic across a separation of almost two hundred years. The stature of the individual, we are shown in *Gulliver's Travels*, is not always of his own choosing and Swift found unexpected ways to make a figure for himself in spite of discouragement, becoming a local hero in the person of the Drapier. The Renaissance was a period of larger potential, with frustrations to match, for men whose activities threw them into the limelight and whose situations were distantly echoed, Swift may have felt, in his own. In the most popular and affectionately remembered writings of those we are considering here there is the same sense of circularity and enclosure, of energies that must be released inside self-imposed barriers, that we find in Swift.[12] They all pay tribute to the concept of *serio ludere*, making use of a classical convention that allows serious matters to be broached in a deceptively playful manner, and which engenders considerable tension in controlling energies that might otherwise be barbarically subversive.[13]

Partly there is some straightforward relief to the scholar or man of affairs in lighthearted literary play of a kind that enhances his knowledge of the classical writers whose ideas and rhetoric he sees as a civilizing influence. Lucian, some of whose satires were translated by Erasmus and More and also by Rabelais, begins his *True Story* with the advice that relaxation is as important for the intellectual as for the physical athlete, recommending "the sort of reading that, instead of affording just pure amusement based on wit and humour, also boasts a little food for thought," and his own book claims just such dual qualities. The fantastic travels of his narrator, motivated by his "intellectual activity and desire for adventure," take him beyond the last footprints of Heracles and Dionysus to a series of topsy-turvy worlds in whose features Lucian can mock the full range of human desires, failings, ideals, practices, beliefs, and weaknesses—most especially those of credulity and the inability to distinguish truth from falsehood.[14] Lucian appealed to the Renaissance satirists because of his lack of illusion and his sense of fun: salutary characteristics to bring to the attention of an age emerging, or failing to emerge, from irrational superstition and misguided reverence for false authorities. Lucian's mockery of unwordly Christian fools could have been incorporated into the *Praise of Folly* without causing Erasmus any offense.[15] His general scepticism could be held up in contrast to overserious interpretations of Plato's idealism and could also be used beside it in the attempt to balance the relationship between reason and faith that exercised Swift as consistently as it did Erasmus—though Swift wore his rue with a difference.

Erasmus describes his *Praise of Folly* as a jeu d'esprit composed so as not to waste time on a tedious journey, and dedicates it to More, punning in his Latin title of *Moriae Encomium* on the similarity of his friend's name to the Greek word for folly (μωρία) and crediting More with an understanding of conventions which include that of the mock-modest apology for triviality. More himself, introducing his *Utopia* with a similar apologetic letter to a friend, gives similar half-serious excuses for his lack of time and skill in tossing off a slight work that he pretends is in any case only secondhand reportage, but he too goes to some lengths to make it clear that the majority of readers will not understand the conventions within

which he writes. Rabelais in his turn plays at confusing the unen-
lightened reader; each of his narratives is preceded by a prologue in
which he alternately cajoles and abuses his unknown readers in
exaggeratedly familiar terms ("Most noble boozers, and you my
very esteemed and poxy friends"; "most illustrious and most valor-
ous champions, noblemen, and others"; "my gouty friends") and in
the first of which he claims to be writing total nonsense that disguises grave mysteries that are not after all to be taken seriously.[16]
Swift borrows such prefatory devices for Gulliver, though he does
not invite the reader to any merriment or intimacy, only to confusion as to what is serious and what is not.

For the serious aspect of his literary frolic Erasmus takes from
classical sources the principle that literature should entertain in
order to instruct. He borrows from Lucretius, for a later defense of
his apparently frivolous work against solemn condemnation, the
particular image of the doctor honeying the medicine bowl to make
the dose palatable to the child.[17] Swift, who claimed privately and
uncompromisingly that he aimed to vex and not to divert the world
(*Correspondence*, 3:102), not only has clearly the same aim with a
savage twist but also used the sterner end of the same Lucretian
quotation for an epigraph on the title page of the 1735 revision of
his book: "Retroq/Vulgus abhorret ab his" (that is to say, without
any mention of honey, that the crowd cannot face distasteful
truths). In the same edition appeared for the first time an especially
Lucianic (and Erasmian) touch with the words "Splendide men-
dax," from Horace, placed descriptively beneath a sober frontispiece portrait of Gulliver. Swift's friend Arbuthnot complimented
the successful author with the words "Gulliver is a happy man that
at his age can write such a merry work", (*Correspondence*, 3:179), and
the ironic senses in which the compliment is deserved depend on a
knowledge and understanding of the mode and the tradition in
which Swift wrote.

In the *Praise of Folly* Erasmus hands over to the person of Folly a
full formal eulogy of herself, delivered from the rostrum in classical
style. The reader smiles at the joke, recognizing that he must
understand everything in reverse, but as the satire develops and
Folly's attributes begin to prove not only universal but also socially
useful, sensible, and ultimately the distinguishing features of un-
worldly Christian behavior, the reader is increasingly a target,
quickwittedly dissociating himself from one category of folly only
to find each alternative position at least as foolish. Erasmus is not
responsible for the offense Folly gives, since it is Folly who speaks

and he can claim to think the opposite. But since the categories of Fools include all mankind, they also include Erasmus as well as the reader, whose criticisms are therefore disarmed on that count as well. The attack on follies and vices is at the same time an earnest moral sermon, a delightful entertainment, an exercise in intellectual gymnastics, and a literary lesson in classical rhetoric. Most of these features are borrowed by Swift from this example of a traditional mode that Erasmus sought to reintroduce after long neglect, except that Swift does not hope to educate the average reader (or Yahoo) and presents him with a figure, a form, and a rhetoric that he will comfortably accept as those of his own time and measure: those of the English traveler who sets out to improve his fortune and solemnly to narrate experiences that may be informative and useful to his country. Swift's moral satire has the same scope as that of Erasmus, but his mood is different and his fool reduced and degenerate by comparison.

Swift, like Erasmus, is both separate from his narrator and implicated with him in the satire. It is as difficult to distinguish between the views of Gulliver and Swift, however, as between those of Thomas More and his fictional narrator Raphael Hythlodaeus, though in the *Utopia* there is an important and perhaps misleading pretense that the two can be told apart. From More's *Utopia* Swift takes the imagining of an ideal world by comparison with which the standards of modern Europe may be criticized, and the figure of an idealizing traveler who rejects the reader's values and must be rejected by him. More's fiction begins with a debate in the Platonic style on the social evils of Europe and includes a central argument on the personal rights and social duties of the philosopher, the traveler, and the counselor. But in book 2 Hythlodaeus takes over with his narrative description of Utopia, which has many features in common with Plato's Republic and with Swift's Houyhnhnmland. Hythlodaeus has an ambiguous relationship with certain illustrious literary antecedents: "his sailing has not been like that of Palinurus but that of Ulysses or, rather, of Plato" (p. 49), but he is also a "real" Portuguese traveler who has given up his domestic commitments, like Gulliver but unlike More, in order to wander with Vespucci in the New World.[18]

Such allusive signposts might direct us but are instead disorientating. We cannot know for sure what More meant by his teasingly conflicting ironies in dismissing the traveler and his ideas at the end of the book.[19] He may have wanted to deny responsibility for proto-communist schemes and unChristian Utopian practices,

whether or not he privately approved of some or any of them. As in
the case of the confusion between Swift and Gulliver, the dreaming
traveler-figure may go too far and absolve his author by becoming
ridiculous; or the author may mock his own imaginative capacity as
well as the general human incapacity to live the life of pure reason.
But the traveling figure that we eventually see in Gulliver is made
up of features from Hythlodaeus, from Ulysses, from real-life
sailors and authors, and from Robinson Crusoe, with all the dubious blending of heroism, idealism, scientific zest, and social irre-
sponsibility that a composite image can convey.

Perhaps the most significant feature that Swift takes from
Rabelais is the device of choosing a sub-literary form as a medium
through which to mock that irresponsible appetite for the fabulous
that both writers plainly enjoy feeding; it is one of the ways in
which the writer becomes a butt of his own satire. A more obvious
borrowing, however, is the giant stature of Swift's traveler. The
sense of restless quest from narrative to narrative and from one kind
of metaphorical experience larger than life to another provides one
structural parallel between the Rabelaisian and the Swiftian giant.
But whereas Gulliver's size turns out to be only the first in a series
of unexpected disadvantages to him, Rabelais's giants, when they
lose that emphasis on size that makes them physically powerful in
the early narratives, progress instead in princely and intellectual
qualities. They triumph over circumstance and exceed their original brief, rather as Erasmus's Folly does. Gulliver is always lonely
and dependent, but Rabelais's giants command a loyal company
with no embarrassment about discrepancies in size (Pantagruel's
name comes jokingly from that of a popular dwarf, Penthagruel).
Swift introduces sudden uncomfortable limits on fantasy where
Rabelais gives it free rein. Gargantua and Pantagruel, father and
son, also portray a continuity of values and a reverence for tradition
even while they are overturning constricting systems of language
and thought. They reform education and establish utopian governments as though from natural inherited principles, not abstract
ideas. As Pantagruel rises in spiritual stature he is offset by the
puny but lovable figure of Panurge, whose human lust for certainty
(in the matter of whether or not he should marry, and whether he
will be cuckolded) obliges Pantagruel to escort him through an
exploration of many systems of inquiry before taking him on the
long voyage to the Oracle of the Bottle. After much aimless wandering and incidental satire of societies along the way they learn
nothing comprehensible. In a sense they discover, as Gulliver

might have done, that travel is not really necessary; neither folly nor wisdom are limited to specific locations.

3

Swift's own choice of form and figure, his attitudes to human society, his teasing of the reader by provoking his engagement with ideas and refusing to confirm his findings, and his concern for the responsible use of persuasive rhetoric make up a set of complex associations with this small body of influential Renaissance satire and with its classical sources. But a further sense of kinship is evident in the relationships between the lives of these men and their roles as writers. Erasmus, More, and even Rabelais had, like Swift, the experience of living close to the centers of political and ecclesiastical power at times of cultural crisis. Each was strong and at the same time helpless. Rabelais had not quite the same opportunity to become intoxicated with the Platonic possibilities of a role as wise counselor to the great, but he expresses as forcefully as Swift does the spleen and disappointment of the Diogenic tubthumper, most notably in his Prologue to the *Tiers Livre*, and his personal fortunes depended on the power of noble patrons.

In each case there is something of the temperament of the ready actor obliged to sit in the audience. The leisured retirement from public affairs, brief or permanent, enjoyed or endured, which each author in turn claims as the condition in which his most imaginative work is conceived is thus not a dignified Horatian choice so much as a protest by the satirist that he can make himself important only in the costume of the fool. He speaks as a ventriloquist through a posturing dummy, keeping his own image more or less politely intact, able or obliged to disown his creation or acknowledging almost grudgingly his reputation as a mere writer. Travelers, giants, and fools, too, are in a sense heroes displaced from their status as guardian founders of the civilized world, but they learn new roles in fables that are even more ancient. To lean on a tradition and claim a pedigree reduces the dominance of the here and now, and Lucian's irreverence becomes as important as Plato's philosophy to men offering otherworldly fictions that combine idealism with scepticism.

Swift may imitate, emulate, or pretend to do either or neither, to show by turns his closeness to these writers and his remoteness from them. Erasmus and More must seem to stand together on a

level of spiritual highmindedness very distant from the earthy
popular images of Rabelais and Swift, and neither would have
expected to be remembered chiefly for his allegedly most lighthearted piece of literary nonsense—or for that matter as a "writer"
at all. The *Praise of Folly* and *Utopia* are genuinely throwaway
works, true at least in part to the jocular spirit in which they were
presented to the world, and they do not convey quite the urgent
defiance of Rabelais or Swift, both of whom pick up and develop
more consciously the ironies involved in being *obliged* to write in a
jokey way: their methods would make less sense if Erasmus and
More had not preceded them. Erasmus and More enjoyed a securer
sense of spiritual reality beside which the material world, though
painfully actual, could finally be discounted. The attitude is not
strictly that of *contemptus mundi*, however. Rabelais, though so
much nearer to them in time, shared Swift's admiration for them
and felt the superiority of their greater freedom. Swift is thus closer
to Rabelais in feelings of loss and frustration. In an alternative
partnering, of course, Swift is closer to More, both of them being
more deeply and publicly committed to local political affairs. Swift
did not have to die for his principles, in a world that lacked heroic
opportunities as much as it lacked heroes, but nor did his temperament allow him to escape as fully as Erasmus or Rabelais do into a
stance of lofty or lowly disengagement. In Swift the stress between
awareness and impotence narrows to an intensity whose forceful
mature expression is a tightly controlled fable, found on the one
hand fit only for children and on the other too obscene for the adult
whose sense of human dignity Swift could not share.

Swift's own view of the Renaissance and his use of its writers is
partly explicable in terms of his Platonic conception of history as at
the best cyclical and at the worst steadily degenerative.[20] The life-
spans of Erasmus, More, and Rabelais extend over a period during
which the physical as well as the intellectual world opened up
enormously to bring potential unity and actual division; the peaceful respite in the early years of the sixteenth century gave Erasmus
a real optimism and might have seemed to Swift equivalent to
another brief potential stasis in his own time—as though the Tory
government of 1710–14 might arrest the processes of decay (the
dates oddly echoing the years 1510–15 during which the *Praise of
Folly* and the *Utopia* were written). Fore or aft, in both periods,
were deep religious and political schisms that revolutionized Christian Europe and Christian England. The Renaissance was also,
however, obviously a good time for thrusting energies of all kinds,

and the humanist scholar might see himself in a powerful authoritative role as quasi-Platonic adviser to rising secular rulers. He could
offer his new knowledge of the ancient world and of historical
parallels with present events to put the modern world in perspective.

For the Christian humanist there were two other worlds: the
unchanging spiritual one that predates classical paganism because it
is timeless, and the changing material one that might move towards
enlightenment as easily as towards decay. The balancing of powers
and goals seemed to require vision of a transcendental and syncretic
kind. At the same time the strangleholds of medieval scholastic and
monastic systems had to be broken, like chains round the ankle,
and one of the ways Swift "parodies" the Renaissance writers in
Gulliver's Travels is through a reversal of the liberating process:
Rabelais's Pantagruel allegorically throws aside medieval constraints as he pulls loose the cables that hold his cradle to the floor
to go in search of precisely immeasurable quantities of food (*Pantagruel*, 4). But other systems equally narrow are restored to power
when Gulliver, in an appropriately imitative allegory of birth,
meekly submits to fragile Lilliputian bonds and waits for nourishment to be carefully calculated for him in portions that never sound
quite adequate (pp. 21–24).

Erasmus, with his uncommitted personal life (like Swift he had
in effect no family, no inherited role or status), could commit himself to the highest aims and make for himself the highest freedoms.
He refused to serve either the temporal rulers who sought his support for their own interests or the increasingly divisive parties
within the single Christian church on which world unity depended,
and he remained the chief representative of an idealism that sought
to unite and to reform, to bring together the spiritual and the
secular. But Erasmus had no illusions in his loftiness and it is as
Folly that he finds his place among the crowd, to ascend thence on
to a plane of religious simplicity that is equally "popular."

Thomas More's life was one of tighter involvements within a
whole series of commitments to family, profession, public service,
and diplomatic office, with the circle of humanist friends as a supporting enclave in which he could be a pupil and the family as a
haven in which he was master. His ideals were those that inspired
Erasmus, and though they were exercised on a lower plane his final
public performance in a real-life trial was that of the fool in Christ.
Complementary features of the two lives show in the imaginative
works: where Folly's role can encompass extremes without self-

division, More presents us in *Utopia* with a split between the contradictory views of his own narrating self and of the separate person
of Hythlodaeus, the imaginary traveler who moves between two
worlds, so that the book works not towards transcendence but
towards the choice of one world over the other. *Utopia*, like *Gulliver's Travels* and the *Praise of Folly* and the works of Rabelais, explores the indulgence of escape and the problem of return.[21] More's
fiction is more somber and urgent and personal than Erasmus's
declamation, its occasion more immediately worldly and political—
but it looks back to Plato, to the essential division and desired
fusion of spiritual philosopher and secular ruler.

In the *Praise of Folly* the consistent presence of the narrator, her
changing expressions mirrored in every face turned towards her, is
a unifying one and the best offers salvation to the worst. In the
Utopia we are taken from More's personal frustrating circumstances
(outlined in his prefatory letter to Peter Giles) to a position of
compromised idealism that is reached through direct reference to
Plato, just as the notion of the ideal world and some of its features
come from him.[22] But fusion of one world with the other, such as
Folly alone engineers, and the contrasting idea of choice between
worlds and spokesmen found in More's fiction are both denied at
the end of *Gulliver's Travels* in a reformulation that offers two impossible worlds and only one unhappy spokesman. Gulliver, setting himself apart from his kind after experiencing the *Republic* of
Houyhnhnmland, is hardly meant to make us expect any kind of
spiritual rebirth as he slouches towards the stable, and he is rather
pointedly not a fool in Christ. The only behavior that will make life
bearable for him is at odds alike with the engagement of Erasmus
and Folly, the freedom of Hythlodaeus, or the compromise of
More. It is suggested to him by Don Pedro, that unassuming
character who fades into and out of the homecoming narrative and
who, though he is a professional Portuguese wanderer like Hythlodaeus, persuades Gulliver to go home since "it was altogether
impossible to find such a solitary Island as I had desired to live in;
but I might command in my own House, and pass my time in a
Manner as recluse as I pleased" (p. 289).[23] It is a piece of advice that
would have carried some poignancy if conveyed by Hythlodaeus to
Thomas More.

Swift might envy Erasmus the spiritual loftiness with which he
could present his figure of Folly and make it include himself and
More and the rest of humankind, unillusioned but also unafraid,
sure of his values and of the all-encompassing range within which

they operate. If Gulliver is a fool-figure he is disguised as a commonsense Englishman; either way he is representative but either way he is cut off not just from his author and the society of his own kind but from any superior system that might lend grace to his situation. Erasmus does not need, as More and Swift do, to confront his readers with other worlds, since the real one is complete and unalienating. Swift's reader feels deprived of the kind of "normal" voice that More allows to intervene between himself and an enthusiastic narrator. More presents us with a split in sympathy between two viewpoints. Swift like Erasmus gives us one viewpoint but makes the inconsistencies and inner disturbances undermine the apparently solid outer form. Gulliver's modern selfhood owes something to two other Renaissance formulations: Pico della Mirandola's universally dignified human being, glorying in its potential for mobility,[24] and Montaigne's personal consciousness, asserting apologetically its own incoherence. Gulliver cannot bear to recognize his own image in the distorted creatures he meets and as a human being he is found physically inferior to the Yahoos, but he is sure that he has secure values and does not question the absolute normality of his own scale of judgment. What in the Renaissance seem open and positive concepts of man go sour in Gulliver, becoming closed and rigid.

The structure of a narrating consciousness in Rabelais involves a relationship between heroic giants whose natures and adventures progress from those appropriate to crude physical stature to those with the metaphorical or moral stature of a princely humanist wisdom.[25] The developing giant figure is all-comprehensive rather than self-contradictory, a figure that can support and shelter lesser mortals and that looks back to the inclusive representativeness of Erasmus's Folly. Swift draws on such figures in making Gulliver representative but also degenerate, all too human just as the Brobdingnagians are. The Brobdingnagians are themselves degenerate giants, "small abortive Births in Comparison of those in ancient Times," according to their own historian (p. 137), and they have none of the superhuman qualities they might be entitled to as creatures of fantasy. Swift's giants are never bigger than himself or the reader. Rabelais's personal life and stature are quite negated in his huge fictions, taken over and altogether transfigured. He writes of his own society and gives us detailed caricatures of its institutions, but they are transformed and elevated in fantasy, made all the more unreal by the presence of a life-sized Rabelais under his own name as the narrative develops. The first "Chronicles" (as Rabelais called

them) were published under the anagrammatic pseudonym of Al-
cofribas Nasier, Extractor of the Quintessence, who, long before he
reverts to François Rabelais, Doctor of Medicine, in the *Tiers Livre*,
recommends in his "Prologue" to *Pantagruel* the therapeutic qualities of such works to those who "ne ont trouvé remede plus expedient que de mettre lesdictes *Chronicques* entre deux beaulx linges
bien chaulx et les appliquer au lieu de la douleur."

Rabelais was not a public figure of the stature of Erasmus or
More. He seems to write almost for the sake of an escape valve for
trapped energies, especially in the allegorical essay on the satirist's
role which makes up the prologue to the *Tiers Livre:* "Prins ce choys
et election, ay pensé ne faire exercice inutile et importun, si je
remuois mon tonneau Diogenic . . . je delibere, je discours, je
resoulz et concluds. Après l'epilogue je riz, j'escripz, je compose, je
boy" (while other men are busily preparing for war with its dubious
glory). Rabelais freed himself from the limitations of a monastery
but achieved giant stature through his words rather than deeds,
provoking censure and risking punishment for the liberties he took
even in fantasy. But his narratives move in a progression that suggests a spiral rather than a homecoming circle: from primitive
popular romance and fable to a mystical world in which the hero
travels free and rootless, no longer establishing his own utopias but
viewing island societies from the ship that has become his home.
The optimism that seemed possible early in the century gave the
impetus to Rabelais's iconoclasm but then left him increasingly
exposed to the power of critical theologians and to the effects of
fluctuating relationships between successive French monarchs and
the Pope and his own patrons; the fantasy contains elements of
propaganda but seems also in part a refuge in which the author can
manipulate words in defiance of facts.

4

Rabelais does release the spirit of man from cramped circumstances: and the giant figures of the early books are a particularly
exuberant expression of that conflict between energy and constraint
which Swift found sympathetic, especially since the constraints
were imposed by just the kinds of system Swift hated and found
barbaric in his turn. Rabelais's narratives, like the others in this
group, have an element of the utopian in their satirical contrasts

between real and imagined worlds. The *Praise of Folly*, however, is an exception both in form and in the fact that its imaginary narrator does not disguise our world or offer an alternative one, though Erasmus satirizes the same range of social institutions under their separate headings.

These targets (government, law, the church; the worlds of learning, science, and medicine) are hardy perennials attacked with a regularity that proves their importance as pillars ensuring the continuance of society, monuments to a central recognition that human nature stays the same and that change can never be fundamental. The satirist, whose business it is to remind his fellows of their dependence on these social structures, is a deeply conservative being; he may claim as Erasmus does merely to lament abuses and hypocrisy, or he may like Rabelais embark on metaphorical destructive purges, sweeping away armies in a flood of giant's urine or pulling apart language and its formulations only to show how irresistibly they bounce back into shape and meaning. The variety of imaginative visions is held together by two constants: the limitations imposed by human nature and human reason on the internal arrangements of the human world, and the centrality of the human figure with his weaknesses and vulnerabilities as a representative of his kind.

Swift, following suggestions for form as well as matter from his Renaissance antecedents, took his basic rules for the structure of an ideal world from Plato, whose intellectual dream took account of natural human limitations and was therefore essentially hypothetical. Plato's premise makes his *Republic* hard to satirize, though it may be mocked for speculating on the impossible too solemnly. Lucian provided a model, to be used alongside that of Plato, for the proliferation of imagined worlds, deliberately free-ranging and fiercely satirical not only of the real world but of the idealizing faculty within it. Hence the importance in each of Swift's models of both world and narrator and the essential duality in each that allows both admiration and mockery. The original Platonic world-model from the *Republic* is the ideal of reason and it is copied in outline by More and Swift but not by Rabelais, whose utopian abbey of Thélème is on the lines of a Lucianic mockery of rational closed societies. Features of Utopia borrowed by Rabelais from More directly are glimpsed more straightforwardly in the governments established by the giants at the beginning of the *Tiers Livre* and the end of *Pantagruel*, but Thélème proves to be a truly en-

closed world when we come to study its principles, whatever freedoms it claims: partly because one man's dream, even of communal
self-indulgence, is not another's.

Some of the most striking features of Plato's *Republic* and the
hardest for members of an ordinary corrupt society to accept are
those associated with Sparta, which was after all a real place,
though mythologized to some extent by troubled Athenians, with
the attraction and fear that a closed enemy society has for an open
one.[26] To fictionalize certain positive characteristics may be a way
of reclaiming them from the enemy and of making them more
authoritative and even more real once purged of associations. In
this manner the actual enemy state becomes the corruption of positive features and their source is instead the writer's imagination,
which he will nevertheless endow with the appearance of truth by
pretending to report at second hand from a distance in time or
place. Thus in the *Timaeus* the story of an idealized ancient Athens
in conflict with Atlantis is welcomed with Socrates saying: "the fact
that it is no invented fable but genuine history is all-important."[27]
The truth of the story is in the authority of those who have handed
it down from one to the other. The legendary Spartan features
become almost obligatory, and are picked up by More and again,
with some modification, by Swift in Houyhnhnmland:

> State restriction of, or control over, private property, the use of money,
> industry, commerce, and foreign contacts; a measure of equality be-
> tween the sexes, with the regulation of sex and marriage in the service
> of the community . . . ; public and primarily moral education, common
> meals, and simple uniform clothing . . . ; regulations against luxury in
> building . . . ; the insistence on few and simple laws . . . ; and the
> tendency to make the imaginary state a republic headed by variously
> elected magistrates and councils with members of great age and experi-
> ence; to make it, too . . . a city-state with a small territory . . . ; and
> lastly, the view that susceptibility to change was a mark of imperfec-
> tion.[28]

In *Utopia* the features that appeal least to most readers are those that
show the degree to which human nature must submit to control in
the realization that it cannot change. More's regulation of family
life, of travel, of leisure time; the supervision and uniformity; the
interchangeability of people as well as houses to keep numbers and
quality equal, produce a two-edged assault on the nature of the
inhabitants who perhaps live well only because they are so controlled and on that of the reader who clings to his own passions and

pride and knows he is only partly ashamed of his values. In the case of Swift's Houyhnhnms the lack of passion and pride is of course natural, not imposed, but this only emphasizes the fact that reason and nature are forever in conflict among human beings. Where in More the reader can hardly resist feeling that the inhabitants of Utopia might revert to ordinary corruption, given the chance (but there is "no lurking hole, no secret meeting place"; p. 147), in Swift's Houyhnhnmland there is simply no place for human beings at all.

More does expose us to a kind of culture shock by making it clear that Utopian civilization is both older than ours ("there were cities among them before there were men among us"; p. 107) and capable of surpassing it technologically—rather as the Houyhnhnms reveal an ability to thread needles: "When we showed them the Aldine printing in paper books [a new peak in the civilized world at the time] . . . without giving a detailed explanation, for none of us was expert in either art . . . they promptly guessed how it was done" and "soon mastered both" (p. 183). The Utopians have also a natural aptitude for Greek and an innate sympathy with Christianity. The development of latent potential is not change or corruption and the Utopians can afford to welcome travelers. Utopia has strong natural and manmade defensive boundaries, however, which ensure control of comings and goings as much as of life on the island. The Houyhnhnms by contrast simply do not believe in life overseas. Their slave class, in spite of speculations about its origin from a pair "who appeared together upon a Mountain" long ago (like Adam and Eve leaving Milton's Eden "down the cliff as fast / To the subjected plain") is something "given," any potential for "improvement" removed by the dismissal of the dangerous Gulliver.

Swift, using a fantastic society which has by nature the qualities that can be only acquired in More's human Utopia but which stems from the same Platonic source, thus sharpens More's point about Europeans to a universal discomfort and increases the distance between ideal and actuality. Houyhnhnmland is the most closed society of all. It cannot be corrupted because where reason is natural, real humans and real animals cannot live and Gulliver, stretching his long-practiced adaptability to the utmost, is obliged to deny his own nature and his own kind just as the horses have lost theirs. The emphasis, as in all these works, is on what can and what cannot be achieved or expected of human nature.

A central concern in each writer is war, not merely as an extreme effect of human pride and greed but as a destructive perversion

unique to the human species. To moralize against war must come
naturally to the satirist who wants stability and permanence the
more comprehensively he divides society up into fragments he can
attack one by one. Plato's ideal society took as a matter of course the
need for defense against aggression and he did not go so far as to
envisage a state in which there might be no need for a trained army
or police force. Taking human nature for granted he is in this sense
as realistic as More in the *Utopia*, or perhaps more so. Plato and
More acknowledge that their ideal societies depend on military as
well as ideological strength if they are to remain invulnerable; they
assume that the rest of the world will remain perversely wicked
beyond their boundaries. More indeed accentuates worldly human
vices among which war is merely the most obviously destructive by
allowing his Utopians to exploit the weaknesses of others. Utopia
grows rich on the greed of other countries for gold that it can spare
in abundance, having no need for money.

One of the most indigestible of Utopia's virtues, or ways to
protect its virtues, is its unChristian willingness to encourage human perversity in other lands—and though Utopia is on the other
side of the world it becomes obvious that Christian Europe in its
zeal for waging war on pagans ("Zeal," "Valour," and "Interest" is
Gulliver's later ordering of respected motives, p. 295) would get the
worst of any encounter without its justifications really being put to
the test. There is, that is to say, no consideration of any motive for
Europe beyond that of materialistic greed. Since long passages in
book 1 are devoted to description of the territorial ambitions of
European kings, their dishonesty and avarice, and the public nuisance created by armies, it is something of a shock to reach as a
central feature of book 2 a protracted discussion of Utopians at war.
There is no place in More's society for indigenous professional sol-
diers (the civilians form an amateur army when needed, including
wives and children who do not fight but keep the men on their
mettle) and the real force consists of mercenaries. The Utopians
would think themselves "the greatest benefactors to the human race
if they could relieve the world of all the dregs of this abominable
and impious people" (p. 209). As long as there are mercenaries (as
particularly from Switzerland in More's Europe) they will turn
against each other, having no loyalties except to the highest and
latest bidder, so that inexhaustible Utopian funds might eventually
clean up the world by using dirt against dirt, purposefully hoarding
cash to mop up the endless willing stream of self-destructive urges.
This striking procedure is only the most vivid example of the Uto-

pians' cunning exploitation of natural viciousness; it seems more an organic process than a final solution. Not only armies are involved, but the Utopians also undermine enemy morale with subversive propaganda among the civilian population.

More's attitude to war as the expression of deeply perverse instincts is one of contempt, and the Utopians protect themselves from what is obviously seen as humanly natural by making sure that only slaves in Utopia may be butchers or go hunting. The depth of the instinct seems to be acknowledged even in the narrator and author, for More describes almost with relish his peaceful Utopians' skill and technology in battle: they have "battle-axes which, because of their sharp point and great weight, are deadly weapons, whether employed for thrusting or hacking. They are very clever in inventing war machines" (p. 215)—which sounds a fairly corrupting activity. The Utopians do allow that war can be just, however; they will fight "to protect their own territory or to drive an invading enemy out of their friends' lands or, in pity for a people oppressed by tyranny, to deliver them by force of arms" (p. 201), and will help other powers in acts of reprisal or to protect the rights of traders. They also maintain a right to colonize other territories, expanding their own dominions when they become overpopulated and justifying aggression when "a people which does not use its soil but keeps it idle and waste nevertheless forbids the use and possession of it to others" (p. 137). The colonization of new territory is a separate and complex issue in which More and Rabelais, like Swift, recognize the difference between the ideal and the actuality. Because Gulliver represents all civilized mankind as it sees itself, and is therefore full of unsorted *idées reçues*, he is capable of squeamish decencies as well as of immoderate praise for the human war machine. He is willing to defend Lilliput against invaders with an aggressive act (finding conventional justifications for war service in a dubious cause) but will not reduce Blefuscu to slavery for a greedy king. He is deeply compromised, however, and neither his size nor his bravely worded principles can preserve him from treacherous schemes couched in equally highflown terms.

The effect of More's discussion of war in *Utopia* is to stress the isolation of the Utopian community in an alien incorrigible world, as though the messy self-destructiveness around could only be held at bay by superior manipulation of its own terms. War is an obvious symptomatic evil to emphasize in a satire that aims to attack the roots of human folly. Erasmus cannot avoid the subject either, but to his mind the effects of war negate all justifications and he does not present an alternative world that must be protected from the real one. In the *Praise of Folly* all worlds are one; there is no hiving off of war instincts on to an enemy, since there are no enemies. Fools and villains are part of a community in which there are no enclaves of vice or virtue. The reforming Christian spirit has power over all and Erasmus touches fairly briefly on war as a contradiction of that spirit, and as practiced most zealously by the church.[29]

The hierarchy that traditionally relates Christians, pagans, and beasts is of course a central issue in *Gulliver's Travels* and Swift's argument on the matter culminates in Houyhnhnmland. In the *Utopia* one is presumably expected to remember from time to time, while considering their moral justifications, that the Utopians are not yet Christians and with their possible Greek origins are nearer to Plato than Erasmus. More must have been aware of Erasmus's views and of his use in the "Dulce bellum inexpertis" adage (1515) of the physical comparison between man and beast that Swift was to modify so alarmingly. Erasmus compares the natural weaponry of various animals with the natural vulnerability of man just as the master Houhynhnm does, which in the latter instance gives Gulliver the opportunity to describe what humans can do by way of perverse compensation for nature. Swift's views seem closer to Erasmus than to More. In the "Dulce bellum inexpertis" Erasmus sums up very precisely the equation that Swift illustrated later in fantasy: "So true it is that anything that diverges from its true nature degenerates into a species far worse than if its vices had been engendered by nature herself."[30] Swift could hardly have wished for a more exact formulation to give authority for his own placing of Gulliver in relation to Yahoos and Houyhnhnms in a context that uses descriptions of war and human ingenuity at a climactic point in the satire, or for better proof that he himself is not uniquely perverse in his uncompromising attitudes. Erasmus, unlike More and Swift, writes without irony in the passage quoted, and it is Swift who translates and brings to life the formula in his savagely ironic ultimate fantasy: there is, or was, a true nature for men as well as for horses but we recognize the distortion of the horse more easily than our own.

Gulliver is not a mean between Yahoos and Houyhnhnms: the classical concept of the golden mean does not describe a mid-point on a scale but is a matter of holding opposites in balance, as Gulliver fails to do when he turns from the Yahoo image but cannot become a Houyhnhnm.[31] Characteristically Swift chooses fantasy

rather than rational discourse as the appropriate mode of appeal to
irrational men. The ironic tradition of the Renaissance satirists,
following in its turn the classical models, provides a context for
recognition that is not available in Swift's contemporary world—
except among those serious Augustans whose imitations were quite
as morally nostalgic as they were aesthetically so. They, like the
Utopians, found the ancients a safer source of guidance for Christian behavior than anything offered by the moderns. In aother of
his "straight" writings Erasmus interestingly had used the
metaphors of war in a guide to Christian conduct: the *Enchiridion
Militis Christiani* (the "handbook" *or* "dagger" of the Christian sol-
dier[32]) translates war, as the *Encomium* gradually translates folly,
into a worldly term for a spiritual state. But this technique, too, is
characteristic of his ability to transform the evil into the good instead of polarizing them.

Where these alternative worlds are used to convey the ideal in
fantasy, war thus plays a part in separating and protecting the
imagined state and creates a gulf as well as opportunity for the most
extreme satirical attacks. More's Utopians, ready to let Europe
wipe itself out, or Swift's Houyhnhnms planning to exterminate
the Yahoos until Gulliver suggests castration as a kinder alternative, are alike rationally savage, but then the satirist has an ancient
right to kill as well as to mock according to his judgment of de-
serts.[33] Gulliver achieves a double reversal of traditional distinctions between man and beast and Christian and pagan at the end of
his narrative. He has finally to play the part of the British patriot
whose duty it is to offer Houyhnhnmland for colonization but who
can also imagine the havoc that would be caused by an equine
defense of its territory if animals were really to behave like men.

Rabelais's giants constantly display a similar awareness of the
place of war in human activities, even when Pantagruel is remote
from Europe. In one episode he meets Messer Gaster, inventor of
arts and of guns that turned back against the firer (*Quart Livre*, 62).
In the first two books Rabelais's giants are often embattled, crude
anachronistic heroes given carte blanche to trample stuffy medieval
institutions underfoot: the grossness of the hero, as in Swift's
fiction, matching the barbarity of the enemy. Battles are either
childlike, totally unruly, or mock-epic in scale and treatment. They
are prehumanist and prehumanitarian. The glory in carnage, the
uncompromising details, might be straight from the *Iliad* but there
is an extra straight-faced mockery in the fact that it is almost impos-

sible for the giant to meet his equal (though in one epic set-piece he
is in single combat with the giant Loup Garou), and he is
specifically compared with Hercules.

The cataloguing of forces and the measuring of size and quantity
have a different kind of exactitude from that which creates balance
and tension in Homer—or which in *Gulliver's Travels* makes Gulliver so dependent on accurate calculations. Logical reasoning and
mathematical measurement belong in fact among Rabelais's enemy
systems, the same that entrap Gulliver, so it is with a delighted
boldness shared with the reader that Rabelais chooses arbitrary
figures whose precision in the final (and smallest) digit and total
carelessness of proportion give an effect of limitless power: release
and control brought to a fine point when a hero may command an
army of "eighteen hundred and fifty-six thousand and eleven, not
counting the women and small children" (*Pantagruel*, 31; p. 271).
Battles celebrated in such prose become fantastically harmless, but
set pieces for their own sake give place to more serious portrayals of
the pettiness of motives for war when the giant princes act like
humanists who have read Erasmus as well as More, bending their
wisdom to the settlements of such disputes as that of the bakers of
Lerné, all the boasting about superior force, epic-style, taken to an
ultimate extravagance and dismissed.

5

War has thus a particular centrality as the ultimate folly and the
symbol of a divided society in these satires. In the *Praise of Folly*
extended discussion, either serious or mock-serious, would be out
of place since Erasmus is interested in showing unity in division.
He concentrates his criticism of it on the war-mongering church at
a crucial point for maximum effect, before Folly embarks on her
climactic   self-transformation   into   true   Christian   other-
worldliness.[34] As in the *Enchiridion* Erasmus restores the image of
the sword to its metaphorical use in the service of the passive
Christian virtues, "gentleness, patience and contempt of life" (with
a special irony in the last). It is "not the sword which serves robbers
and murderers, but the sword of the spirit which penetrates into
the innermost depths of the bosom and cuts out every passion with
a single stroke, so that nothing remains in the heart but piety"
(Folly's Christian ecstasy and its rhetoric are to be distinguished
from the passions that inspire Gulliver or Raphael Hythlodaeus in

similarly heightened culminating speeches). For Erasmus the single weapon becomes divided and misused through misinterpretation that "fits out the apostles with spears, crossbows, slings and catapults" (p. 193). The satiric pen is also transformed in the description of holy ecstasy, until we are abruptly reminded of the mocking framework of Folly's declamation: "But I've long been forgetting who I am."

Folly is Folly in any guise and there can be no real split like that between Thomas More and Raphael Hythlodaeus after the latter's peroration at the end of the *Utopia*, where two individuals have personal names and divisive contradictory experiences. Folly invites and includes all; More's reader must apparently make choices. But More finally suggests an open middle way: "I readily admit that there are very many features in the Utopian commonwealth which it is easier for me to wish for in our countries than to have any hope of seeing realized." The final phrase of the book is one of concessions and conditions constructed like a set of Chinese boxes: Realization nests within Hope within Wish within Admitted Partial Desirability ("ita facile confiteor permulta esse in Utopiensium republica, quae in nostris civitatibus optarim verius, quam sperarim"). Gulliver in his turn seeks an all-encompassing authority equal to that of Folly, and denies us any capacity to judge for ourselves. He has told the truth, knowing we expected wonders; he intends the "PUBLICK GOOD," knowing the treachery of personal fame. He dutifully considers the idea of colonization, but more dutifully rejects it. He shows Europe recognizably barbaric— and then exempts England; he settles into domestic life, and will allow no one near him. Where Folly united apparent opposites and More showed a way between them, Gulliver presents two faces so incompatible that he ends up with no face at all.

Swift produces an effect of fragmentation that amounts almost to cancellation, and an essential structural feature of his satire is its proliferation of worlds and contradictory experiences. Like Lucian, and Rabelais in his later books, he often describes good and bad, the realistic and the outrageously fantastic as though there were no distinction, in a series of deadpan reports. Apart from the impossible coherence of Houyhnhnmland the ideal appears in glimpses (as in the "original Institutions" of Lilliput). Lucian made his Island of the Blest a brief satirical sketch that is no more distorted than other episodes, in mockery of the human desire to escape to a paradise of sensuous self-indulgence. Rabelais sketched a utopian antimonastery in his Abbey of Thélème (*Gargantua*, 52–57). It has no walls and the only rule is "Fay ce que vouldras," but it is in fact closed to all but young people who are well bred, well educated, and virtuous by nature, and though the inhabitants dress gorgeously for their amusing life they choose to dress all alike and all to play the same game—as though even fantasy cannot escape regimentation.

Pantagruel's experiences in the final books are for the most part loosely episodic and unrelated except by a generally satirical treatment of various isolated societies. The *Quart Livre* and the *Cinquième Livre* (which is only dubiously by Rabelais)[35] deserve the same criticisms that have been showered on Swift's *Voyage to Laputa* by readers disappointed in similar ways, but the restless traveling makes a satirical point in the kaleidoscopic equation of one fantastic experience with another. Swift's imitation of a structural device that may also link his would-be hero with the wandering Odysseus is more important than the noted borrowing of narrative details from Rabelais's Kingdom of the Quintessence for the Academy of Lagado (a satire on scientific experiment that also alludes directly and indirectly to the modern royal Society and its fictional "origins" in Bacon's College at Bensalem in the *New Atlantis*).[36]

Form is itself a rhetorical device and Swift's concern with persuasive and deceiving rhetoric, with credibility and credulity, owes its motives as well as expression to Erasmus, and through him to Lucian whose irreverence for superstition and its exploitation provided such important examples of satirical treatment. As a truth-seeker Erasmus was primarily interested in making the word of God clear enough to negate the effects on the church of confusing and divisive interpretations and of the authority that unchallenged erroneous readings could acquire. But his secular handbook of rhetoric, *De utraque verborum ac rerum copia*, was in some ways as influential as his study and translation of the Greek New Testament (since ideas depend for their power on expression in words), and rhetoric was no longer considered an irrelevant ornamental art, as in earlier medieval thought.[37]

Swift's interests might seem more worldly than spiritual but one of his few treatises on style is his *Letter to a Young Gentleman, Lately enter'd into Holy Orders*, with its central tenet of "Proper Words in proper Places" (*Works*, 9:65).[38] In both Swift's period and the Renaissance, religious power and fervor took the brunt of the humanist attack on irrationality, the language of unreasonable persuasion depending on either simplified emotional appeal or a mystifying obscurity in the expression of anything that might otherwise be challenged by intellectual inquiry. But the narrow reasoning of science (as it appeared to the humanist mind described in the quotation earlier from C. S. Lewis), of further closed systems of esoteric thought and method that bring dubious ethical benefits, was also subject to ridicule.

The humanist satirist sought to show his superiority and unillusioned imperviousness to humbug by taking command of his enemy's weapons. So Swift mocked and imitated the "inspired" prose in which the unsound subversive ideas of freethinkers and religious zealots were conveyed, and also made the solemn reports of projects by the Royal Society seem ludicrously unrelated to spiritual or worldly realities. He could borrow from Rabelais or from contemporary writings with equally and deliberately indiscriminate ease, making a fantasy of would-be facts. Rabelais's own iconoclastic prose aims to reduce the authority of language systems, playing ostentatiously with the widest possible range of styles, juxtaposing set-pieces so that they become inconsequential through comparison or equal weighting. Whole chapters in Rabelais may consist of lists in which, for example, 168 epithets each for Panurge's and Friar John's testicles take *copia* to exhaustion point (*Tiers Livre*, 26, 28). At the same time such lists, set neatly on the page in parallel columns, have a satisfying exhaustive formality, the ordering of nonsequiturs giving control to the writer, *verba* inflating *res* only to the extent of his arbitrary will. Another episode in Rabelais (*Quart Livre*, 55, 56) makes uncontrolled words seem threatening when hailstorms of frozen barbarisms frighten Panurge by thawing into sound, yet Pantagruel shows them to be harmless, an abundant surplus they can afford to ignore.

Much Renaissance concern with language, including that of Erasmus, was with the power of the writer, what he should write and how. Rabelais's use of the vernacular was a new freedom (and responsibility) to be explored and wielded. The invention of printing gave a kind of autonomy to the published word (as Gulliver complained when presented with a text he hardly recognized as his own): like gunpowder it also extended the writer's arm mechanically to frightening or exciting limits. Swift looks back consciously (and askance at modern Grub Street) when choosing the appropriate rhetoric for the *Tale*'s hack or sailor Gulliver or the Drapier, as well as for his own sermons, poems, and letters, according to the recipient and the occasion. When Swift uses lists as a device, as he does so forcefully in the penultimate paragraph of *Gulliver's Travels*, juxtapositions only seem arbitrary; "a Lawyer, a

Pick-pocket, a Colonel, a Fool," etc., achieve amoral equality only to be forced back into a moral hierarchy by the reader, who resists the "likeness" in the terminal "or the like." Where Rabelais had only to end his list to make it seem complete and controlled, Swift's list drifts off into an unorganizable infinity. His words choose for themselves unexpected and irresistible relationships. For Gulliver the sum of the parts of the whole human race becomes "a Lump of Deformity, and Diseases both in Body and Mind," and the foregoing listed segmentation into qualities that would actually overlap (leading to the kind of erroneous total that Gulliver would reach when he computed the number of Englishmen by their religious and political loyalties, in Brobdingnag [p. 128]), should be compared with that initial inventory from Gulliver's pockets that ought to describe an individual but instead makes him barely intelligible.[39]

Words are treacherous in other parts of the book, too. The Houyhnhnms have no words for things outside their experience, which they thus can neither believe nor imagine; the Academy at Lagado has a project for doing away with words altogether, and another for the production of infinite knowledge by the mechanical arrangement of words. Throughout the narrative the reader is dependent on Gulliver's choice of words and his style and must take into account what Gulliver does not say and what he interprets wrongly, measure his overstatements and understatements, supply alternative formulations for what is really going on, as the plain man's words reduce or inflate the matter.

There is a sense in which association with a particular style or manner is itself reductive, however judiciously chosen. So the frequent changes and shifts of persona by the humanist satirists are a device by means of which they can stand outside their own varied performances in order to judge rather than be represented by them. The more thorough and engaged the exploration of rich and positive ambiguities and of various modes of deceit and humbug, the more versatile the tongue and the sharper the ability to measure the value of what is said. The plain language of simple sincerity cannot often be used, since it is no guarantee against deceit or error and may expose limitations; only in a fantasy world like Houyhnhnmland, where truth is obvious and incontrovertible because nature and reason are the same, can direct expression go unquestioned in a way that would be dangerous in a real human world of error and deception and hopeful possibility.

Erasmus's Folly claims the right to sing her own praises in a learned traditional form; her misuse of it is both harmless and edifying, a salutary exercise that shows her audience the extent to which value depends on rhetorical skills and forms, the ease with which a learned and persuasive tongue can gain authority for the craziest recommendation by knowing the rules of presentation. An apparently irrelevant and irreverent pagan discourse can serve, with its witty appeal to rational judgment, the real Christian truths that might otherwise founder in superstition, leaving reason to the ungodly whose use of it must be feared. Erasmus's intellectual exercise is optimistic; while he anticipates criticism he is nevertheless sure of his appeal, first to More and other likeminded scholars, and then to those who, though they "are offended by frivolity and fun in a thesis," should also consider that "the same thing has often been done by famous authors in the past." They must recognize the moderation and delicacy of his intention "to give pleasure, not pain" in attacking "the ridiculous rather than the squalid" (pp. 57, 60).[40]

More was more cautious with his *Utopia* but apart from the implications for his own public career he, too, commented on the narrowness of the reading world and needed enlightened friends to support his appearance in such unexpected guise. Every reader will dissociate himself from More's comprehensive list of the unappreciative and philistine: "The barbarian rejects . . . whatever is not positively barbarian. The smatterers [like only] obsolete expressions. . . . This fellow is so grim that he will not hear of a joke; that fellow is so insipid that he cannot endure wit. Some are so dull-minded. . . . Others are so fickle," etc. (p. 45). The technique is that conventional one of overcoming the enemy before he can attack, by breaking him down into segments that conflict and cancel each other out.

Swift in *Gulliver's Travels* characteristically reverses procedures that are well enough known because the tradition and the conventions exist. Contradicting the optimism of Erasmus and the caution of More he allows Gulliver an offensive certainty that refers to no external authority but that of the fictional "Richard Sympson" and the anonymous "Neighbours at Redriff." In the 1735 edition there is added to the simple reportage of the honest sailor an exaggerated instructive aim (in the new prefatory letter) that has outraged Gulliver by failing. The reader is properly warned (and offended) but his judgment is undermined by the sheer entertainment of the initial *Voyage to Lilliput*, its fulfilment of expectations that Gulliver did not invite seeming a kind of treachery. Swift used a form and style that needed no introduction to the common reader, that were readily acceptable and did not have to be explained. They are those of the real-life travel narrative, the style being close to the flat prose of William Dampier, whose dedicatory preface to his *New Voyage round the World* declares a modest aim that his "plain piece" may show his "hearty Zeal for the promoting of useful knowledge, and of anything that may never so remotely tend to my Countries advantage."[41] Dampier's zeal for truth is equal to Gulliver's; he apologizes for his style ("it cannot be expected, that a Seaman should affect Politeness"), but above all he records the buccaneering exploits of his company, its survival of extreme dangers and discomforts, its pirating of Spanish treasure ships, its exploitation of trusting natives, its killings and treacheries and mutinous divisions, totally without moral comment, so that the effect of modest discretion is to give all value to the accurate representation of facts (a good deal of very careful and useful description of flora and fauna).

Gulliver seems to aim for the most part at unbiased reportage, but he cannot always resist making moral observations on things he usually gets wrong. The danger is that because he is good at accurate measurement of physical objects the reader will trust his judgment on more important matters; Gulliver has close at hand the unacknowledged example of Robinson Crusoe as the fictional traveler who usurps a claim to wisdom. The reader's discovery of irony and of the unacceptability of most of Gulliver's opinions comes gradually as he makes adjustments between what he expects of a certain kind of narrative and what he is actually given. Swift can let Gulliver attack and alienate his reader (as those he imitates or parodies do not) to enforce the realization of how strong his attraction and command would otherwise be if there were no tradition of reference to other standards and of comparison with other works.

Rabelais's mockery of popular and vernacular fictions, along with their gullible readers, also enhances them and gives them literary status in the attempt to awaken a robust new life. As Folly is both on the rostrum and among the crowd, so Rabelais's giant is both the learned writer and the fabulous clown, with a similar unifying comprehensiveness. Where the Renaissance writer could bring ancient and modern, simple and erudite together, Swift aggravates the battle between them, and his modern fiction, like his modern giant traveler, is a monster self-generated, cut off from its ancestors in an arrogant self-sufficiency of self and world, self-alienating and self-divided in consequence. Yet Gulliver is also representative and all-encompassing. He completes a progress that works in paradoxical parallel to the commoner sense of the progress of man towards civilization in that comfortable hierarchy of beast, pagan, Christian—by expressing in his own person a characteristally Swiftian view of degeneration. After the ancient heroes and philosophers, after the Renaissance scholar-fools and giant-clowns, and the societies that produced and accepted them, finally comes the representative modern English sailor and traveler and would-be empire-builder who, as Walter Scott recognized, like "any other nautical wanderer of the period, endowed with courage and common sense . . . sailed through distant seas, without losing a single English prejudice which he had brought from Portsmouth or Plymouth, and on his return gave a grave and simple narrative of what he had seen or heard in foreign countries."[42]

The modern travel narrator has a particular importance to Swift, because in a sense he usurps the role of the ancient philosopher and is another manifestation of degeneracy. Isolated men, even in Socratic dialogue, who assume authority by virtue of superior human wisdom, like those who claim special divine inspiration, traditionally arouse suspicion when they cut themselves off from common values and refuse to serve or share the limitations of their fellow men. The uneasy relationship with society is evident in the portrayal of More's Hythlodaeus and is taken to an extreme with Gulliver. At the heart of the matter is the role of the leader and educator who is required to be something other than hero, saint, or hermit, whatever admirable lonely examples these may set; Odysseus as a traveler is a dubious figure whose heroic reputation is earned by the achievement of getting home to resume government (though without his travels there would be no epic).

In the Renaissance, with its expanding opportunities, handbooks abounded for the education of Christian princes according to classical precepts. Travel could bring power and material advantages of a kind very easily abused and of obvious corruptive potential, as classical history also showed. But the idea of travel could also be used imaginatively to make moral comparisons between a corrupt Europe and a clean new world. Even before the inevitable discovery of noble savages there might be opportunity for the establishment, perhaps rediscovery, of ideal social systems. Admired societies of the remote past as well as those known to be mythical might be presented as future possibilities through the temporary medium of fantasy (as Bacon's *New Atlantis* sketched a fictional outline for a projected real Royal Society). So fantasy could be used responsibly with a moral purpose, especially when it was carefully advertised as such so as not to mislead the reader. Thomas More's prefatory jokes are intended to be quickly understood and his ironic deceptions respected. As a homebound humanist scholar he can stand between the traveler and the vulnerable reader in an interpretative social role.

But to Swift the travel narrator is a dangerous figure in a world where science takes responsibility for itself. The traveler becomes an authority by virtue of his unique personal experiences, presenting facts that cannot easily be questioned, telling tales that cannot be verified, and building for himself a heroic reputation without reference to society. Swift, comparing the narratives of real and fictional travelers as he must have done, would see what powers to mislead and to exploit could be acquired by such figures as Dampier on the one hand and Robinson Crusoe on the other. Dampier offers information, and any entertainment is incidental to his declared purposes. The reader is not invited to ask the value of the information, or to judge the behavior that made its acquisition possible. The traveler sets his own standards and creates his own horizons; he also begins to determine what is valuable (the new and the strange) and to direct the requirements of society—and the tastes of readers. Dampier's deadpan reports are remarkably similar in tone to those of Lucian, but Lucian's satire is aimed at just such autonomous figures and at those who accept uncritically what they are given. Defoe might have created Robinson Crusoe (surely the most morally conscious traveler ever) as a nervously defensive answer to such spirits as Lucian's and Swift's but his deception is deliberate whereas Dampier's motivation is naively (if culpably) uncritical of itself. Defoe attempts to make Crusoe respectable by having him retain his civilized social standards in the wilderness and by allowing him to find God through an inspired random use of the Bible. Swift, as if to punish those who believe in Crusoe, gives us Gulliver instead, a figure we have earned and courted, so to speak, by our susceptibility to Dampier's facts and Crusoe's prayers.

Gulliver represents his reader, who is his patron and has chosen him. Swift is implicated as a writer serving anonymously the figure he has been obliged to create. He resists identification with Gulliver through the same ironic ploys that Erasmus used and is subsumed equally helplessly but much less willingly into the fool-figure of his own age. The tradition of variations on a theme enforces our recognition of differences through similarities. It is in this sense that Swift praises Gulliver, with the deepest irony: that is, he lets the reader praise Gulliver as he has probably praised Robinson Crusoe, with less honesty than Folly praised Folly. The degeneration, the sinking into the one figure with its one viewpoint, perhaps goes even further, since the reader decides that he is after all superior to Gulliver. He learns to dissociate himself gradually from Gulliver as a norm, delighting in his own faculty not only to register exact proportions and reversals of scale but to restore to man an absolute value as mean between Houhnhnm and Yahoo. From praising Gulliver the reader moves on to praise himself.

Erasmus and More needed patrons, too. A dedicatory address creates an ideal reader, telling him the qualities he needs to appreciate the work, obliging him to take responsibility for it, and allowing him to rise nevertheless above its shortcomings and those of the writer (just as Swift's reader rises above Gulliver). For Erasmus the first reader was More. For More it was Peter Giles, with other friends (including, of course, Erasmus). These patrons are implicated in the narratives along with the authors themselves. More makes his friends take part in the debate of book 1 and afterwards credits them with more up-to-date knowledge of Hythlodaeus than he has. Rabelais also creates readers and patrons and ostentatiously forces upon them an intimate relationship with the author-figure he creates in his prologues. The prologues are fully self-conscious exercises in the setting up of a fictive reader who recognizes himself as such by means of the inconsistencies and rapid role-changes forced upon him.[43] Swift's first reader is a bored armchair traveler who has been vicariously excited by the perversions and conversions of Robinson Crusoe. His patronage and taste are expressed through the person of the fictional "Publisher" who serves him and recommends Gulliver—no Ulysses, no Plato, no Hythlodaeus but a figure that Sympson knows he can sell, tailored to the measure of the reader's self-image. In the end Gulliver's reader may realize his own fictionality as he recognizes Gulliver's; by splitting himself in two he may be released from the conflicting forces of mutual antipathy and shared identity and learn through fantasy what he is and what he is not.

Satiric fantasy is not a high literary mode, but it can carry a high charge of moral indignation in the writer who is forced into a pretense of frivolity in order to address serious matters in the terms of a fallen world. Erasmus cites classical authorities for his formal mockery. More debates the wisdom of publishing "something that may bring profit or pleasure to others, who nevertheless receive it with disdain or ingratitude" (p. 43). Rabelais and Swift play defensively with elaborate prefatory jests to mask the suspicion of serious authorial intentions. For Swift perhaps the greatest value of these Renaissance antecedents is the authority they provide for attacking the low in a lowly style, showing the world its debasement by offering it what it deserves, but at the same time alluding directly or indirectly to inherited values that an élite at least will recognize and applaud and confirm. Where Swift's causes seem less dignified and more local by comparison, his imitations make the point that that is society's fault, not his. Swift's major statements on man in *Gulliver's Travels* and those made by the Renaissance humanists in comparable works show Swift alluding to an earlier manner but also adding invariably a further savage twist to the satire. Energies that had worked in mitigation or alleviation of folly seem as though they can be released only in the service of vice; features echoed in Swift's narrative have to be recognized, but it is a recognition of deliberate contrasts and inversions and not of emulation or borrowed hope for fallen man.

John Traugott has suggested that in drawing up Gulliver's "sextumvirate of worthies" and regretting the impossibility of a seventh name Swift may "modestly nominate himself."[4] The folly of Gulliver is not in the same class as that of Erasmus's Folly, but in inviting this and other comparisons his author may claim his place in another sextumvirate: Plato, Lucian, Erasmus, More, Rabelais—and Swift.

Notes

1. See Peter Steele, *Jonathan Swift: Preacher and Jester* (Oxford: Clarendon Press 1979), for discussion of some of these themes.

2. One inevitably speaks of "Erasmus's *Praise of Folly*," though the pun in his title is also meant to suggest "Erasmus's Praise of More." Quotations are from the Penguin edition, translated by Betty Radice (Harmondsworth, 1971). Subsequent page references in the text are to this edition. There are no universally recognized divisions within Erasmus's text to make general reference possible. The new Latin edition (Amsterdam: North-Holland Publishing Company, 1979) and a translation (New Haven, Conn.: Yale University Press, 1979) are by Clarence H. Miller, but there is as yet no translation in the Toronto edition of Erasmus's works.

3. C. S. Lewis, "Addison," in *Essays on the Eighteenth Century Presented to David Nichol Smith* (Oxford: Oxford University Press, 1945), pp. 1–14.

4. This point is made by Denis Donoghue in his introduction to *Jonathan Swift: A Critical Anthology* (Harmondsworth: Penguin Books, 1971), pp. 23–27.

5. See also a letter to Bolingbroke (14 September 1714): "The poor dead Queen is used like the giant Lougarou in Rabelais" (*Correspondence*, 2:129). Here Swift does relate the anecdote in explanation of the allusion.

6. Page references for *Gulliver's Travels* are to the revised edition, 1959. Pope is quoted as saying "Dr. Swift was a great reader and admirer of Rabelais, and used sometimes to scold me for not liking him enough" (see Joseph Spence, *Observations, Anecdotes, and Characters of Books and Men*, ed. James M. Osborn, 2 vols. [Oxford: Clarendon Press, 1966], 1: item 133).

7. See Harold Williams, *Dean Swift's Library* (Cambridge; At the University Press, 1932).

8. See, for example, Jonathan Smedley, writing with some malice in *Gulliveriana* (1728), p. 331. This spurious fourth volume of the Pope-Swift *Miscellanies* is reprinted in facsimile as *Swiftiana VIII* by Garland (New York and London, 1974). See also John Dunlop, *The History of Fiction*, 2d ed., 3 vols. (Edinburgh: for Longmans, Hurst; 1816), 3: 488–91, and Sir Walter Scott's comments in his edition of Swift's *Works*, 2d ed. 19 vols. (Edinburgh: Constable 1824), esp. 1:338–40, 488–91; 11: 5–6. Modern comparisons of the two fictions include Nigel Dennis, *Jonathan Swift: A Short Character* (London: Weidenfeld and Nicholson 1964), esp. p. 123; John F. Ross, *Swift and Defoe: A Study in Relationship* (Berkeley, Calif. University of California Press, 1941); and Maximillian E. Novak, "Defoe's Use of Irony," in a Clark Library Seminar entitled *Irony in Swift and Defoe*, (Los Angeles, Calif.: University of California Press, 1966).

9. Swift had referred to the vanity of searching for Utopia in "A Tritical Essay . . ." (1707) and had listed "Utopian *Commonwealths*" among figments of the fanatic imagination in the "Mechanical Operation of the Spirit" of 1704 (*Works*, 1: 174, 248). But it would be as dangerous to dissociate Swift from serious aspects of the Utopian idea presented in the original book as to accept More's own apparent disclaimers.

10. For discussion of this point see C. J. Rawson, *Gulliver and the Gentle Reader: Studies in Swift and our Time* (London: Routledge, 1973), p. 9, in an essay first published in 1968. L. J. Morrissey, in *Gulliver's Progress* (Hamden: Archon Books, The Shoestring Press, 1978), builds an entire thesis on Gulliver's complaints to the printer about misrepresented dates, but he takes them out of their context of other textual complaints in the same "Letter to Sympson." He believes that Swift intended to reveal his meaning through hidden references to set scriptural readings in the church calendar.

11. Deane Swift, *An Essay upon . . . Swift* (1755), Anglistica & Americana facsimile reprint (Hildesheim, 1968), pp. 217 (numbered 189)–25.

12. See Emrys Jones, "Pope and Dulness," *Proceedings of the British Academy* 54 (1968): 231–63.

13. The origin of the term *serio ludere* is hard to trace but it was apparently in common use among Renaissance writers, who took the concept from Plato (see Rosalie Colie, *Paradoxia Epidemica: The Renaissance Tradition of Paradox* (Princeton, N.J.: Princeton University Press, 1966), and Edgar Wind, "The Concealed God," in *Pagan Mysteries in the Renaissance*, rev. ed. (Harmondsworth: Penguin Books, 1967). The title page of More's *Utopia* describes it as a work "nec minus salutaris quam festivus."

14. Lucian, *A True Story*, trans. A. M. Harmon, Loeb edition, vol. 1 (London: Heineman, 1913), pp. 249, 253.

15. Lucian mentions the Christians briefly in his *Alexander* (25, 38) and comments on them in the *Peregrinus* (13) where their gullibility is exploited. He sees them as foolish because "the poor wretches have convinced themselves . . . that they are going to be immortal" but he grants them some not necessarily despicable qualities: "in no time they lavish their all" (to help a friend) and "they despise death." See Loeb edition, vol. 5, trans. A. M. Harmon (London: Heinemann 1955), pp. 14–15, and a discussion of these passages in Marcel Caster, *Lucien et la pensée religieuse de son temps* (Paris: Les Belles Lettres, 1937), pp. 348–57.

16. I have used Pierre Jourda's edition, 2 vols. (Paris: Garnier, 1962), but in cases where archaic French slang is not instantly comprehensible to the average reader I have turned gratefully to the Penguin translation by J. M. Cohen (1955). Page references to the appropriate version are given after quotations.

17. *De rerum natura*, 1. 945. See the "Letter to Martin Dorp" (1515) usually printed with the text (Penguin edition, p. 216).

18. Page references for quotations are to the Yale edition of *The Works of Saint Thomas More*, vol. 4, *Utopia*, ed. Edward Surtz, S.J., and J. H. Hexter (New Haven, Conn.: Yale University Press, 1965).

19. For recent discussion see Thomas I. White, "Festivitas, Utilitas, et Opes: The Concluding Irony and Philosophical Purpose of Thomas More's *Utopia*," *Albion* 10, Supplement (1978): 135–50.

20. For relevant theories of history see C. A. Patrides, *The Phoenix and the Ladder: The Rise and Decline of the Christian View of History* (Berkeley, Calif.: University of California Press, 1964).

21. See W. B. Carnochan, *Confinement and Flight: An Essay on English Literature of the Eighteenth Century* (Berkeley, Calif.: University of California Press, 1977), for interesting exploration of these complementary themes in *Gulliver's Travels* and other texts.

22. Hythlodaeus cites only a part of the relevant passage: "Plato . . . shows why philosophers are right in abstaining from administration of the commonwealth," p. 103. Plato actually goes on to say (through Socrates) that this is not the philosopher's ideal, since in a state that suits him he will grow more in himself *and look after public affairs as well as his own:* "καὶ μετὰ τῶν ἰδίων τακοινὰ σώσει" (*Republic.* 6. 497).

23. William J. Kennedy sees Peter Giles as a norm in *Utopia*, a subsidiary but important character (as Don Pedro is in the *Travels*) against whom More and Hythlodaeus may be measured (*Rhetorical Norms in Renaissance Literature* [New Haven, Conn.: Yale University Press, 1978], p. 95).

24. See *Oratio de dignitate hominis*. One choice offered to man there could be seen in ironic relation to Gulliver's final position: "And if he is not contented with the lot of any creature but takes himself up into the center of his own unity, then, made one spirit with God and settled in the solitary darkness of the Father, who is above all things, he will stand ahead of all things. Who does not wonder at this chameleon which we are?" (*On the Dignity of Man*, trans. Charles G. Wallis [New York: Bobbs-Merrill Co., 1965], p. 5). Paul Oskar Kristeller has a useful chapter on "The Dignity of Man" in *Renaissance Thought and Its Sources*, ed. Michael Mooney [New York: Columbia University Press, 1979], esp. pp. 173–78.

25. For the development of concepts of the heroic, see W. B. Stanford, *The Ulysses Theme: A Study in the Adaptability of a Traditional Hero*, 2d ed. (Oxford: Basil Blackwell, 1963); and G. Karl Galinsky, *The Herakles Theme: The Adaptations of the Hero in Literature from Homer to the Twentieth Century* (Oxford: Basil Blackwell, 1972).

26. For definitions, and for the background to the relationship between Athens and Sparta, see K. R. Popper, *The Open Society and Its Enemies*, vol. 1, *The Spell of Plato*, 5th ed. rev. (London: Routledge, 1966), pp. 173–201.

27. *Timaeus*, 26. Loeb edition, vol. 7, trans. R. G. Bury (London: Heinemann, 1961), p. 47.

28. Elizabeth Rawson, *The Spartan Tradition in European Thought* (Oxford: Clarendon Press, 1969), p. 171. My attention was drawn to this useful summary through its quotation by John Ferguson in *Utopias of the Classical World* (London: Thames & Hudson Ltd., 1975), p. 29.

29. "War is something so monstrous that it befits wild beasts rather than men . . . so impious that it is quite alien to Christ; and yet they [i.e. churchmen] leave everything to devote themselves to war alone . . . though they turn law, religion, peace and all humanity upside down" (*Praise of Folly*, p. 181).

30. The translation is from Margaret Mann Phillips, *The "Adages" of Erasmus: A Study with Translations* (Cambridge: Cambridge University Press, 1964), p. 315.

31. See M. A. Screech, *Rabelais* (London: Duckworth, 1979), p. 254.

32. Liddell and Scott give (1) "hand-knife, dagger" in fourth-century usage; (2) "handle" in the third century; and (3) "manual, handbook" as a title in Epictetus, Longinus, and other later writers.

33. See Robert C. Elliott's account of the history of satire in *The Power of Satire: Magic, Ritual, Art* (Princeton, N.J.: Princeton University Press, 1960), esp. pp. 4–8, 285–92.

34. M. A. Screech, *Ecstasy and the Praise of Folly* (London: Duckworth, 1980), sees Christian ecstasy as the fundamental theme and inspiration of Erasmus's book and thus gives it an altogether more otherworldly aspect.

35. Screech leaves aside discussion of the *Cinquième Livre*, treating it as a separate text for a future edition (see his explanation of the problems, *Rabelais* p. xvii). Those who like to

include the fifth book in Rabelais's œuvre in spite of sound arguments against its authenticity, as I do, are tempted to do so for the sake of resolution to a text otherwise "flamboyantly unresolved" and for the "consonance of [its] conclusion with the thematic structure of the earlier books" (see Terence Cave, *The Cornucopian Text: Problems of Writing in the French Renaissance* [Oxford: Clarendon Press, 1979], pp. 118–21; Dr. Cave, spotting a weakness that critics may soon have to grow out of, rightly recommends caution).

36. I have discussed some possible allusions in "The Unity of Swift's *Voyage to Laputa:* Structure as Meaning in Utopian Fiction," *Modern Language Review* 72 (1977): 1–21 (pp. 7–11).

37. See Kennedy, *Rhetorical Norms*, p. 13.

38. For Swift on style, see Charles A. Beaumont, *Swift's Classical Rhetoric* (Athens, Ga.: University of Georgia Press, 1961), ch. 1.

39. C. J. Rawson discusses lists in Swift and Rabelais in *Gulliver and the Gentle Reader*, esp. pp. 101–7.

40. Compare (or contrast) Swift's aim to vex rather than divert (*Correspondence*, 3:102) and his pointedly opposite emphases generally.

41. William Dampier, *A New Voyage Round the World* ed. Sir Albert Gray (1697; reprint ed., London: Adam and Charles Black, 1937), p. 1. William Hallam Bonner, in *Captain William Dampier: Buccaneer-Author* (Stanford, Calif.: Stanford University Press, 1934), has a whole chapter on Swift's possible use of Dampier's *Voyages* in *Gulliver's Travels* (pp. 156–81). See also W. B. Ewald, *The Masks of Jonathan Swift* (Oxford: Basil Blackwell, 1954), pp. 125–28.

42. Scott's edition of Swift's *Works*, 1:339.

43. See Kennedy, *Rhetorical Norms*, pp. 4–7 and 109–23 for extended discussion of the fictive reader in Rabelais.

44. "A Voyage to Nowhere with Thomas More and Jonathan Swift: *Utopia* and *The Voyage to the Houyhnhnms*," *The Sewanee Review* 69 (1961): 534–65 (p. 535).

10

Gulliver's Travels: Some Structural Properties and Certain Questions of Critical Approach and Interpretation

Ricardo Quintana

Foreword

To what, it may be asked, are we referring when we speak of *Gulliver's Travels?* A moment's thought will assure us that the question is not a farfetched one, not one that is solely the preoccupation of philosophers of meaning and semiotics. At the level of ordinary, everyday experience we know that no book, least of all a famous one like Swift's, is possessed of a uniform, unchanging significance. It presents different questions, different meanings as our cultural eras succeed one another. In a period of relative cultural stability it conveys messages that vary in accordance with the temper and intelligence of particular readers, and even for the same reader encountering it at different stages of his experience it can undergo suprising atmospheric change. Indeed, is a *Gulliver's Travels* always the same thing for its author? For him there is a time before composition, another during the actual writing and thereafter a nonending period of retrospection.

We may ask the same question—to what are we referring?—in respect of the precise text of a given work when more than one text is available. In the case of *Gulliver's Travels* it happens that two texts have come down to us, an earlier one found in the London edition of 1726 (the Motte edition) and one given in the Faulkner edition appearing in Dublin in 1735. It is the latter that is now generally preferred by modern editors and the one used in the eleventh volume of the standard Davis edition of Swift's Collected Works. Is it a matter of any significance which of the two we have in mind while discussing the *Travels?* It would seem to be. To the many readers who have found the work the grimmest of all satiric commentaries on the human scene it may come as a surprise to observe that to the 1735 version has been added what in effect is a kind of comic prelude—a prelude in three parts.

To put this as briefly as possible. In 1726 the prefatory matter consists of a single piece, "The Publisher to the Reader," signed by a Richard Sympson, who represents himself as a cousin and friend of the author and the one who as "publisher" has made the manuscript of the *Travels* available to the printer. The later edition adds two further pieces to the front material: an "Advertisement" and "A Letter from Capt. Gulliver to his Cousin Sympson." In so doing it creates a comic scenario engaging an everflowing cast of characters. Present here are Lemuel Gulliver, who now complains of his great want of judgment in ever allowing his *Travels* to be published; Richard Sympson; "a Person now deceased"; "a gentleman in London"; the "several worthy Persons" mentioned by Sympson; two printers; and the "judicious candid Reader" of the present edition. These in one way or another, assisting or by their blunders hindering, have been engaged in the enterprise that has finally resulted in a new edition designed to be free of the textual errors of the previous edition. But it would seem that an errorless text is something not to be realized in this world. The writer of the opening "Advertisement" speaks of Sympson's letter to Gulliver, which should be Gulliver's letter to Sympson: in his "Letter to Sympson" Gulliver corrects the spelling *Brobdingnag* which should be *Brobdingrag* (though, to compound the error, the incorrect spelling *Brobdingnag* runs throughout the text itself), while Gulliver's assertion that everything set forth in his book is true beyond dispute because this truth immediately strikes every reader with conviction is stridently out of tune with the characterization accorded him on the frontispiece of the new edition, where he is called, by way of Horace, a superb liar. The final touch is the short quotation from Lucretius now added to the title page: "Retroq; Vulgus abhorret ab his" from book 1 of the *De Rerum Natura.* Swift had in mind, and we should have, the entire passage in which these lines occur: the philosophy which I, Lucretius, am setting forth is a bitter one and the multitude back away from it; yet my verses are full of light and touched with the muses' charm, for I have followed the practice of those healers who, in administering wormwood to children, rim the cup with sweet, golden honey, and through bitterness bring them to health. It was honey and wax in the *Tale of a Tub;* now it is honey and wormwood, the charming manner and style of the *Travels* coating their bitter truths. Frontispiece, title page, "Advertisement," the "Letter from Capt. Gulliver," and "The Publisher to the Reader," taken together, add up to Swift's own comment on his *Travels.* The tone is typical of him, something between jest and earnest.

Some Formal Properties

Whatever *Gulliver's Travels* means, or has meant, or may in future times come to mean, it shows as do all literary works certain invariant features, most obvious of which are its basic structural elements.

To begin, the *Travels* is a satire taking the form of four imaginary voyages. There is a traveler; there are detailed descriptions of strange lands encountered and their inhabitants; there are the traveler's own feelings amidst these foreign settings, his reactions to the natives, theirs to him. As a type the imaginary voyage owes its being to the genuine travel book, but it does not exist to give us a truthful image of its parent. *Gulliver's Travels* is no exception. It is an imaginary voyage asserting itself to be genuine throughout but in so doing telling us otherwise. It is a parody of the true voyage. But we cannot let it go at that. With another turn of the screw its status as an imaginary voyage is called in question; it outdoes, preposterously, what it is imitating; it becomes a parody of a parody. Swift's wit, delighting, in ambiguities, is at work here.

In any event, it is to the travel book and its spinoff, the imaginary voyage, that the basic compositional features of the *Travels* may be said to owe their being. Swift, we know, was a longtime reader of books of travel, both genuine and fictional, and he drew on both sorts for many of the details that are to be found in his account of Gulliver's adventures. But he was clearly less interested in details than in the particular kind of fictional situation hinted at in this popular literature of travel. It was this that caught his attention. Seizing on it, as he ultimately did, he exploited the possibilities it held forth with all the resourcefulness and power of his satiric imagination.

The crucial feature here has really little to do with who the traveler is or the exact place where he finds himself—any traveler and a great many different places will do for a start. It lies in the manner in which a person responds to strange surroundings, or in the way the people of differing cultures behave when brought face to face.

We can see Swift coming gradually to a perception of the possibilities inherent here. In the days when Steele was writing his *Tatler* papers Swift offered him what he later described to Stella as "a noble hint . . . about an [American] Indian supposed to write his travels into England." A little later, in a political pamphlet of 1711, the *New Journey to Paris*, he devised a kind of Ur-Gulliver in the person of a French servant, one du Baudrier, supposedly an attendant accompanying Matthew Prior while the latter is making his way to Paris. As the two men converse, Prior points out the truly sorry state of things in France resulting from the war in progress; the effects of scarcity and poverty are visible everywhere, but in England things are different. Du Baudrier responds to this blow dealt his nationalistic pride by delivering an impassioned but ludicrously miscalculated defense of his native land.

By the time Swift came to the *Travels* he already had in mind the structural pattern that was to shape the four voyages. It was one that afforded countless opportunities for thematic development and ingenious improvisation: descriptions of places visited, and of the physical characteristics of the creatures coming under observation; different customs, habits, and forms of social and political organization; the varied comedy of behavioral dissimilarities; parodies of European ways; life—good, ridiculous, deplorable. And throughout, counter to the narrator's matter-of-fact style and delivery, extraordinary and sometimes outrageous happenings. The element of tension that we make so much of today in our discussions of works of art and that everywhere informs the *Travels*, arises out of what Swift found in embryonic form in the voyages he had perused.

A second aspect has more to do with the construction of the four voyages when seen as an unfolding sequence of occurrences. An exhaustive study of the way in which details, events, experiences parallel one another from voyage to voyage, or stand as obvious variants or clear reversals, is to be found in Kathleen M. Swaim's *A Reading of Gulliver's Travels*. This is an interesting and able study, notable for the method it employs, and one which those taking a similar line of approach will find suggestive though not indispensable. What, in the case of each voyage, causes Gulliver to take to sea? What are the misfortunes that put him ashore? In Lilliput, Brobdingnag, and the country of the Houyhnhnms, what kinds of problem does he bring upon his hosts?

Pursuing this line of analysis further, we see that each voyage presents a realized situation, fully and systematically explored. The multiplicity of details encourages an air of reality even when the absurdities that amuse us are most in evidence. Gulliver passes through a series of extraordinary experiences. Is there, in this respect, a connected sequence of psychological reactions on his part? Save in the third voyage—though here the episode of the Struldbruggs is a notable exception—his involvment is apparent. It becomes increasingly intense, and this fact is communicated to us through his behavior as, at the end of each voyage, he finds himself home again. After Lilliput he is much his usual self; the Brobdignagian experience leaves a deeper mark; his sojourn among the Houyhnhnms and his expulsion from their country effect a lasting change of personality. It is a planned scheme, ascending by degrees to a climax that is, however else, we may choose to describe it, quite unusual, as Swift in one of his wrier moods might have called it.

Part of an overall scheme is also evident in the different patterns of action contained in the separate parts. In the "Voyage to Lilliput" Gulliver is mistaken as to the true nature of the little people, finding them charming and admirably competent in all their affairs; the things that come to pass during his stay among them leave him of an entirely different mind. In the second voyage he is overwhelmed by the physical size of the giants and fearful of the treatment he may receive at their hands, but when transported to their metropolis and placed among people of the Court he finds them considerate and civilized; unfortunately, the opinion they conceive of European ways as these are described to them proves so offensive to Gulliver that he turns against all Brobdingnagians and from then on can find nothing good in any of the forms of their society. In the meantime, and at another level of experience, he is being forced to endure not only the odor exuded from the bodies of these huge beings, but the repulsive sight of their skin and flesh, protuberances and blemishes enormously blown up as though viewed through one of the microscopes that so delighted the members of the Royal Society and other modern scientists seeking to inquire into the reality of things. Contrary to Gulliver's experience in both Lilliput and Brobdingnag, first judgments undergoing radical change, in the final voyage he comes to the instantaneous and unalterable conviction that the Houyhnhnms are living embodiments of the Good, the True, and in a horsey way the Beautiful—a striking example of Locke's immediate certitude by intuition.

Commentaries and Problems of Interpretation

There are other structural properties besides those just discussed that will be taken up later. At this point, a number of recent critical items may be considered with profit. Some of these are directed at the *Travels* as a whole, others at themes running through it, or at one another of the separate parts, or at psychological questions concerning Swift. The special interests of these writers and their different critical postulates are self-evident. If structural properties are not to the fore, they can be said to lead into the matters under discussion.

Kathleen Williams has contributed to the collection of critical papers edited by Roger Lonsdale—*Dryden to Johnson*—a penetrating and sanely balanced essay on Swift and his best-known works. Her orientation is a humanistic one in the sense that she views Swift as a person deeply "engaged" and *Gulliver's Travels* as a wide-ranging commentary on the nature and circumstances of human life and society. Her statement concerning the ordonnance of the *Travels*, short but emphatic within its set limits, is an admirable one. The analysis moves from voyage to voyage; the formative themes, their manipulation and the effects produced are noted. Particularly striking is the handling of the moral symbolism of the *Travels* and the forms this takes in the course of the narrative. In the third voyage, for instance, the satire bears less on science per se than on the misuse of the intellectual faculties. The projectors and their kind are toiling meaninglessly, metaphors of futility. There is a darkening of tone as Houyhnhnmland draws near. The treatment of the fourth voyage rests on an interpretation that if not accepted by all present-day Swiftians, is increasingly favored. Consensus on this, the most controversial section of the *Travels*, seems to be emerging as to the true meaning that Swift wove into it.

The form given the *Travels*, with the interests and ideas indigenous to foreign countries constantly on display, ensures the appearance in the narration of a number of topics having to do with learning, forms of government, politics, and the course, upward or downward, that civilization may be taking.

Political references in the *Travels* have, since the day of the book's first publication, excited curiosity and drawn a variety of interpretations from critics and historians. It is in parts 1 and 3 that persons and events suggestive of the political scene of Swift's time are most frequently in evidence, and the question arises whether the characters and the episodes appearing in the narrative refer to actual persons and incidents. It was in 1919 that Sir Charles Firth in a paper entitled "The Political Significance of Gulliver's Travels" set in motion a discussion of these matters that has continued to this day. The main points of his interpretation were these: In the first voyage, Lilliput is England and Gulliver is at first Swift himself. But later, when his misfortunes set in, Gulliver becomes Bolingbroke and his flight from Lilliput signifies Bolingbroke's fate after Queen Anne's death. In the third voyage the flying island represents England and Balnibarbi stands for Ireland. The story of the resistance to royal authority is to be taken as an allegorical reference to Ireland's opposition to Wood's halfpence, while Munodi is probably meant to suggest Lord Midleton.

The attempt to discover carefully worked-out political allegory in parts 1 and 3 reached a climax in an essay by Arthur Case appearing in 1945, "Personal and Political Satire in *Gulliver's Travels*." Case would have it that the first voyage contains a hidden history of the Oxford-Bolingbroke administration that lasted from the latter months of 1710 down to Queen Anne's death at the beginning of August 1714. The references here, he contended, are not to scattered events but rather form an extended and consistently maintained political allegory: "Swift is telling a story which began in the reign of Anne and ended in that of George I" (p. 76). Case saw the third voyage as an attack on "learned folly, or 'pedantry,' to use the word in its eighteenth-century meaning" (p. 80), the focus of this attack being the Whig ministry under George I, and the rebellion of Lindalino constituting without doubt "an allegorical description of the controversy over Wood's halfpence" (p. 81). Throughout his discussion, furthermore, Case proceeded to link character after character in the story with historical personages figuring in the political events of Swift's time.

Though for a while these Firth-Case interpretations and their engendering assumption that the *Travels* was the kind of work that admitted intentional allegorical references gained wide acceptance, they have since come to be roundly challenged and in greater part rejected. It has been shown, for one thing, that certain of the identifications given by Firth and Case simply do not hold up under historical analysis. But chiefly, and more important, it has been argued that the *Travels* does not contain nor was meant to contain sustained or for the most part occasional allegory; if any references to real people were intended they were, with a few exceptions, incidental and purposely vague. This is the general purport of Phillip Harth's "The Problem of Political Allegory in *Gulliver's Travels*" (1976). Harth points out that before Firth and Case advanced their theories, common readers did not find continued allegory in the work; they did indeed see certain allusions—Harth observes that no one is now disposed to dispute the presence in the third voyage of the England-Ireland allegory—but it was not imagined that Swift was telling a story that matched point by point the political events of the early eighteenth century.

Much the same view as Harth's is to be found in J. A. Downie's "Political Characterization in *Gulliver's Travels*" (1977). Downie accepts a few of the identifications that have in the past been offered (e.g., Flimnap stands for Walpole), but after rigorous analysis rejects most of them as historically impossible. Much of the time Swift's hints and characterizations are vague, sometimes contradictory, and they are intentionally so, it would seem. Yet there is clear and direct political satire in the *Travels*, and the heart of it lies in the conversation between Gulliver and the King of Brobdingnag. The questions put by the King to his interlocutor constitute no less than "a full-bodied attack on Walpole's administration," and the views thus expressed, which Swift himself endorsed, are those professed by Bolingbroke and others who in the 1720s were attempting to form a parliamentary opposition to Walpole and his policies. The fact that in this episode Swift is giving voice to criticism based on broad positive principles that are his own, and that he does this precisely, emphatically, and with no attempt at disguise or concealment shows the foolishness of looking for specifics in the many vague references.

The most recent study of these matters and the most comprehensive is F. P. Lock's *The Politics of "Gulliver's Travels"* (1980). Lock has no patience with attempts to establish similarities between Swift's characters and historical figures, and one of the stated purposes of his study is to clear away "the accumulated weight" of allusions, personal and particular, that have been read into the *Travels*. He rejects exact historical similarities between, for instance, Bolgolam and the Earl of Nottingham, Flimnap and Walpole, and Gulliver's experiences in Lilliput leading up to his flight from that country and actual events at the time of Queen Anne's death and thereafter. Nor does he find any valid grounds for supposing that the episode in part 3 describing how Lindalino defied the King of Laputa and survived the threat of the flying island contains references to the Wood affair. The Lindalino incident, he would have it, is rather in

the nature of a "genuine fable of successful resistance to tyranny."
The political commentary in *Gulliver's Travels*, he asserts, is mostly
by way of fables and paradigms illustrative of general principles
and impelling forces—not allusions and allegories pointed at
specific figures and events.

Lock does not deny that there is political satire in the *Travels*, but
he believes that the satire was originally intended to be "unlimited
in its application by time or place." However, as Swift proceeded
with the composition of the *Travels* he became increasingly involved in public affairs, and after the appearance of the Motte
edition in 1726, his bitterness towards Walpole and the Whig regime was intensified, and this resentfulness was registered in the
textual additions largely incorporated in the 1735 edition. (It may
be observed that Lock's theory as to how Swift saw to it that the
1735 edition printed the additions is a novel one and will in all
probability be the subject of further discussion on the part of
scholars interested in these textual problems.)

But only part of *The Politics of "Gulliver's Travels"* is devoted to
questions of specific allusions. Another of Lock's purposes has been
to relocate the *Travels* "in a wider context of politics and political
thought," and this purpose he has carried out effectively. The influences shaping Swift's political thought are summed up briefly
and skillfully: contemporary conditions in the European scene (in
Ireland and France as well as in England); ancient and modern
philosophers and writers (chiefly Plato, More, Clarendon, and
Temple; and regarding practical politics, Polybius, Tacitus,
Machiavelli, and Harrington). What Lock has to say about the
treatment of Kingship in the *Travels*, though not strikingly new, is
clearly put. Vehemently rejecting absolutism, Swift saw in a mixed
or balanced government the form best suited to serve the general
welfare. The Brobdingnagian King is the type of sovereign who
heads the state impressively, exercises firm control—there are no
disruptive factions—and through conviction places his power
within due limits. The King of Luggnagg is the absolute despot. In
Lilliput the political atmosphere is one of secrecy and perpetual
intrigue. The King of Laputa, a limited monarch, is subject to
practical restraints, as the resistance on the part of Lindalino makes
clear. Lock gives us much more than these bare details, and altogether he succeeds in suggesting the richness of the *Travels* as
broad political commentary.

That the section on the science of the moderns found in the third voyage is leveled at the Royal Society and their *Transactions* has long been understood. But some have felt that there is more here than has been fully accounted for. Reactions to the new science before and during Swift's time are now better understood than in the past, and it is possible to make out with greater accuracy Swift's position and that of others in respect, for instance, to Cartesianism, Baconianism, Newtonian theory, and English empiricism. In his "Swift: Laputians as a Caricature of the Cartesians," David Renaker remarks that more work still remains to be done on the scientific satire of Book 3, and he tries, with some success, to define the difference between science in Laputa and that in Balnibarbi. The Laputians are Cartesians, wholly theoretical and in consequence absurdly impractical. This is science as interpreted in France. The Balnibarbians, on the other hand, represent what has taken place in England, which suffers from "an addiction to insane experiments and projects" by reason of a kind of infection originating among French Cartesians.

An approach by a different route to science and satire in the time of Swift has been mapped out by Donald Davie in a seminal monograph *The Language of Science and the Language of Literature, 1700–1740*. Davie accepts all that Marjorie Nicolson and her associates have established concerning Swift's indebtedness for satiric material to the Royal Society and their publications, but he protests that for Swift, Pope, and other Augustan satirists science came to serve as more than the butt of their direct, frontal attack. The order of language characteristic of the various scientific writers of the period carried with it a new vocabulary and implicitly a new worldview. Science-based terms and references lay at hand for eighteenth-century writers, not only for those welcoming and promoting the new science but for those who rejected it as a whole. For Swift and others of his persuasion the scientific style presented irresistible opportunities for satire delivered in the idiom of the scientific writers. Episodes, indeed whole compositions, could be given a metaphorical turn. Thus Pope's Kingdom of Dulness has been conceived and described in terms that fuse science and the forms of human perversity and folly.

It is a short step from Davie's satiric metaphors derived from science to more extended metaphors reflecting feelings of surprise, shock, and dread in the presence of the revolution taking place in European thought and sensibility. These latter metaphors are not exactly those brought to our attention by Davie; they are less directly linguistic, more in the nature of symbolistic idiom. Caves, prisons, flights from the familiar and the confining, concepts of time, of space, of the relativity of sense experience—images and concepts such as these are not uncommon in Enlightenment literature, and the increasingly sophisticated criticism of today has seized on them with enthusiasm as offering fresh insights into the art and psychological sources of English writers of post-Restoration decades.

In 1977 two exceptionally penetrating treatments of this kind of literary symbolism appeared. One is Hopewell Selby's article "The Cell and the Garrett: Fictions of Confinement in Swift's Satires and Personal Writings." In the *Tale* Swift gives us Bedlam, which is confinement for madmen. In the *Travels* there is the abandoned temple where Gulliver is chained up by his Lilliputian captors and the box in which he is carried about by his Brobdingnagian nurse, and the end of the *Travels* finds him seeking self-confinement in a stable with his two horses. In the interpretation given in this article, Swift's enclosures "inevitably resemble the madman's Bedlamite cell." Gulliver suffers a disintegration of personality typical of "all the trapped speakers of Swift's satires." But punishment by confinement functions in Swift not only in an uncreative, repressive way but as admonition to accept the sanity of the established norms of society. He himself, threatened by the terrible void and haunted by anxiety, suffered nightmares where disappearance and loss of sanity impended.

To what extent all this is present in the open text of the *Travels* cannot be settled dogmatically. There are episodes and incidents singled out in the criticism that are indeed a part of the work. One is free to choose between different ways of accepting the instances of confinement. The structure of the *Travels* accommodates them, or to put it more forcibly, calls them forth. Or they may be taken as symbols, expressive of more than lies on the surface. If we believe them to be symbols, we have to decide whether they were introduced by Swift by design or were unconscious intrusions, deep metaphors subrational in nature. It ought not to be forgotten that in *A Tale of a Tub* Swift made sport of symbolic writing, whether with open or arcane symbols. The person writing the "Preface," explaining how the *Tale* came to be written, speaks of the practice that sailors have of flinging out an empty tub to divert a whale from attacking their ship, and he points out how this has been allegorized with symbolic meanings for the ship, the whale, and the tub. Again, the three oratorical machines form a "Physico-logical

Scheme," which is "a Type, a Sign, an Emblem, a Shadow, a Symbol."

The other publication of 1977, not dissimilar from Selby's in subject matter and treatment, is W. B. Carnochan's *Confinement and Flight: An Essay on English Literature of the Eighteenth Century.* The scope here is broader, and in the second section ("Islands of Silence") Swift appears in company with Defoe and Sterne. Foucault's *Madness and Civilization,* specifically referred to, looms large in the background. Carnochan's informing topic as he states it concerns the "cultural sea-change associated with the onset of the modern world." The shape of experience came to be discerned in the shape of prison life; escape and flight were corollary metaphors. Locke's epistemology had the effect of confining men to the prison-house of the mind; the mind was screened off from reality and the external world. The closed world in which man had previously lived had given place to an infinite universe. One wanted to escape, to find freedom in the unconfined; yet, ambivalently, one yearned for the safety, the assurance of enclosure. The way in which Carnochan comes to Swift, finding in him telltale symptoms of anguished ambiguity, is complex, subtle, and frequently brilliant. In his last voyage Gulliver is existing in an Island of Silence, the condition towards which the sense of displacement moves, the condition of speechlessness or of linguistic meaninglessness. Reality is things, language is only names of things. How can we in speech reach beyond the words, the names, to what lies beyond them? "The real world and uncreating word," as Carnochan puts it. In part 4 Gulliver is in danger "of schizophrenic withdrawal."

Is it indeed this way? What I think is more provocative than this psychopathetic approach is Carnochan's perception that matters of language, of linguistic theory, are playing an important part. Gulliver's language, Swift's language in and out of the *Travels,* is a subject that undoubtedly will be more closely treated than hitherto. We must of course avoid imputing to Swift those feelings of scepticism and bewilderment that people in our own time, exposed to contemporary inquiries into the nature of reality, language, and meaning, are known to experience. Swift was by no means unaware of trends in epistemology since Descartes, but his reactions impress me as those of a satirist confident of his base of attack, not of one Angst-ridden.

It scarcely needs saying that it is the fourth voyage that has

occasioned the longest and sharpest of all the critical contentions as
to the proper interpretation of what Swift has bequeathed us. In
1974 James L. Clifford summarized the course that the battle over
Swift, Gulliver, the Houyhnhnms, and the Yahoos had taken since
the time when, at the close of the last century, something like
sanity had at last begun to assert itself among those writing on
Swift. Edmund Gosse, who in 1889 wanted the *Voyage to the
Houyhnhnms* banished from proper households because of the
Yahoos, was no longer in good company. Swift was not Gulliver,
Houyhnhnms and Yahoos carried meanings of more subtlety than
simplistic moral criticism allowed. But questions remained. What
do the Houyhnhnms mean, and the Yahoos? What is Gulliver's
role, caught as he is between the rational horses and the filthy,
apelike creatures? What Clifford calls the "soft" school of criticism
took over for a while, and a new interpretation of the Houyhnhnms
began to emerge. Perhaps it was they, typifying "reason" in all its
constricting inflexibility, who were the real objects of the satire, not
the Yahoos. Such a reading was soon rejected by critics of Clifford's "hard" school, who came forward to affirm that the
Houyhnhnms, in their rationality, reflected tragically on the bestial
irrationality to which human beings could and did fall when they
no longer respected reason.

Since Clifford offered his summary of the battle over the fourth
book, greater agreement appears to have been reached, not so much
over "soft" or "hard" versions—the old dispute was losing much of
its significance—but about the way in which Swift came to this
dramatization of the human situation.[1] Something of what had
been passing in Swift's mind when creating the situation and the
symbols around which the "Voyage to the Houyhnhnms" turns is
revealed in his famous letter to Pope of 29 September 1725. He has
ever, he declares, hated all nations, professions, and communities,
his love having always been towards individuals. "Principally," he
protests, "I hate and detest that animal called man, although I
heartily love John, Peter, Thomas and so forth." Then follow the
much-quoted words applying to *Gulliver's Travels:* "I have got Materials Towards a Treatise proving the falsity of the Definition
animal rationale; and to show it should be only *rationis capax.*" Man,
that is, taken in the bulk, is not a rational animal; he is only capable
of reason, as individual men bear witness. It is important to understand that in this context reason is not that mental instrument by
which we seek to arrive at truth. To Swift it was primarily the
voice of common sense, restraining our undisciplined emotions and

"irrational" impulses, directing us to live by the guides given in experience.

It was R. S. Crane who followed a lead he perceived in this letter and traced Swift's reference to "John, Peter, Thomas and so forth" to the logic books widely used in the universities, and specifically to the *Institutio logicae*, written by Narcissus Marsh when he was a tutor at Trinity College, Dublin, and almost certainly known to Swift. Marsh, following established tradition, placed *homo*, a rational animal, against *animal brutum*, an irrational one, but in giving Christian names to his individual men he chose John, Peter, and Thomas, Swift's trio, instead of one of several more customary groupings. Swift was remembering from his undergraduate days at Trinity College, and now rejecting, the old Marsh formula of man as a rational animal and brute as an irrational one. And it was *equus*, possessed of the *facultas hinniendi*—the whinnying ability—that had often been given in works in logic as an instance of *brutum*.

C. T. Probyn has since followed up the subject of Swift and the logic tradition, and in a recent discussion, "Swift and the Human Predicament," has brought a wealth of pertinent scholarship to bear on it. But we may say that even without such guidance to the precise context of Swift's rational man-irrational brute contrast, careful readers of the *Travels* were not left wholly in the dark about the thrust of the fourth part. What happens to Gulliver here has not happened to him either in Lilliput or Brobdingnag. At his return from Houyhnhnmland he has no curiosities to exhibit and does not fancy himself a giant shouldering his way like a bully through English pygmies; he lives instead in a stable, preferring the company of horses to that of men. He is no longer a normal human being. His misanthropy, induced by his exposure to the Houyhnhnms, has not been in the least mitigated by the kindness shown by Pedro de Mendez, the captain of the ship that picked him up at sea and took him to Lisbon. He has forbidden his family to come near him, and "to this Hour they dare not presume to touch my Bread, or drink out of the same Cup." The Sacrament, becoming private, has lost its meaning. Gulliver is alone in his folly.

Throughout the metaphorical episode that is the "Voyage to the Houyhnhnms," the Houyhnhnms and the Yahoos are each performing a given function. The Houyhnhnms have admirable qualities, and as living, moving beings they are as amusing as the Lilliputians and often as ridiculous. The Yahoos are not the human race, though they are a shockingly close imitation. Gulliver's ultimate failure of nerve can be taken both as tragic and comic, or as

tragic covered over by the comic. It is a failure of determination to
act in the way that human beings, neither impossibly perfect nor
utterly abhorrent, are capable of acting. The message is not different from what Swift gives us in his epitaph: assert your strength to
the utmost, act in the cause of freedom.

Further Structural Elements:
The Presences in the Narrative

Besides the structural properties already discussed—which can
go unnoted only by the most unobservant reader—there are other
less obtrusive ones, which give rise to a steady play of half-
submerged wit. In the *Travels* Gulliver, as the narrator, is always
present. Yet Swift himself—or, as will be made clear, one of the
several Swifts—can and frequently does make himself known. And
we the readers must be considered constant participants until we
choose to put the book down. We may say that there are three
"presences" here—Swift, Gulliver, and the reader—and as is the
case with the oratorical machines in the *Tale of a Tub*, there is "a
strict and perpetual Intercourse between all three."

During the past few decades a shift in critical interest has occurred, diverting attention from the broader aspects of literary
structure towards structural elements found in particular areas of
literary composition. Paul Goodman's *The Structure of Literature*
appeared in 1954. Meanwhile, critics were becoming increasingly
alive to the fact that each distinctive literary genre works in its own
special ways and that the precise nature of these ways invites close
analysis. Sheldon Sacks's *Fiction and the Shape of Belief* appeared in
1964, preceded by Wayne C. Booth's *The Rhetoric of Fiction* in 1961
and followed by Booth's further study, *Critical Understanding: The
Powers and Limits of Pluralism* (1978). For both Sacks and Booth,
certain eighteenth-century works of fiction hold particular interest
as pointing to a central critical problem. *Gulliver's Travels, Tristram
Shandy,* and the *Vicar of Wakefield* are alike in that in each of them
the narrator is not telling a straightforward story, but is one whose
presence raises questions about his role in the narrative. Tristram's
story has two dimensions, the story itself and Tristram's running
comments on the narrative in progress and on himself. Goldsmith's
Parson Primrose is constantly revealing his own intimate engagement in the plot. In cases such as these, how do we view the role of
the author? How do we situate him in reference to the narrator

within the story and to the reader? Both Sacks and Booth have interesting observations about Swift and *Gulliver's Travels*, Sacks devoting an entire section (pp. 31–49), besides scattered passages, to Swift and the *Travels*, and Booth taking up the *Travels* briefly in his *Rhetoric of Fiction* and *Critical Understanding*.

SWIFT

Addressing himself in his *Critical Understanding* to questions of who or what an author is, Booth distinguishes five entities. This sounds forbiddingly complex, yet two of his five "authors" are readily understandable and are in fact taken for granted by everyone. These two are the real historical person who is a recognized author by virtue of his writings and the person whom Booth calls the "implied author," the creative writer we instinctively recognize as present in and responsible for the text holding our attention. (Booth's three other entities receive our assent almost as quickly. The "dramatized author" is the "I" who is the purported narrator, the "career author" is the author of all the works produced by him; the "fictitious hero" is an author's popular image, independent of his actual achievement.) In suggesting that with the *Travels* in mind we may therefore count five different Swifts, I do not believe I am leaving common sense behind.

1) Swift is a historical personage. Although we know a great deal about his activities, the motivated man inside the public person remains largely a figure of conjecture; witness the endless guesswork about Swift's true motives throughout his life.

2) When we speak of "Swift the writer" we are usually pointing to Swift the author of the complete body of works known to be his. Any problems here are bibliographical—for example, is *A Letter of Advice to a Young Poet* genuine Swift?—and textual.

3) "Swift the satirist" is a convenient and necessary label, but one is constantly tempted to use it loosely. The satirist who wrote *all* the satires is not the satirist who wrote one particular satire. Swift may have a habitual satiric manner, an authentic signature, but recognition of this can never replace direct encounter with a specific work, which artistically and intellectually is an entirely singular construct.

4) Swift is the author of *Gulliver's Travels*. We know approximately when he wrote it; the important circumstances of its publication have been described by Swift and his friends. These, however, are only outward and superficial matters. We ought not

to withhold attention from the Swift within the *Travels*, the way he functions as one of the "presences," the relations he establishes between himself and Gulliver and the reader.

5) Finally, there is Swift positioning himself outside *Gulliver's Travels* and commenting on it, as in his letters: the *Travels* are "admirable Things, and will wonderfully mend the World"; "expect no more of Man than such an Animal is capable of, and you will every day find my Description of the Yahoos more resembling"; "Upon this great foundation of Misanthropy (though not Timon's manner) The whole building of my Travells is erected." Caution is to be exercised in interpreting such remarks. They were doubtless genuine enough but they were occasional observations drawn forth by the mood and condition of the moment. Extrapolation is too easy.

Turning back now to the fourth of the figures, the Swift present in the *Travels*, we now take it for granted that Gulliver is not Swift. But the relationship between the two does not rest on a single formula; it varies from one situation to another. Swift is Gulliver's maker, and the created character frequently gives the impression of proceeding under his own endowed power, yet there are moments when Swift seems to take over. We have a relatively unimportant instance of a change of voice at the beginning of the sixth chapter of the "Voyage to Lilliput." The Lilliputians' manner of writing is described as "very peculiar; being neither from the Left to the Right, like the Europeans; nor from up to down, like the Chinese; nor from down to up, like the Cascagians; but aslant from one Corner of the Paper to the other, like Ladies in England."[2] Gulliver has little humor in him—not enough, surely, to hit upon the Cascagian analogy.

There are significantly wider gaps. Glumdalclitch, Gulliver's nurse in Brobdingnag, kept in her bedchamber "a little old Treatise" on morality and devotion in which it was maintained that nature "was degenerated in these latter declining Ages of the World, and could now produce only small abortive Births in Comparison of those of ancient Times" (chap. 7). "For my own Part," writes the narrator, "I could not avoid reflecting, how universally this Talent was spread of drawing Lectures in Morality . . . from the Quarrels we raise with Nature." This is not Gulliver but Swift himself, who has taken the opportunity to interject very effectively his own commentary. The essential Swift is speaking. In Christian terms, which with one part of his mind he would seem to have accepted implicitly, man is a fallen creature. In the state to which he has now come, his reliance must be upon his own moral capabilities, God-given and still undestroyed. This is his freedom. It is not in nature's control.

The widest gap of all is found in the fourth book. Indeed, it extends through the entire "Voyage to the Country of the Houyhnhnms" and is the real source of the conflicting interpretations that have been placed upon it. What are the Houyhnhnms supposed to signify? Do the Yahoos represent human beings like ourselves? To answer such questions is to presume certain conditions. One is that Swift himself did not have the answers. Most people seem to have believed that he did, in which case he either failed to make clear to us what they were—a failure of communication—or chose for reasons of his own to leave them obscure, or placed them unmistakably within the metaphorical situation that is the whole of the fourth book. It has been suggested that he purposely left obscure what to him was the heart of the matter in order that the reader might make his own discoveries. This is the position taken by C. N. Manlove in *Literature and Reality: 1600–1800:* Swift refuses all valuation of his own; his purpose is "to push the reader back on his own resources" and force him to rethink his values. On the other hand, as we have seen, certain recent critics whose conclusions carry weight believe that Swift had defined his meanings clearly and that these are borne in upon us by everything in the Voyage.

GULLIVER

Gulliver's role is more complex than at first we are apt to perceive. What happens to him through the series of satiric episodes that is the *Travels* holds our interest but does not, and is not supposed to, arouse sympathy. He is one of Swift's notable comic-satiric figures. Though he bears no resemblance to the religious enthusiasts of the *Tale of a Tub* nor to a Partridge or a Modern Proposer, he grows in folly in the course of his experiences as a world traveler until at the end of his adventures he develops a most bizarre kind of irrational behavior. He is a necessary presence in the narrative, manipulated with great cunning in accordance with the demands presented in turn by the different situations that form themselves as the story takes us to Lilliput, to Brobdingnag, to Laputa and the other places encountered in the third Voyage, and to the land of the Houyhnhnms. His most obvious function is that of a traveler who observes and reports—who observes, as he believes, the plain, unvarnished facts and reports them without embellishments. That he became increasingly involved in the events that come upon him is one of the humorous strains enlivening the *Travels*.

Gulliver's involvement may be said to take two forms. On the one hand he arrives at moral judgments about the people and the societies he meets with, while on the other he suffers increasingly acute emotional reactions. It is Gulliver's psychological experience that is the effective means of drawing us into the story. We know how he felt in all the nerves of his body upon awakening to find himself bound fast by the Lilliputians. We share the pain and disgust he felt when exposed to the body odors of the Brobdingnagians and the feces of the Yahoos.

Gulliver's prose style is still another point to consider, but until Swift's views on style and his stylistic practice are better understood than they have been in the past, the question of style in the *Travels* remains an unsolved critical puzzle. It is in his *Letter to a Young Gentleman, Lately enter'd into Holy Orders* (1721) that Swift wrote most clearly and directly about the matter of style, but here he was discussing pulpit oratory, and his demand that in sermons the style be simple and that it set forth a Christian's duties clearly and reasonably and without recourse to emotional fervor had behind it a tradition established by a long line of Anglican clergymen, one of whose favorite topics was the form and style of the proper sermon. But the *Travels* is not this kind of sermon. Gulliver's factual style has been seen by some critics—e.g., Frederik N. Smith in his *Language and Reality in Swift's "A Tale of a Tub"*—to betoken Swift's acceptance of Locke's theory of the reality of the external world, of which our senses give us a true report. I think it is doubtful that this is Locke's theory and still more doubtful that Swift ever accepted Locke's linguistic views. It seems to me more likely that Swift was to some degree influenced by his friend Bishop Berkeley, and that like Berkeley in the *Treatise Concerning the Principles of Human Knowledge*, he found Locke's theory of perception and of language simplistically false. Hugh Kenner strikes me as hitting closer to the truth in his *Flaubert, Joyce, and Beckett: The Stoic Comedians*, where he remarks that *Gulliver's Travels* has been constructed as a satire on mindless empiricism, Gulliver existing "in the center of a universe of objects" to the physical properties of which he is infallibly responsive.

Clues found in the *Travels* itself would seem to indicate that Swift was both amused and irritated by the superabundance of nautical terms present in the voyage literature of the period. He made his point, as he often did, by way of parody, lifting from Samuel Sturmy's *Mariners Magazine* (1669) the description of the storm at sea given in the opening chapter of the second Voyage; and in case we should miss the fact that the style of the *Travels* is sometimes meant to ridicule the language found in the travel books of the time, we are told in the "Letter . . . to Sympson" that Gulliver's "Sea-Language" has been faulted by some readers. The reference in the 1735 "Advertisment" to the author's "plain simple Style" and in the notice of "Publisher to the Reader" to the fact that the style of the *Travels* is "very plain and simple," the only fault being that the author is "a little too circumstantial," may point ironically to Gulliver's "Sea-Language" or again to his resolutely empirical, nonimaginative style. In short, today's critics and readers alike must come to their own conclusions concerning the style of the *Travels* with a minimum of explicit guidance.

THE READER

It will not, perhaps, be a matter of regret to those who have been following this essay that of the three presences in the *Travels*, that of the reader must here receive short shrift.[3] Swift and Gulliver each lays a burden on him, but they do so in different ways. If he proves unequal to the challenge, where does the blame lie? The critic would like to know, but the common reader is probably indifferent. If his response to the *Travels* is a loose and impressionistic one, that is how it has been over the years with most of the literate public. A book draws its lifeblood from its imperfect readers.

And with this the critic must bid adieu to all who have felt or in the future may come to feel the power, however it be described, of the comic-satiric-tragic masterpiece formally entitled *Travels Into Several Remote Nations of the World.*

Notes

1. Donald Keesey has an amusing commentary on Clifford's schools of criticism in "The Distorted Image: Swift's Yahoos and the Critics," *Papers on Language and Literature* 15 (Summer 1979):320–32. If we are to believe Keesey, the battle between the two schools has by no means ended, and further he points to the appearance of a "middle-state" school of criticism, somewhere between "soft" and "hard". Keesey is himself of the "hard" persuasion, scorning both the "soft" and the "middle-state" positions. The *Travels*, he holds, is a discontinuous

structure, to be read detail by detail, but with man's pride the ever-present target of Swift's satire.

2. R. W. Frantz has shown ("Gulliver's 'Cousin Sympson'," *Huntington Library Quarterly* 1[1938]:329–34) that for this handwriting passage Swift was indebted to *A New Voyage to the East-Indies* (1715; 2nd ed. 1720), given as the work of a Captain William Symson. This Symson never existed, the *New Voyage* being drawn in part (including a version of the handwriting passage) from John Ovington's *Voyage to Suratt* (1696). But the "Cascagians" do not make an appearance either in the *New Voyage* or the *Voyage to Suratt*. If they are not of Swift's invention, no one has as yet discovered in what work Swift came upon them.

3. I should note, however, that what I have said in connection with the "presences" of Swift the author and of Gulliver has necessarily pointed to significant relationships with the reader.

In 1961, in his *Rhetoric of Fiction*, Wayne C. Booth wrote that the act of communication by author with reader in fictional art "has in modern criticism often been ignored, lamented, or denied" (p. 89). He himself saw the rhetoric he was analyzing as this kind of communication, and he had a number of interesting things to say about the reader and readership. In the years since 1961 there has been no lack of criticism, some of it exceptionally interesting, devoted wholly or in part to the role of the reader. One of the most extensive and detailed critical studies is Wolfgang Iser's *The Implied Reader: Patterns of Communication in Prose Fiction from Bunyan to Beckett* (1974); cf. also his "Indeterminacy and the Reader's Response in Prose Fiction" in *Aspects of Narrative: Selected Papers from the English Institute* (1971), and *The Art of Reading: A Theory of Response* (1978).

One practical result of this recent critical discussion—some of it highly theoretorical—is the recognition that "the reader" can be broken down into several different "readers," the relationships between reader, author, and text being discerned as multiple and variable. Does such criticism bear upon *Gulliver's Travels*? Iser, in his *Implied Reader*, makes no mention of Swift or of the *Travels*, presumably because he does not associate them directly with what he regards as prose fiction. Wayne Booth, however, remarks that his *Rhetoric of Fiction* is concerned with nondramatic fiction as represented by *Tom Jones*, but that the problems he takes up are also present in didactic works like *Gulliver's Travels*, *Pilgrim's Progress*, and *1984*.

Works Cited

Booth, Wayne C. *Critical Understanding: The Powers and Limits of Pluralism*. Chicago: University of Chicago Press, 1978.

————. *The Rhetoric of Fiction*. Chicago: University of Chicago Press, 1961.

Brady, Frank. "Vexations and Diversions: Three Problems in *Gulliver's Travels*." *Modern Philology* 75 (1978):346–67.

Carnochan, W. B. *Confinement and Flight: An Essay on English Literature of the Eighteenth Century*. Berkeley, Calif.: University of California Press, 1977.

Case, Arthur E. *Four Essays on "Gulliver's Travels"*. Princeton, N.J.: Princeton University Press, 1945.

Clifford, James L. "Gulliver's Fourth Voyage: Hard and Soft Schools of Interpretation." In *Quick Springs of Sense: Studies in the Eighteenth Century*, edited by Larry S. Champion. Athens: University of Georgia Press, 1974.

Crane, Ronald S. "The Houhyhnhnms, the Yahoos, and the History of Ideas." In *Reason and Imagination: Studies in the History of Ideas, 1600–1900*, edited by J. A. Mazzeo. New York: Columbia University Press, 1962.

Davie, Donald. *The Language of Science and the Language of Literature, 1700–1740*. London: Sheed and Ward, 1963.

Downie, J. A. "Political Characterization in *Gulliver's Travels*." *The Yearbook of English Studies* 7 (1977): 108–20.

Firth, Charles H. "The Political Significance of Gulliver's Travels." (1919). In Firth's *Essays Historical and Literary*, Oxford: Clarendon Press, 1968.

Frantz, R. W. "Gulliver's 'Cousin Sympson'." *Huntington Library Quarterly* 1 (1938):329–34.

Harth, Phillip. "The Problem of Political Allegory in *Gulliver's Travels*." *Modern Philology* 73 (1976):S40–S47.

Iser, Wolfgang. *The Act of Reading: A Theory of Aesthetic Response*. Baltimore, Md.: Johns Hopkins Press, 1978.

————. *The Implied Reader: Patterns of Communication in Prose Fiction from Bunyan to Beckett*. Baltimore, Md.: Johns Hopkins Press, 1974.

————. "Indeterminacy and the Reader's Response in Prose Fiction." In *Aspects of Narrative: Selected Papers from the English Institute*, edited by J. Hillis Miller. New York: AMS Press, 1971.

Keesey, Donald. "The Distorted Image: Swift's Yahoos, and the Critics." *Papers on Language and Literature* 15 (1979): 320–32.

Kenner, Hugh. *Flaubert, Joyce and Beckett: The Stoic Comedians*. Boston, Mass.: Beacon Press 1962.

Lock, F. P. *The Politics of "Gulliver's Travels"*. Oxford: Clarendon Press, 1980.

Manlove, Colin N. *Literature and Reality: 1600–1800*. London: Macmillan, 1978.

Nicolson, Marjorie H. "The Scientific Background of Swift's *Voyage to Laputa*." In Nicholson's *Science and Imagination*, Ithaca, N.Y.: Cornell University Press, 1956.

Probyn, Clive T. "Swift and the Human Predicament." In *The Art of Jonathan Swift*, edited by C. T. Probyn. London: Vision Press, 1978.

Renaker, David. "Swift's Laputians as a Caricature of the Cartesians." *PMLA* 94 (1979): 936–44.

Sacks, Sheldon. *Fiction and the Shape of Belief*. Berkeley, Calif.: University of California Press, 1964.

Selby, Hopewell. "The Cell and the Garret: Fictions of Confinement in Swift's Satires and Prose Writings." In *Studies in Eighteenth-Century Cul-*

ture. vol. 6, edited by Ronald C. Rosbottom. Madison, Wisc.: University of Wisconsin Press, 1977.

Smith, Frederik. *Language and Reality in Swift's "A Tale of a Tub."* Columbus: Ohio State University Press, 1979.

Swaim, Kathleen M. *A Reading of "Gulliver's Travels."* The Hague: Mouton, 1972.

Williams, Kathleen. "Johnathan Swift." In *Dryden to Johnson*, edited by Roger Lonsdale. London: Sphere, 1971.

11

The Ironic Tradition in Augustan Prose from Swift to Johnson

Ian Watt

When the Steering Committee of the Clark Library Seminar honored me with an invitation to initiate a discussion in the general area of eighteenth-century prose, it occurred to me that, surprisingly enough, there was one fairly large and reasonably germane topic—that of the tradition of irony in the eighteenth century—which had not, as far as I knew, received any general treatment. It is surely true that in no other period does irony loom so large upon the literary scene: many of the acknowledged masterpieces are ironic both in their basic strategy and their local style—the *Tale of a Tub*, *Gulliver's Travels*, the *Rape of the Lock*, the *Dunciad*, *The Way of the World*, the *Beggar's Opera;* nor can we look long before finding an important ironical element in many others: the indulgent mockery of the *Spectator* or the Citizen of the World; the lofty awareness of the narrow limits placed on man's endeavor in *The Vanity of Human Wishes* and the *Decline and Fall of the Roman Empire;* the comic counterpoint of action and comment in *Tom Jones* and *Tristram Shandy:* similar tonalities are everywhere, from the speculative heights of Berkeley and Hume to the abysses of Grub Street, with all its jaded poems about nymphs and its pamphlet wars between ninnies.

What are the reasons for this virtual omnipresence of irony? How is it connected with the many other characteristics of the period which we have learned so much about in the last few dec-

Reprinted, with a few slight alterations, from *Restoration and Augustan Prose. Papers delivered by James R. Sutherland and Ian Watt at the Third Clark Library Seminar, 14 July 1956,* William Andrews Clark Memorial Library, University of California, Los Angeles, 1956, pp. 19–46. By permission of the author, © copyright 1956, Ian Watt.

ades? Does it shed any light on the relation of the eighteenth century to what comes before and after, to the Restoration and to
Romanticism? These are the directions in which I would like to
initiate a few tentative explorations.[1]

1

There seems no doubt that, as he himself claims in the *Verses* on
his own death, Swift inaugurated the ironic tradition in eighteenth-
century literature.

> Arbuthnot is no more my Friend,
> Who dares to Irony pretend;
> Which I was born to introduce,
> Refin'd it first, and shew'd its Use.

Swift does not, however, help us very much to understand *how*
he refined it. His few remarks about irony—like all those I have
come across in other writers of the period—are very casual, and
stay well within the classical treatments of irony in Aristotle, Cicero, and Quintilian. There is perhaps a little more help—some
negative tangential clues at least—to be found in Swift's letter to
the *Tatler* on "the continual Corruptions of our English Tongue."
There, singling out two of his favorite lexical *bêtes noires*, he writes:
"I have done my Utmost for some Years past to stop the progress of
Mobb and *Banter*, but have been plainly borne down by Numbers."
    "Mob" and "Banter" are being singled out as vulgar neologisms:
but, as notorious recent additions to the speech of the time, they are
also significant I think, of certain new forces in the Augustan
scene—forces that help us to isolate some of the elements of Swift's
irony, merely because Swift, and his irony, were diametrically
opposed to them.
    "Mob," of course, was the modish abbreviation of *mobile vulgus:*
and Swift objected as much to the thing as he did to the abbrevia-
tion. Roger North says in the *Examen* (1740) that the word first
appeared, in place of "rabble," when the London crowd became the
"beast of burthen" of Shaftesbury and his Green Ribbon Club,
which met at the King's Head Tavern, and which is attacked in the
Second Part of *Absalom and Achitophel.*
    The word was naturalized, according to the *Oxford English Dic-
tionary*, in 1688, the year of the Glorious Revolution: and for the

following century most of the great men of letters remained on
guard against the mob, against all those who threatened to subvert
the established order, whether in politics or in literature or in manners. To say that the Augustans invented the dichotomy of the elite
and the mob would obviously be exaggerated; but they certainly
went further than ever before in conceptualizing and applying the
distinction. Indeed, the idea seems to have defined their basic conception of their role as writers: they were a small band, a righteous
minority, ever battling for truth against every kind of deviation
from the norm; against the Dunces and the Foplings and the Vir-
tuosos—almost any page of Swift or Pope will supply confirmation
and additions.

Out of this there arose a vision of a double, a divided audience
that made irony, in the sense of speaking by contraries, a possible,
and almost an obligatory mode of discourse.

The chosen few—the men of wit and judgment and learning—
could be assumed to have considerable identity of attitude and
understanding: to them you could speak as subtly and elliptically as
you wished. But to the many, the mob—you obviously could not
and in any case would not use the same language; in Johnson's
delightful phrase, they had "no claim to the honour of serious
confutation." There was, therefore, a strong pressure towards
shaping every element of discourse, from the single word to the
total work, with two different and opposite categories of people in
mind. For example, there were the people in the largest category,
the literary mob, who could be persuaded that Gulliver was a real
person, and they were provided with the most elementary kind of
narrative interest in the simplest kind of prose—if you played the
game well enough you might even take in an Irish bishop. While
those for whom Swift really wrote were allowed to savor simultaneously, not only the ironical interpretation of the fable—the
book's real meaning—but also the literary skill with which the less
percipient were being hoodwinked. The ironic posture, in fact, was
both a formal expression of the qualitative division in the reading
public and a flattering reinforcement of the sense of superiority that
animated one part of it.

This separation of the true wits from the mob, incidentally, had
the great advantage of flexibility: in any given context it was
defined merely by the absence or presence of proper standards. So
if, for example, the Hanoverian boors and the vulgar millionaires,
along with their political toadies and their poets laureate, seemed to
most people to be the great ones of their time, Pope could put a

brave face on the situation and announce that "Scribblers or peers alike are mob to me"; Swift could reserve his choicest scorn for the "better sort of vulgar"; and Fielding could continue the tradition by explaining in *Tom Jones* that "wherever this word [mob] occurs in our writings, it intends persons without virtue or sense, in all stations; and many of the highest rank are often meant by it."

The mob, then, was the perfect antitype of proper standards: the more so as, being mobile as well as vulgar, it could naturally represent sentiment, enthusiasm, every kind of fashionable novelty, as opposed to the unchanging norms of nature and tradition espoused by the Augustans. Finally—and perhaps most significantly—the mob, as an ancient symbol of irrational forces, could stand for passion, as against reason.

If "mob" could stand for the complete antithesis to the kind of audience and outlook that Swift esteemed, and thus dictated something of the content and basic strategy of his irony, "banter" helps us, also by contradiction, to describe the tone and the attitude that characterize his ironic technique.

In *A Tale of a Tub*, Swift, after promising us a treatise entitled "A modest Defense of the Proceedings of the *Rabble* in all Ages," turns briefly, in the prefatory "Apology," to the subject of banter. "This Polite Word," he tells us, "was first borrowed from the Bullies in *White-Fryars*, then fell among the Footmen, and at last retired to the Pedants." Swift then goes on to illustrate the difference between "Bantring" and genuine "Productions of Wit" from the works of his antagonist William Wotton: "it is grievous to see him . . . going out of his way to be waggish, to tell us of *a Cow that prickt up her Tail*, and in his answer to this Discourse, he says *it is all a Farce and a Ladle*."

Swift, then, thought of banter as open personal attack cast in the vulgar dialect of the marketplace: both in manner and matter it violated the decorums of social and intellectual refinement. Irony, we can see, is the exact opposite. Its rhetorical aim, perhaps, is the same: to expose your enemy to shame and ridicule; but the game is played in much more seemly fashion. Aristotle had written in the *Rhetoric* that the role of *eiron* befits a gentleman more than that of the buffoon, and the reasons are not far to seek. Irony tends to understatement, to meiosis, which itself insists on the difference of social rank: the mob are little people. And while the gentleman is disposing of his foe by the method of irony, his serenity need never be discomposed, even by laughter: the true gentleman, like Fontenelle, "n'a jamais fait ha ha ha." Whether Swift, as reported, never laughed, we do not know; I think he probably did, but not, certainly, in his prose. Puttenham defined irony as "the dry mock"; and Swift's prose rigidly obeys the code of irony which, like that prescribed for Prussian officers, allows no more than "ein kurzes militärisches Lachen"—a single, chilling, "Ha!"

Irony is better suited to the gentleman and the wit than banter in many other ways: it is rude to stick your tongue out in public, whereas, it is the very pink of politeness to praise your enemy with your tongue in your cheek; and this obliquity of insult is, moreover, much more difficult to counter. As Max Beerbohm said long ago of the father of irony, the Socratic method is not a game at which two can play.

Such are some of the ways in which Swift's irony may be seen as the complement of his opposition to mob and banter; and the basic situation I have sketched is closely related to some of the characteristics of his prose style. If a sentence is to be susceptible of two contrary interpretations, the simplest kind of predication will be best: to get the opposite we only have to supply a "not" for the verb, or an antonym for the noun; and it is therefore likely that eighteenth-century irony both required and stimulated the development of a kind of prose perspicuous enough for its double meanings to be sufficiently transparent. Swift's conciseness, his avoidance of adjectival ornament, his subordination of all the rhetorical arts to an easy conveyance of meaning—all these are prerequisites of his irony.

With such a staple established, prose could, of course, become capable of emphasis with much less expenditure of effort; and this, too, is necessary for irony. If we compare Swift's method of emphasis with those of earlier writers, with Lyly or Nashe or Donne or Milton, it is surely apparent that in this case, at least, Henry James's law—"economy of means—economy of effect"—does not apply. Consider, for example, the famous line in the "Digression on Madness": "Last Week I saw a Woman *flay'd*, and you will hardly believe, how much it altered her Person for the worse."

Shocked into a full realization of the inner-outer, appearance-reality dichotomy with the very slightest of verbal pressures from Swift, we cannot withhold from him the honor that Dryden claimed for the true satirist: he is the very Jack Ketch of his art, without rival in making "a malefactor die sweetly." Swift's "you will hardly believe" so casually ranges us with the mob, with those habitually blind both to the realities below the surface of things, and also, perhaps, to the actual cruelties and miseries of this world, however much they may fancy themselves to be "brimful of that *Modern* Charity and Tenderness" ironically alluded to at the end of the "Digression." And, of course, the ominous modulation would lose its effect if we did not know that the pretended author was actually an obtuse spokesman of the mob; or if Swift's prose were not so beautifully lucid, that our attention was deflected from his double range of implication by being occupied with the difficulty of deciphering the sentence's bare meaning.

"Proper words in proper places"—such was no doubt Swift's greatest legacy to eighteenth-century prose. If we look for a more specific indebtedness to Swift's irony in later writers, it seems most obviously to reside in two other characteristics of the passage that are closely connected with its economy of effect.

First, it surely is evident that the device of understatement might formerly have passed unnoticed. In Jacobean prose, for example, the competition for our attention would be much too energetic for the meiosis of "how much her person was altered for the worse" to serve as effective climax: Swift's fastidious aversion—at once ironic and real—to anything more than a spare, analytic notation of an effect—requires to be set in much more equable and unemphatic surroundings if it is to strike home.

Swift's perfectly controlled lucidity, combined with his habit of understatement, probably did much to attune the ears of succeeding generations of readers to similar ironic effects in later writers: and to the duplicities of calculated hyperbole as well as of meiosis. When Hume, for example, spoke of the "hideous hypothesis . . . for which *Spinoza* is so universally infamous," a good many readers could be expected to see that the adjectives were ironical: Hume's normally restrained vocabulary being what it is, "hideous" and "infamous" could only be wanton hyperboles, which the deist minority would delightedly recognize—and find their pleasure increased by their recognition of the author's straightfaced parody of the overstrained indignation of the—this time orthodox—mob.

Perhaps the most significant ironical characteristic of Swift's style, however, is that exemplified in the cool, distant generality of "how much it altered her person." A degree of abstraction would seem to be necessary for ironic diction. Partly because the number of nonabstract nouns that have an opposite is fairly limited: there is no antonym, as far as I know, for "Ian Watt": but there is one for "human" or "wisdom," as I am aware.

Even more important, perhaps, and certainly so in the present case, is the fact that the use of abstract words in itself often creates an ironical effect: if anyone who knows my proper name calls me "Professor," I at once suspect him of intending a certain ironical distancing. So one constantly finds the strong abstract element in eighteenth-century prose connected with one of the characteristic features of its irony—the lofty, analytic, and slightly supercilious command of the entire human scene. When Shaftesbury, for example, after proclaiming the great benefits of "raillery"—the banter of the elite—for composing differences among educated gentlemen, goes on to confess that "the mere Vulgar of Mankind . . . often stand in need of such a rectifying Object as *the Gallows* before their Eyes"—there is surely an implicit social and literary alignment of Shaftesbury with his ideological opposite, Swift. Both, at least, give us a vision conspicuously removed from the ordinary man's concrete apprehensions.

Abstract diction, in fact, has dissolved the terror of the gallows, like the bloodstained agony of the flayed woman, into the metaphysical air; the witty compression of "rectifying object" is a whole world away from the crowds on Tyburn Hill; generality of diction functions as the verbal expression of the vast distance between the wit and the mob.

2

So much for the connection between the opposition to "mob and banter" and some of the essential features of Augustan irony. Before passing to a somewhat more detailed—but necessarily still rather schematic—consideration of three of its constituents that, I think, were both problematic in themselves and contained the seeds of major literary developments in the tradition of irony, I would like to suggest that what I have already said provides some clues as to the reasons for the difference in tone between Restoration and Augustan literature. Swift's predecessor Samuel Butler, for example, invites the mob as well as the elite to jeer at Sir Hudibras, and his verse aims at stimulating his audience into the loudest possible guffaw. Similarly Dryden—in *MacFlecknoe*, for instance—comes much closer to banter than Pope ever does, and the barrier between himself and his satiric targets is not normally the unsurmountable one of irony: his verse implies that both he and they are human beings, and this is not always the impression we get from Pope. Finally—to take a third example from the domain of literary genre—it is surely the instinctive preference for meoisis over hy-

perbole that explains why the Augustans were given to mock heroic
rather than to travesty.

Looking forward, now, I would like to single out as the first of
the problematic elements in Augustan irony the tendency already
noted towards general and abstract statement. When Johnson, for
example, gave us his immortal definition of gin as "a compendious
mode of drunkenness," the context—a serious attack in the *Literary
Magazine* (no. 13) on the "enormous and insupportable mischiefs"
arising from intemperance—proves that he did not mean to be
ironical. "Compendious," like Shaftesbury's "rectifying," is merely
an abstract modifier, but taken in conjunction with its concrete
referent "gin," the terse abstractness arouses a suspicion of irony,
merely because of the absence of the expected moral connotation:
compendiousness, which he defined in the *Dictionary* as that "by
which time is saved and circuition cut off," is normally a welcome,
useful quality, and what approbative connotation exists in the word
is therefore somewhat contrary to expectation. But the main reason
for our surprise is, I believe, the generality of the diction itself,
which involves an absence of the powerful connotations we would
normally expect from the referent concerned, an absence that is so
conspicuous as to generate irony.

The analytic, generalizing tendency of the eighteenth-century
vocabulary may itself be regarded as ironigenic then, as tending to
produce irony whether intended or not; partly because it lacks
connotation, excludes the normally attendant feelings and evalua-
tions with which its concrete referent is usually associated; and
partly because generalized diction has its own kind of connotation,
always suggesting a cool, unemotional, and hence sceptical evaluation of what it describes.

A passage from Swift's *Letter to a Young Gentleman Lately Enter'd
into Holy Orders* may serve to illustrate this tendency: Swift is ear-
nestly advising his charge against attempting to explain the mysteries of the Christian religion: for, he says, with impeccable logic,
"If you explain them, they are Mysteries no longer; if you fail, you
have laboured to no Purpose." Taken out of context, this could well
come from an ironical deist tract; and the effect is heightened when
Swift goes on to say "For my part, having considered the Matter
impartially, I can see no great Reason which those Gentlemen you
call the *Free-Thinkers* can have for their Clamour against Religious
Mysteries; since it is plain, they were not invented by the Clergy,
to whom they bring no Profit, nor acquire any Honour." I pass

over Swift's apparent chagrin that Providence has dealt the Deists all the theological aces, to emphasize how the mere application of rational argument and the reduction of the essential terms of Christianity to such general abstractions as "mysteries," "profit," "honour," cannot but have a sceptical effect.

A similar tendency—the tendency of the cool absence of connotation in any discourse concerned with things fraught with emotion, to create a disturbing ironical ripple even where it is not intended—is discernible in Shaftesbury's epithet for God—"the best natur'd One in the World"; and it similarly subverts his own beloved avocation, philosophy, when he asserts that "to Philosophise, in a just Signification, is but to carry Good-Breeding a Step higher." In a sense, then, Swift's refinement of expression and especially his easy manipulation of general terms may have helped—quite unintentionally—to prepare the way for works so totally contrary to Swift's ideas as Hume's essay "Of Miracles" in the *Enquiry Concerning Human Understanding*. Hume's tone, as indeed his logical method, have a very close kinship to Swift's coolly abstract treatment of the Christian mysteries: "So that, upon the whole, we may conclude, that the *Christian Religion* not only was at first attended with miracles, but even at this day cannot be believed by any reasonable person without one."

It would be possible, I think, at this stage, to show how Swift's rather exaggerated belief in the extent to which words, and indeed the human mind, operate, or rather should operate, by means of single, logical meanings—actually extends far beyond the question of diction. If Voltaire—no innocent when it comes to irony—took the *Tale of a Tub* as an attack on religion, it was surely in part because the total effect of allegorical and metaphoric devices can no more be rigidly circumscribed to the single logical effect intended than can that of single words. The analogy of the coats as such is not forgotten once we have discerned its application to factional quarrels in the Church: the prestige of the Church itself is likely to be—no doubt irrationally—diminished by the association. Words, images, the human mind, will not always keep to the single track marked for them by irony, especially when—after a lapse of time— we have only a hazy recollection of a few concrete images divorced from their logical structure: the Bishops had their own kind of alogical wisdom when they feared that the true religion had been besmirched by the company it had been made to keep in the *Tale of a Tub*.

3

The meaning—whether of a single word or of any larger unit of expression—cannot, then, be wholly restricted to the role that it is allotted by the logic of the ironist: and the same difficulty occurs in the case of the largest ironic weapon of all—that of the author'x pretended narrator or protagonist—the ironic mask or *persona*.

The use of a fictional *persona* would seem to be a structural necessity in any extensive piece of ironical writing: the actual author must remain invisible, for we would lose our interest in the chase if we could see from the beginning that it was the same man who was running with the mob of hares and hunting with the witty hounds. The ironic *persona* can be on either side: most often he is with the hares, making us see which way the author's hunt is going by speaking or acting the contrary: such is the Grub Street hack who writes the *Tale of a Tub*, for example. But the *persona* can also be a huntsman, as long as he is in disguise: he may speak direct truth, that is, but by some naïveté, some Cassandra-like disablement, some apparent inferiority to ourselves as a witness, what he says sounds false, except to the initiated: such, essentially, is the role of the clairvoyant Chinamen, penetrating Persians, and existentialist Abyssinians who smile at us mockingly from the pages of Goldsmith, Addison, and Johnson; and they are close literary kinsfolk to the King of Brobdingnag, and of the even wiser nags of the Fourth Part.

The use of the *persona* is, of course, a very ancient device; and we must remember that the element of actual pretense was still strong in the eighteenth-century usage of the term *irony*. Swift, however, is surely unrivaled both in the number of *personae* he adopted, and in the imaginative completeness with which he merged himself into them.

There, I think, is the rub. In many of Swift's satires the *personae* are so convincing that, in addition to our awareness of the two levels of interpretation intended, the fictional world of each *persona* also takes on a reality of its own: the mask looks perfectly lifelike. This, of course, has some great advantages: in the *Drapier's Letters*, for example, or the *Modest Proposal*, Swift enlists to his purpose the force of the immediate, personal participations and revulsions that are normally either weak or absent in expository prose. But in other circumstances—and we come now to the rub—this surely places a double responsibility on the *persona* that he cannot easily discharge. In so far as he is an ironic device, his effectiveness is directly proportional to the completeness of his disciplined subordination to his creator's purpose; while, *qua* individual character, the *persona* can become living and effective only by transcending the role he is allotted as the vehicle of the transparently dual or multiple presentation of reality that irony requires. This implicit contradiction becomes manifest if the plot requires that the *persona* not only be lifelike, but actually come to life and be changed by his experiences, just like a real person or a character in a novel; and I believe that it is this which has caused the climax of Swift's career as an ironist—the Fourth part of *Gulliver*—to tease two centuries of critics: an ironical fate, be it added, for a writer whose main literary intention was the enforcement of truths which he believed to be universally available to the common sense of mankind.

I cannot even begin to consider the complex problems that arise when you have several *personae* engaged in ironic counterpoint, as in *Gulliver's Travels;* nor am I proposing here yet another solution to the problems offered by the Fourth Part; I wish only to suggest that such a solution must take account, not only of the inherent contradictions between the functions of the ironic *personae* and the fully developed literary character, but also of the philosophical problem that underlies it—how to handle the individual-class dichotomy.

One modern tendency in Swift criticism has been to articulate the hypothesis of a progressive ironical structure in *Gulliver's Travels* by tracing the developing sequence of the hero's reactions to his experiences. It seems to me that there are many difficulties in doing this. Theoretically, for example, it depends upon the premise that you can have flat and round, static and developing ironic *personae*, just as you do characters in a novel; and Part Four seems to me to present undeniable evidence that the possibilities of combining the effects of character and *persona* are strictly limited; that as readers we cannot, in fact, maintain the separation between the pretended ironic *persona*, and the actual suffering person. Swift, I have little doubt, merely intended Gulliver to exhibit a climactic reaction to a never-before-glimpsed vision of the squalors of passion—the Yahoos,—and the splendors of reason—the Houyhnhnms: and the blinding brightness of the vision was to be brought home by making his *persona* end his days in a comically hyperbolic revulsion from the actual human scene. But—in the very process of shattering the complacency of the dullest reader— Swift's narrative genius gave the episode a psychological reality so deeply disturbing that many initiated readers find it difficult not to allow their gaze to be deflected from the relentless intellectual pressure of Swift's ironic tenor to the pathos of the fate of its literary vehicle; in so far as Swift made Gulliver convincing as a character, our possession of his logical meaning was necessarily disturbed by our sorrow that a fellow human being, who had, after all, no harm in him, should, as the fruit of his labors in life have become a candidate for the madhouse.

The duality of *persona-character* is essentially the special case in the field of ironical narrative of the general problem of the duality of general and individual, which is the topic of Swift's famous letter to Pope about Gulliver's Travels:

> I have ever hated all nations, professions and communities, and all my love is toward individuals; for instance, I hate the tribe of lawyers, but I love Counsellor Such-a-one and Judge Such-a-one; so with physicians—I will not speak of my own trade—soldiers, English, Scotch, French, and the rest. But principally I hate and detest that animal called man, although I heartily love John, Peter, Thomas, and so forth. This is the system upon which I have governed myself many years.

I must confess that, as a commentary on *Gulliver's Travels*, I do not find this by any means self-explanatory or unambiguous. I can share Swift's general feeling only too well, but, at the risk of calling down very varied thunders on my head. I must confess that, judged as a statement of "system" or set of correlated principles, I find the passage hyperbolic, if not ultimately illogical; while as a gloss, I find it mainly helpful as an example of a confusion that rather closely parallels that which I find in Swift's handling of his *persona* in the Fourth Part.

Briefly, Swift seems to be qualifying the blank misanthropy of his preceding assertion that "the chief end I propose to myself in all my labours is to vex the world rather than divert it" by explaining that his reaction to man in his collective aspect is the complete opposite of his reaction to man in his individual aspect. But since the common qualities of "John, Peter, Thomas, and so forth," constitute whatever may be denoted by the collective term "man," it is surely to invert the fallacy of the class to assume that there can actually be any total contradiction between them. It follows, then, that the whole force of Swift's distinction must lie, not in the existent, objective properties of the individual and the group, but in the different ways they are regarded; it is, in fact, all a matter of two opposite ways of looking at what is ultimately the same thing.

This seems to offer a suggestive parallel to the analogous shift in the way we see Gulliver: mainly, and most of the time, he is an ironical *persona*, essentially a general representative of man collectively considered, but in the Fourth Part he becomes a man individually considered, with a particular wife and a particular problem, and our feelings change, if not from hate to love as in Swift's letter, at least from amused detachment to a much closer emotional involvement.

Swift's letter seems to me to support this interpretation in another way: for, just as it suggests a tendency—and not, I think, in the interests of paradox alone—to make the dichotomy of the individual and the general more total than it can actually be, so it also exhibits a certain lack of discrimination between the different ways we address ourselves to philosophical and to human objects. Swift's basic paradox depends for its effect on making the words *love* and *hate* antithetic: and so, indeed, they normally are, except perhaps in the abysses of the unconscious. But in the context of the letter, they are antithetic in direction but not in degree, because they apply to rather different levels of feeling: the "hate" that Swift bears to all collectivities must surely be a somewhat abstract, philosophical kind of aversion, since it is directed to an entity that does not exist except in the mind: while the "love" he bears the individual members of the species is presumably much closer to the realm of passion and emotion, closer to what we normally mean by "love," although it is surely still hyperbolic to talk of love when the circumstances can at best allow a general disposition to be benevolent.

The hyperbole in the use of "love," it is true, disappears if we read "I heartily love John, Peter, Thomas, and so forth" as meaning a finite listing of Swift's actual friends, rather than as an infinite series of individuals considered as such, which the paradox requires for its maximum force: but there remains a lesser hyperbole in the antithetic collocation of *love*—of particulars—and *hate*—of collectives; and this alone tends to confirm my previous suggestion about *Gulliver's Travels*. If Swift was prone to apply the same emotional terms to abstract ideas as are applied by most people only to their feelings towards a few individual persons, he may not have foreseen what would happen when, in the Fourth Part, he involved Gulliver for the first time in situations that, though intended to represent abstract issues, were actually such as to provoke intense emotional participation, rather than cool and rational observation, in his readers. For the same reason Swift may not have seen how his erstwhile *persona* had become a character, and thus lost the element of distance from the reader, which is so essential to the *persona's* ironic function: may not even have noticed how his puppet Lemuel had turned into a human being, and, just as he was being hustled off the stage, observed on his own behalf that irony could be cruel.

Ultimately, I suppose, the problem of the *persona* in relation to the individual-general dichotomy is connected with Swift's whole conception of irony as a weapon against the mob, which is after all a pejorative way of looking at man in general. But I have no time to pursue this, nor to consider whether there is not an ultimate contradiction between this steady animus against collectivities, and Swift's neo-classical preference for the general rather than the particular, of which the ironical mode is perhaps the central literary expression.

The tension between Gulliver as *persona* and Gulliver as individual character also looks forward. We can perhaps see in it how an age that did not find the lyric or dramatic modes wholly congenial was naturally tending towards a fuller realization of the individual character than either the ironic *persona*, or the neoclassical preference for the general as opposed to the individual, would allow: was tending, in fact, to the novel. This again, is too large a topic to be developed here; but one of its aspects—the problem of how the experiences of man individually considered could find literary expression in an age whose operative critical assumptions were towards general truth—cannot be avoided, since it is closely related to a new tendency in the ironic tradition that is characteristic of the succeeding period: the development, that is, of Romantic Irony.

4

To a writer wholly given over to the cultivated complicity in human pettiness that the consciously ironic perspective requires, the subjective world of feeling, and even what Wordsworth called "the primary affections and duties"—these will seem meager and unimportant. Such a writer will tend to see himself and his affections ironically, and write—with Gibbon—"I sighed as a lover, I obeyed as a son." The abstractions, the conventional roles, the mighty framework for the eternal littleness of man—they surely damp our resolution to live our own lives. Mr. and Mrs. Gibbon, I fancy, found little more satisfaction in their son than Mademoiselle Suzanne Curchod in her lover. I observe in passing that the greatest eighteenth-century ironists—Swift, Pope, Hume, and Gibbon—were all bachelors.

We can, of course, pretend to make the best of the void, and take *Vive la Bagatelle* as our motto—*faute de mieux*. But, in Swift at least, we are aware that he has settled for long walks and dirty poems, not out of weakness, but out of an honest conviction that the possible alternative would be wrong, would be unworthy of a human being. Have no fear: I will proceed no further in speculative biography: my intention is only to suggest one explanation of Swift's attitude, and this only because I think it throws some light on the development of romantic irony.

The explanation, I think, lies in what I see as the basic schism in neoclassicism, the antithesis of reason and passion. Not, of course, that the opposition is by any means peculiar to it, but it became particularly influential when it was combined with the generalizing and antithetical mode of thought that is so characteristic of the Augustan period. The problem is a complex one, and particularly so in Swift, but the Fourth Part surely suggests that the later Swift accepted the reason-passion antithesis hook, line, and sinker, especially sinker: all allowances made for the needs of dramatic heightening, there is surely nothing else in human thought that equals the violence and the starkness of the dichotomy of Yahoo and Houyhnhnm. There is a similar completeness and a barely less unconcealed violence in the opposition between Reason and Passion in one of the most familiar of Swift's "Thoughts on Religion":

> Although Reason were intended by Providence to govern our Passions, yet it seems that, in two Points of the greatest Moment to the Being and Continuance of the World, God hath intended our Passions to prevail over Reason. The first is, the Propagation of our Species, since no wise Man ever married from the Dictates of Reason. The other is, the Love of Life, which, from Dictates of Reason, every Man would despise and wish at an End, or that it never had a Beginning.

The antithetical mode of thought made absolute excludes the mixed motives of actuality; the literal and absolute attitude to words dictates that "govern our Passions" should mean, not—as was traditional—adjudicate or balance or restrain them, but annihilate them: such are the logical confusions we must accept before we allow ourselves to be overwhelmed by the specious finality of Swift's paradox. It would surely be better to apply to the passage the words of the Russian poet Alexander Blok: "In the vodka of

irony the mocker drowns his hope along with his despair." Poised
between the squalors of passion and the inoperancy of reason Swift
sat so long on the fence that the the irony entered into his . . . soul.

After Swift, the problem of how the writer should speak of
himself and deal with the life of the emotions came to the forefront
of literary interest. There was, of course, Sentimentalism, of which
I will say nothing except that the reigning habit of reifying abstractions and speaking of them with cool elegance makes it difficult not
to read the most ardent professions of love or benevolence without
smiling. Henry Brooke's *The Fool of Quality*, and Mackenzie's *Man of
Feeling*, to a modern reader at least, overflow, not with tears, but
with unconscious irony.

The great eighteenth-century novelists—of course—make the individual and his feelings their central subject: and this, on the
whole, meant excluding the ironic *persona*, though not, of course,
irony. Here—until we get to Sterne—Fielding's *Jonathan Wild* is
perhaps the most interesting work, because it is so curious a mixture of genres: in the satirical part, about the "Great Man" (no one
in the eighteenth century seems to have spoken about great men or
heroes without irony), we find an undeviating maintenance of the
double role very similar to that in Swift, but the sentimental part,
centering on the Heartfrees, seems to be open to objections very
similar to those against the sentimentalists proper: the abstract vocabulary makes the whole thing unreal, especially when the reader
carries over to the pathetic part, as he cannot but do, the habit of
ironical interpretation in which the satirical part has set him.

The two attitudes—sentiment and satirical irony—come together more convincingly in Sterne, and we get the new kind of
irony, romantic irony. There is neither time nor need to describe
the complexities of romantic irony: for, whether we are thinking of
Byron or the German Romantics, and whether or not we can follow
Friedrich Schlegel, any conception of the idea must include the two
points that, I have been trying to argue, the developing tradition of
irony had brought to the forefront. Romantic irony, that is, always
involves the writer himself, and his attitude both to the world and
to his creation; and it is subjective in another sense because it
usually involves the writer in an internal counterpoint between his
feeling and his reason: "hot baths of sentiment followed by cold
douches of irony," as Jean Paul said.

Sterne was accepted as a great forerunner of romantic irony by
Tieck, Schlegel, and others; he is, of course, continuously ironic
about what he is writing. In itself, this is often only a continuation

of the "Cervantick manner," although of course Sterne pays ironical lipservice to the Augustan impersonality by pretending that it is not he, but Tristram, his character—or is he no more than a *persona?*—who is addressing us. More significant for our purposes is Sterne's treatment of sentiment, the unrestrained expressions of feeling suddenly terminated by a deft rational undermining: to take the most famous case—Le Fever's death—we have:

> The pulse fluttered—stopp'd—went on—throb'd—stopp'd again—moved—stopp'd—shall I go on?—No.

It is interesting, I think, to see how this ironic mode was foreshadowed. Something very like it is found in Swift's private letters—especially in the *Journal to Stella,* with its playful yet tender central relationship. The reason, I think, is obvious. The private letter was largely free from the inhibitions on the expression of personal and emotional feelings that neoclassical literary decorum, and the dichotomy of reason and passion, imposed on public discourse. Nevertheless, their effects were felt, because in the last analysis the inner life, unsupported by the main orientations of eighteenth-century culture, seemed to lack any authorized standing; it was difficult to know how to assess its importance, and so its expression—even in letters to close personal friends—tended to be rounded off by a gesture of depreciation or apology, a closing obeisance to rationality.

Gray, for example, is habitually ironical about his own most real interests as a man and a poet. In one letter, to Thomas Warton the Younger, after giving vent to his enthusiasm for Ossian, he expresses the feat that "you will think I am grown mighty poetical of a sudden." In another somewhat similar passage we are given, in addition, an insight into the prosaic conception of prose, the sense that it was not the proper vehicle of feeling, which did so much to lead eighteenth-century writers into their ironical manner: Gray is ending a long description of the Kentish landscape to Norton Nicholls:

> In the east the sea breaks in upon you, & mixes its white transient sails & glittering blew expanse with the deeper & brighter greens of the woods & corn. this last sentence is so fine I am quite ashamed, but no matter! you must translate it into prose.

When Horace Walpole describes his enthusiasms there is usually a similarly ironical concluding evaluation of them: as when, for

example, after revisiting Houghton after sixteen years, the thought
of his father's death, and the dubious future of his great mansion,
makes him ask:

> For what has he built Houghton? For his grandson to annihilate, or for
> his son to mourn over! If Lord Burleigh could rise and view his repre-
> sentative driving the Hatfield stage, he would feel as I feel now—poor
> little Strawberry! at least it will not be snipped to pieces by a descen-
> dant!—You will think all these fine meditations dictated by pride, not
> by philosophy—pray consider, through how many mediums philoso-
> phy must pass, before it is purified.

There is a more complex kind of ironic wisdom here, as indeed in
many of Walpole's letters, and in those of several other writers of
the period, but the point has by now been established that it is in
the private writing of the eighteenth century that we get the most
direct expression of personal feeling; and that even there it is frequently qualified by a persistent irony of tone, which brings it very
close to what was later to be called romantic irony. Horace Walpole, indeed, almost foreshadowed the term itself when, after an
enthusiastic description of the Grande Chartreuse to Richard West,
he stopped short, fearing that he must sound "too bombast and too
romantic."

5

I come, finally, to a great exception, as I believe, to much of what
I have been saying: to Dr. Johnson. One may not think of him
primarily as an ironist, but his pre-eminence among the eighteenth-
century prose writers can perhaps be illuminated by a glance at his
position in the tradition of irony.

In it, he and Swift, of course, are the mighty opposites, although
they at least start from similar positions: from Christianity and a
deep pessimism about human life. After a discussion of man's natural goodness, Lady McLeod accused Dr. Johnson of being "worse
than Swift"; and if in the *Tale of a Tub*, Swift had called happiness
"the sublime and refined Point of Felicity, called *the Possession of
being well deceived*: The Serene Peaceful State of being a Fool among
Knaves," Johnson so little liked "any one who said they were
happy" that when on one occasion his judgment was challenged, he
thundered: "I tell you, the woman is ugly, and sickly, and foolish,

and poor; and would it not make a man hang himself to hear such a creature say, it was happy?"

The tone of Johnson's retort points to the distinguishing feature of his irony: it usually operates through fairly conscious hyperbole, and this in itself humanizes it by breaking with the decorous impersonality that was so important a part of Augustan irony; Johnson brings himself—his own anger, not to say unhappiness—into the irony: he is not outside the ironic contradiction of attitudes but within it: he knows and relishes the folly of his own hyperbolic impatience, and this qualifies what might otherwise appear to be an assertion of his own superiority to the wishful deceptions of fallible humanity.

Bringing himself into the ironic contradiction of attitudes was easy enough for Johnson—was indeed inevitable—when he was merely being reported by Boswell, or, as in the present case, by Mrs. Thrale; but Johnson locates himself within his ironic vision almost as consistently in his writings for publication. The letter to Lord Chesterfield one might call half public; and there we notice how the brilliance of his ironies at Chesterfield's expense is qualified, humanized, by the confession of his own earlier personal humiliation: "no man is well pleased to have his all neglected, be it ever so little."

In Johnson's published works, in the *Lives of the Poets*, and *The Rambler*, for instance, we have the same refusal to locate himself permanently on the Parnassian eminence, above and beyond the mob, from which Swift and Pope had looked down. This I know is contrary to the opinions of those who see Johnson's magniloquence as arrogant and impersonal. It is, in a sense, both, but we may perhaps change T. S. Eliot's phrase about Donne and say that Johnson could be as personal as he pleased because he could be as impersonal as he pleased: he could introduce his own experience and his own mixed and fallible human nature into his public prose without any violation of classical decorum, because his perspective on himself and on the world was broad enough and impersonal enough to avoid any reflection of our attention from the subject to the personality involved in it.

As an example of this, perhaps the famous passage about Shenstone's gardening will serve:

> Whether to plant a walk in undulating curves, and to place a bench at every turn where there is an object to catch the view; to make water run where it will be heard, and to stagnate where it will be seen; to leave

intervals where the eye will be pleased, and to thicken the plantation where there is something to be hidden, demands any great powers of mind, I will not enquire; perhaps a sullen and surly speculator may think such performances rather the sport than the business of human reason. But it must be at least confessed, that to embellish the form of Nature is an innocent amusement; and some praise must be allowed by the most supercilious observer to him, who does best what such multitudes are contending to do well.

Johnson's wish to be just does not let him go so far as to allow us to envisage for a moment that he will ever turn into the man with a hoe. But he does refuse to range the full force of his mind against Shenstone and the multitudes who are contending in the sports of human reason. Those who mock must remind themselves that they may be sullen, surly, or supercilious; and that to set the just bounds of speculation is not easy. Johnson does not see the situation in the general terms of an elite and a misguided mob, but rather in terms of a very specific contrast of particular and equally human attitudes: in the present case, a degree of folly on the part of the doers is at least free of the charge of malignity that might be leveled at the seers and judgers: and so Johnson "rejoices to concur with the common reader"—with the mob—as far as he honestly can.

The Shenstone passage illustrates many other distinguishing features of Johnson's irony. There is the Ciceronian amplitude and ornament that also makes its contribution to the humanization of the irony. The very complication of the syntax is necessary to enable Johnson to re-enact all the gradations of attitude in the judging mind, and to allow of such incidental ironic felicities as "stagnate where it will be seen," where the formidable analytic power is shown easily constrained to a suitably comic antithesis— "stagnate," incidentally, is calculated to enlist the rich variety of sensory connotations that Swift tends to avoid. Later we have the more outright jeer of "thicken the plantation where there is something to be hidden," archly prepared for by the earlier portion of the antithesis "to leave intervals where the eye will be pleased"—we are already primed to congratulate ourselves at the trickery whereby Shenstone avoids "displeasing" the eye. The whole conception of prose, indeed, allows for the complex organization of a wider range of feeling and attitude than that of Swift, and its final ironical surprise—the placing of Shenstone above the multitudes— is in the direction of magnanimous allowance rather than of direct climactic derision.

The passage can, perhaps, not unfairly be compared with an equally famous passage in Swift—the judgment of the King of

Brobdingnag: "I cannot but conclude the Bulk of your Natives to be the most pernicious Race of little odious Vermin that Nature ever suffered to crawl upon the Surface of the Earth." Swift here allows himself more latitude than usual for adjectival qualifications, but it is only for steadier bringing home of the single rational judgment: the taxonomist, at first baffled, has at last found proper words; man is pernicious—harmful, but harmful, not as lions or natural catastrophes are, but as cockroaches are, or bedbugs. No complication of the verdict is allowed. I must confess that I find something obtrusive about the consistent clarity, the intense delimitation of intention, in Swift's prose; the tone, the words, the syntax, the logic—all are aseptic; all bespeak what Johnson characteristically called Swift's "oriental scrupulosity" about his ablutions. Is not Swift, in short, a cook who cares so much for cleanliness that all his dishes taste of soap?

Several other general points about Johnson's irony must be made very briefly. First, he was a true sceptic: "prodigies are always seen in proportion as they are expected" surely rivals Hume in its serene repudiation of popular credulity. In a sense Johnson was even more sceptical about reason than the romantic ironists; after all, they assumed in their heart of hearts that reason was truer than feeling, even if it wasn't so nice. Johnson made no such *a priori* assumptions, and therefore avoided letting the dichotomizing habit, whether in the Swiftian or the romantic way, become his master: "I hope . . . that I have lived long enough in the world, to prevent me from expecting to find any action of which both the original motive and all the parts were good." All is mixed; one cannot merely present a system of erroneous or inadequate ideas and leave the reader to elicit the truth by working out the opposite *per contrarium* in the obvious ironical manner; the universe is not logical; it is certainly not disposed in an endless series of exact linear contradictions; and so to discern what is false or foolish will not in itself give us any grip on reality. Johnson never forgot this: if he uses antithetical polarities their status is provisional, exploratory, pragmatic; and his irony in general is the product of a continually fresh attempt to perceive and express the total setting of any perception; perhaps we can call it an open irony, as opposed to the more predetermined and closed dichotomies within which Swift tends to work.

For this open irony Johnson had the full, indeed the unequalled, possession of a truly philosophical analytic power that could embody itself in the unexpected but logically convincing metaphor as easily as in the intricately appropriate abstraction. Consider, for the first, the famous epigram on Gray: "He has a kind of strutting dignity and is tall by walking on tiptoe," and for the second—the manipulation of the intricately appropriate abstraction—the passage in the "Life" where Johnson considers Swift's treatment of his domestics: "That he was disposed to do his servants good on important occasions is no great mitigation; benefaction can be but rare, and tyrannick peevishness is perpetual." Johnson enlists the full weight of abstraction and impersonality in his wounding judgments, but there is—to use Bronson's fine phrase—a "yeast of insobriety" behind "tyrannick peevishness" that makes us marvel at the powers that could both observe the phenomenon and make the expression fit the crime. The judgment, of course, is contrary to the apparent, the commonly accepted scale of values, but its subversive paradox gains total authority from the fine balance of the phrasing: "benefaction can be but rare, and tyrannick peevishness is perpetual."

Here, perhaps, we have the major ironical characteristic of Johnson's style: the almost continual contrast between the poised, philosophical assurance of the manner, and the "yeast of insobriety" that informs the matter: while the grand generality of the manner functions as the hallmark of Johnson's public *persona*, the matter reveals a deep commitment to the particularities of a personal vision of reality; and somewhere within the dichotomy reason and passion are made one.

I cannot get any further in defining Johnson's irony. The *Life of Pope*, for example, does no more than set before us the infinite disparities and discontinuities of an individual life, and then place them in a larger context of generalization: but it is done so justly that we are continually moved to a rapture of assent. The irony, I suppose, is of the kind that has no special label but with which modern criticism has been most concerned: it demonstrates nothing because it finds that it cannot truly do more than enlist all the resources of experience, understanding, and art to create a dispassionate image of the endless incongruities that seem to be the condition of life in this vale of tears, and which are, I do not doubt, the most truly universal norms in what the eighteenth century called Nature.

Note

1. I am deeply grateful to Harold D. Kelling, John Loftis, and Henry Nash Smith, who read drafts of this paper and made valuable suggestions and criticisms.

Selective Bibliography

Bibliographical Aids

Berwick, Donald M. *The Reputation of Jonathan Swift, 1781–1882*. 1941. Reprinted New York: Haskell, 1965.

Landa, Louis A., and Tobin, James Edward. *Jonathan Swift. A List of Critical Studies Published from 1895 to 1945*. 1945. Reprint. New York: Octagon Books, 1975.

Stathis, James J. *A Bibliography of Swift Studies 1945–1965*. Nashville, Tenn.: Vanderbilt University Press, 1967.

Teerink, H., and Scouten, Arthur H. *A Bibliography of the Writings of Jonathan Swift*. 2d ed. Philadelphia: University of Pennsylvania Press, 1963.

Vieth, David M., *Swift's Poetry 1900–1980. An Annotated Bibliography of Studies*. New York: Garland, 1982.

Voigt, Milton. *Swift and the Twentieth Century*. Detroit, Mich.: Wayne State University Press, 1964.

Williams, Harold, *Dean Swift's Library*. Cambridge: At the University Press, 1932.

Concordance

Shinagel, Michael. *A Concordance to the Poems of Jonathan Swift*. Ithaca, N.Y.: Cornell University Press, 1972.

Modern Editions

COLLECTED EDITIONS AND SELECTIONS, INCLUDING LETTERS

Correspondence. Edited by Harold Williams. 5 vols. Oxford: Clarendon Press, 1963–65.

Gulliver's Travels and Other Writings. Edited by Louis A. Landa. Oxford: Oxford University Press, 1976. Reprint of the Riverside edition, Boston: Houghton Mifflin, 1960.

Poems. Edited by Harold Williams. 3 vols. 2d ed. Oxford: Clarendon Press, 1958; *Collected Poems* edited by Joseph Horrell: 2 vols. London: Routledge, 1958; *Poetical Works* edited by Herbert Davis: Oxford Standard Authors. London: Oxford University Press, 1967; *Complete Poems* edited by Pat Rogers. Harmondsworth: Penguin, 1983.

Prose Works. Edited by Herbert Davis et al. 16 vols. Oxford: Blackwell, 1939–74. Vol. 14, index by Irvin Ehrenpreis et al.; vols. 15–16, *Journal to Stella*, edited by Harold Williams. Standard edition, normally referred to as *Works* in the text. Mainly unannotated. Important introductions.

A Tale of a Tub and Other Satires. Edited by Kathleen Williams. Everyman's University Library. London: Dent, 1975.

The Writings of Jonathan Swift. Edited by Robert A. Greenberg and William Bowman Piper. Critical Edition Series. New York: Norton, 1973. Best one-volume selection.

INDIVIDUAL WORKS

A Discourse of the Contests and Dissentions Between the Nobles and the Commons in Athens and Rome. Edited by Frank H. Ellis. Oxford: Clarendon Press, 1967. Annotated.

The Drapier's Letters. Edited by Herbert Davis. Oxford: Clarendon Press, 1935. Annotated.

An Enquiry into the Behaviour of the Queen's Last Ministry. Edited by Irvin Ehrenpreis. Bloomington: Indiana University Press, 1956. Annotated.

Gulliver's Travels. The Text of the First Edition. Edited by Harold Williams. London: First Edition Club, 1926.

Gulliver's Travels. Introduction by Michael Foot, edited by Peter Dixon and John Chalker. Harmondsworth: Penguin, 1967; edited by Robert A. Greenberg: Critical Edition Series (revised). New York: Norton, 1970; edited by Louis A. Landa: London: Methuen, 1965, reprint of the Riverside edition, Boston: Houghton Mifflin, 1960.

Gulliver's Travels. Edited by Paul Turner. London: Oxford University Press, 1971. Best annotated edition.

Journal to Stella. Edited by Harold Williams. 2 vols. Oxford: Clarendon Press. Reprinted as vols. 15 and 16 of *Prose Works*, above.

Memoirs of Martinus Scriblerus (with Pope et al.). Edited by Charles Kerby-Miller. 1950. Reprinted 1962, New York: Russell and Russell. Annotated.

A Modest Proposal. Edited by Charles Beaumont. Merrill Literary Casebook. Columbus: Charles E. Merrill Publishing Company, 1969.

Polite Conversation. Edited by Eric Partridge. London: Deutsch, 1963. Annotated.

A Tale of a Tub. Edited by A. C. Guthkelch and D. Nichol Smith. 2d ed. Oxford: Clarendon Press, 1958. Annotated.

Biography and Criticism

GENERAL STUDIES

Bullitt, John M. *Jonathan Swift and the Anatomy of Satire: A Study of Satiric Technique.* Cambridge, Mass.: Harvard University Press, 1953.

Carnochan. W. B. *Confinement and Flight: An Essay on English Literature of the Eighteenth Century.* Berkeley: University of California Press, 1977.

Craik, Henry. *The Life of Jonathan Swift.* 2d ed. 2 vols. London, 1894.

Davis, Herbert. *Jonathan Swift. Essays on His Satire and Other Studies.* New York: Oxford University Press, 1964.

Donoghue, Denis. *Jonathan Swift. A Critical Introduction.* Cambridge: At the University Press, 1969.

Ehrenpreis, Irvin. *Literary Meaning and Augustan Values.* Charlottesville: University Press of Virginia, 1974.

————. *The Personality of Jonathan Swift.* London: Methuen, 1958.

————. *Swift: The Man, His Works, and the Age.* Vol. 1: *Mr. Swift and His Contemporaries.* London: Methuen, 1962. Vol. 2: *Dr. Swift.* London: Methuen, 1967. One volume to follow.

Elliott, Robert C. *The Power of Satire.* Princeton, N.J.: Princeton University Press, 1960.

————. *The Literary Persona.* Chicago: University of Chicago Press, 1982.

Johnson, Samuel. "Swift." In *Lives of the English Poets.*

Landa, Louis A. *Essays in Eighteenth-Century English Literature.* Princeton, N.J.: Princeton University Press, 1980.

Leavis, F. R. "The Irony of Swift." In *The Common Pursuit.* London: Chatto, 1952; Harmondsworth: Penguin, 1962. Essay frequently reprinted in collections of critical essays on Swift.

Paulson, Ronald. *The Fictions of Satire.* Baltimore, Md.: Johns Hopkins Press, 1967.

Price, Martin. *Swift's Rhetorical Art.* New Haven, Conn.: Yale University Press, 1953; Carbondale: Southern Illinois University Press Arcturus paperback, 1973.

————. *To the Palace of Wisdom: Studies in Order and Energy from Dryden to Blake.* Garden City, N.Y.: Doubleday, 1964.

Quintana, Ricardo. *The Mind and Art of Jonathan Swift.* 1936. Reprint. Gloucester, Mass.: Peter Smith, 1965.

————. *Swift: An Introduction*. London: Oxford University Press, 1955. The best short introductory book, reliable and lively.

————. *Two Augustans: John Locke, Jonathan Swift*. Madison: University of Wisconsin Press, 1978.

Rawson, C.J. *Gulliver and the Gentle Reader: Studies in Swift and Our Time*. London: Routledge, 1973.

Rogers, Pat. *Grub Street. Studies in a Subculture*. London: Methuen, 1972; abridged as *Hacks and Dunces. Pope, Swift, and Grub Street*. London: Methuen, 1980.

Rosenheim, Edward W. *Swift and the Satirist's Art*. Chicago: University of Chicago Press, 1963.

Steele, Peter. *Jonathan Swift, Preacher and Jester*. Oxford: Clarendon Press, 1978.

Thackeray, W. M. "Swift." In *English Humorists of the Eighteenth Century*. London, 1853. The best-known and most controversial nineteenth-century discussion.

Ward, David. *Jonathan Swift. An Introductory Essay*. London: Methuen, 1973.

Williams, Kathleen. *Jonathan Swift and the Age of Compromise*. London: Constable, 1959.

———— ed. *Swift. The Critical Heritage*. London: Routledge, 1970. Collection of early criticism of Swift.

COLLECTIONS OF ESSAYS (EXCLUDING VOLUMES DEVOTED TO SINGLE WORKS)

Donoghue, Denis, ed. *Jonathan Swift. A Critical Anthology*. Harmondsworth: Penguin, 1971. The best single collection of essays; includes a historical section with comments from Swift's time to 1934, followed by a section entitled "Modern Views," including George Orwell, "Politics vs. Literature: An Examination of *Gulliver's Travels*," J. C. Beckett, "Swift as an Ecclesiastical Statesman," R. S. Crane, "The Houyhnhnms, the Yahoos, and the History of Ideas," and extended pieces by Louis A. Landa, Norman O. Brown, Irvin Ehrenpreis, Herbert Davis, Robert M. Adams, Ronald Paulson, Hugh Kenner, Geoffrey Hill, Denis Donoghue, A. E. Case, C. J. Rawson, Hugh Sykes Davies.

Jeffares, A. Norman, ed. *Swift. Modern Judgments*. London: Macmillan, 1968. Reprints F. R. Leavis's important essay, "The Irony of Swift," George Orwell's essay "Politics vs. Literature," Majorie Nicolson and Nora M. Mohler's "The Scientific Background of Swift's 'Voyage to Laputa'," and other essays.

————. *Fair Liberty Was All His Cry. A Tercentenary Tribute.* London: Macmillan, 1967. A larger book than the preceding one, reprinting many essays, notably Leavis's, Orwell's, and Nicolson's and Mohler's, as above; part of Yeats's introduction to his play about Swift, *The Words upon the Window-Pane;* and J. C. Beckett's important article of 1949, "Swift as an Ecclesiastical Statesman." There are also a survey by Ricardo Quintana and a checklist by Claire Lamont of writings about Swift from 1945 to 1965.

Probyn, Clive T., ed. *The Art of Jonathan Swift.* London: Vision Press, 1978. A collection of new essays, including W. B. Carnochan, "The Consolations of Satire" (on the poems); essays by Angus Ross and J. A. Downie on the Irish and English political writings; David Woolley on the Armagh copy of *Gulliver's Travels;* Jenny Mezciems, "Gulliver and Other Heroes"; and essays by David Nokes, Clive T. Probyn, and Pat Rogers.

Traugott, John, ed. *Discussions of Jonathan Swift.* Boston: D. C. Heath, 1962. Reprints extracts from Johnson's *Life;* Thackeray's *English Humorists;* W. B. C. Watkins's *Perilous Balance;* the whole of Leavis's and Orwell's essays; part of Yeats's introduction to *The Words upon the Window-Pane;* Norman O. Brown's important Freudian reading from his *Life Against Death;* J. C. Beckett's "Swift as an Ecclesiastical Statesman"; and useful discussions by A. E. Dyson, Martin Price, and A. E. Case. One of the best paperback collections.

Tuveson, Ernest, ed. *Swift, a Collection of Critical Essays.* Englewood Cliffs, N.J.: Prentice-Hall, 1964. One of the best paperback collections, reprinting Leavis, Brown, and Joseph Horrell's "What Gulliver Knew," Ricardo Quintana's "Situational Satire," John Traugott on Swift and Thomas More, and good pieces by Maynard Mack, Ernest Tuveson, and others.

Vickers, Brian, ed. *The World of Jonathan Swift.* Oxford: Blackwell, 1968. An expensive hardback, mostly of new essays, but reprinting a 1967 essay on Swift's politics by W. A. Speck and a 1966 essay by Herbert Davis on Swift's irony. Important new pieces are Pat Rogers, "Swift and the Idea of Authority," essays on the poems by Roger Savage and Geoffrey Hill, and Brian Vickers on Swift and Thomas More.

"A TALE OF A TUB"

Clark, John R. *Form and Frenzy in Swift's "Tale of a Tub."* Ithaca, N.Y.: Cornell University Press, 1970.

Harth, Phillip. *Swift and Anglican Rationalism: The Religious Background of "A Tale of a Tub."* Chicago: University of Chicago Press, 1961.

Paulson, Ronald. *Theme and Structure in Swift's "Tale of a Tub."* New Haven, Conn.: Yale University Press, 1960.

Smith, Frederik N. *Language and Reality in Swift's "A Tale of a Tub."* Columbus: Ohio State University Press, 1979.

Starkman, Miriam K. *Swift's Satire on Learning in "A Tale of a Tub."* Princeton, N.J.: Princeton University Press. Reprinted New York: Octagon Books, 1968.

POLITICAL AND ECCLESIASTICAL WRITINGS

Beckett, J. C. *Confrontations. Studies in Irish History.* London: Rowman and Littlefield, 1972. Includes "Swift: The Priest in Politics" and some historical studies in Swift's period.

————. "Swift as an Ecclesiastical Statesman." In *Essays in British and Irish History in Honour of James Eadie Todd*, edited by H. A. Cronne, T. W. Moody, and D. B. Quinn. London: Muller, 1949.

Cook, Richard I. *Jonathan Swift as a Tory Pamphleteer.* Seattle: University of Washington Press, 1967.

Downie, J. A. *Robert Harley and the Press. Propaganda and Public Opinion in the Age of Swift and Defoe.* Cambridge: At the University Press, 1979.

Ehrenpreis, Irvin. *Acts of Implication. Suggestion and Covert Meaning in the Works of Dryden, Swift, Pope, and Austen.* Berkeley: University of California Press, 1980. Essay on Swift deals with *Examiner* and *Drapier's Letters*.

Ferguson, Oliver W. *Jonathan Swift and Ireland.* Urbana: University of Illinois Press, 1962.

Foot, Michael. *The Pen and the Sword.* London: MacGibbon and Kee, 1957.

Goldgar, Bertrand A. *The Curse of Party: Swift's Relations with Addison and Steele.* Lincoln: University of Nebraska Press, 1961.

————. *Walpole and the Wits: The Relation of Politics to Literature, 1722–1742.* Lincoln: University of Nebraska Press, 1976.

Kramnick, Isaac. *Bolingbroke and His Circle. The Politics of Nostalgia in the Age of Walpole.* Cambridge, Mass.: Harvard University Press, 1968.

Landa, Louis A. *Swift and the Church of Ireland.* Oxford: Clarendon Press, 1954.

Lein, Clayton D. "Jonathan Swift and the Population of Ireland." *Eighteenth-Century Studies* 8 (1975): 431–53.

Molyneux, William. *The Case of Ireland Stated* (1698). Introduction and afterword by J. G. Simms and Denis Donoghue. Dublin: Cadenus Press, 1977. Important source of Swift's thinking on the constitutional status of Ireland.

Rawson, C. J. "The Injured Lady and the Drapier: A Reading of Swift's Irish Tracts." *Prose Studies* 3 (1980): 15–43.

————. "A Reading of *A Modest Proposal*." In *Augustan Worlds. Essays in Honour of A. R. Humphreys*, edited by J. C. Hilson, M. M. B. Jones, and J. R. Watson. Leicester: Leicester University Press, 1978.

POEMS

Barnett, Louis K., *Swift's Poetic Worlds*, Newark: University of Delaware Press, 1982.

England, A. B. *Energy and Order in the Poetry of Swift*. Lewisburg, Pa.: Bucknell University Press, 1980.

Fischer, John Irwin. *On Swift's Poetry*. Gainesville: University Presses of Florida, 1978.

———— and Mell, Donald C., eds. *Contemporary Studies of Swift's Poetry*. Newark: University of Delaware Press, 1981.

Jaffe, Nora Crow. *The Poet Swift*. Hanover, N.H.: University Press of New England, 1977.

Johnson, Maurice. *The Sin of Wit: Jonathan Swift as a Poet*. Syracuse, N.Y.: Syracuse University Press, 1950. Still the standard introduction.

Rawson, C. J. "'I the Lofty Stile Decline': Self-apology and the 'Heroick Strain' in Some of Swift's Poems." In *The English Hero*, edited by Robert Folkenflik. Newark: University of Delaware Press, 1982.

————. "The Nightmares of Strephon: Nymphs of the City in the Poems of Swift, Baudelaire, Eliot." In *English Literature in the Age of Disguise*, edited by Maximillian E. Novak. Berkeley: University of California Press, 1977.

Schakel, Peter J. *The Poetry of Jonathan Swift*. Madison: University of Wisconsin Press, 1978.

"GULLIVER'S TRAVELS"

Brady, Frank, ed. *Twentieth-Century Interpretations of "Gulliver's Travels."* Englewood Cliffs, N.J.: Prentice-Hall, 1968. Mostly brief extracts rather than complete essays.

Carnochan, W. B. *Lemuel Gulliver's Mirror for Man*. Berkeley: University of California Press, 1968.

Case, Arthur E. *Four Essays on "Gulliver's Travels."* Princeton, N.J.: Princeton University Press, 1945.

Crane, R. S. "The Houyhnhnms, the Yahoos, and the History of Ideas." In *Reason and the Imagination: Studies in the History of Ideas, 1600–1800*, edited by J. A. Mazzeo. New York: Columbia University Press, 1962. Reprinted in Crane's *The Idea of the Humanities and Other Essays*. 2 vols.

Chicago: University of Chicago Press, 1967. Contains important information crucial to a proper understanding of the Fourth Book.

Eddy, W. A. *"Gulliver's Travels," a Critical Study*. Princeton, N.J.: Princeton University Press, 1923. Despite its title, concerned mainly with sources.

Elliott, Robert C. *The Power of Satire: Magic, Ritual, Art*. Princeton, N.J.: Princeton University Press, 1960. A brilliant book in general, with a very good study of *Gulliver* in particular.

————. *The Shape of Utopia*. Chicago: University of Chicago Press, 1970.

Foster, Milton P., ed. *A Casebook on Gulliver among the Houyhnhnms*. New York: Crowell, 1961. An important collection of essays on the interpretation of the Fourth Book.

Goldgar, Bertrand A. *Walpole and the Wits: The Relation of Politics to Literature, 1722–1742*. Lincoln: University of Nebraska Press, 1976.

Gravil, Richard, ed. *"Gulliver's Travels." A Casebook*. London: Macmillan, 1974. Collection of essays that usefully supplements Milton P. Foster, 1961.

Lock, F. P. *The Politics of "Gulliver's Travels."* Oxford: Clarendon Press, 1980.

Mezciems, Jenny. "'Tis not to divert the Reader': Moral and Literary Determinants in Some Early Travel Narratives." *Prose Studies* 5 (1982): 1–19; also in *The Art of Travel: Essays on Travel Writing*, edited by Philip Dodd. London: Frank Cass, 1982.

————. "The Unity of Swift's 'Voyage to Laputa': Structure as Meaning in Utopian Fiction." *Modern Language Review* 72 (1977): 1–21.

————. "Utopia and 'the Thing which is not': More, Swift, and other Lying Idealists." *University of Toronto Quarterly* 52 (1982): 40–62.

Orwell, George. "Politics vs. Literature: An Examination of Gulliver's Travels (1946)." In *Collected Essays, Journalism, and Letters of George Orwell*, edited by Sonia Orwell and Ian Angus. Vol. 4, London: Secker and Warburg, 1968. Included in several collections of essays on Swift: see above.

Index

Acts of the Apostles, The, 105
Adams, Robert M., 56–57, 330
Addison, Joseph, 124, 130, 278, 314, 332; *Freeholder, The*, 247
Alcibiades, 129
Alemán, Mateo, *Guzmán de Alfarache*, 224–25
Alexander the Great, 118
Angus, Ian, 334
Anne, Queen, 17–18, 47, 90, 102, 130–31, 139, 145–46, 149–51, 236, 278, 288
Arbuckle, James, 201
Arbuthnot, John, 18–19, 134, 241, 247, 252, 306; *History of John Bull, The*, 134
Aristides, 129
Aristophanes, 109–10
Aristotle, 229, 306; *Rhetoric*, 308
Arnold, Matthew, 85, 95
Atterbury, Francis, 210, 212, 214, 224
Augustine, Saint, 107

Bacon, Francis, 224, 291; *New Atlantis*, 270, 275–76
Balzac, Jean-Louis Guez de, 229
Barnett, Louise K., 333
Bate, W. J., 23, 40–41, 44
Baudelaire, Charles, 202, 333
Beaumont, Charles A., 281, 328
Beckett, J. C., 165, 330–32
Beckett, Samuel, 25, 201
Beckwith, Charles E., 226
Beerbohm, Sir Max, 309
Bennett, G. V., 149
Bentley, Richard, 88, 92, 95, 97–98
Berkeley, earl of (Charles), 15
Berkeley, George, 300, 305
Berwick, Donald M., 327

Biddle, Sheila, 149
Blake, William, 109, 115
Blanchard, Rae, 150
Blok, Alexander, 319–20
Boileau (Despréaux), Nicolas, *Le Lutrin*, 76
Bolingbroke, Viscount (Henry St. John), 17–19, 66, 132–33, 137, 141, 143, 146, 149–50, 278, 288–89, 332
Bonner, W. H., 281
Booth, Wayne C., 296–97, 302
Bosch, Hieronymus, 88
Boswell, James, 23, 48, 323
Brady, Frank, 302, 333
Bronson, Bertrand H., 326
Brontë, Charlotte, *Shirley*, 205, 211
Brooke, Henry, *Fool of Quality, The*, 320
Brown, Norman O., 45, 330–31
Brutus, Lucius Junius, 188
Bullitt, J. M., 66, 125, 329
Bunyan, John, 72; *Pilgrim's Progress*, 302
Burgess, C. F., 244
Burke, Edmund, 57, 153–54
Burnet, Gilbert, 122–23, 128, 144
Butler, Samuel, *Hudibras*, 311
Byron, Lord George Gordon, 44, 203; *Don Juan*, 204, 223

Calvin, Jean, 81
Camus, Albert, 81
Carnochan, W. B., 280, 293, 302, 329, 331, 333
Carroll, John, 244
Carteret, Lord John, 179–82
Case, Arthur E., 288, 302, 331, 333
Caster, Marcel, 279
Cato, Marcus Porcius (the Younger), 188

335